Falwell
An Autobiography

Liberty
HOUSE
PUBLISHERS

P.O. Box 10307 • Lynchburg, VA 24506

FALWELL
An Autobiography

Cover and Book Design: Eric Cashion and Lee Fredrickson

Library of Congress Cataloging-in Publication Data

Jerry Falwell
Falwell: An Autobiography/ By Jerry Falwell
p. cm.
1. Falwell, Jerry 2. Baptists—United States—Clergy
Biography 3. Title

ISBN 1-888684-04-6

Printed in India at Indira Printers, New Delhi-110 020.

Acknowledgement

To my wonderful family—Macel, Jerry Jr., Becki, Trey, Wesley, Jeannie, Paul, Jonathan, Shari and Jonathan, Jr.

Jerry Jr. spent three years of his very busy life researching the Falwell family history. Without this effort, *Falwell: An Autobiography* would not have been what it is. Thank you, Jerry.

Table of Contents

Foreword

Jerry Falwell has said often through the years that he has had three mentors: Francis Schaeffer, B.R. Lakin and me. Since, at age 82, I am the only one of those mentors still in the land of the living, I assume this is the reason I was asked to write this preface to his autobiography.

I am honored to do so since I consider Jerry Falwell to be "at least" the second most influential American clergyman of this century. I believe the nature of Dr. Falwell's ministry in confronting the culture and in building a major Christian university may ultimately cause him to impact history and future generations above any Christian leader of the 20th Century.

I first met Jerry when, as a 19 year-old student at Baptist Bible College in Springfield, Missouri, he was a roommate with my son, Herb. At the time, I was executive vice-president of the college and also pastor of Landmark Baptist Temple in Cincinnati. This young man caught my attention immediately. I learned that he was not only a straight A student with a photographic memory, but that he had volunteered to teach a Sunday School class of 11 year-old boys in a local church. That class grew from an attendance of two boys in September to 56 boys the following May. Herb told me that Jerry was the "spark plug" of the campus. During those days, Jerry Falwell and the Rawlings family became friends and have been for the past 44 years.

Jerry graduated at the top of his class three years later, as he had in his high school class back home in Lynchburg, Virginia. He then went back to his home-town and started the Thomas Road Baptist Church. During the past 40 years, God has used this man to impact the world. While building one of the largest congregations in America, he has also spoken to the nation almost daily on television and radio for four decades. He has conducted a continuing weekly telecast for 40 years, without interruption, which is much longer than any other religious broadcaster. He has written 12 books. He founded Liberty University 25 years ago and it is now the largest Christian university of its kind in the world. He has raised over $2 billion for his

7

various ministries, which include Elim Home for Alcoholics, Liberty Godparent Home for Unwed Mothers, his church and schools.

In 1979, Religious Heritage of America selected Jerry as America's Clergyman of the Year. In 1980, Israeli Prime Minister Menachem Begin presented him the prestigious Jabotinsky Centennial Medal for his friendship to Israel. He has been on the covers of Time and Newsweek and has been featured on countless print and broadcast outlets. U.S. News and World Report listed him as One of the 25 Most Influential People in America in 1983. That same year, he was chosen The Most Admired Man Not in Congress by The Conservative Digest. He was voted the Second Most Admired Man in America, behind President Reagan, in 1982, 1984 and 1986, by the readers of Good Housekeeping Magazine. He has met privately numerous times with U.S. Presidents George Bush, Ronald Reagan, Gerald Ford and Richard Nixon. He has also met often with world leaders such as Egyptian President Anwar Sadat, Jordanian King Hussein, South African President P.W. Botha and Israeli Prime Ministers Begin, Shamir, Rabin and Peres.

He has spoken at dozens of colleges and universities, including Harvard, Princeton, Oxford, Yale, Dartmouth, UCLA and Notre Dame. He has appeared many times on ABC's Nightline, Larry King Live, Phil Donahue, and most of the networks' news shows and talk shows. I believe I am not exaggerating when I say that no clergyman of any faith has appeared in the media as much as Jerry Falwell...ever.

However, Jerry Falwell is best known worldwide for his virtual single-handed organizing of what the media refers to as the "Religious Right." He founded the Moral Majority in 1979 to counter the rapid secularization of America by certain forces. He brought together over seven million religious conservatives around a pro-family, pro-life, pro-strong national defense and pro-Israel platform. Over 100,000 pastors and priests joined hands in the 80's to rise up against the moral and social decay that was overwhelming the nation.

These religious conservatives made Ronald Reagan their hero and set about registering, informing and mobilizing millions of

8

new voters. In November 1980, pollsters gave them credit for making the difference in electing President Reagan and voting out 12 liberal U.S. Senators. Jerry had created the largest voting bloc in America— the Religious Right.

Believing this to be true, I go one step beyond giving Falwell credit for Ronald Reagan's presidency and also grant him a significant role in bringing about the collapse of the Soviet Union and the end of the Cold War, since these were unquestionably Reagan accomplishments.

Further, the Christian Coalition, Concerned Women for America, the Rutherford Institute, Focus on the Family, the Family Research Council and hundreds of other conservative groups of the 90's owe their genesis and/or inspiration to Jerry Falwell and the Moral Majority. The Pew Research Center conducted a survey in the summer of 1996 and reported that the Religious Right now comprises one-fourth of the total electorate, by far the largest single voting bloc. Jews make up 2% and African-Americans 9%.

One of the reasons I believe Jerry Falwell is probably the most influential American clergyman is that the Religious Right and, particularly, the evangelical pastors of the nation, still look to him almost exclusively for direction in the vital social and moral issues facing them. Add to his political strength the lasting spiritual and moral influence of the huge and growing Liberty University on future generations, and it is difficult to rank the influence of Falwell behind that of anyone else.

Any honest treatment by historians of the final 40 years of the 20th Century will give Jerry Falwell a positive and significant role in providing moral and spiritual compass to America and the world during this crucial era. I am hopeful that the decision-makers of the nation will read this book. I encourage young people to carefully read this book. In a day when America so desperately needs heroes, I submit that Jerry Falwell is a true role model for this generation to follow.

Dr. John W. Rawlings
Pastor and Christian Educator

Introduction

Why this updated and revised version of my autobiography? Nearly ten years have passed since Simon and Schuster published my autobiography, *Strength for the Journey*. The book has enjoyed wide circulation and has been read by thousands.

Many have told me how the Lord has used my experiences to help them find strength for their journeys. That is precisely why I wrote the book originally. I wanted others to know what God had done for, with and through me and that He could repeat His mercies in them. Stuart Hamblen told the truth in his song *It is no Secret*: "what He's done for others, He can do for you."

So much has happened since 1987 that I have felt compelled for quite some time to update *Strength for the Journey*. In this renamed revision, I have not only provided an update but I have also made some slight edits and additions (of words and pictures) designed to make my personal testimony more usable by our Lord as we enter the third millennium.

None of our children were married when *Strength for the Journey* was first published. All three have since married fine Christian spouses and Macel and I now have three grandsons... Jerry, III (Trey), Charles Wesley (Wesley) and Jonathan, Jr. Needless to say, the past decade has produced radical changes at our house.

The fallout from the television ministry scandals in the late 1980's impacted all Christian media ministries dramatically and permanently. Following the PTL debacle and the Swaggart affair, the Old Time Gospel Hour experienced a $25 million loss in annual revenues. Since the Old Time Gospel Hour had been the leading benefactor of Liberty University, having provided hundreds of millions of dollars in subsidies to Liberty during the 70's and 80's, major financial pressures were set in motion. As I will share in the latter pages of this book about God's miraculous provision during these recent and difficult times, I believe your faith will be strengthened to keep looking up in the midst of your personal storms.

Jerry Falwell   January 1997

11

Having obtained strength for the journey during my first 40 years as pastor of Thomas Road Baptist Church and my first 25 years as chancellor of Liberty University, I believe God has now prepared me for the best that is yet to come. I face the 21st Century with great expectation and excitement.

— Jerry Falwell

CHAPTER ONE

The Falwells

W e Baptists don't spend much time in graveyards. Grieving is not our style. I suppose that is why I have spent so little time at the Falwell family cemetery, on a barren little hillside just outside the city limits of Lynchburg, Virginia. Except for May 2, 1977, when we buried my mother there, June 12, 1981, when we buried my brother Lewis, and September 20, 1988, when we buried my sister Virginia in the family graveyard, I have paid few visits to that place where so much of my history and the history of my family lies forgotten.

Few people even know that the graveyard stands there, isolated from the old Falwell family home on Rustburg Road by Virginia State Highway 501. Today I drove the distance from my Liberty Broadcasting Network office on Langhorne Road in just nine minutes. Of course I had to drive slightly faster than the posted speed limit to guarantee green lights all the way, but that was a small, safe sin. I could drive the distance blindfolded. Langhorne Road becomes Campbell Avenue just before it crosses Bypass 460, the highway to Richmond. Then, disguised as Business 501, the road exits Lynchburg city limits and disappears

13

into the rolling Virginia countryside, dropping almost due south in the eastern shadow of Liberty Mountain.

If you see signs pointing toward Eastbrook, you've gone too far. Just after passing the Lynchburg city limits, you have to make a U-turn on 501, take the rutted pathway that parallels Little Opossum Creek, and bump your way to the crest of that wet, weeded hillside where the bodies of my family lie buried.

You may have trouble finding it. There is no sign to mark the spot where my grandfather Charles and my grandmother Martha are buried alongside my father, Carey Hezekiah; my mother, Helen; my three uncles, Warren, Carl, and Garland; my older brother, Lewis; and my baby sister, Rosha.

A rusted wrought-iron fence guards the small garden of marble markers barely showing above the weeds and wildflowers. Stinging nettles and wild ivy vines threaten to bury the place forever. I visited this Falwell family plot many times as a child, but in the busy adult years as pastor of Thomas Road Baptist Church I have almost ignored this important place, if not forgotten it altogether.

My grandfather Charlie Falwell personally tended this little plot until his death in 1939. My uncle Warren Falwell took up the task and kept the undergrowth at bay until he died in 1976. For the past decade my cousin Calvin Falwell has tried gallantly to rescue the family plot from the sea of weeds and wildflowers that would claim it.

Then, in early 1987, while attending the University of Virginia Law School, my oldest son, Jerry Jr., rediscovered our unkempt family graveyard on the weeded hillside and led me back there for a nostalgic visit for the first time in several long, busy years.

"We ought to spruce it up, Dad," he said, forcing open the rusted iron gate. Cut back the weeds, polish the stones, and paint the ironwork," he added. "After all, you and I will end up here one day." He paused for effect like an attorney before the bar or more likely like his own father in the pulpit. Then he grinned and asked quietly, "We wouldn't want our graves to be overgrown like these, now would we?"

For a moment my son stood in the ruins of our old family

graveyard looking at me. He was grinning his own bashful grin, but his eyes were deadly serious. For the two years, prior to his graduation from Law School, he had spent more time in the Virginia State archives digging out the family roots than in the University of Virginia library reading civil or criminal law. I knew the Falwell family history well enough, or so I thought, but unearthing the stories of the people buried here and in the four Falwell plots in Lynchburg's Presbyterian Cemetery or in the Tyreeanna Methodist Church Cemetery, the Spring Hill Cemetery, or the smaller Falwell plot across 501 has become a kind of passion to my oldest son.

"There are fifty-six Falwells buried in Lynchburg alone," Jerry reminded me on the first journey back to this quiet, lonely place upon the hill, "and dozens more in Campbell, Buckingham, and Goochland counties," he added. "They go back to the 1600's," he said, his voice rising in concern. "They were pioneers with the first immigrants from England to America. They fought in the Revolutionary and Civil wars. They were our family, and we have forgotten them."

After reminding me of my long neglect during that first visit to the Falwell family cemetery, my son smiled at me and without another scolding word knelt down to part the tall wet grass so that we could read the names on the gray stained marble tombstones.

After that weekend, Jerry drove back to law school and I returned to work. On Monday I flew to Washington, D.C., for a press conference and a guest appearance on the ABC television network's "Nightline." On Tuesday I videotaped inserts for the "Old Time Gospel Hour," met with my staff at Thomas Road Baptist, and flew to Chicago for a television appearance. On Wednesday I spoke to a convocation of 7,500 students and faculty at our Liberty University, met with the university trustees, and en route to my office on Langhorne Road had a sudden urge to return alone to that little cemetery on the hill.

"They were our family, and we have forgotten them." For three days Jerry Jr.'s words had echoed in my brain. Sunset was just an hour away when I turned up that rutted road past Little Opossum Creek and walked alone toward the rusty iron fence around my family's past.

This time I stamped down the weeds myself. On this visit I used my handkerchief to wipe away the dried and splattered mud from the marble headstones. Finally, alone on that quiet hill, I asked myself the questions my son had asked of me.

How could I have forgotten this hill and the graves upon its crest? How could I have let the grass grow, the iron rust, and the memories fade? There is too much to be learned about sin, sorrow, and life from this simple graveyard and from the fields and forests surrounding it to let them be forgotten.

Sin? I confess it is an ugly word, quite out of style these days, and such a bad choice to begin a book, let alone my own autobiography. Yet I suppose it's what most people would expect of me, to talk of sin in the beginning and to take the risk that all but my Baptist friends and family will put down the book and walk away. But sin is what I think about in this quiet, almost forgotten graveyard, sin and its consequences in my life and in the lives of my extended family.

Written upon several of the ten marble stones in the Falwell cemetery is the name of an adult member of my family who spent his or her life struggling against sin and its effects, knowing both victory and defeat along the way. Each pair of dates on each headstone signals the beginning and the end of one person's lifelong human struggle against sin. And each grave holds the body of someone for whom the destiny of his or her soul was determined for all eternity by the choices made during that lifetime of struggle.

Don't misunderstand. Those generations of Falwells that went before me were not a saintly bunch. Certainly the men in my family would not sit still for a discussion of sin or its consequences. My grandfather was a self-avowed atheist. My father was an agnostic who hated preachers and refused to enter the doors of a church. Most of my uncles inherited the enterprising, tightfisted spirit of those Virginia pioneers who were too busy building a new world to have much time to take seriously the questions of religion.

But their stories, like yours and mine, are replete with painful lifelong struggles. And though they might not call the Enemy by his Biblical name, they knew in their hearts that there was an enemy. And it takes only a few moments in this old cemetery on a hilltop outside Lynchburg to remember what awful crippling damage the Enemy caused those members of my family who are buried here. Until we understand their Enemy and ours, until we call him by his name, we cannot understand sin or its consequences.

I am the first preacher in the Falwell family. So I suppose it's only natural for me to be the one to call our family enemy by his given name. His name is Satan. Some call him the Devil. Others call him Beelzebub, Belial, the Obstructor, the Tempter, the Evil One, the Accuser, the Prince of Demons, the Ruler of this World, the Prince of the Power of the Air. Whatever you call him, he is the Enemy and he is real!

I know how difficult it is for modern men and women to take seriously the notion of a personal devil. Halloween stories and Hallmark cards have made him a cute and harmless fiction. But in fact our Enemy wears no black cape, he grows no pointed horns, and he carries no bloody pitchfork to give away his presence. He is not a childhood myth that we outgrow with age and maturity. He is not the imaginary darkside counterpart to Santa Claus or the Easter Bunny. And though we cannot see him with our eyes, he is a real being who takes a real and deadly interest in each of us.

And though the stories of each man and woman in my family graveyard illustrate the Enemy's power in the individual human life, it takes the Old Testament writers to help us understand who he is and how our struggle with sin began. Satan did not begin life as an evil God-hating, human-destroying being. According to the prophets Isaiah and Ezekiel, he began life as Lucifer, son of the morning, the most beautiful of all of God's created hosts. And though he was created by God he was capable of disobeying Him and turning against his own Creator. Lucifer's sin was pride. He rebelled against the almightiness of God and desired to be His equal. That first act of disobedience in the history of creation the prophets call sin. Sin is any act of rebellion against the will of God. Sin was the Enemy's idea. In fact, he was the first to try it.

Lucifer soon learned the price of disobedience. When he exalted himself above God, he was cast out of heaven and away from the presence of his loving Creator. From that moment unto this day he has stalked the earth seeking revenge on God through the domination and destruction of God's creation. Just after the creation of man and woman, Satan appeared in one of his endless disguises and tempted those first creatures to disobey God as he had disobeyed. God had given them a law: "Thou shalt not eat of the tree of the knowledge of good and evil." Misled by Satan, Adam and Eve broke God's law. Their sin, too, was pride.

Other sins soon followed on the earth. Early in human history the ancients named seven of the world's favorites: envy, anger, pride, sloth, avarice, gluttony, and lust. The modern list of sins grows longer with each night's evening news: rape, incest, child molestation, corporate theft, political perjury, arson, kidnap, drug dealing and drug abuse, divorce and violence in our homes, robbery and murder on the streets, terrorism and all-out bloody warfare between races and nations.

Our little graveyard was built on a hilltop that has seen centuries of sin, suffering, and death. No one knows for how many centuries, even millennia, tribes of the Sioux Indian nation occupied this territory. The Monacan Indians, a Siouan tribe and a confederacy of Virginia, were the last Indian peoples to pitch their tents on this hilltop in the early seventeenth century. Arrowheads, clay bowls, and other artifacts found buried in the soil are the only reminders of this once great people who lived here.

During the Monacans' last century of existence the Enemy was very busy in this place. He rejoiced when the Monacans warred with their neighbors, the Powhatans of Tidewater, or suffered bloody raids by the fierce and ambitious Iroquois who rode down from the north and ravaged the Monacans after crossing the James River at the Horse Ford, just north of our family graveyard. There were only thirty bowmen and perhaps a hundred souls still remaining here in 1669 when our Falwell ancestors were settling at the mouth of the James. By the turn of the century, the Monacans had disappeared altogether, victims of war and bloodshed, victims of the Enemy.

It is not difficult to imagine, in the early years of our nation's history, the slaves who may have been beaten or even murdered in the woods around this hilltop site or the boys in blue and gray who were wounded or killed nearby. The Quakers who first settled this place fled here to escape persecution and death in the northern colonies and then were forced to flee the discrimination they found here as well. It doesn't take much to imagine the centuries of sin and suffering that this lonely hill has witnessed. The Enemy knows well this place and celebrates his accomplishments here.

And though our modern world is still a blood-splattered battlefield that we can see with our own eyes in headlines and on the evening news, the real warfare is the invisible war between the Enemy and our loving Father that has been waged on our planet from the beginning of its creation. Wherever children suffer, wherever young men and women die, wherever there is hatred, selfishness, lust, greed, pride, there is sin. And behind each act of disobedience there is Satan using every trick in his book to destroy God's creation, each of us, one by one.

The Bible clearly warns us that Satan is a roaring lion who travels about our planet seeking to devour those whom he will. Don't ask me to explain it. I cannot. But the Bible tells me it is true and when I stand alone in this little family cemetery I have all the proof I need of Satan and the war he is waging to dominate and destroy every human life he can, including the lives in my family and in yours.

To understand my own struggle with sin is to first understand the struggle of my parents and of their parents and of their parents before them. Satan pursued and tempted each of them. And their struggle with sin, their victories and defeats, went a long way in shaping me for my struggle.

We Falwells have been in Virginia from the early 1600's. Apparently we sailed from England with the pioneer settlers and established our first foothold in the new world on Chesapeake Bay near the mouth of the James River. Each Falwell generation moved farther inland up the James from Goochland to Buckingham to Campbell counties. Hezekiah Carey Falwell my great-grandfather, and his brother John were the first

Falwells to move to Lynchburg—in 1850. Before that the history of our ancestors is sketchy at best.

Because so many Virginia courthouses and their priceless records were burned by soldiers in the Revolutionary and Civil War periods, the only hard data we have on any of those early pre-Lynchburg Falwells is rather embarrassing to confess. Whereas my friend Pat Robertson traces his roots in Virginia from the chaplain of the first permanent English-speaking settlement in the New World, through a signer of the Declaration of Independence, an officer on George Washington's staff, two American presidents, and his own father, our distinguished long-term senator from Virginia, the only war hero we Falwells can find is James Falwell, who after being blinded in battle during the Revolutionary War ended up spending the last twenty years of his life as a guest of the poorhouse in Buckingham County, Virginia.

To better understand my father's family it is necessary to understand the rivalry between what my father considered the "rich Republicans" who migrated from the North to live in the more fashionable areas of uptown Lynchburg and the native Democrats of rural Virginia who were my family's ancestors. It wasn't long after 1757, when Quaker John Lynch built the first ferry across the James River, that Lynchburg became a thriving commercial center. Thomas Jefferson called Lynchburg "the most interesting spot in the state" and praised the city for its enterprise and correct course. He even predicted that the Lynchburg area would be one of the nations three major cities in the distant future, along with Philadelphia and New York. Jefferson spent much of his time in his later years near Lynchburg at this summer home, Poplar Forest, and even considered locating the University of Virginia in our town.

Until the Civil War, it looked like Jefferson's dreams for Lynchburg were certain to come true. The James River-Kanawha Canal, conceived by George Washington as a water link between the James and the Ohio rivers, was completed from western Virginia through Lynchburg and Richmond to the Chesapeake Bay by the 1830's. Until the late nineteenth century, Lynchburg was a major tobacco center, serviced by the canal and three different busy railroad lines. By 1859, Lynchburg was the second-wealthiest city per capita in the nation. In 1910, it was third, and it remains high on the list today, with a strong and diverse manufacturing base. Industries from iron foundries to shoe manufacturing plants sprang up in Lynchburg during the industrial revolution. The city became a cultural center for wealthy industrialists and workers migrating from the North. City folk resembled Northerners in ancestral roots, culture, and customs.

But the country folk living in the rolling hills around Lynchburg were farmers descended from the same British migrant families that produced Thomas Jefferson, George Washington, James Madison, John Marshall, Patrick Henry, and Robert E. Lee. These native Virginians came to the New World not for religious freedom like the poor but devout Puritan and Pilgrim peoples but to make money on cash crops like tobacco. They built a prosperous agrarian economy that was destroyed by the Civil War and Reconstruction. After the war my ancestors, the Beasleys and the Falwells, along with millions of their Southern neighbors, were trapped in an economic cycle of despair. Their farm-based economy was in ruins, and they watched with growing resentment as newcomers from the North replaced them in their former positions of power and prosperity in the South.

The Falwell history that begins to inform and to form me really begins with my great-grandfather Hezekiah Carey Falwell and his brother John. John Falwell fought for the Confederates in the Civil War. And though he came home alive in 1865 from the battlefields of that bloody War Between the States, he was shot and killed by burglars in the front yard of his home just months after arriving safely back in Lynchburg. Jerry Jr. found this brief article describing the murder of my great-grandfather's brother in the *Lynchburg Daily Virginian,* dated November 10, 1865.

Mr. John M. Falwell, who was shot on Tuesday night by some unknown persons, died Wednesday night of his wounds. Two persons named Phelps and Layne have been arrested on suspicion and lodged in jail. The murder of this inoffensive citizen, without cause, as far as is known, is one of the greatest outrages ever committed in the community....It is a deplorable state of society when a citizen is thus waylaid on his own premises and ruthlessly murdered. We trust that avenging justice will hunt out the perpetrators of this foul deed and visit the deserved punishment of their crime upon them.

I don't know whose struggle with the Enemy was affected by John's tragic and untimely death. But looking back, John's murder is just one more personal reminder that the Enemy pursues us even in the quiet paradise of Lynchburg nestled safely in the shadow of the Blue Ridge Mountains where the Blackwater Creek meets the James River. Man was not created to murder his fellow man. Something has gone terribly wrong with the creation. Evil is at work in the world, and no family can be protected from it.

Four thousand years before John Falwell moved to Lynchburg, God made His law clear to Moses: "Thou shalt not kill." But two persons named Phelps and Layne refused to obey God's commandments. Somehow the Enemy got through to them. They disobeyed God. They sinned, and that sin caused the death of a man whom God loved. And who can estimate the rings of evil circling outward like ripples in a pond from that tragic murder affecting friends, family, and strangers alike. In all probability it also created a long struggle against hatred and revenge-seeking by his brother, my great-grandfather Hezekiah Carey Falwell.

Unfortunately, we don't know much about Hezekiah Carey. In 1851 he bought the almost one thousand acres on which our family graveyard stands. Dozens of Falwells like myself have grown up in comfortable tree-shaded farmhouses on that rolling countryside, and up to this present day most of the Falwell family businesses were built on that same plot of land. My great-grandfather Hezekiah Carey Falwell grazed cows and horses in the meadows and built a large farm that fed the Southern soldiers during our nation's Civil War. He was a wheelwright who made and repaired wagon and buggy wheels by trade and a slaveowner who allowed the Confederate forces to build a huge fort on his property to defend the city. Seventy years later that old fort would become a favorite Lynchburg tourist attraction and the site of some of my own father's most successful business ventures.

Hezekiah Carey Falwell's son, my grandfather Charles William Falwell, built a large dairy and dirt farm on the hill just east of the graveyard. Horse-drawn wagons delivered milk from my grandfather's Meadow View Dairy and fresh vegetables from his farm to the people of Lynchburg. It was no small risk for my great-grandfather to buy those almost one thousand acres in 1851, yet his investment is still paying dividends to the generations of Falwells that followed him.

The announcement of my great-grandfather's death was the second time the Falwell named appeared in Lynchburg's little paper, the *Daily Virginian*. On December 1, 1886, his short obituary appeared on page four. It read simply,

> Carey Falwell, a respected citizen of Campbell county, who lives four miles from this city, on the Campbell county road, died yesterday morning at three o'clock from dropsy of the heart.

I wish I had known my great-grandfather. I wish I had asked his friends and family to tell me the story of his spiritual struggle before they took it to their graves. I didn't even think to ask them. Jerry Jr. and I have searched for clues in the stand of oak and red myrtle where my great-grandfather built his house in 1850 upon moving into Lynchburg. An early surveyor's map showed it standing on the crest of the hill due east of our family graveyard, but we couldn't even find a foundation stone. Every trace of the man and of his spiritual journey is gone.

I was too young to ask his son Charles William Falwell, my grandfather, about the story. He died in 1939, when I was only six. His burial was the first I remember in our family graveyard. At the wake in our home following his funeral, I remember seeing my father cry for the first time. I remember wandering

through the kitchen past great platters loaded down with fried
chicken and roast turkey, salads and cooked spinach greens,
hot corn on the cob, home-baked breads, and a table covered
with pies and cakes and cookies. It seemed like a party, but the
grown-ups were crying.

At six years old, I couldn't understand their tears. When
my seven-year-old cousin Peggy Falwell joined me in the tree
swing, I asked her about the family grief. "They're just cry-
babies," she answered, and I remember nodding in agreement.

Now I know more about the reasons they cried that day.
My Grandpa Falwell had been a kind and loving man. My twin
brother Gene and I were the last little children in his life. I
remember how he sat on our front porch and held us. He would
ask us quiet, thoughtful questions or hold and rock us gently in
the silence. It was ten years later that I learned why there was
no Grandma to hold us boys, why Grandpa Falwell visited us
alone. In 1914, Grandpa's young wife, Martha Catherine Bell
Falwell, contracted a painful crippling illness. Grandpa watched
helplessly as she struggled to survive. Apparently he prayed
long and hard for her recovery from the cancer that had metas-
tasized and spread from her uterus throughout her body. When
she died, Grandpa Falwell turned his back on God forever.

The Enemy used Grandma's death to destroy Grandpa's faith
and cause him a lifetime of anger and bitterness. Four years
after his wife's death, Grandpa's favorite nephew, Thomas
Falwell, died in the forests of Argonne, one of the 320,000 American casualties of World War I. In the tragic mystery of disease
and war, Satan won the victory. Those painful, tragic events in
Grandpa Charles' life turned him permanently against God.
Those who remember say that if the issue was ever raised
Grandpa would say angrily, "I don't believe in God." Grandpa
Charles refused to enter a church and relentlessly ridiculed any-
one who did.

Mom came from a totally different world with totally different standards. Her people, the Beasleys, were Baptists from
the beginning of time. Reading the Bible, praying, going to
church, giving a generous offering, working in the Sunday
School, and avoiding places like the Merry Garden were as

natural and habitual to my mother as sleeping, eating, or working. She was born in Hollywood, Virginia, a town of just one hundred souls. In earlier America the Beasleys lived in gracious colonial houses on plantations farmed by slaves, but the Revolutionary War and the War Between the States impoverished the people of eastern Virginia including my mother's ancestors.

The Civil War destroyed the Beasley plantations and killed or wounded many of the Beasley men. My mother's grandfather Thomas Davidson was killed in the Civil War on June 15, 1864, at the Battle of Petersburg, Grandmother Rhoda Ferguson Davidson moved in with her daughter Sarah Ann, her son-in-law King David Beasley, and their sixteen children.

Mom's parents were dirt poor, but every Sunday morning Mr. and Mrs. Beasley loaded the family wagon with their sixteen children and drove them to the Hollywood Baptist Church for Sunday School and morning worship.

Sunday mornings at the Beasleys' must have been a fascinating experience. All sixteen children took turns bathing in one tin tub and then dressed in their Sunday best. Each of the nine girls' hair was brushed and braided. Each of the seven boys was spit-polished and gleaming. Each child had a well-marked New Testament. Each could pray out loud, quote long Bible passages, and sing at least a dozen hymns by heart.

The sixteen Beasley children sat beside each other in two long pews in the old Hollywood Baptist Church. Mother Sarah Ann Davidson Beasley sat proudly beside her husband King David Beasley at the end of the long family pew. Helen Virgie Beasley, my mother, sat among them until she moved to Lynchburg in search of employment.

I don't know how my father met Helen Beasley. But in a conversation with Frank Burford, an eighty-five-year-old neighbor who was an eyewitness to those days, my son Jerry Jr. heard a story about Mom and Dad's courtship that opened up at least a tiny window on those days almost seventy-six years ago.

"Your dad had a black stallion horse," Mr. Burford remembered, "and a shiny single-seat buggy with a leather top and bright red wheels."

According to Mr. Burford, the first time my father called on his sweetheart in that spanking new buggy, something spooked the stallion just as he was riding up to the old Beasley place. The stallion reared. Out of control, he ran blindly up onto the sidewalk pulling the buggy behind him and tangling in his own slack harness. Through it all, somehow, Dad managed to hold on to the reins and to keep his seat in the wildly careening buggy.

Helen and her parents were watching from the open door. My dad was just nineteen. He wanted to impress his girl. He finally got the stallion settled and untangled and the horse and buggy back down off the sidewalk and onto the street again.

The commotion brought the neighbors running. Burford remembers one of them shouting over to Helen, "You aren't going to ride behind a horse as rowdy as that one, are you?" But Helen Virgie Beasley wasn't afraid to get up on the buggy and ride behind that rowdy stallion, nor was she afraid to risk her future on the man who rode beside her. Dad was twenty-two and Mom was just twenty when they married in Lynchburg, August 7, 1915.

After a secret six-month search through three Virginia counties, Jerry Jr. found the old buggy, repaired and repainted it, and gave it to me for Christmas 1984. It is without doubt one of the greatest Christmas gifts ever given me. I knew nothing about that historic old buggy until my son opened our front door and presented it to me on that unforgettable Christmas morning. The buggy now stands proudly in a covered portico at our home in Lynchburg.

My grandpa and grandma are buried in that little family plot not far from the graves of my own mom and dad. The simple marble stone my parents share has only the Falwell name carved large between two dogwood blossoms above their names, Carey Hezekiah and Helen Beasley, and the dates of their birth and death. There is no epitaph, no word or phrase to capture their spiritual journey. I don't remember who made that decision but in searching each of the ten headstones in that rusty little enclosure, I found no extra words on any one of them.

Before I was born, my father's spiritual journey was shaped for all time by two other people buried near him in the family graveyard. Rosha Geraldine, my sister, is buried next to Mom and Dad. She was just ten when she died in 1931 two years before Gene and I were born. I know almost nothing about her except the tragedy of her death and the way the Enemy used her death to affect my father.

Dad was an energetic and ambitious entrepreneur. In 1915, when he was just twenty-two years old, he opened his first business, the C. H. Falwell Grocery and General Store. Six years later he built his first service station and within a decade owned seventeen stations around Lynchburg and Campbell County, many with little stores and restaurants attached. In 1922 he built oil-storage tanks on a spur of the Norfolk and Western rail lines that passed just north of our family home, and he founded the Power Oil Company with the Quaker State oil franchise rights for sixteen Virginia counties.

During the 1920's. and 1930's. my father ran and promoted cockfights and dogfights in a large empty barn on the Falwell family property outside Lynchburg. These illegal events attracted gamblers from across the county and around the state. Often the bloody fights ended in death for an animal and great financial losses or sudden wealth to the bettors present.

In 1927 my father began the American Bus Lines, which ran from Lynchburg to Washington, D.C. One year later he began the Piedmont Bus corporation and the Lynchburg-Durham Bus Line, covering routes and owning terminals in cities from Lynchburg to Danville, from South Boston to Durham, North Carolina. These lines later became Trailways and Greyhound. He was the first bus line operator I know of to supply his buses with primitive battery-operated movie projectors to show old black-and-white Charlie Chaplin and Laurel and Hardy motion pictures to his riders.

Nearly a hundred years earlier, in 1834, my father's great-grandfather George M. Bruce started Lynchburg's first stage-coach lines. His business partner was Virginia's Governor William Smith. George Bruce later operated livery stables on Main Street and provided horses to Confederate troops.

In 1929 Dad opened the Old Fort Cottage Inn near one of Lynchburg's three surviving Civil War Confederate fortresses.

Built on a hilltop east of town with a spectacular view of the
Blue Ridge Mountains and easy access to the nearby intersection of U.S. Highway 460 and Business 501, the Old Fort Cottage Inn was actually one of the first motels in our state.

Each cottage of Dad's Old Fort Inn had a private garage. It
was one of the first hotels in the South to feature twenty-four
hour room service, a swimming pool, radios and telephones in
every room, as well as private shower baths and thermostat-
controlled steam heat. Dad solved the problem of maintaining
the sprawling lawns around the thirty-two brick and wood cottages on four acres of land by grazing sheep to keep the grass
down, by selling their wool for profit, and by buying back at low
cost the blankets to use in his Old Fort cottages.

And though Dad was proud of his success in business, he
found his real joy in the company of his wife, his two young
daughters, and his first son, Lewis, born in 1924. My sister
Virginia, born in 1917, and my sister Rosha, born in 1921, were
my father's pride and joy. Virginia remembers Rosha as a bright,
energetic, exuberant child with sparkling brown eyes and long
auburn hair. When Dad's black chauffeur drove him up the long
circular driveway to our family home on Rustburg Road, Rosha
would race down the gravel roadway to meet them at the bottom of the hill and ride with her daddy up the last hundred
yards. Often Dad carried Rosha on his shoulders up the stairs
and sat rocking her on the front porch as she chatted happily
about school or church or her favorite kitten.

When Rosha suddenly grew ill, Dad was the first to notice.
She seemed tired and rundown. Immediately he called the family physician. Dr. Davis first diagnosed Rosha's symptoms as a
serious cold, then pneumonia. The doctor was still fumbling for
an accurate diagnosis when Rosha's appendix burst. She died
painfully of peritonitis before Dad got her to the hospital.

I suppose that event was Dad's first spiritual crisis and the
beginning of his lifelong struggle with the Enemy. Dad mourned
my ten-year-old sister's death and, like his father, couldn't understand why a loving God would allow such a stupid tragedy.
He never trusted doctors or hospitals again after that, and his
mind and heart seemed forever closed to the possibilities of

Christian faith.

After all, Dad grew up in the home of an atheist. And though my mother was a devout Christian, my father would silence any attempts she made to discuss God in their early years together with his quiet reply, "I just don't know." Finally she quit trying to share her faith with him and spent her life loving him as an example of God's love and praying for his spiritual renewal.

Six months after Rosha's death the second tragedy occurred that shaped my father's spiritual struggle for the seventeen remaining years of his life. On December 28, 1931, my father shot and killed his kid brother Garland in the office of his brother Warren's restaurant on the intersection of Routes 10 and 18, just east of Lynchburg.

In the far corner of our family graveyard stands the marble headstone marking the burial spot of my uncle Garland W. Falwell, "Born December 9, 1906. Died December 28, 1931." He was just twenty-five years old when my father killed him and ruined his own life in the process.

In the archives of the *Lynchburg Daily Advance* and the *Lynchburg News*, my son Jerry Jr. has documented the full story of the brothers Garland and Carey Falwell and their running battle with each other and with the Enemy. The account begins on Monday evening, October 28, 1929, the day before "Black Tuesday" when the stock market crashed and the nation was plunged into its Great Depression.

The Enemy was having a field day in Lynchburg and around the world during those dark Depression days. The "roaring twenties" had fizzled out. An era of apparent prosperity had in effect benefited only the rich. Sixty percent of the nation's 122 million people lived on annual incomes of less than $2,000, estimated by the government as the bare minimum for the "basic necessities of life." During the past two months the four million stockholding families in the nation had lost more than $100 billion. In those next tumultuous months, at least 20,000 American businesses would fail, 5,000 American banks would close, and unemployment would rise from 1.5 million people in 1929 to an estimated 16 million people in 1933. In 1932 thousands of Americans would lose their homes to foreclosure. The people of Lynchburg, like the people of the world, were poor, angry, and afraid.

The country craved a good stiff drink to drown its sorrows and temporarily dissipate the growing fear. In 1919 liquor had been made illegal by the Eighteenth Amendment, but the rules and regulations of that Prohibition era were easy to get around. My father and his brother Garland, seeing the opportunity, became the leading distributors of bootlegged liquor in Campbell County. Young Garland had friends down in Franklin County, where the hidden stills produced high-quality illegal booze. Apparently the liquor was hidden in false bumpers and empty panels in my dad's oil trucks and even in his buses, delivered into Lynchburg, and served and sold in the Falwell family restaurants, stores, the Old Fort Inn, and even through his gasoline service station outlets.

My father was a businessman who bought and sold whiskey on the black market as he bought and sold cereal, bread, and meat in his country stores. To Dad, bootlegging was just another business. But the extra flow of cash had gone to Garland's head. The younger Falwell drove a fast black roadster. He drank heavily and began to use a drug known then as Veronal to keep him high and wide awake. He caroused with a growing number of shady characters, and his hell-raising reputation around Lynchburg was well deserved.

Still my dad loved his little brother. He excused the faults he could not correct. When Garland got in trouble with the law, it was his brother Carey who bailed him out of jail and hired the lawyers to defend him in court. He had escaped any serious consequences from his unpredictable and sometimes violent outbursts until Sunday, October 27, 1929, when Garland's rage got out of hand.

Garland owned a filling station in Pleasant Valley near Lynchburg. That Sunday afternoon two young male students from Washington and Lee University with their dates from Randolph-Macon Woman's College parked their red convertible roadster at Garland's pump, ordered the car serviced, and entered Garland's cafe for drinks and a bite to eat. Apparently the young men knew that Garland served illegal whiskey, and they ordered drinks for themselves and their dates. Garland already drinking heavily himself, suddenly grew suspicious. He accused one of the students of being a Prohibition agent. A scuffle followed. In the confusion, Garland dropped his wallet and one student dropped a pair of glasses. As the students fled Garland's cafe, they picked up both the glasses and the wallet by mistake and drove away quickly.

Garland and two of his friends followed after the frightened students in his souped-up roadster. The two cars careened down country roads toward Lynchburg. Garland pulled a pistol and began to fire wildly at the students. Before the police could intervene, Garland had fired more than forty rounds of ammunition into the students' automobile, practically destroying it and seriously injuring the son of one of West Virginia's leading citizens.

The Lynchburg headlines describing the arrest of G. W. Falwell were as large as the headlines heralding the stock market's continued decline that day. The story concludes with the reporter's account of the Keystone Cop-like chase and Garland's eventual arrest:

> The pursuit continued into Lynchburg, and down almost to the heart of the business district—three or four miles from the city limits. At the sight of a policeman standing at the corner of Twelfth and Clay streets, the girl driving stopped the car and screamed for help. Falwell stopped at the same time and ran back.
>
> "Arrest that man," Falwell shouted to patrolman L.J. Horsley, pointing toward the car in which Gus B. Witshire (a Washington and Lee student from Martinsburg, W. Virginia) lay bleeding dangerously from his wounds. "He held me up and tried to rob me of $200."
>
> Patrolman Horsley instead arrested Falwell on the girl's information and took him to police headquarters....A search of Falwell's auto revealed it to contain three guns: a double barrel shotgun, a .32 caliber repeater of high power and a pump gun popularly known as a "six shooter."

In addition to those weapons, Falwell is alleged to have had a .32 caliber pistol in his hand when arrested and another strapped about his neck by a shoulder holster.

On Wednesday, October 30, 1929, there was no news of the stock market crash on the front page of the *Lynchburg News*, but a two-column headline described the case against Garland Falwell, and his brother Carey's attempts to save him from the full force of the criminal charges.

...the attempt of Carey H. Falwell, a brother, to procure a warrant against Gus Wiltshire, 22, Washington and Lee student, charging him with attempted grand larceny were new angles added yesterday to the investigation of a shooting affray at Pleasant Valley filling station which nearly ended disastrously for a party of college students.

Carey got his younger brother out on bail during the duration of the two-month trial that followed. He hired lawyers and worked tirelessly on Garland's behalf. On December 6, 1929, full-page banner headlines in the *Lynchburg News* read: "Jury Gives Garland Falwell Two Years in Penitentiary; Motion for Another Trial Denied and Prisoner Sentenced."

In fact the verdict was appealed. And in early February 1930 a compromise was reached between lawyers of the Commonwealth of Virginia and the defense attorneys Carey Falwell hired for his brother. On the felony charge of shooting with intent to kill, Garland Falwell would be given a $100 fine and three months in the custody of Lynchburg authorities.

The judge, Don P. Halsey, was shocked by the attorneys' agreement. "I suppose you know more about this case than I do," he told the lawyers in his chambers, "and I accept your judgment, but from what I've heard of it [the crime] I think the punishment is extremely light."

Eleven days later an even bolder full-page headline read: "Garland Falwell Makes Break from City Jail." That story in the February 20, 1930 edition of the *Lynchburg News* revealed that Garland had walked past his jailers boldly during the delivery of his evening meal and escaped in the car of a waiting friend. An all-points bulletin had been issued for his capture and return. In the same article, the police admitted that it wasn't the first time Garland had tried to escape. "On the return from Rustburg," the story reads, "Falwell secured permission to enter his home, and, while there, secured a gun and attempted his getaway but was persuaded to desist at the insistence of Warren Falwell, his brother."

Garland had three brothers. My father, Carey, was the oldest, followed by Warren, another Lynchburg businessman. The youngest, Carl "Mutt" Davis, was still a teenager. All three brothers had intervened at various times on Garland's behalf. But Garland seemed determined to alienate and anger them all.

When Garland wasn't taking pills or drinking, he was a real charmer. Everyone liked him. He was a very kindhearted, often compassionate person. He was bright and clever, a loyal if boisterous buddy. But during those wild, intoxicated times, Garland took on another personality altogether. His brothers and other members of the Falwell family had stood by Garland faithfully, and when he misused or abused their friendship he was able to charm and manipulate them to get back into their good graces. Even the jailer from whom he escaped called Garland "a good-hearted boy" who was willing to keep the jail clean.

For years the Falwell family had tolerated Garland's drunken rages, his painful and malicious pranks, and his increasing problem with drug and alcohol abuse. But the family's patience was growing thin. Garland's escape from jail was a final blow. Three days after his escape, my father obtained papers committing Garland to the state penitentiary. Garland was being hunted across the state. Dad simply walked into the county clerk's office, asked for a copy of the court order incarcerating his brother, and delivered Garland and the papers into the hands of the state police on the front porch of our family home on Rustburg Road.

Once again my father intervened to save his younger brother. City officials and the police were outsmarted by my dad in yet another of his almost blind and desperate attempts to save his

Garland from self-destruction. He was released to family custody after serving his brief three-month term. Together the family reached out to give Garland yet another chance. But the Enemy had other plans, and those plans were realized on December 28, 1931. One Lynchburg headline read: "Carey Falwell Kills Brother He Defended." Secondary headlines outlined briefly the painful story: "Garland Falwell Dies of Gunshot Wounds While on a Two-Gun Rampage; Hand of Fratricide Pierced by Bullet; Slayer Had Stood by Younger Brother in Many Escapades; Dope Blamed."

In spite of his many run-ins with civil authorities and his prison record, Garland had achieved considerable success for a twenty-five-year-old. He had earned and spent thousands of dollars during those Depression years on legitimate and illegitimate business enterprises. He was president of his own small oil company. He had a prospering restaurant and service station of his own. Still, Garland was not happy.

Garland's mother had died of cancer of the uterus when he was just eight years old. He had been raised by his father and older brothers who practiced tough love but knew little of gentle intimacy, warmth, or quiet understanding. When Garland began to attend the Jehovah Jireh Presbyterian Church, his father ridiculed him for his softness. Garland overreacted to prove that he was strong. He adopted a tough outer core to protect and hide his growing inner hurt. While still an adolescent, Garland began to drink heavily. Eventually he experimented with drugs. He felt like the black sheep of the Falwell family and grew jealous of his older brothers. Gradually the Enemy fanned that fire of jealousy until it blazed up within him. Garland tried to put out the fire with alcohol. He drank heavily from the moment he was released from prison. When alcohol proved inadequate, Garland began using the drug Veronal again.

The night Garland died, he and his friends had been celebrating in front of his gas station and restaurant on the edge of the Falwell properties. Someone confusing the explosion of fireworks with the sound of gunfire, called officer W. A. Farmer of the Lynchburg police department. The police raced to the scene and found Garland and his friends exploding harmless firecrackers and tubes filled with gunpowder.

Garland, already high on whiskey and Veronal, flew into a rage at the officers, demanding they tell him who called in to report "the disturbance." Since his release from prison, Garland already had half a dozen complaints pending against him with the police and the sheriff's department. He suspected that his brother Carey had telephoned the police, hoping they would send him back to prison. The police assured Garland that it had not been his brother who had phoned. It was too late for truth. Garland had already convinced himself that Carey had called them. He armed himself with two loaded pistols and walked with his friends to Warren's restaurant, where Carey often met for drinks with his friends after hours.

Carey was in Warren's upstairs office speaking to his Piedmont Bus Line dispatcher when Garland broke in with both pistols cocked and aimed in his direction. Richard Glass, Carey's cousin and longtime friend and employee, distracted the nearly hysterical Garland just long enough that my father could run from the room. Garland fired both pistols at his retreating brother. Bullets grazed his right hand and his left side. Carey, realizing the seriousness of his predicament, ran to the back of the building, kicked out a window, and jumped fifteen feet to the ground below. As he ran for the safety of a nearby clump of trees, Garland appeared at the broken window firing and cursing.

According to eyewitnesses, he shouted, "Damn you!" into the darkness. And as he reloaded his weapons he yelled again, "I know you're there."

Then Garland fired wildly into the trees and nearby parking lot. Carey hid in the dark shadows until the shouting and the shooting stopped. Then he began to run toward the nearby home of Robert Johnson, one of his employees. My father had loaned Mr. Johnson a shotgun for duck hunting and wanted desperately to reclaim that gun to defend himself against Garland's attack. Just as he approached the Johnson home on Route 10, Carey saw Garland's car speeding toward the family home on Rustburg Road. It was clear to my father that this time the danger was real. He woke the Johnsons, asked them for his shotgun, and loaded it hurriedly.

"I don't need my gun to kill somebody," he promised them. "I just need it for my own protection."

Carey returned to Warren's restaurant on a path through the woods. My grandfather Charles was there with worried office personnel and close friends. Carey warned them of the danger just as Garland reappeared. With both pistols firing, he chased his older brother back into Warren's office. My father stumbled against the wooden desk, whirled, raised the shotgun, and fired blindly.

The *Lynchburg News* story dated December 29, 1931 reports what happened next: "A load of shot fired by his own brother, Carey H. Falwell, in self defense, tore a hole through Garland's body just above the heart. Death was instantaneous."

The article concluded the matter simply: "Garland Falwell is dead....Thus his turbulent career of terrorizing the police and populace was brought to an abrupt close."

Garland was a victim in that invisible war the Enemy wages to destroy each of us with sin, uncontrolled and unforgiven. Satan was present in young Garland's life from the very beginning, as he is present in every life, working to damage and destroy God's dreams for humankind. Satan was in the cancer of the uterus that killed his mother when Garland was just a child. Satan was there in the laughter and the ridicule of his father when Garland tried to attend Sunday School, and he was there in the quiet prodding of his chums to join them in another glass of whiskey or another dose of drugs. And Satan was there in Garland's drunkenness urging him to kill what he could not conquer.

But the Enemy was also present in the silence of the church. Not one Christian that I know about came forward to share the good news with Garland or my father in those early troubled days. No one stopped my father or his young brother on the street to tell them of God's loving plan for their lives. No one knocked on the door of their homes or offices to share the plan of salvation or to place a Bible in their hands. Nobody stepped forward while there was time to save them. Then suddenly it was too late. The Enemy had won the battle; and though Garland's wider family all grew up to know God's forgiveness, Garland, as far as anyone knows, died in the hands of the enemy.

In the early-morning darkness before the sun streaked through the trees and cast bright shadows on the little country graveyard, my father would park his car on the hillside, turn off his lights, and make his way to the place where his younger brother lay buried. My father visited this tragic place at dawn or just after sunset so that no one would notice him. But there are those who still remember seeing my dad standing alone on the hillside early in the morning or late in the afternoon outlined against the horizon. They say he stood there for five or ten minutes just looking down at the grave, his hat gripped tightly in his gnarled hands.

I get tired and bored with all those "enlightened" souls who smile and turn away when I speak of sin as though evil and the Enemy were ancient outdated ideas that died with this new modern age. People who don't believe in sin or its consequences need to remember my father standing brokenhearted at his brother's grave. They need to remember their own fathers, mothers, brothers, sisters, husbands, or wives staring down at shattered dreams and broken lives. And they need to think about the deep, hurtful consequences of their own personal failures before they reject the idea of sin or give up believing in the very real presence of evil.

People who do not believe in sin are already well on their way to being its victim. The first and greatest self-deceit is the fantasy that any one of us is invulnerable to deception by the Enemy. I am not ashamed or embarrassed to speak of sin, because I have seen its power in my own life, in the lives of my family, and in the daily lives of most of the people of this planet. I speak of sin at the beginning of my story because I am convinced that life is the battlefield upon which God and Satan war for the control of each of us. And those who refuse to acknowledge that battle are in deadly danger of losing the war and of bearing the consequences for all eternity.

Ask our first ancestors, Adam and Eve, what sin is all about. I believe that Adam and Eve were actually the first man and woman on this earth. But you don't have to believe it to get the full emotional impact of their story or to relate to its meaning in your own life. In Hebrews, Adam means "first man" and Eve means "mother of life." If you can't believe in Adam and Eve as the actual mother and father of humanity, at least read and consider seriously their beautiful and poetic story in Genesis. Moses' account is a moving and prophetic warning about the power of sin and the need for forgiveness from the very beginning of life on this earth.

The ancient Biblical text claims that God placed Adam and Eve in the garden of Eden. "Of every tree of the garden thou mayest freely eat," God told them. "But of the tree of the knowledge of good and evil thou shalt not eat of it." And if you eat of that tree, God warned, "thou shalt surely die" (Genesis 2:16-17).

Spend all the time you want debating if the tree was real or just a symbol. I personally believe in a literal interpretation here. But don't get so bogged down in questions about talking snakes and shiny apples that you miss the truth in this ancient story. That truth affects believers and skeptics alike. At the heart of the account is a fact known to everyone: Each of us is prone to sin. We may have plenty to eat from the heavily laden trees around us, but we are restless and unhappy until we've tasted the fruit of the one forbidden tree. There are few real limits placed on us by our Creator. And the limits exist to protect us from suffering and death. But we refuse to stay within the limits. As the Apostle Paul reminded us: What we know to do, we do not. And what we know not to do, we do anyway. We sin—every one of us—and in our sinning we cut ourselves off from each other and from God.

What is sin? You define it. Whatever you say or do that results in damage to yourself, to your relationship with another human being, or to your relationship with God is sin. We Baptists make lists of sins, but our lists—no matter how long or unwieldy—tend to be inadequate at best. The first Old Testament list of sins is really quite small and precise. It can be summarized in the Ten Commandments received by Moses upon Mount Sinai:

1. I am the Lord thy God: thou shalt have no other Gods before me.

2. Thou shalt not make or bow down to any graven images.
3. Thou shalt not take the name of the Lord thy God in vain.
4. Remember the sabbath day to keep it holy.
5. Honor thy father and thy mother.
6. Thou shalt not kill.
7. Thou shalt not commit adultery.
8. Thou shalt not steal.
9. Thou shalt not bear false witness against thy neighbor.
10. Thou shalt not covet thy neighbor's house, or his wife, or his servant or his animals.

When this first list of guidelines was given, it was God's gift to His people, Israel. This was not a negative list, a list of "sins" as we see it now, but a list of positive behaviors that led to closeness to God and to one's neighbors. Not killing, though you had the urge, was a positive, life-giving act. Not committing adultery, though you were driven by lust, preserved relationships and prevented further sin. The Ten Commandments are, in fact, a list of positive behaviors meant by God to foster peace and happiness upon the earth.

God had just rescued His people from slavery in Egypt. They were beginning their journey to the promised land. God gave them this list of positive acts to guide them in their relationships with Himself and with each other during their long, difficult journey.

Look over these ten simple commands. Four refer directly to the people's relationship with God. Six commands refer to their relationship with each other. This small, loving list was not given to limit human freedom but to protect it. These commandments were not given to stifle human joy but to help maintain it. The list was not petty, unreasonable, or restricting. To the contrary, these limits lead to life. Still the people rushed to disobey them.

Sin is the Biblical name for the act of transgressing God's law; and sinful (full of sin) describes succinctly the condition of

the human heart. It didn't take many generations to realize
that humankind was sinful at the core and determined to disobey God's commandments whatever the cost. And it cost
plenty to disobey. From that first act of disobedience in the
Garden of Eden, we learned that sin has terrible consequences.
The sinner is estranged, cut off, isolated from God and from
humankind. Adam and Eve were cast out of paradise for eating
the forbidden fruit. Their son Cain was marked by his crime
forever. By Noah's time, the epidemic of sinfulness threatened
the very existence of humankind.

Four thousand years ago the Psalmist David cried out this
universal prayer: "Have mercy upon me, O God according to
thy loving-kindness: according unto the multitude of thy tender
mercies blot out my transgressions. Wash me thoroughly from
mine iniquity and cleanse me from my sin. For I acknowledge my
transgressions: and my sin is ever before me" (Psalms 51:1-3).

Read the entire Psalm. David confesses that he sins: "Hide
thy face from my sins," he prays, "and blot out all mine iniqui-
ties" (Psalms 51:9).

But he also confesses his larger sinful condition: "Create in
me a clean heart, O God; and renew a right spirit within me"
(Psalms 51:10).

In 1863 President Lincoln sounded very much like the Psalmist in his proclamation for a national day of prayer: "It is the
duty of nations as well as of men to own their dependence upon
the overruling power of God, to confess their sins and transgressions in humble sorrow, yet with assured hope that genuine repentance will lead to mercy and pardon."

In his important little book *Whatever Became of Sin?* the
esteemed American psychiatrist Dr. Karl Menninger reminds
us that since 1953 no President has mentioned sin as a national
failing. Menninger quotes an article in *Theology Today:* "Since
1953, no President has mentioned sin as a national failing. Neither Kennedy, Johnson, nor Nixon. To be sure, they have
skirted the word. The Republicans referred to the problems of
'pride' and 'self-righteousness.' The Democrats referred to 'short-
comings.' But none used the grand old sweeping concept of sin. I
cannot imagine a modern President beating his breast on behalf

of the Nation and praying, 'God be merciful to us sinners,' though experts agree this is one of the best ways to begin" (Frederick Fox of Princeton University, *Theology Today*, 29:260, October 1972).

What happens when we refuse to acknowledge our sins or our sinfulness? When the idea of sin disappears, the possibility of forgiveness goes with it. And without forgiveness, the world is lost. Our relationships with God and with each other deteriorate and we live miserable, hopeless lives. But when we admit the possibility of sin, we hold up the possibility of forgiveness as well. And with forgiveness, there is hope that our relationships with each other and with God can be restored again.

I begin my story standing among the bodies of my ancestors buried in our little Falwell graveyard on a lonely, quiet hill just outside the city limits of Lynchburg, Virginia. Each member of my family began his or her journey in this life with no idea how life would end. Nobody started out to be a victim of the Enemy. No one planned to sin along the way. It just happened. It happens to everybody. The Apostle Paul wrote to the first-century church in Rome that "all have sinned, that all have fallen short of the glory of God."

Too bad so few of us believe it. Then suddenly life is over and the next generation looks back and sees that there really is an Enemy and that sin is a sign that he is winning. Why don't we see it while there is still time to change? Why don't we confess our sins at least privately and put the Enemy in his place before our body ends up in our own family graveyard on a lonely hill like this one?

Today I stood in the midst of their graves and tried to remember those who sinned and were destroyed by it and those who sinned and found forgiveness and new life. The body of my grandmother who died of a terrible disease is here next to the body of my grandfather Charles who quit believing in God because his prayers for her healing were never answered. The body of my ten-year-old sister Rosha lies between the body of my dad, Carey, and the body of Garland, the younger brother that he killed that tragic night more than half a century ago. My mother's body lies nearby, beside my father's.

And we must not forget those who suffered and died in this

place before my ancestors were born: the Monacans and the Iroquois, the teenaged soldiers dressed in blue or in gray, the Quakers and the slaves.

Of course I want to rush past the sin and suffering. I want to hold out the promise of resurrection and eternal life. I am a Baptist, and that is expected of me. But not just now. For this moment I want to stand in the graveyard at the beginning of my story and remember the tragic, human side of their stories without rushing past them to forget and even to deny the power of the Enemy in their lives while they lived.

It all happened before I was born; yet I stand today in the midst of those tragic memories thinking about the Enemy and of the pain he caused them all. And I wonder why it is so hard for those of us who follow to remember their stories of sin and suffering and to seek a better way.

You do not determine a man's
greatness by his talent or wealth, as
the world does, but rather by what
it takes to discourage him.

— Jerry Falwell

God is not impressed with buildings, budgets or programs. The only
thing in this world that impresses
God is people.

— Jerry Falwell

CHAPTER TWO

A Family Sin

Just moments after firing the shotgun blast that killed his brother Garland, my father called the Rustburg sheriff, R. L. Perrow, to report the shooting. Dad was arrested and released immediatcly on $10,000 bail. One day later he was acquitted by trial judge David S. Blankenship of the technical charge of the murder of Garland W. Falwell and released on the grounds of self-defense.

The hearing was in the judge's tiny chambers in Rustburg, Virginia, just minutes from the Falwell family home. Spectators mobbed the courtroom, spilled down across the front lawns and even into the street. After the hearing, my father tried to avoid reporters from newspapers and radio stations across the state of Virginia who had gathered to interview him. He was thirty-eight years old, lean and muscular. He was a successful businessman, respected, even held in awe by the people of Campbell County and throughout the commonwealth. He wore a brown striped business suit to the court hearing, with a dark silk vest and his brown felt dress hat. People who remember that moment say he looked pale and exhausted, fighting to hold back

45

his tears.

"I have nothing to say," he mumbled, trying to crowd past the reporters who surrounded him. "It was an awful thing," he added, hurrying away. "I am sorry that it happened."

That was Tuesday morning, December 29, 1931. The sorrow had just begun. Eventually, it would destroy him.

From the beginning of my father's agony, my mother was there to calm his angry outbursts, to hold him through those dark, difficult hours, and to wipe away his tears. Still he grieved. Even she could not comfort him. Then one night in November 1932, in a moment of intimacy between them, my twin brother Gene and I were conceived. My parents had determined not to have another child, but the death of my ten-year-old sister Rosha the same year that Garland died caused them to reconsider their decision. My mother had suffered a miscarriage earlier in 1932. This time, her pregnancy went full term. On August 11, 1933, Gene and I were born in Lynchburg's Guggenheimer Memorial Hospital.

After almost two years of melancholy and grief, my dad seemed to come to life again. At least for the moment our birth and his growing business enterprises distracted him from the unforgiven sin still gnawing at his conscience. And though sin and the Enemy continued working in my father's heart, he was too busy and too productive to take much notice.

Those years that corresponded to our childhood and adolescence were so filled with business and family duties that Dad never had time or never took time to face up to the consequences of that unforgiven sin still working in his life.

Apparently, the birth of twins was a rather rare event in our little community. We were driven home from the hospital in a dark gray Buick sedan chauffeured by my father's black driver, Thomas Good. The nurse who helped deliver us had ridden from the hospital to help mother carry the squirming heavy bundles wrapped in blue. Gene and I weighed in at seven and one half pounds apiece. Mom was still too weak to carry us both, so our proud and beaming father intervened. My older sister Virginia remembers how Dad took Gene and me in his arms and carried us across the wide lawn and up the front stairs through a crowd of family and neighbors waiting to celebrate our arrival.

My sister Virginia was sixteen, and my brother Lewis was just eight years old the day they and their childhood friends welcomed us to the old family home on Rustburg Road. Dad's sister Blanche was there. The family remembers her as a rather mysterious woman who always wore black and eventually owned her own little filling station. My dad's brothers, Warren and Carl, were there to greet us with their wives and young families. Grandpa Falwell sat in his rocker in his place of honor on the front porch. A handful of Mom's family, the Beasleys, had dropped in from their homes in Hollywood, Virginia. Mom had fifteen brothers and sisters with husbands, wives, and children of their own. With our curious and excited neighbors and our black workers, their children, and assorted members of their families, quite a crowd had turned out for our welcome to life in Lynchburg.

With all the people and the mounds of food and drink, there was still plenty of room in the old three-story, Falwell family farmhouse for twin babies, even fifteen pounds of us. Actually, the home-place we were taken to that day was more than just a farmhouse yet somewhat less than a country mansion. It was a gracious, comfortable wooden farmhouse built in the late nineteenth century by George M. Jones, a wealthy industrialist, on a hillside at the northwest end of the Rivermont Bridge in downtown Lynchburg. In 1908, Mrs. Jones commissioned the Jones Memorial Library to be built in her husband's memory on the crest of that same hill.

For years, the old country mansion that became the Falwell family home sat in the shadow of that grand library building with its six giant Ionic columns supporting a shallow dome, a gabled roof, a block main building, and two wide wings. On his visits to the library to check out books on business and the law, my father studied the old house that seemed so out of place next to Lynchburg's version of the Parthenon. Finally, in 1923, he bought it, had his workers painstakingly number each board in it, tore it down, moved it to the edge of Lynchburg, and rebuilt it on the country acreage where I spent my childhood.

Our home still stands on a hill overlooking old Rustburg Road just one mile from the Lynchburg city limits. A circular driveway ascends the hill through a half acre of lawn. The house is still surrounded by red oaks, Virginia pines, and mulberry trees. Six steps on the western corner lead from the cement walkway up to a wide veranda that crosses the entire front of the house. The master bedroom on the second floor juts out over the front porch, with windows looking out across the creek and up the northeastern slope of Candler's Mountain, now Liberty Mountain, the home of Liberty University. From the third-floor attic window one can still see the green meadows in the distance where sheep and cattle graze; and the forest of chestnut, white and red oaks, pines, and mulberry trees stretches south-southwest in the direction of Bocock and the open countryside beyond.

About nine months before we were born, Franklin Delano Roosevelt had been elected the nation's thirty-second President. Mr. Roosevelt had promised in his inaugural address to fight the economic emergency as though it were a "foreign foe." Fifteen million Americans were unemployed. Millions had lost their life savings. Thousands of businesses had gone bankrupt. The banks were just beginning to reopen and the national economy was in chaos.

My father was a loyal Democrat who believed with all his heart that F.D.R. was the only hope for America's economic ills. To my dad, the rich Republicans who lived across Lynchburg in the Rivermont section of our town were carpetbaggers who threatened the future of the nation. My dad used his buses to transport registered Democrats black and white who were poor or disabled to the polls to help effect the Roosevelt landslide. Like his President, my father fought the Depression like a general fights a war. In fact, my father's most prosperous days as a businessman were during those hard fought Depression years.

My father, Carey Falwell, was the first generation of Falwells to break out of this cycle of despair. He succeeded by beating the Lynchburg business establishment at its own game. He scrambled to build a little business empire of his own, and he often said that the wealthy men of Rivermont were surprised at

his success. He was a self-made man without a "proper education." One of his lawyers, Thomas J. O'Brien, remarked often
that Carey was a success in business "for the very reason that
he didn't get a proper education."

Judge R. I. Overbey wrote a letter to a friend describing the
legal skills of my self-taught father. "Carey Falwell never went to
law school," the judge wrote, "but he has more sense about the
law than two-thirds of the lawyers I see in court."

My father's success in building a rather considerable business empire in Virginia made him an enigma to the business
establishment and a folk hero of sorts to his native rural neighbors. One old man told me that "your dad was the only one of us
who made it big, and we loved him for it."

Dad returned that love. He used his influence on the courts
to get fines lowered and friends and family members like his
own brother Garland out of jail. He helped other friends start
businesses of their own. Men like Roland Hamner, president of
the Virginia Outdoor Advertising Company, credited my father
with helping him get his own successful business launched. Older
members of the black community like Chauncey Spencer remember my dad as a kind of philanthropist who dispensed gifts
and loans of money, houses, and pieces of land to needy blacks.

Even the economic woes of those long Depression years
didn't seem to affect my father's growing business success. In
our matched handmade wooden cradles on the second floor of
our family home, my brother Gene and I knew nothing of the
economic suffering that gripped the country. Dad and his brother
Warren had sold or merged their bus lines with Greyhound and
Trailways. His Fort Early Company dealt profitably in real es-
tate, stocks, bonds, and vending machines. His gas stations
across sixteen counties distributed gas and oil products for Shell,
Standard, Texaco, and Quaker Oil.

Dad had invested wisely in land and rental properties around
Lynchburg; and his stores, restaurants, and the Old Fort Cottage Inn were booming. And though the Beer-Wine Act of
March 22, 1933, had legalized beer and wine and ended the
years of Prohibition, Dad still bought and sold bootlegged liquor to meet his customers' growing demands. Everybody

knew about the illegal stills in Piney River, Virginia, but there was so much bootlegging going on in those later Prohibition days that the local or state police and the officers from the federal government were helpless to stop it.

In 1935 Dad built the Merry Garden Dance Hall and Dining Room high on a hilltop overlooking Lynchburg with a spectacular awe-inspiring view of the Blue Ridge Mountains in the distance. Immediately the Merry Garden became the center of Virginia's swing society. One thousand patrons could dine on regional and European cuisine in the restaurant. A nine-piece orchestra with celebrity singers performed at dinner and entertained customers for late-night ballroom dancing. The big band era came to Lynchburg via Dad's Merry Garden. Old-timers remember the week Tommy Dorsey's band played there. People drove from cities all across the South to dine and dance to his fabled big-band sound. Others remember listening to the music of Claude Thornhill or Jack Teagarden in my father's night spot on the hill.

My sister Virginia earned extra money working for Dad at the Merry Garden as a hat-check girl. She was an eyewitness to the Garden's moments of glory in the 1930's.

"I was just eighteen when Dad hired me to work in the Merry Garden," she remembers. "Some nights I checked hats and coats in the lobby checkroom. Other nights I sold one-dollar admission tickets at the door."

My sister went on to describe a typical night at the Merry Garden. As she remembered it, the crowds of excited customers were greeted by maitre d's in tuxedos. The gentlemen checked their topcoats and the ladies their furs, and they were ushered to their tables. Long lines of waiters dressed in formal wear stood on either side of the ballroom. The polished wooden floors gleamed from modern inverted triangles of lights hung down from the ceilings and sparkled from the reflections of a turning mirrored ball high overhead. The bandstand was at the far end of the dance floor. Large round dining tables circled the floor, covered with linen cloths and formal china. The room was huge, with more than 10,000 square feet of floor space. And the lobby and dressing rooms were elaborately furnished with brocade curtains, hidden lighting, plush carpets, and over-stuffed chairs.

Dad became a kind of P. T. Barnum in our city, producing special events as well. He hosted traveling circuses, sponsored musical concerts in the Merry Garden, organized the first walk-athons in Lynchburg, and even owned a huge bear that was chained near the Old Fort for picture taking and an occasional match with a tourist or local who tried to win Dad's prize of $50 for throwing the bear in a wrestling match in his large steel cage.

My cousin Calvin Falwell, Warren's son, told me recently that Dad even arranged for the great Houdini to appear in Lynchburg. Before a crowd of several hundred people, Sheriff Jack Miles locked Houdini into chains and bound his hands in official police handcuffs before locking him inside a Campbell County mailbag and dropping him from a crane into Dad's public swimming pool near the Old Fort Cottage Inn.

"The bag hit the water like a ton of bricks," Calvin told me. "And before the bag could reach the bottom, Houdini had opened every lock and escaped entirely from the sealed mailbag." Jerry Jr. has investigated this event to see if it actually was the great Houdini who dropped into our pool that day or an impostor. No one seems certain; nevertheless, it was a stunt old-timers still remember, and the publicity only added to the lines of people already ascending Falwell Hill for its scenic view and its varied services.

Within 200 yards of each other, guests could dine in four different Falwell restaurants, stay in a Falwell cottage or hotel, have their cars filled with gas and serviced in a Falwell filling station, pick up their emergency sundries and supplies at a Falwell grocery or general merchandise store, swim in the large Falwell pool built just below one of Lynchburg's Civil War fortresses, or dine and dance in the elegant Merry Garden on the hill.

As the nation's economy improved, so the Falwell families flourished. We weren't millionaires during those Depression and pre-war years, but we didn't suffer either. Dad presided over a bustling local business empire while Mom built a quiet, peaceful home at the center of the storm.

Looking back, it isn't difficult to understand why Dad loved Helen Beasley and wanted to share his life with her. Though she was poor, like her father King David Beasley, Helen stood tall and walked proud. Actually she was tall—five feet eight and one half inches in her stocking feet. And though she never cut her waist-length auburn hair, she braided it or rolled it tightly into a bun held in place by pins and only took it down at night.

The few pictures we have of my mother during those World War I years of courtship and early marriage show a kind, sweet, tender face. Apparently she smiled her shy little smile all the time. It was not a laughing smile, but she was obviously bright, sensitive, and filled with hope for the future.

She always wore her dark below the knee dresses to church, to parents' nights at school, and even to the few formal occasions when she and Dad entertained or were entertained in a Lynchburg home or restaurant. Actually, Mom was not a society type. Sunday worship, weddings, and funerals were about the only times I remember Mom actually dressing up. On those occasions she always wore a black short-brimmed hat. Mom was totally unaware of fashion changes and never really felt comfortable dressing up. She was perfectly satisfied to stay at home to tend her house and family.

She covered her long dress with an even longer white apron when she worked in the kitchen or about our family home. The apron came around both sides and tied in the back and would hang down below her knees to cover her dress completely. I can remember limping into the kitchen with another fresh scrape or bash, crying at full volume. She would reach out her arms and wrap them around me, and I would bury my face in that warm, soft apron and feel totally comforted.

I still remember the warmth of her kitchen, the brightness of the early-morning sun as it flooded the room with light, and the smell of her homemade bread baking in the oven or fresh rice or banana pudding cooling on the wooden bake table. Mom would bustle about the kitchen lowering or raising the oven temperature, stirring a fry pan, blowing foam off a boiling pot, or getting fresh supplies from the icebox or the pantry. She presided over a large and busy household: the black woman who helped in the kitchen, the black men who cleaned our house and yard, David Brown, who tended us children, Dad's driver, and countless other employees who painted, repaired, and kept up the huge old family place. Everybody who knew my mother loved her. She never seemed to be without a smile. She hummed or sang softly in the midst of chaos. She had a grateful word for every little act of kindness, and best of all, she had her way with my father. Family, friends, and employees all looked to Mother to calm him in the storm.

Her patient, loving style was beautiful counterpoint to my dad's ambitious, often intemperate, sometimes belligerent approach to daily life. And though their personalities were light-years apart, she could work as long and as hard as he could. Mom cooked three full meals a day for the family and often fed Dad's employees, friends, or drop-by guests at our long dining-room table. She listened attentively to his business woes, but she never allowed his problems to become her own. And never once did she discuss his problems with any one of us in the family. In fact, I don't remember ever hearing my mother say a negative word about my dad. She was loyal to him and kind, but she maintained her own private world and refused to be overwhelmed by his powerful personality or to be unnerved by his various professional or psychological battles.

She was a Falwell by marriage, but she remained an active, loving Beasley from her birth. That large, wonderful Beasley family was the source of a great deal of comfort to me during my childhood years. Mom had brothers and sisters, uncles, aunts, and cousins all over six Virginia counties. The Beasleys were a Southern clan, a tribe, a kind of mini-nation with their own language and customs. They loved each other faithfully and stood by each other through thick and thin. Nobody could out-celebrate a Beasley. Any occasion was excuse enough; and birthdays, baptisms, engagements, and marriages required full-scale celebrations. Every event, major or minor, from birth to death was reason enough for a Beasley clan reunion. I remember fondly attending these reunions as a child and eating so much at that great family table that I could hardly stagger away.

Mom would scurry about the house getting us children ready and her share of the food prepared. Dad seldom if ever took time to attend one of these Beasley "blowouts." He would send a driver and we would bundle into the car, summer and winter, for the journey to one Beasley home or another. People used to say that you could drive on any road in any direction in Virginia and eventually find a Beasley. The Beasley family had the most creative names: Elcester, Aurelius, Cornelius, Elester, Sylvester, Ben Walker, and King David. All were Beasleys and all loved a good party.

Sylvester Beasley was my granduncle. He was the unofficial patriarch of the Beasley clan. He owned an old country store in Appomattox County. His house was the only Beasley house that could handle the bunch of us in a rainstorm. All the other Beasley reunions spilled out of their various little wooden houses, down across the rickety front porches, and even onto the adjacent streets or fields.

We especially loved to visit Sylvester Beasley's huge old farmhouse at the end of a dirt road near Appomattox. The woods around Uncle Sylvester's were filled with chinquapin bushes. The chinquapin nut was a rare and tasty little morsel, and we filled our pockets or aprons with chinquapins and ate them with iced tea and homemade ice cream on Sylvester's shaded long porch.

On Sundays he would call the children together and march the army of us down that old dirt road to his general store. With great pomp he would take his long brass key from his Sunday overalls, flash it to the cheers of us children, and open the door to his treasure house of wonders. There were bolts of bright cloth, piles of tin and lumber, school supplies, shoes and clothing, picks, shovels, groceries, and jars filled with every kind of candy imaginable. I loved the licorice jar and always ran straight to it. There were long black sticks of licorice all stuck together in a bundle. I would pull a stick free, put it into my mouth, and bite down hard upon it, pulling and twisting until the licorice broke apart flooding my taste buds with that wonderful sweet, somewhat astringent taste. On those early visits to Uncle Sylvester's I developed my lifelong taste for real licorice. He bragged about his special licorice even then.

In all probability Sylvester Beasley never spent a day in a formal classroom; yet he could tell fascinating long stories about every item on his shelves. Licorice was his specialty. He told us how the Italians extracted the black sugary paste from the crushed and boiled roots of the Glycyrrhiza plant, how they rolled the warm pulp into long strings and cooled it in the shade. In the last ten years, I've sampled licorice in almost every state hoping to find another stick of Uncle Sylvester's original licorice imported from Calabria, Italy. So far the search has been futile.

Sylvester had one son. He was a strong, handsome young man with the wit and charm of his father. When Lafayette Beasley was just sixteen, he drove his father's old car into a deep ditch. Determined to retrieve the car himself, the boy bent low, gripped the front bumper in both hands, and pulled the rear wheels back onto the roadway.

Apparently as he strained to save his daddy's car, the young boy's spinal cord snapped and left him almost totally paralyzed. For the rest of his life, Lafayette Beasley sat helplessly on his chair on his daddy's front porch. I still remember him sitting there during our Beasley reunions. His head lay back against a bright red pillow. His eyes sparkled, and his mouth was slightly opened in a smile as each arriving Beasley kin crowded around to greet him with a cheery word or a sloppy kiss on the cheek.

I was just a child. Lafayette Beasley was the only quadriplegic I had ever seen. He was in his late thirties or early forties then, but he looked old and wrinkled and wise. There were no wheelchairs, no electric beds, no body braces or hand grips to help him through the day. And though he sat there for the rest of his life, the Beasley clan didn't let a day go by that someone in that loving family didn't appear with a friendly word or a fresh homemade lemon pie.

Luther Ferguson and his unmarried sister Ada lived in a shack at the edge of Appomattox County. They were very close relatives and friends of the Beasleys. In my memory, Luther and Ada were part of the Beasley clan. Periodically, Mom, Virginia, Lewis, Gene, and I would drive by to visit with a box of fresh vegetables or a freshly baked pie to give them. They were poor as church mice, but they loved each other and they loved us. Luther would guide us into their little two-room shack with a tin roof and rough wooden walls as though into a palace. We crammed ourselves around their kitchen table and talked with Luther while Ada made dinner. Pictures of their nephews and nieces, parents, and even distant relatives stared down smiling upon us. Mementos of other visits, Christmas cards, and long handwritten letters from family around the world were stacked among the memories in that happy little place. I remember sitting there as a child in that clean but shabby place feeling safe and loved.

I suppose it was the love I felt for Luther and Ada that caused another childhood memory that haunts me still. One visit, late in summer, as we were about to drive away from that Beasley shack at the end of the road, I waved, smiled, and slammed the door full on Cousin Luther's bony hand. He fell to the ground from the shock and pain of it. I was terrified and embarrassed and wanted to die. Mom and Ada helped Luther back into his shack. I sat alone in the car sobbing and waiting until my mother returned. There was nothing more she could do for him, and we drove away in silence.

Weeks passed before we drove out to Cousin Luther's home again. He and Ada were sitting on the front porch waiting. Arm in arm they hurried toward the car. I hung back while the rest of the family hugged and kissed the Fergusons. Finally Cousin Luther noticed me sitting in the back seat staring at him through the window. He walked quickly to the car, leaned down, and smiled through the open window. He looked at me for a moment, trying to understand my strange behavior. Then he smiled broadly, held his bruised but healing hand through the window, and said quietly, "See, Jerry. Good as new."

He just laughed about the accident and hugged me close. But I will never forget the hurt I caused him and the joy I felt when I saw that he was well again.

The Beasleys were poor and self-taught, but there wasn't an ignorant man or woman among them. Titus Beasley was another brother to Sylvester and King David Beasley. Titus was the only university-educated Beasley in the bunch. He became professor of history at Southwest Baptist College in Bolivar, Missouri. There is a hall out there that bears his name. He was held in loving awe by the rest of the Beasley clan. Apparently Titus was a scholar. He never married or had a family. His family were his history books. For many years I had hoped that someone in the Beasley family would help me attain Uncle Titus's wonderful library for Liberty University, but a terrible winter fire destroyed his whole collection. Now Beasley Hall is about the only public memorial to that warm, wonderful family, except perhaps the living memorial they left in each of us who knew them and who love them still.

My mother inherited her spiritual roots from the Beasleys. Before most Beasley reunion meals, the entire clan would gather around the heavily laden festive tables and bow their heads while one of the senior Beasleys prayed a long, sincere prayer of gratitude for food and family. And on Sundays, Baptist churches all over Virginia had at least one Beasley in the pews.

Mom met the Lord when she was just a child sitting in the family pew. She learned to read her Bible and to pray in those preadolescent years and never stopped reading and praying until the day she died. It was my mother who planted the seeds of faith in me from the moment I was born. And though they didn't take root until I was a sophomore in college, my mother continued to water and fertilize those little faith buds all through my years of childhood and adolescence. For a while she tried to get my father interested in the Christian faith. Eventually, she decided that her faithful, silent testimony would be the only witness he would tolerate.

She didn't dream that one day the man she married would be so rich or so strong-willed. However, in spite of their differences, by the time Gene and I were born Mom and Dad's life together had developed into a safe and rather comfortable routine. I remember only being loved during those first five years of childhood. I remember no great conflict, no pain, not even any real tensions in our home on Rustburg Road. But my sister Virginia was old enough to notice that there were subtle changes in my father from the day that Garland died.

"Dad began to get up earlier," she told me recently. "He

worked harder and longer hours than before. He grew more introspective. And," she added quietly, "after shooting Garland, he began to drink."

The celebration of new life in the Falwell household was not enough to wipe away the growing pain my father's unforgiven guilt was causing him. Still he bluffed, bantered, and braved his way through it, hiding the painful symptoms from all but those who knew him best.

In the morning Mom would dress and hurry down to the kitchen before sunrise while Dad shaved and dressed in suit, tie, and vest. While she baked oversized hoe-cake biscuits and fried eggs and fat-back bacon, he sat in the kitchen near her reading the morning edition of The News and drinking his first cup of her strong fresh brewed coffee. Then she poured the sizzling gravy on the huge hot biscuits, served up his eggs and fat-back, and sipped her coffee beside him at the kitchen table as he ate.

I remember waking almost every morning of my young life to the smell of sizzling bacon and the whispered sounds of their conversation. They seemed to love each other and to love each of us during those quiet, happy years of our childhood. Dad would be gone to work before the sunrise. And Mom would return to the stove to prepare breakfast first for Virginia and then for Lewis. Virginia would be driven to Lynchburg High School by one of Dad's drivers in the family limousine while Lewis rode to the Campbell County School in nearby Tyreeanna. Each would be bundled off with lunch in hand by the time Gene and I were squealing for attention.

David Brown was a black man hired by my father to help Mom with us children. Dad delivered us from the arms of our nurse into the arms of David Brown. He was tall and muscular, as I remember, but very gentle. In the mornings he bathed and dressed us. He held and rocked us at nap time. He fed and changed us. He helped us with our first faltering steps and he picked us up off the ground when we stumbled or fought and fell. He was practically a member of our family, but he ate alone on the back porch and sat in the shadows when he wasn't needed.

During those preschool years, David Brown and Mom would take turns watching over our play and presiding over nap times. Dad always returned home for lunch. His chauffeur would turn up our driveway at almost the exact same time every midday. Mom would have a hot lunch prepared, and they would sit and eat together. David Brown kept us energetic twins out of harm's way while Mom and Dad were eating. After lunch, Dad would carry us around the yard explaining how the farm worked, naming trees and flowers and animals, tussle with us on the lawn, and then as quickly as he had appeared he would disappear again.

As Gene and I grew older, stronger, and more independent, we began to explore on our own the meadow and the forest near our home. Huge oil-storage tanks were built on the Norfolk and Western Railroad line that ran through a northern section of our property. Dad built a pipeline from those tanks down through our meadow, and gravity pulled the oil to similar storage tanks on Rustburg Road just south of our front yard. We could sit on our swing and watch as Dad's oil and gasoline drivers filled up their tanks and drove away to make their deliveries throughout the commonwealth. The drivers would honk their air horns when they noticed us on the lawn above them signaling for attention. When we could escape the watchful eye of Mother and David Brown, Gene and I would even climb up the metal ladders on the tanks to watch the oil being pumped from tank cars or into trucks on Rustburg Road.

During the late 1930's Dad began a firewood and coal business in a huge barn directly west of our family home. As the threat of a world war made gasoline and heating fuel more scarce and expensive, the firewood and coal business flourished. Gene and I played in the piles of timber and wood stacked to the ceiling of the barn.

Scattered about our property were the homes of our father's black employees. The South was strictly segregated at the time. Black people could order food in my dad's restaurant but couldn't sit in the dining room to eat it. A strict protocol was maintained in the grocery stores and even at the filling stations. But in spite of the formal sense of separation between our family and the black families that lived in the shadow of the main house during our childhood years, Gene and I spent hours each day in those little wooden homes playing with black children, eating fresh baked sweets, and gnawing stringy chunks of sugarcane. Most of our friends during those elementary school years were black children, and though we did not attend the same schools, we spent most of our after-school and weekend hours together.

We played hide and seek under, over, and behind the slaughterhouse, the smoke-house, the chicken coops, and the tool sheds. We dug forts in the damp earth or sledded down the hillsides covered with fresh powdery snow. We picked wildflowers in the springtime and carried home to Mother great armfuls of lobelia, blue lupine, May apple, trumpet vine, morning glory, and goldenrod. We climbed in the apple trees and ate green apples until we turned green ourselves from eating them. And we sat side by side in the rope swing that hung from a high branch on an oak tree in the front yard and pumped higher and higher until Mom or Dave Brown would come running to catch us in their arms and to scold us for flying so high.

Every evening at six-thirty or seven o'clock Dad would arrive home, take us in his arms, and walk with us around the home-place while Mom and Virginia made the dinner. We always dressed for the evening meal and sat together around the long formal table in the dining room. Dad always wore a three-piece suit. In his lower right vest pocket he carried a gold railroad watch with a chain that hooked onto his belt. I don't think I ever saw him go outside without wearing his necktie. He always had overalls nearby to slip on when he helped the workmen with a load of oil barrels or boxes of supplies, but the overalls were slipped off again immediately when the dirty task was done. And regardless of the season, my dad wore a brown or gray flannel dress hat with a two-inch silk hatband. He turned down both brims, front and back, just slightly like a Depression version of Indiana Jones. Like Jones, my father always wore his hat.

Dad didn't like too much informality. He wouldn't let us come downstairs in the morning or the evening in our pajamas. He insisted that we "be presentable" and scolded us if we tried to get away with even a quick infraction of the rule.

But in the evening, when the whole family was ready for bed, it was a tradition for Gene and me to jump into Mom and Dad's large downy bed and tussle wildly with our father until Mom would call a halt to the proceedings. She hated to see us fighting, but Dad loved and encouraged "a good little family brawl." He encouraged it, that is, unless Gene was winning. At that moment the fight would be cancelled in no uncertain terms.

Gene and I began elementary school together. And though I skipped grade two and advanced one class ahead of Gene that second year, he put on height, weight, and muscles more quickly than I did. Believe it or not, I was the skinny kid in those early photos of the two of us, and Gene was tall and husky. Dad was afraid that I would grow soft, so the fights he encouraged between us were strictly regulated for me to win. I've often wondered why Gene seemed so willing to go along with those lopsided, unfair rules. Even then there were signs of the loving, generous spirit that would mark my brother Gene through his entire lifetime and even to this day.

Dad also had a loving, generous side. Often during the Depression years when friends and neighbors with financial problems ordered food in one of Dad's small restaurants or groceries in his country store, he would whisper to the clerk, "Don't charge them this time. They're old friends."

In 1932 alone thousands of Americans lost their homes to foreclosure. When our neighbors had no place to live, Dad fixed up old barns, a garage or two, and even a hen house for his homeless friends, white or black, to live in. And he loaded his payroll with men who were out of work even if he really didn't need them.

Dad was a rather strict segregationist when it came to business, but there wasn't a black man or woman who knew him that didn't consider him their friend. Percy Coles, a black neighbor in those days, still remembers my father's generosity.

"Whenever folks got in trouble," he told me recently, "your dad would help them. He never turned them down. Like with money or with the law, nine times out of ten he got you out of it."

Dad was very proud of his children and often bragged about us to his friends. Sometimes when Gene and I visited his office, he would jump up from his desk, take us in his arms, place us on a file or table, and ask us to sing for his bemused employees. I can still remember the opening lines of one song we sang over and over for him. "I washed my hands this morning. They were very, very clean." If anybody knows the rest of that song, I would be grateful to hear it. My brother-in-law Lawrence Jennings swears that on one such occasion when Dad had us standing on a table before a roomful of employees, he put one hand on Gene's head and one hand on mine. Then he said, "Gene will be my farmer and Jerry will be my preacher."

I find it hard to believe that my father singled me out for the ministry during those early years. He refused to darken the doors of a church, but provided Mom a car and driver to take the rest of us to Sunday School. I remember Dad warning Lewis about the ministry.

"Don't be a preacher, son," he said. "When a preacher walks into a room, people start acting funny."

Whatever advice Dad gave us or failed to give us along the way, each of us knew that he loved us. He showed his love in so many different ways. Sometimes Gene and I would fall asleep in our room before Dad returned from counting the receipts at a restaurant or closing up a distant filling station or cutting a deal with a new business partner. Many times in the middle of the night he would enter our room, lift us from our beds, carry us still sleeping into the master bedroom, and lay us on his bed. We would awaken in the morning with Dad's arms around us and his head beside ours on the pillow.

My father was a strange and always surprising mix of love and mischievousness. When he grinned, it was a warning. His brown eyes sparkled when he was up to something wicked. He loved to tease, and anybody in the vicinity was fair bait. Everyone knew he meant no harm, but there was an underlying element of cruelty in his pranks that I didn't recognize as a child. In fact, I remember collaborating with him in a joke against a boy named William, a friend of mine from the neighborhood.

"Daddy," I said late one Saturday afternoon, "I have William out there and he's really scared of you. I'm going to bring him in in a few minutes," I added, almost goading my father into another of his infamous pranks.

I remember the excitement I felt when my daddy winked as I ran back out the front door to invite my friend William in for milk and cookies. William hesitated at the door. He knew my father carried a gun, and there were too many stories circulating about that gun to leave William feeling easy about entering our home. Quickly I pushed my friend inside and closed the door behind us. Dad was still sitting at the kitchen table reading a newspaper. Suddenly he looked directly at us and shouted.

"Both of you, stop!" William froze in his tracks, and I leaned forward eagerly to see what Dad was up to. William's eyes opened wide as Dad drew his gun and pointed it at the floor just in front of my friend's trembling legs.

"Don't move," he said quietly. Then he took careful aim and pulled the trigger. The shot from the .38 Remington pistol blew a fairly impressive hole in the kitchen floor. Calmly, Dad blew smoke from the barrel and placed the pistol back on the table.

"I've been trying to get that fly all day," he said, looking back down at his paper. "And finally I got it."

There was a moment of silence. Then, with a gasp, William bolted out the door. I never got him back inside our house again, and the legend about my father continued to spread throughout the neighborhood. Later Dad and I laughed ourselves hoarse just remembering William's startled look and sudden exit.

There were times that Dad's pranks bordered on cruelty. One of his oil company workers, a one-legged man he nicknamed "Crip" Smith, complained about everything. Dad and Crip's coworkers got tired of the old man's bellyaching and decided to take revenge. One morning Crip called in sick and Dad volunteered to have lunch delivered to his grateful but suspicious employee. Dad and his chums caught Crip's old black tomcat, killed it, skinned it, and cooked it in the kitchen of one of Dad's little restaurants. They called it squirrel meat and delivered it to Crip on a linen-covered tray. When Crip returned to work the next morning, Dad and his coconspirators asked him how he liked his meal. They knew he would complain even about a free home-cooked lunch, and when Crip called it "the toughest squirrel meat" he had ever eaten, they were glad to tell him why.

Dad had a mean streak, and when he reached his limits it was wise to stay out of his way. A tough young drunk who had been harassing patrons in a Falwell restaurant, insisting he could "beat up anybody in the place," was pulled outside by my father, who supposedly shouted at him, "You want to fight? Fight him!" With that, my father threw the startled drunk into the bear cage. An eyewitness told me that Dad waited until the bear nearly scared the life out of that poor unsuspecting drunk before he dragged him from the cage screaming and pretty well mauled.

People didn't mess with my father. Even those who didn't respect him feared him. They knew he had shot his brother in self-defense, but couldn't help wondering whom he might shoot next. Dad always carried his gun, either in his belt or in a drawer or on a shelf a arm's length. He slept with his gun on the table by the bed. Nobody came close to Daddy when he was resting. They were afraid that if disturbed he might wake up shooting. Actually, Dad grew up carrying a gun. He was born in 1893 and wore a gun into the fields even during his adolescent years. Too many little Southern towns had no police departments and a sheriff that might drop by once a month or less. "Nobody will protect you or your family or your property if you don't protect them yourself," Dad used to tell us.

My father worked for the Burns Detective Agency in Roanoke, Virginia, before World War I and was appointed a special policeman in Campbell County. In 1916, my dad and mom barely escaped death when their first house behind the C. H. Falwell grocery store roared into flames in the middle of the night and burned quickly to the ground. Awakened with only seconds to run from the rapidly burning wood-framed building, they lost everything they owned except for the night clothes they were wearing.

During World War I my father was hired by the Norfolk and Western Railroad to guard the bridge crossing the James River and the various little trestles and bridges scattered about the county. He was glad to take the rail detective job. And though it seemed highly unlikely that the German Kaiser would send spies to blow up the railroad bridges of Campbell County,

Virginia, my father knew that protecting those bridges would exempt him from combat in Europe. During World War I, Dad shot a local man caught stealing from a boxcar who tried to get away. It was the only real combat that he saw during the war years.

The Prohibition era only reinforced Dad's need to carry fire-power. He was a "legitimate" bootlegger. He didn't make the stuff. He only bought and sold it. Still, the company he kept worked outside the law. Whether they were big-time crime fami-lies trading in liquor across the nation or small-time operators with one primitive still, they carried guns; and early on Dad refused to leave home without one. He even carried his pistol to the office.

Jerry Jr. learned just recently that my father, his grandfather, carried hundreds of thousands of dollars in life in-surance policies on himself during the 1930's, more than any other man in our entire state of Virginia. He had enemies and apparently no small fear that they might do him in. Even as a child I could see why people might hate him.

When I was just ten years old, I remember visiting my fa-ther at his office on payday. Dad was sitting at his desk passing out paychecks to his employees. Dad's drinking had increased measurably during those last few years. By the time I entered school, he was drinking a dozen beers a day and downing a fifth or more of whiskey on top of them. He usually hid his drinking and seldom showed the slightest sign of being drunk. But when he had been drinking heavily and was surprised or angered at the same time, it was dangerous to cross him.

"I'm not paying you today, Red," Dad said to one of his em-ployees just as I walked into the office.

Red was one of Dad's drivers. He had torn up a transmission that week. And his careless driving cost my father money.

"Why?" Red asked, his freckled face flushing pink with an-ger and surprise.

Red had been on Dad's payroll for many years. He was a friend of our family, and his wife and children had been invited to our home for supper. Dad liked Red and so did I.

"Because you cost me more this week than you earned me,"

my dad replied, brushing Red aside and passing checks to the next man in line.

I stood against the wall watching my friend Red and hurting for him. I knew he and his family needed the money badly. I decided that I would ask my father to pay Red anyway when I saw Red walk to a tool crib behind my father and pick up a heavy sledgehammer with a short wooden handle.

"Look out, Dad," I shouted, and without blinking, my father pulled his gun from his desk drawer, wheeled around in his swivel chair, placed the gun not three inches from Red's forehead, and said quietly, "Swing it, Red. Go ahead and swing it!"

Red stood there with the hammer held above Dad's head. The office emptied while both men faced each other. Dad was smiling. Red began to shake. Suddenly he dropped the hammer and walked quickly from the room without saying a word.

On Monday Red was back at work as usual. Dad paid him the next week and never spoke of it again so far as I know. Dad's rages appeared often without warning like a summer storm, and then disappeared again.

From that moment in 1931 when my father killed his brother, there were signs like this one of great emotional conflict growing deep within my father's soul. The court had found Carey Falwell "not guilty." And technically the court was correct. My father had committed no crime. There would be no trial. He would not serve time in a federal penitentiary or risk the gallows or the electric chair. He was free to return to his home and family. The fatal shot he fired would not cause him to miss one day of work. He was innocent in the eyes of the law and in the eyes of the community.

Jerry Jr. recently discovered this touching letter to my father written by Mr. B. F. Ginther on December 30, 1931, just one day after Dad's acquittal.

It is with a heart full of sympathy and understanding that I write you [the letter begins]. I am with you, as all good people are or should be. I am sure your friends understand, and that all sensible people understand. Don't be uneasy. Let your mind rest free. No sensible person is going to point you out in the future. You are going to be treated as a gentleman by all sensible folks who understand. The rest don't make any difference. So, don't pay any attention.

> PS. You owe it to yourself and your wife and your children and your business to square your shoulders, hold your head up and look the world square in the face like the man that you are. Don't forget your friends believe in you!

Mr. Ginther was the managing editor of the Brookneal newspaper, the *Union Star*. He expressed the general sentiment that my dad should feel guilty of no crime. But my father was guilty in his own eyes, and no acquittal by a Rustburg judge and no acceptance by the general public could end the years of agonizing guilt that would follow him to his grave. There were signs along the way that Dad was suffering from his unforgiven guilt, but Dad hid the signs, and most of the family suspected nothing. All through the 1930's and into the tragic years of World War II, the silent secret war raged inside my father.

Eventually, it destroyed him.

It is an ancient story as true today as it was true in the Garden of Eden at the beginning of creation. It is the problem of sin; and though we modern types try to bury the word beneath a mountain of psychological garbage, there is no other word for it. Whatever you call it, sin is real. Nobody called Garland's death a sin. The court did not call it sin. The police did not call it sin. The family did not call it sin. Even my father would not call it sin. Not knowing what to call it, he labeled his brother's death "an awful thing." It was self defense by everybody's standards, but in my father's heart it was sin. And regardless what you call it, sin has its inevitable consequences.

When the angel Lucifer sinned, he was cast out of heaven and doomed to stalk the earth. When Adam and Eve sinned, they were forced to leave the Garden of Eden and make their home in the wilderness. When Cain killed Abel, he was marked forever by his crime. When the ancient King David fell in love with Bathsheba, he knew his adulterous acts were sinful. But he never dreamed that the consequences of his sin would be so disastrous. One sin invariably leads to another. Adultery, for David, led to deceit, to dishonor, and to murder. Warned by the prophet Nathan that even kings have to pay for their sinfulness, David watched his family destroyed and his son murdered as a direct consequence of his sinfulness.

When will we learn? When we sin, we pay a price. And our only hope to minimize that price is to be forgiven of our sin and thus to be made right with God, with those we've wronged, and with our own conscience once again.

My father had been acquitted, but he had not been forgiven. For whatever justifiable reason, my father had broken God's law. He had sinned; and unless he found forgiveness for that sin, it would grow inside him like a cancer and eventually prove fatal. The Enemy would see to that. And my father's own story proves it true.

During my childhood and adolescent years, the unforgiven sin was like a small fire burning undetected in my father's heart. One day it would explode into a conflagration and consume him. But until that day, he got along just fine. He was a wonderful father. I look back on our short time together with great gratitude and many happy memories. Sin didn't destroy his effectiveness as a husband, father, friend, businessman, or community leader. But it must have been a whole lot harder for him to achieve all that he achieved with that cancer growing in his heart.

Dad was temporarily distracted from the problem of unforgiven sin during my childhood years by his family and his growing business enterprises. And when the distractions of home and office didn't work, he drank until the alcohol distracted him and eased his pain. At first he was in total control of his drinking. Then slowly the drinking got out of hand. It became harder and harder to distract him from the problem in his soul. He was crying out for forgiveness and didn't know where to find it. So he tried to drown out the misery with liquor and to bluff away his growing fear with wild pranks and acts of bravado. Violence and anger were not qualities basic to his character but fruits of the unforgiven sin still growing in his life.

Now we can see clearly how sin worked inside my father

for all those years. But then it was hard to notice or to identify even the subtle signs of the Enemy at work in him. If you look back over the picture albums of those first fifteen years of my life, no single picture would show what was happening to Dad. But Dad was being eaten away by the unresolved grief and the unforgiven sin working within him. And he and most of the family were just too distracted by life to see death approaching.

Almost two thousand years earlier, the Apostle Paul wrote the simple formula that would describe what happens if sin goes unforgiven. "The wages of sin is death," he wrote in a letter to Rome; and from that moment on December 28, 1931, at about seven o'clock in the evening when my father pulled the trigger and watched in shock and horror as his brother slumped to the floor and died, my dad began to die as well.

One fall night when Gene and I were still just children, a transient sitting near the large oil tanks on the rail line just above the house dropped a burning cigarette into the dry grass. Apparently he fell asleep; and by the time he noticed the flames, they were silently licking their way toward the coil of oil hoses that led to the main access valves. Apparently the transient had just time enough to run away before the tank exploded with a huge roar. It seemed like the end of the world. The ball of fire lit up the skies above Lynchburg and left us with exaggerated childhood memories of that sudden, frightening conflagration.

We were too young then to realize that in those next six years between 1939 and 1945 most of Europe and great portions of Asia and North Africa would also explode into flame. And we were too young to see the secret war already raging in my father's broken heart. Our childhood days were spent in our quiet, happy Valley of the Virginias. And though the Enemy was dealing death across the world and in my father's heart, the sun still rose above the apple orchard and set behind the nearby Blue Ridge Mountains. The James River still flowed silently past the seven hills of Lynchburg. The spring wildflowers still painted the hills on each side of Rustburg Road, and the fall still set the forests ablaze with leaves of red and orange and gold.

I have an obligation to my children, and to their children, to see to it that when I am gone I have left behind a legacy called freedom, liberty, morality and decency.

— Jerry Falwell

CHAPTER THREE

The Prodigal
Father

In the Fall of 1940 when Wendell Willkie was campaigning against President Roosevelt's third term in office and the Japanese were signing military pacts with Germany and Italy to form the Axis alliance, Gene and I were entering first grade at Mountain View Elementary School in Lynchburg, Virginia. I loved those elementary school days, especially the bus ride to and from our red-brick school building on Campbell Avenue. Sometimes Dad had his chauffeur drive us, but most of the time we caught the bus in front of Mrs. Burford's store on Rustburg Road.

From the earliest days, we gathered with the other children from our neighborhood at Burford's store early enough in the morning to buy Pepsi Colas and bags of peanuts with our lunch money. Before school, my friends from seven or eight neighborhood families stood on the porch outside that store waiting for the bus, talking excitedly about the day ahead. And after school we bought more Pepsis and more peanuts and sat talking until it was time for dinner. We were a miniature community, and Burford's store was our meeting place.

From that porch we could see the world. In the fall we could

71

look up Candler's Mountain at the wildly changing colors of the maple, birch, elm, sweet gum, and dogwood trees. In the winter we sat around the old wood-burning stove and watched the silent snow cover the hills and forests in white. In the spring-time the world blazed again with color; and the fragrance of dogwood, apple, and cherry blossoms mingled with the many wonderful smells of Mrs. Burford's general store.

She was a Christian lady who used our time in her store to share her Christian faith with us children. Often she turned up her radio so that even as we sat there chatting about the day at Mountain View Elementary, we would hear the sounds of Gos-pel music or the exhortations of Dr. Bob Jones, Sr. or some other preacher.

My six years at Mountain View Elementary are just a happy blur of memory fragments now. There's nothing left of the old brick building where we held our classes. A community recre-ation center stands on the site where I spent those years be-tween 1940 and 1946. I do remember that awful moment my brother Gene and I were separated by our second-grade teacher, Mrs. Hunter. She didn't think I belonged in the second grade; so, with the principal's approval, she skipped me on to third. From that day my brother and I were in different classes. We never knew exactly why she advanced me one whole year. Looking back, I think she knew that one Falwell twin was enough for any teacher to handle and she preferred Gene to me.

I especially remember the principal of Mountain View, Mr. Thomas W. Finch. He is eighty-four years old now and remem-bers all too well my elementary years. I confess that I had a mischievous streak even then. I am glad to say that most of my third- and fourth-grade pranks were harmless, even though I came close to injuring my best friend Wallace when I pulled his chair out from under him just as he sat down in it. Instead of being turned off by my occasional rowdiness, Mr. Finch seemed drawn to it.

He was a devout man and believed that even children needed to be developed spiritually alongside their physical and intellec-tual education. He sponsored weekly chapels for the student body. We learned hymns and sang them lustily. We read and quoted in unison great passages from the Scriptures, including the first and twenty-third Psalms, the beatitudes, the "Golden Rule," and Paul's definition of love in I Corinthians 13. Mr. Finch invited guest preachers and lay leaders to address his elementary children, and together we learned to pray the Lord's Prayer once a week before classes.

Of course that all happened before the Supreme Court made it illegal to read the Bible or to pray in the public classroom. But looking back on Mr. Finch and those spiritual experiences I shared with several hundred classmates, I feel a deep sense of loss for the children in elementary school today.

However, my real spiritual development took place at home. Mom led us in a prayer of thanksgiving before our meals. Often she prayed with us a bedtime prayer at night. And she insisted that we accompany her every Sunday morning to Sunday School and worship whether we wanted to attend or not. My grandfather was an atheist and my father was an agnostic who didn't support my mom in any of her spiritual plans for us children; although he did provide a car and driver for our weekly trip to Sunday School.

Dad's disinterest in Mom's Sunday plans never seemed to affect her. Like those of every Beasley, my mother's Sunday morning habits were fixed from childhood. After Dad had eaten breakfast and headed off to work, as he did seven days a week, Mom would feed us children and load us into the car for the short trip to the Franklin Street Baptist Church in Lynchburg.

I was no more excited about attending Sunday School than I was about attending church, but there was no arguing with my mother. During the war years, Virginia and her husband, Lawrence Jennings, lived with us on Rustburg Road and drove the family to Sunday School. For much of my childhood our older brother Lewis was in the Navy or too adult for Mom to charm into attending Sunday School. But Gene and I never found an excuse that would work with our determined mother. We carried our unread, unmarked Bibles to Sunday School every Sunday morning, but sometimes the minute the car was parked and everybody else had headed into their different classrooms, we ducked out the back door and headed south on Franklin

Street to the little home of my uncle Matthew Ferguson. He had married Carrie Beasley, one of my mother's sisters, and he was the only Beasley kin we know who didn't go to church.

We called Mr. Ferguson Uncle Ricker. Like us, he held out against the Beasley Sunday tradition. He didn't like church any more than we did, and his house was just seven or eight doors down Franklin Street from the little red-brick Baptist church with its flat-topped tower and mock stained glass. He must have watched for our appearance, because the minute we broke stride and ran for his front door it would swing open from inside and he would stand grinning in the shadows behind it to greet us.

Uncle Ricker always had sweet rolls and orange juice waiting. The News wasn't thick and the comics weren't printed in color, but it was a joy to read that paper on Sundays, flopped on the floor beside Uncle Ricker with the sound of poor trapped children singing in the distance.

There were occasions when Mother found us there and with a rather pained look at Uncle Ricker marched us back up Franklin Street to morning worship. Actually, the Reverend Robert L. Randolph was a very effective Gospel preacher. He is still remembered in Lynchburg for his positive and caring influence on our community. The Randolph Memorial Baptist Church now stands in Madison Heights, named in his honor.

And Richard Logwood, the teacher of our fifth-grade Sunday School class, was such a good Bible teacher that we actually looked forward to his classes. There were ten or eleven of us who gathered in little rows with our Bibles and our Southern Baptist Quarterly in hand. He assigned us homework for the week and rewarded us when we came prepared the following Sunday.

To us children, the Bible was the most boring book in the world, but to Mr. Logwood the Old and New Testament stories were more exciting than the Green Hornet or the Shadow. When he began the morning lesson, he took off his coat, threw it on the back of a chair, and got us in rows of little chairs around him. He started the story sitting down, but as the excitement mounted he would jump up and begin to pace. Suddenly that bare white-walled classroom came to life. We didn't have television then. We didn't have full-color books and magazines scattered around our bedrooms. So Mr. Logwood became the best if not the only entertainment in our town.

When Logwood taught, we listened. And though I never accepted his invitation to give my young heart to Jesus, I was impressed by the stories that he told me from the Gospels and often puzzled over their meaning. Through his exciting stories, he introduced us fifth-graders to the heavy stuff of Christian theology.

"See that cross standing there?" he said one Sunday the week before Easter. And we all looked at the whitewashed wall with the faded painting of Jesus dying on Golgotha. "That cross was like the electric chair or the gas chamber," he explained. "The Romans killed criminals on it. Was Jesus a criminal?"

Nobody answered. We leaned forward in our chairs.

"If He wasn't a criminal," Logwood asked, "why did the Romans kill Him?"

Suddenly we were there on Skull Mountain looking up at Jesus with the nails in His hands and feet and the bloody wound in His side. Suddenly thunder shook the earth beneath us and lightning lit up the pitch-black sky.

"Look closely at the man on the cross," Logwood whispered. "That is no criminal dying there. That is God Himself taking on the sins of the world."

Ten little boys stared up at the painting with eyes wide open and hearts beginning to pound. Mr. Logwood explained carefully that God was just. He couldn't condone sin. He must punish it. But that God was also merciful. It was His nature to forgive. So, to bring together God's justice and His mercy, a penalty had to be levied. A payment had to be made.

Logwood had already told us the story of the Jewish tradition of sacrifice. We had followed him in our imaginations to the top of Mount Moriah, where Abraham offered his son Isaac as a sacrifice, but God had provided a ram in a thicket instead. He had read us God's warning in Leviticus that without the shedding of blood there is no forgiveness of sin. And we had watched him sprinkle imaginary blood of an imaginary lamb on an imaginary doorpost as he recounted the ancient story of Passover.

Sacrifice a lamb, ordered God's angel to his people while they were slaves in Egypt, and when the angel of death sees the sacrificial blood on your doorpost he will pass over you, but in those houses where there is no sacrifice the firstborn son shall die.

He read from Psalm 16 and Psalm 22 the Biblical prophecies that one day in Christ's death the ultimate sacrifice would be made. And as we stood staring up at that man dying on the cross, he said, "This is God Himself saying in His death on the cross, You are forgiven. The final sacrifice has been made. My act of mercy has satisfied my need for justice."

Slowly Mr. Logwood sat down on his chair. "Has anybody here ever done anything bad?"

We grinned back at him and then looked down at the floor.

"Do you remember how hard it was to say 'I'm sorry'?" he asked after grinning back at us knowingly.

"And do you remember how good it felt when your dad or mom said 'That's okay. I forgive you'?"

I did remember, so I nodded.

"The death of Jesus on the cross," he said, "made it possible to know that whatever bad thing you do, He has forgiven you already."

Then Mr. Logwood asked if we would like to ask God to forgive us. One girl raised her hand. I remember others peeked around the class and giggled. I just sat there staring at the picture on the wall, trying to make sense of it. And though Mr. Logwood made it very tempting "to give my heart to Jesus," I held back during those elementary school years. When we outgrew Mr. Logwood's class, I lost interest in God and in the church again. I spent as many Sundays as I could reading the paper and drinking orange juice with Uncle Ricker.

Actually, attending Sunday School and church was about the only time demand Mom placed on us. After school and on weekends we were free to explore the wonders of our world on Rustburg Road. We had all kinds of animals to play with, from rabbits and dogs to goats, cows, sheep, and horses. When I was just seven, Dad put me on my first pony and trotted me around the farm. In a few days he turned the reins over to me and watched from the porch as I rode the pony up and down the front yard all by myself. One hot afternoon a snake spooked the pony. She rose up on her hind legs and came down running. I remember grabbing her mane and holding on tightly as we ran into the front yard past my startled father. When he saw that the horse was heading for the drop-off to Rustburg Road, Dad yelled, "Jump off!"

I remember how far the ground seemed and how frightened I was clinging to that runaway pony. But when my dad yelled out at me, I jumped without a moment's hesitation and rolled off the pony's back. The soft grass cushioned my fall, and I looked up just as the pony went over the hill and onto, Rustburg Road. With all Dad's weaknesses, even when I was just seven years old I knew that I could trust him.

Dad worked day and night, seven days a week. The time he spent shaping us directly was crowded into his already over loaded schedule. He just took enough time off work to aim us in a direction before he disappeared back to work again. For example, Dad gave us both .22 rifles when we were very young and encouraged us to practice with targets and to hunt game in the woods around our home.

Gene soon proved to be a natural hunter. Dad gave him a double-barreled shotgun for a Christmas gift when Gene was ten or eleven. I was afraid to shoot it. I hated the loud noise and the sudden recoil. But Gene wandered alone into the woods and practiced until he became quite skilled with the gun. He wore Dad's old hunting jacket and returned from a morning in the hills with his pockets filled with squirrels or rabbits he had killed.

Before he was twelve years old, Gene taught himself to skin and clean game. He loved to hike alone through the country side near our home in search of deer, squirrel, rabbit, turkey, and even quail. Occasionally we hiked together, climbing trees or Icing in wait for the animals. It was exciting to see a red fox with her pups or a brown deer grazing in a distant meadow, but I couldn't shoot anything, and watching the hunters skin and clean a carcass almost made me ill. I envied Gene his love for hunting and the out-of-doors skills he learned, but I just couldn't pull the trigger.

Over the years we had a garden variety of mixed-breed dogs to play with. I especially loved a little Scotch terrier named Pep. She was the real hunter in our family. Pep would chase anything, but her specialty was snakes. There are a variety of snakes in Virginia. Most, like the green and the black snakes, are harmless. Others including the copperhead, moccasin, rattlesnake, and cottonmouth are deadly. Pep didn't even bother to distinguish.

When a snake appeared anywhere near our home, Pep would rush up to it barking furiously. She would circle the snake growling and pawing the earth. The snake would rise to the bait. Keeping a careful eye on Pep, the snake would slowly lift its head above the ground to meet the little Scottie's challenge. Then, just when the snake's head was high enough in the air, Pep would quit barking, bare her teeth, and lunge for a hold just beneath the darting tongue. Then she would shake the snake angrily until it died and drag it proudly to the feet of any horrified person who happened along.

Pep and I used to walk across the fields on summer evenings to the sugarcane processing plant near Little Opossum Creek, just below the family cemetery. Grandpa Falwell was the first in our family to raise sugarcane and to process it into the sweetest natural molasses you ever tasted. The only problem was that every year it got harder and harder to find a foreman who knew the secrets of making sugarcane molasses. Finally Dad found an old black man in prison serving a life sentence for murder and robbery. He was the best molasses man in Campbell County. Every year the Falwells would get permission from the state prison board to take the man into their personal custody during sugarcane harvest time.

I can still remember the smell of that sugarcane boiling under pressure and the taste of those sweet molasses samples the old foreman would give me with a toothless grin and a proud shake of his head. I would sit on the hillside in the early evening talking to that wonderful old man about his early memories of Lynchburg. His grandparents had been slaves freed by the Quakers, who, like John Lynch, the city's founding father, hated slavery and refused to support it.

Even in our earliest years of childhood, Dad was determined that Gene and I would be industrious. From the be ginning of our lives, he tried to pass on to us his entrepreneurial ways. I don't remember how our minnow business got started, but it turned out to be one of our first successful attempts at earning our own money during those childhood years.

A narrow, slow-moving creek flowed past the front of our boyhood home on the other side of Rustburg Road. Fishermen en route to the James River, Isaak Walton Lake, or one of the many ponds or streams around Lynchburg would drive past our home every morning. I don't remember who suggested that we open up a little stand selling live minnows for bait, but Dad supported the idea enthusiastically.

He loaned us a truck and driver to go to the larger creeks around our home to seine for minnows. He helped us find a seining net that hung vertically in the water with floats on the top and weights on the bottom. He taught us how to use the net to catch the tiny wiggling fish and how to transfer them to tanks that held them on the short sloppy ride home. He helped us build a minnow box with screens on both ends and helped us place it securely in the stream that ran parallel to our family home. He showed us how to fill the box, carefully separating into different wired sections the various sized minnows and the larger "mud kittens" (baby catfish) that we trapped and carried home.

Before sunrise, fishermen would see our LIVE MINNOWS FOR BAIT sign, stop on Rustburg Road, and honk their horn for service. Gene and I took turns on the night shift. The twin on duty would hear the horn, jump into coveralls and a woolen sweater, switch on the front lights illuminating the sidewalk, the driveway, and even the distant creek and minnow box. He would cross the road, walk the fishermen to our bait tank, and use a handy net to scoop up minnows at fifty cents a dozen. Mud kittens cost more, selling as high as $1.25 for twelve.

The big bass and Virginia perch loved our live bait; so the fishermen loved us. We could make $25 to $30 a day each dur- ing fishing season. Between 1945 and 1948 we earned and banked a minnow fortune. We may have smelled of fish. And each morning sale with its loud honking and sudden flash of lights may have awakened Mom and Dad, but they never complained. In fact, often in the early morning we could see Dad grinning down on us from his bedroom window. Apparently he told the story of our "minnow millions" with embellishments to everyone who would listen.

Dad got us motorbikes when we were just twelve years old. Today's generation would call them dirt bikes. We roared up and down the hillsides, jumping over mounds of earth, spinning in the mud, and crashing through the underbrush.

When we were still in elementary school, Dad taught us how to drive. He was a good teacher. But Gene and I could hardly see above the wheel of his beat-up work truck or his Buick sedan. We would race about the Falwell acreage doing spinouts and "wheelies" when we could barely reach the accelerator or the brakes. Chickens flew screeching into the air and sheep ran for the hills as we sped past. Mom could tell where we were driving from the dust cloud that followed us around the property.

We were just thirteen years old when Dad decided to get us driver's licenses. I think he thought us safer on the highways than bumping over creeks and up and down the hillsides behind our home. We were still two years under the official driving age, but Dad went to the county seat in Rustburg, signed a statement that we were fifteen years of age, and got us our official driver's licenses anyway.

While we explored the back roads of Campbell County, Gene and I got interested in the Civil War history of Lynchburg and her environs. We climbed over the old walls of Fort Early, built in 1864 by Confederate General Jubal A. Early to guard the Salem Turnpike (Route 460) and to keep the approaching Union Army from Lynchburg's inner defenses.

We read the accounts of the battle for Lynchburg and stood gaping up at the pointed obelisk memorializing General Early's courageous and creative defense against the North. When we decided to build a mock Civil War cannon out behind the house, Dad supplied an old steel casing about six inches in diameter that he found lying in a pile of used casings near his oil-storage tanks. He helped us mount it on a wooden platform and taught us how to load and tamp our steel casing with gunpowder and a giant steel ball bearing that he gave us to use for a cannonball.

It is a wonder we didn't blow up the family home let alone half the neighborhood with that cannon. We learned to aim the thing, to light the powder through a hole in the top of the casing, and to hold our ears. We could fire that heavy ball bearing with amazing accuracy at dead trees clear across Rustburg Road. The startled neighbors would duck automatically from the loud explosion that echoed through the valley and then shake their trembling fists in our direction. Dad heard their complaints but only smiled. "Boys will be boys," he said, and I can still remember how proud he looked while saying it.

In those wonderful carefree years at Mountain View Elementary School, World War II seemed light-years away. Then our older brother Lewis received his letter from Uncle Sam.

"Dad nearly had a fit when Lewis received his draft announcement," Virginia remembers. "He walked up and down the living room waving the telegram and muttering about the 'idiots' who run the War Department."

Apparently Lewis and his buddies were excited about joining their destroyer escort at the Norfolk naval base. Virginia remembers how they walked down the driveway, arms around each other's shoulders, bending and swaying like drunken sailors, bragging about the ports they soon would visit and turning one last time to wave to Mom and Dad, who watched them go with sadness and with fear.

Early in the war, my sister Virginia married her high school sweetheart Lawrence Jennings. Lawrence's brother Ralph was drafted, trained, and shipped into combat immediately. A million boys were being sent away to fight the enemy. Lawrence thought he might be next. There was no time for him to establish a new home for his young wife, so they moved together into our home on Rustburg Road. Lawrence and Dad often sat in the kitchen talking and drinking until late at night. Lawrence drank very little, but by the war years my dad was drinking a pint of scotch whisky a day on top of his dozen bottles of beer during the late morning and early afternoon and a bottle or two of wine at dinner.

"Your father and I sat at the kitchen table," Lawrence told me recently, "after you and Gene were put to bed. We sat and talked together until two or three o'clock in the morning. Actually, your dad talked," Lawrence remembered, "and I listened. Usually he talked about shooting Garland.

"'I didn't really kill him, Lawrence,' he said over and over again. 'He killed himself, you know.' Then he would lean across the table, look into my eyes, and say, 'If you ever have to kill anybody, kill yourself instead.'

"Then," Lawrence recalled, "he would sit in silence for a long time, sipping whisky and staring into the past. Tears would form in his eyes and roll down his face. He didn't even bother to wipe them away. I would sneak away to bed leaving him there alone with his tears and his unhappy memories."

Lawrence's brother was killed on D-Day at a Normandy beachhead. Six weeks later his parents received the news in a telegram from President Roosevelt himself. The two families shared their mutual grief, and my father grew more and more anxious about my brother Lewis, sailing with his buddies somewhere in the waters of the Atlantic.

Every day at noon when Dad returned for lunch with Mother, he would stop at the mailbox at the bottom of the hill and search through the first and second-class mail, the bills and advertisements, for a letter from his son. None came. Dad's anger and impatience grew. Finally, worried about the silence, he called the Pentagon and asked to speak to the Secretary of the Navy. No one in Lynchburg believed that Dad would actually do it let alone get through. They didn't know my father.

"My boy is out there somewhere on a destroyer named the J. Douglas Blackwood," Virginia remembered Dad shouting into the telephone. "He's been out there three months without a word, and I will not tolerate one more day of silence."

Believe it or not, the Secretary of the Navy got word to my brother's ship and the commander ordered that every member of the crew write home once a week from that day forward. When Lewis finally returned on leave, he and Dad had a long, hot conversation about that telephone call to the Pentagon.

Apparently, when the word leaked out that it was Lewis Falwell's father who had caused them all their weekly discomfort, it made my brother the most unpopular man on board during the ship's long Atlantic patrol.

During Lewis's first Navy furlough Mom planned a festive welcome-home dinner in his honor. The family gathered around the dining-room table and ate sumptuously of the food Mom had prepared. Following dinner, we pushed back our chairs to hear the stories of Lewis's adventures in the Navy. Our older brother had left Lynchburg for the war in the Atlantic still a teenager. He returned home determined to be a man. He wore his white sailor hat jauntily over one eye. He swaggered about town like the Great Gatsby, bragging of his romantic exploits to his high school chums. I still remember how every shiny black hair on his head was greased permanently into place with Vitalis.

That first night home, after two pieces of Mom's French apple pie loaded down with scoops of home-churned vanilla bean ice cream, Lewis leaned back in his chair, took a pack of Camels from his breast pocket, jauntily lit a match with a quick flick of his thumbnail, and took a long drag on his cigarette. Just that quickly my father reached across the table without a moment's warning and hit Lewis squarely in the mouth. The blow came with such surprising force that our older brother flew backward out of his chair and sprawled face up on the dining-room floor.

Dad didn't say a word at first. He just sat there sipping his after-dinner coffee as Lewis blinked his eyes, stroked his painful jaw, and eventually took his place back at the table. Gene and I were speechless. Frankly, we didn't know whether to laugh or cry, but the mood was shifting toward twin bursts of laughter when Dad finally interrupted the long strained silence.

"Nothing's changed around here, Lewis," he said quietly. It was all that needed to be said. Dad hated the smell of cigarettes. No one ever smoked in our home. The rule had been long established. We all knew how much Dad loved his oldest son, how worried he had been when there was no word from him during his first months at sea. And when the war ended, my father gave Lewis his prime Hilltop Restaurant and bragged about his son's "courageous wartime record." Still, that first family dinner of our brother's long-awaited furlough ended painfully with Dad's violent outburst against him.

Those occasional violent outbursts were dramatic proof of Dad's growing problem with the bottle. Over the years, his guilt about Garland's death continued to plague him. He tried to drown the memories with great quantities of beer and whisky. The alcohol was being delivered to our home in ever increasing amounts. He packed the refrigerator with beer and wine bottles and stowed his flasks and decanters of whisky in various oft-visited locations in the rooms of our family home and in his desk at the office.

At night Dad stayed up later and later with his handful of longtime friends and employees, drinking in the back rooms of his restaurants or in his private inner office. Mother waited up for him each night. She always had a full dinner warming for him in the oven when he returned, regardless of the hour. Before long the other wives began to call my mother asking when they could expect their husbands to return from Dad's latenight drinking bouts. Mother was always hurt and embarrassed by their calls.

Dad seldom showed any signs of drunkenness. He continued to manage the businesses that remained, but his dark moods and occasional violent outbursts were increasing. Sometimes he struck with words alone. David Brown had been our faithful, loving nurse from infancy. He was a model employee, but when Dad came home raging about a problem in a restaurant or filling station, he often took it out on David. Mom would rush to David's side and defend him.

"Leave him alone, Carey," she would say quietly. "You know he's a good man. You're just not feeling well."

And though my father was typically generous and supportive of his black employees, in those drink-induced, guilt-ridden rages he might call my mother "a g— - d—— nigger lover" in David's presence and then turn to walk away.

As the drinking increased, Mom learned to control his violent outbursts with a quiet word or a loving embrace. In the midst of Dad's alcohol-fueled rages, she would say firmly, "Why, Carey, you know that's not right." He would grumble and groan at her, but gradually, as he sobered, he would come to his senses once again.

Occasionally angry words were not enough and Dad would strike out with his fists before thinking. Only once in my childhood do I remember my father actually striking me. I was thirteen years old. Mom and Dad were in the kitchen late one evening. He was pouring himself another scotch from his hidden home supply. Mom was taking his warmed meal from the oven. Gene and I had been wrestling in our bedroom when Dad arrived.

I raced down the steps to greet him in the kitchen. Gene chased after me shooting spitballs from a rubber band. Just as I approached my father, one of Gene's errant missiles hit him in the neck. That sudden surprising sting whirled my father in my direction. Without thinking, he smacked me hard with his open hand.

I didn't say a thing. Gene and Mom were stunned momentarily into silence. I left the room and went to bed. Gene followed. I lay in the darkness feeling the sting of his hand across my face. But I didn't hate him or fear him or mistrust him for it. I loved and trusted my father even in times like this. He was not a violent man. Even as a child I knew intuitively that he hated those occasional bouts with violence and rage as much as we hated them. I couldn't understand his secret struggle. I didn't know then that it was the predictable result of unforgiven sin boiling in those secret, miserable places of his heart. I knew that by morning he would be sober and himself again.

That night Mom sat beside Dad as he downed several more whiskies chased by a bottle of cold beer. Slowly, lovingly she explained to him what had really happened. Apparently he began to feel great remorse. Before sunrise that next morning Dad awakened me.

"I'm sorry, son," he said, sitting on the edge of my bed. Actually, after a few moments sulking the night before, I had forgiven him and gone to sleep without another thought about it. It was an easy mistake to understand, but Dad had never hit me before. He was grief-stricken. He took my hand and tried to make it right.

"Your mother told me what happened," he said quietly. "I'm sorry, son," he mumbled again. "Real sorry." Then he kissed me on the cheek and walked toward the door of our bedroom. For a moment he stood in the light of the hallway looking back at me. I muttered something and smiled back at him. Then he turned and walked away. As I watched him, I realized my father had grown old. His shoulders were stooped. His hands trembled. He looked tired and lined and pale. Now, looking back, I am convinced that it was that unforgiven sin that was undoing him. He had killed his brother. And though everyone else had forgiven him, he still could not forgive himself. Only God had the power to forgive him adequately, and my father did not believe in God.

About the time General MacArthur signed the truce with the Japanese ending World War II, our family began to realize that my father was an alcoholic. Doctors and ministers did not know much about helping alcoholics in 1945. Christian homes for alcoholics were still years away. Most of our Baptist friends saw drunkenness as a sin and condemned it roundly. They attacked the alcoholic for his drinking and forgot that often drunkenness is a symptom of a much more serious, often hidden struggle with the Enemy.

Fortunately, my mother understood Dad's real problem. She never scolded Daddy for his drinking. She just loved him faithfully, refused to be hurt or angered by his drunken rages, cleaned up his empty whisky bottles, and prayed that one day he would find the forgiveness he was seeking.

And though Dad drank great and growing quantities of beer, wine, and whisky every day, he still managed to run his various businesses around the county and to be a responsible and loving husband and father. When Dad did explode at the end of a working day, Mom simply calmed him with her quiet, careful warnings.

"I'll shoot that so-and-so," Dad would say, drunk and angry about an employee who may have stolen from the cash register or an IRS inspector who seemed to be snooping into Dad's past tax records.

"You would like to shoot him, Carey," Mom would answer calmly. "But you won't. You aren't a stupid man."

She knew just the right thing to say when alcohol fueled my father's anger and frustration. Within minutes he would be himself again. And because my mother never seemed thrown off balance by his surprising and sometimes vicious tirades, the whole family managed to stay on an even keel during his last three years of struggle.

"Your daddy's going to be all right," she would reassure us. "Now don't you get bothered by it. He's just fine. After a good night's sleep, he'll not remember anything about this, and," she added, winking, "neither will we."

My father saw his business empire begin to collapse during those painful years of World War II. More than one million American men and women were killed or wounded on the battle-fields. There was little to celebrate in the Merry Garden Dance Hall above Lynchburg. Business dwindled. Finally in 1942 Dad sold his great dining room with its polished floors and starched tablecloths to his brother Warren. The once great night spot became a dusty roller-skating rink on the edge of town.

The war had cost the nation billions in war equipment and supplies. Every extra drop of oil was needed on the battlefields, and gasoline was rationed for civilians, so my father's domestic oil supplies began to dry up. He closed his Power Oil Company in 1942 and that same year sold many of his filling stations across the state. There was little discretionary money for vacations and no fuel for vacation driving or rubber for tires, so my father sold off the Old Fort Cottage Inn that same year.

After the war, Lewis's Hilltop Restaurant continued to prosper for several years. Dad kept several filling stations and the restaurant on Bedford Avenue, but he moved his offices into the barn behind our house and presided there over his last really thriving business in firewood and coal. Trucks would unload large piles of logs in our backyard. Workers would trim the logs and feed them into the giant rip saw and then cut and bundle large loads of firewood.

About that time, my father began his slow, painful death of

cirrhosis of the liver. I was just fourteen. I couldn't know then
that my dad actually had begun to die seventeen years before
on that night in 1931 when he shot and killed his brother Garland. Often Dad stayed in his office over the huge barn late into
the night with one or two of his cronies drinking and remembering.

During all those years Dad was plagued by a recurring series of "if onlys." If only he had taken more time to be with
Garland. If only he hadn't teased Garland out of attending Sunday School and church when his little brother was a child. If
only he had loved his brother more. If only he hadn't panicked
when Garland entered Warren's office firing those pistols. If
only he had remained calm, reasoned quietly, and taken those
guns out of his brother's hands. If only he had put his arm around
Garland and talked him to his senses. If only he hadn't jumped
from the broken window, run to the neighbors' house to get
back his shotgun, or fired the shotgun in a moment of anger and
fear.

I've talked to several of his old friends who remember those
late-night drinking times together. Apparently, after Dad joined
in the conversations about Roosevelt and Truman, the Marshall
Plan, and the growing Cold War with the Soviet Union, he would
almost invariably begin to talk about his brother Garland and
that night in Warren's restaurant when Garland died.

His friends told me that my dad's eyes would fill with tears
as he talked about shooting Garland and the years of regret
and remorse that followed. Then he would grow silent. His
drinking chums would eventually steal away. Apparently my dad
would sit in the old barn alone with his memories and his bottle,
sometimes for hours before turning off the lights and walking
across the field to our home on Rustburg Road.

I can still remember finding him lying on the path between
the barn and our family home when I was thirteen or fourteen
years old. Dad had left his office after spending the afternoon
drinking alone behind its locked doors. He was so tired and so
drunk that he slumped down along the pathway to rest. I found
him lying there unconscious on the ground. It really upset me
to find him sprawled out in the cold and damp. I woke him up

and then, with his arm around my shoulder, I helped him home. Money was falling out of his pockets, coins all over the ground.

Mom saw us coming. She stood at the window looking up the pathway. She wasn't angry. She didn't lose her temper. She didn't scold or humiliate him further. She just watched faithfully and when she saw us coming she rushed to open the door.

"Carey," she said, "you're home now. It's time for bed."

I still remember how Dad opened his eyes and looked at her. Then he looked at me. He didn't say a word. He just sat on the steps looking back and forth between us. Then Mom helped him up the stairs and into bed.

I didn't understand it then, but Dad's unforgiven guilt for killing his brother was in the process of killing him. Though it was entirely understandable, Dad had made a terrible mistake. Apparently he was hoping that if he tried hard enough he could find a way to undo the damage that had been done. Of course there was no way. In a moment of terror he had pulled the trigger. My father had killed his own brother. He had sinned, but he had no idea that his sin would be fatal to himself as well.

The once strong, proud man had become a victim of his unforgiven sin. God loved my father, but my father did not believe in God. Little by little the Enemy had won. I didn't dream it then, but within a few short months we would bury my dad in the family graveyard near our home.

During his seventeen years of suffering, I don't know one man who thought to explain to Dad what the Apostle Paul made clear almost 2,000 years ago. "The wages of sin is death; but the gift of God is eternal life through Jesus Christ our Lord." My father desperately needed to find God's forgiveness. Gradually his unforgiven guilt led to alcoholism, and his alcoholism led to death.

There was one woman besides my mother who tried to help Dad understand. Her name was Virginia Glass McKenna. Virginia was my father's cousin. They had been friends as children and spent at least one vacation with their families on Lake Erie in 1913. Virginia was a descendant of Lynchburg's great Carter Glass family. She married Emmett McKenna, a Lynchburg industrialist who owned the McKenna Meat Packing Plant and other businesses in the Lynchburg area. Virginia was a member of the Bethesda Presbyterian Church, a committed Christian woman and a determined witness to her faith.

In her later years, Virginia was an ebullient round-faced, heavy-set woman known about town for her aggressive soul-winning tactics. Nobody intimidated Virginia. Nobody was too important or too busy or too far gone to hear the good news. She was the only person I know who tried to witness to my father from the first day that she met him.

"Now, Carey," she would say, surprising him in our kitchen with a third or fourth whisky highball in his hand. "You need to stop all this. You need to go to church and make things right."

Somehow, Virginia never offended my father. He seemed almost glad to spot her in a crowd. And though he grinned down at her when she witnessed, as a parent might grin down at an errant child, I am convinced that all those years she was laying the groundwork for a kind of miracle.

Virginia was a friend of Billy Sunday and at least an acquaintance of most of the traveling evangelists during the first half of this century. One of Dad's boyhood friends told me that Virginia had convinced my father to attend a tent meeting in the early 1930's. In fact, she persuaded Dad to allow the evangelist to pitch his tent on Falwell land. Several people remember how my father surprised them one night when he actually dropped by the meeting, sat in the shadows, held a hymn-book while the people sang, listened to the preacher's sermon, and watched the seekers kneel and pray around the mourners' bench. Then, just as quietly as he came, he disappeared again.

Virginia was never discouraged. She and Mother prayed for Dad daily. They both believed with all their hearts that one day he would find God's forgiveness. But time was running short. My father was dying. During the spring and summer of 1948 the poison accumulating in his liver from his excessive drinking began to spread throughout his system. The poisonous fluids were causing Dad to swell. He grew jaundiced, weak, and very ill.

After my sister Rosha's death, Dad hated hospitals and was suspicious of doctors and their mistakes. And though he was dying of the poisons in his system, he refused to be taken from our family home on Rustburg Road. He did allow a doctor in to tap and to draw off the deadly fluids. It was a painful process that left him even more weak and helpless. Mom and Virginia waited. They had done their best to present the Gospel to him, but he had not responded. So they sat by his bedside, tried to make him comfortable, and prayed for his spiritual and physical recovery.

One afternoon in late September 1948, Virginia met Frank Burford at a grocery store. Frank was a longtime business associate of my father and a good friend. He died in March, 1987 at age 85, but when my son Jerry Jr. and I interviewed him about that conversation with Virginia McKenna thirty-eight years ago he remembered every word in detail.

"Virginia walked up to me and my wife in the store," Frank told us. "'Carey's awful sick, Frank,' she said to me. 'Why don't you go round to see him?' Then she said one more thing, looking me in the eye and talking serious. 'And if you will, Frank, please mention something to him about his soul.'

"I remember the chrysanthemums were in bloom," Frank told us. "My wife cut a big bunch of them flowers for Carey and packed a whole basket with fresh fruit. Carey had been good to us over the years. If he liked you, he'd get up out of bed in the middle of the night and walk to Lynchburg in the snow to do you a favor. We were sorry he was dying. But I didn't know exactly what to say to Carey 'bout his soul."

Frank Burford took the plunge. With a huge bunch of white chrysanthemums in one hand and a basket of fresh fruit in the other, he arrived in Dad's bedroom looking more like a delivery man than an old friend come to say good-by. Frank remembers worrying about what he would say all the way to our home on Rustburg Road.

"The Lord says just open your mouth and He'll put words in it," Frank told us. "So I did. Carey wasn't an easy man to talk to about his soul. I didn't know what to say nor how he'd answer."

"Carey, you told me once if ever you could do something for me, you would do it," Frank began quietly sitting in a chair beside my daddy's bed.

"Well, boy," my father answered, "you see me lying here in this bed, don't you. But if there's anything I can do, I'll do it."

"I want you to join the church," Frank remembers blurting out, feeling kind of foolish as he said it.

"Boy," my dad answered from his pillow without a moment's hesitation, "I'm going to do it."

Frank was stunned by the sureness and the suddenness of Dad's reply. Virginia and Mom looked at each other across the room, their eyes beginning to fill with tears.

"Well, good, Carey," Frank answered. "When you gonna do it?"

"Any time you bring the man down," Dad replied. "Anytime."

Frank remembers whispering to my mother, "Mrs. Falwell, would it be all right for me to bring the preacher down here to see Carey?"

"Any hour of the day or night," my mother answered gratefully.

"So I drove straight over to the old Jehovah Jireh Presbyterian Church in Bocock," Frank remembers. "Andrew Ponton was the preacher. It was after nine o'clock at night and he was sleeping on a cot in the little parsonage right next to the church. Just a short while back brother Ponton had suffered a heart attack. He didn't get around too easy after that and talked to me through the door still laying on his cot.

"'Brother Ponton,' Frank recalls saying, 'I want you to come with me down to see Carey, Carey Falwell. You know he's sick.'"

"I can't go tonight," the Reverend Ponton answered weakly, still quite ill himself.

"Well, just when can you come?" Frank asked.

"I'll go with you in the morning," brother Ponton replied. "I'm just not feeling up to going over there tonight."

"What time then?" Frank asked, feeling disappointed and afraid that either one of them might die before the business of Carey Falwell's soul was taken care of.

"Any time you come for me," the preacher replied.

"I was there at nine o'clock in the morning," Frank remembers. "I had to carry the old man into your daddy's bedroom," he added. "I sat him in a chair at the end of your daddy's bed."

After my father repeated his desire to join the church, the preacher answered, "This Sunday afternoon, we could have the elders here-"

"Don't wait till Sunday, Carey," Frank remembers cutting in.

"No," my father said, agreeing. "I'm going to make my confession right here and now."

Thirty-nine years have passed since that day my father confessed his sins and found God's forgiveness. Mom and Dad are dead. Virginia and the Reverend Ponton are dead. Frank Burford died in March, 1987. After almost four decades of silence, Frank Burford still would not share anything my father confessed that night.

"And I'll carry his story to my grave," Frank told us. "I promised your daddy I would never tell anybody. And I have kept my promise. But I will tell you this," he added. "He just opened up and told God everything. Pretty soon he was crying. And I was crying. And brother Ponton was crying. I didn't even try to stop my tears, because I knew the presence of the Lord was there. And when Carey prayed and asked God to forgive him, I thought my heart would break. Cause I knew what your daddy had suffered over killing his brother. Everybody knew. And to see him get that right with God at last was something special."

"Mrs. Falwell," the Reverend Ponton asked at the end of my father's prayer, "would you bring us a bowl of water?"

My mom hurried to the kitchen, poured warm water into a bowl, and took it to the preacher.

"Carey Falwell," Andrew Ponton began, "because you have confessed your sins and been forgiven by the Lord, as He has promised, I baptize you in the name of the Father, the Son, and the Holy Ghost. Amen."

"Nobody moved after that," Frank remembers. "We all just sat there around Carey's bed praying silent, thankful prayers and staring at your daddy through our tears."

In the life, death, and resurrection of Jesus my father found the only possible solution to his sinfulness. That solution to my dad's grief and guilt had been there waiting through all his years of suffering.

The need to be forgiven, to be reconciled with God and with each other, began at the beginning of time. From that first day in the Garden of Eden when Adam and Eve sinned, God had been working to rescue from the power of sin His first two creatures and all of us who would follow.

Thousands of years ago, during ancient Old Testament times, God was there to forgive human sin through the blood of a sacrificial lamb. The old sacrifice system may seem strange, even hideous, to us now, but it is important to try to understand it. The reasons behind the ancient sacrificial system are as valid today as they were those thousands of years ago.

God is holy. He cannot condone sin. God is just. He must therefore punish sin. But God is also merciful. It is His loving nature to forgive sin. In order to synchronize God's holiness, His justice, and His mercy, a payment had to be made. What good is a law if it cannot be enforced? What good is a criminal justice system, if injustice is not punished? Moses wrote simply that without the shedding of blood there is no remission of sin.

In Exodus 12 Moses tells a story that helps us understand how the Old Testament sacrificial system began. To save the world from sin, God needed a people who would love and obey Him. He chose a motley crowd of twelve different tribes who were slaves in Egypt. He decided to rescue those tribes and unite them in a plan that would lead the world to salvation. To effect the rescue, God called Moses to be His spokesman to the King of Egypt.

Pharaoh, Moses cried in obedience to God's command, let God's people go! And when Pharaoh would not listen, Moses assembled the elders of those little enslaved tribes and whispered God's amazing instructions to them.

Sacrifice a perfect lamb, he commanded. Splash its blood on the upper doorpost of your house. Then roast and eat the lamb with unleavened bread and bitter herbs. But eat with your shoes on your feet and your staff in your hand and eat in haste: It is the Lord's Passover.

That same night, to punish their disobedience and to

convince them of His power, God's angel of death killed the firstborn sons of Egypt. This terrible, moving story illustrates how seriously God takes the matter of sin and disobedience. Pharaoh had disobeyed God's servant. The Egyptian king had refused to set God's people free. So God plagued Pharaoh for his disobedience. But the people of God were spared because they did as they were told. The blood of the sacrificial lamb that they had spread on the doorposts of their homes signaled the angel of death to pass over and spare the people inside. From that night, Jews have celebrated the Passover feast, a memorial to God's promised deliverance from death and slavery.

By Jesus's time, sacrifice had become a complex ritual at the heart of Jewish faith. Birds and animals, fruit and grain, oil and spices, were given to God in the temple on appointed feast days or as an act of thanksgiving, for tribute, for worship, or for forgiveness of sin.

As the sacrificial system evolved, the penalty for a person's guilt for breaking the Law of God could thereby be temporarily removed. The tainted body and mind of the sinful person could be reconditioned by the shed blood of a sacrifice dropped by a priest on the ear, thumb, and toe of the offerer - as prescribed in Exodus 29:20. Since the blood had been consecrated by its contact with God's altar, the procedure of washing with blood signaled the regeneration or rebirth of the guilty, tainted person, and the death sentence was thus removed. The guilty one was literally made alive again, at least in type.

How can we modern men and women understand this ancient Hebrew rite of sacrifice? It is difficult if not impossible to understand it. But we can know this. By Jesus's time, the temple, its priests, and their sacrifices had become a corrupt and exploitative system. Money changers shortchanged and cheated the poor. Merchants charged grade A prices for scrawny, sickly sacrificial animals. Priests and Sadducees increased their own wealth and power by demanding that the people buy their way to salvation.

The sins of priests and laymen alike increased until the sacrificial system, meant to alleviate sin, became a sin itself. The law condemned the people for their sinfulness but provided no way for their guilt to be removed. Jesus came to provide the new, authentic way of forgiveness. Jesus Himself was the new sacrificial lamb of God having no spot or blemish. He lived a sinless life. He was totally God but not so much God that He ceased to be man. And He was totally man, but not so much man that He ceased to be God. He experienced all the pain and agony, the suffering, testings, and trials that we experience. The Apostle Paul wrote, "He suffered in all points like as we yet without sin."

Jesus was the merciful God Himself meeting His own demands of justice and holiness. Like the Passover lamb, on that cross of Calvary, Jesus's blood was shed for our sins. And from that day to this, the forgiveness of sins comes to anyone who dares to believe that the application of His blood upon the doorposts of our hearts is adequate to satisfy God's justice and holiness and to obtain God's mercy. Jesus's death on the cross is God's gift of salvation. We do nothing to earn it. He holds it out to all who will confess their sins, admit their need for His forgiveness, and accept that gift into their hearts.

Unfortunately, my dad waited until just days before he died to accept God's loving gift. Those who were in the room with him that day remembered well the immediate and incredible change that God's forgiveness brought to him. The load of guilt that he had carried finally dropped away. He was forgiven. He was reconciled with God and with his family. He found peace in his troubled heart at last.

Jerry Jr. and I interviewed Frank Burford on tape to get the whole story of my dad's deathbed conversion. Apparently, after my father prayed the sinner's prayer, my mother wiped away her tears of gratitude, walked over to the bed, and kissed Dad on the cheek. Then she turned and led everybody from the room.

At the front door as her guests were leaving, Mom took Frank Burford's arm and smiled up at him gratefully.

"Frank," she said, tears welling up in her eyes, "if you don't have but one star in your crown, you are going to have a mighty big one."

Life is filled with glorious
opportunities brilliantly disguised as
insoluble problems.

— Jerry Falwell

God never promised to keep you out of trouble; but He does promise to be with you through all your troubles.

— Jerry Falwell

CHAPTER FOUR

The Prodigal Son

During the last two weeks before he died, my father's life showed remarkable change. He continued to fail physically, but his spirit was literally reborn. The heavy burden of guilt that he had carried those seventeen years just fell away. In his short, honest prayer of confession Dad had discovered God's forgiveness, and it made a difference that was obvious even to me.

Before his conversion, my father had an explosive temper with a very short fuse. He was often demanding and used rough, profane language to get his way. But after his conversion, my father quit his demanding ways. He became grateful for every little act of kindness and his profanity ended altogether.

During those last few weeks, Dad's body was still swollen from the poison in his system. He was in constant and intense pain, but his eyes were warm and alive. When Gene and I walked up to his bed, he would smile at us and grab our hands. Often, tears welled up in his eyes when Mother approached his bed, and when he spoke we hardly recognized his gentle, quiet voice.

Just two weeks after Frank Burford's visit, my father faced

his final crisis. He contracted pneumonia and his lungs filled with fluid. The doctor took our family aside late on the evening of October 9, 1948, to warn us. "Carey won't make it another twenty four hours," he told my mother. "You should alert the family."

The Falwells began to gather at our home on Rustburg Road early the next morning. By afternoon the house was filled with relatives, food, and flowers. Throughout his illness, Dad had remained in a downstairs bedroom just off the kitchen. Mom, my sister Virginia, and my brothers Lewis and Gene joined close friends and family around Dad's bed that last evening. There must have been fifty other people spread throughout various rooms of the house, with dozens of neighbors dropping by just to offer their best wishes along with a gift of fried chicken or a deep-dish apple pie. They would stand on the porch holding Mother's hands and whispering quietly. Then they would hug her tenderly and disappear down the driveway.

I had just left Dad's bedroom and walked into the kitchen when the house grew very quiet. I turned from the sink and ran toward my father's room. "He's gone, Jerry," someone whispered as I pulled up just short of the bedroom door. People were crowding in to comfort my mother. I remember standing there wanting to be alone with Mom but unable to even reach her through the crowd. Finally I bolted up the stairway and down the hall to my own bedroom to escape the scene. My father was dead, and with all his weaknesses, I loved him. I was just fifteen years old. I would never see my dad again, and already I missed him terribly.

Dad had not spent a great deal of time with us over the years. He certainly wasn't the kind of doting parent who ends up at every parents' night or spelling bee, music recital or football game. I don't think he attended a PTA meeting in his lifetime. But he loved us, and the rare times we shared were often adventures worth remembering.

I closed the door, switched off the light, and flopped down across my bed. I remember crying quietly for a few minutes and then lying there in the darkness thinking about Dad, wishing he hadn't died, wondering what his death would mean to our life together as a family.

Then suddenly there was a quiet tapping on the door. One of my mother's sisters entered the bedroom and sat down beside me. She didn't say anything. She just sat beside me with her hand resting on my shoulder. I wondered if my mother had sent her. I think I'll always remember how much my aunt's silent, loving presence meant in that time of grief. Now almost forty years have passed, but I still think of her sitting there beside me in the darkness. And when I feel the urge to speak words of comfort during someone else's grief, I remember how much more silence and a loving touch can mean than a torrent of words.

We gathered around Mom in the living room after most of our friends and family had gone. Mother had many decisions to make, but my older siblings, Virginia and Lewis, helped her make them. Gene and I were too young to be involved in the business side of dying. I remember watching my mother during that long night, wondering why she didn't cry.

Dad had been in such physical pain that his death was almost a relief to her. And because he had found the Lord in that prayer of confession two weeks earlier, she knew that death was only the beginning of Dad's new life in the presence of his heavenly Father.

I had little interest in eternity in those days. Heaven was not a place I cared to visit let alone to think about very seriously. I avoided church when I could. I didn't read the Bible or pray. I had no real interest in God let alone a personal relationship with Him. But I felt no strong feelings against God either. I didn't blame Him for my father's death. In fact, after those first tears in my bedroom the night Dad died, I don't think I cried again about his passing.

I do remember greeting the undertaker at the door and watching as my dad's body was taken away for the embalming and then returned again for those two days of viewing in our living room. It was a Falwell tradition based on years of Southern practice for family and friends to assemble around the open casket in a living room or bedroom of the family home. I remember those two days and how strange it felt at first to be in the room with my dad's body. The family laughed and cried together. We talked about Dad and we sat in silence remembering him. And though that old Southern tradition seemed uncomfortable at first, looking back I realize now how much I was comforted by it. Whatever had been left unsettled by my father's death was settled in that family circle around his open casket.

The funeral was held at home. The house and grounds were crammed with hundreds of people. Chairs were set on the front porch and all across the long front lawn. The minister, Dr. John L. Suttenfield, pastor of the Fairview Christian Church, was pastor to the entire Falwell clan. Even those uncles and aunts and cousins and nephews who didn't belong to Dr. Suttenfield's church were married and buried by this distinguished Lynchburg clergyman. He conducted my father's funeral standing in the open doorway on the west side of our front porch, addressing simultaneously the crowds inside and outside the house. It was the door Gene and I had used to service our minnow business during the early morning hours when Dad was still alive. As I sat listening to the minister's big booming voice eulogizing my father, I remembered Dad standing in that same doorway in his robe and slippers smiling proudly at us as we ran toward the little creek and the minnow tank he had helped us build to serve the waiting fishermen.

My dad's funeral procession was so long that it stretched from our home more than a mile up the Old Rustburg Road and at least another mile down the New Rustburg Road, winding around the country lane up to our old family cemetery on the hill. As we walked toward the little iron fence that surrounds the Falwell graveyard, I looked back down the hillside at the steady stream of people that were gathering to pay tribute to my father.

The grass had been mowed and smelled fresh and sweet. Great garlands of flowers surrounded the casket with color and fragrance. It was October 12, 1948, and the trees were changing from green to burnished orange, bright red and yellow. Nature seemed decked out for a celebration, but all the mourners were dressed in black. Mom wore her long dark Sunday dress, a large wide-brimmed black hat with a veil, and her dark winter coat. She smiled and greeted everyone as we walked to the two rows of chairs that had been placed for the family near Dad's grave.

Dr. Suttenfield waited until the long line of cars had parked and the mourners had assembled on the hill. I remember that he smiled at my mother, opened his Bible, and began to read from the book of John, Chapter 11.

It was the story of Jesus's special friend Lazarus of Bethany, whom Jesus loved. Apparently Lazarus had grown ill quite unexpectedly, and before his sisters Mary and Martha could get word to Jesus, Lazarus had died.

The Apostle John, an eyewitness at the scene, remembers how Jesus wept when He was led to His dear friend's tomb. And how the people watched in disbelief and joy as Jesus said, "Lazarus, come forth!"

"I am the resurrection and the life," Jesus said to them that day. "He that believeth in me, though he were dead, yet shall he live."

I listened to the story from John 11, but I don't remember being moved by it then. I was more interested in the crowd of people stretching out in all directions from my father's casket. They had come to honor him. He had been a leading business-man in the city. He had owned the oil company, the bus lines, various stores, restaurants, and filling stations. During Prohibition he had kept a steady flow of illegal whiskey moving to his friends and customers in Lynchburg and across Campbell County. During the Depression he had loaned money to many of them, given them food, provided a job or a place to live.

But through it all, the killing of his brother haunted my father mercilessly. Recently, in a pile of old family treasures, Jerry Jr. found my dad's last wallet. It was crammed with business cards, little lists of figures and important appointments he had scheduled. Hidden beneath it all was just one picture, a photo of his kid brother Garland.

Dr. Suttenfield finished his address with a stirring reminder that God's forgiveness made an incredible difference in my father's life, but it still had not made a difference in mine. I was just fifteen. I hadn't committed any grievous sins that I could remember. I certainly had not killed my brother. I didn't really need to be forgiven, or so I thought.

On those occasions when I had broken a family law, Mom had been there to correct and punish me. She had always been the disciplinarian in our family. And though she set few rules, bad language or disrespect were strictly off limits. Even worse, she hated for Gene and me to fight with each other.

"If you are going to fight," she would say when a fresh war broke out between us, "I am going to switch you." She also threatened a switching when Gene or I swore or talked back offensively. Dad always encouraged the fights between us. He even liked to see us get angry a bit and seldom if ever scolded us for bad or profane language. He smiled at our offenses, but Mom didn't see the humor. She simply walked to the kitchen door, broke a thin willow branch from the tree near the back porch, and applied that willow switch briskly to our buttocks. The punishment stung and left red marks on our posteriors that faded with her forgiveness. She never hit angrily or out of control and certainly left no scars. When she really wanted to make her point, Mom made us pick our own willow switch and deliver it to her for our punishment.

Dad never supported Mom's attempts to discipline us any more than he supported her attempts to get us to go to church. Still, she tried. After seeing their prayers for my father answered, Mom and Virginia McKenna, her collaborator in the spiritual underground, went to work on me. Mom never preached or lectured me, but every Sunday morning she turned on the Mutual Broadcasting radio network to Charles Fuller's "Old Fashioned Revival Hour" program. I awakened in the morning to the cheery Gospel music of Rudy Atwood and the Revival Hour Choir. While I bathed, I could hear Mrs. Fuller ("Honey") read the letters. And during breakfast while I ate my hoecakes, eggs, and ham, Charles Fuller preached and I was forced to listen.

After Dad's death, my mother, with my sister Virginia's help, moved immediately into managing the few businesses that were left, especially the firewood company in the huge barn behind our home. After cutting the best wood into building lumber, the Lynchburg sawmill would deliver rough side slabs to our barn, where our saws would rip them into firewood-sized logs. We had a daily ad in the Lynchburg paper. People would call our home to place firewood orders any time of the day or night. At the height of the business, Mom had fifteen or twenty trucks hauling cords of firewood throughout the city and county. And because it was strictly a cash and carry operation, it was not unusual for her to handle two or three thousand dollars in cash every day.

My sister Virginia and her husband Lawrence had moved into their own home nearby. Lewis lived near his Hilltop Restaurant. Gene, Mother, and I were the only Falwells left in the family home on Rustburg Road. David Brown still lived in a little house on our property and helped Mom manage the household. Each morning Mother would prepare the family breakfast and kiss Gene and me good-bye as we walked down Rustburg Road to Mrs. Burford's country store where we would catch the bus to Brookville High School. Then she bundled up for the short walk to her office in the barn adjacent to the firewood business, where she managed the books and kept track of Dad's remaining business interests throughout Campbell County. In the evening she would close the office and return home to begin our evening meal.

There was little time for mourning after Dad died. In 1948 I was a junior at Brookville High School. I enjoyed my studies and graduated valedictorian of my senior class; but during those last two years at Brookville I conserved most of my energy for my extracurricular interests. I was first a reporter, then the editor in chief of our high school newspaper, the Brookville Bee; and I was addicted to after school sports, especially football and baseball.

Until my junior year, I was a skinny little kid who had to struggle to put on weight. My 148 pounds left me looking rather vulnerable in a football jersey. And because I didn't relish being tackled by the two-hundred-pounders who charged me from the line, I really worked on speed. I ran up and down Rustburg Road almost every morning before school and almost every evening before going to bed. I did exercises in my bedroom:

sit-ups, push-ups, and running in place. I had a metal bedstead with a round metal bar crossing the end of the bed. I remember pointing my toes, arching my back, and pulling on that bar until my feet almost touched the ceiling. I did chin-ups and arm stretches from that bar until it sagged.

After school and on Saturdays I drove around town looking for a sandlot baseball game I could join. If there was a touch, flag, or tackle football game in progress in the county, I could find it. And if there was no action around town, I would run up and down the country roads around our home, lift weights in our backyard, or do my own crude gymnastics on the bent bar in my bedroom.

Gradually I began to put on muscle in my arms and shoulders. And with the right combination of speed and body strength I could run head-on into almost anybody and lay him out. So, during my junior and senior years at Brookville, I played fullback on offense and safety on defense. In those days you could play both ways, and in my senior year I was elected captain of the team and played both offensive and defensive positions in every single game. We must have had a small team in those days, because I don't remember once watching a play from the sidelines.

Brookville High School stood on a beautiful oak-shaded campus on Timberlake Road. The school is gone now. A new school was erected many years after my 1950 graduation, and the old building was left behind. In fact, our Liberty University, then Lynchburg Baptist College, used the newly vacated, about to be razed high school for our first classrooms during the 1970's. Later the wreckers destroyed that gracious old school on Timberlake. Now the campus of Heritage High School stands on the spot where so many of us came of age.

Every morning a yellow Campbell County school bus would pick us up at Burford's store and deliver us to that three-story red-brick building shaded by oak trees and surrounded by lawns, a parking lot, and an athletic field. Usually as we arrived, the black janitor, Marshall, would be raising the American flag up a tall white flagpole near the school's front entrance. We often stopped and waited quietly as Marshall pulled the flag into place. I remember how he treated that flag, unfolding it gently at the beginning of the school day and refolding it just as gently when the day had ended. And in the morning, after he wound the rope securely into place, Marshall would take a few slow steps back from the flagpole, look carefully to see that the flag was flying freely in the breeze, and then salute smartly before turning to greet us students with a cheery "good morning."

Brookville, like all Southern schools at that time, was segregated. Marshall was just one of several black employees hired to maintain that all white campus. He was friendly and outgoing to each of the hundreds of students who attended Brookville, but he was especially kind to Gene and me after our father's death. Apparently my dad had been good to relatives or close friends of Marshall during the Depression years, and the white-haired custodian never forgot his acts of kindness.

Marshall called us Mr. Jerry and Mr. Gene. We often took our lunches to eat with Marshall in his "office" in the furnace room in the basement. He would greet us cheerily, pat us on the shoulder, and ask us about our classes, our teachers, and our friends.

I worked hard in the classroom and at every extracurricular task, but I don't remember taking any of it very seriously. I was my father's son. Nothing stood in the way of a good prank. And as with my father, some of my pranks teetered close to the edge of impropriety. Marshall knew my father well and understood his prankster side in me. I suppose that's why I fled to Marshall's warm "office" in the school basement near the old coal furnaces when I needed my own place to hide or recuperate.

I could not resist an occasional practical joke. I knew I would pay the consequences when I teased or tormented a student or a teacher especially a teacher. And though it cost me plenty, I entered into each new prank with abandon. And though this might sound like a halfhearted attempt at self defense, some of my victims deserved it.

I shall never forget one particular teacher who will remain unnamed. He was a mean little man who pranced about our physical ed classes squeaking out orders, humiliating students, and generally trying to lord it over all of us. I led the growing resistance movement to this teacher and his prissy, falsetto ways. He forced students who were terrified of heights to climb up a rope attached to the ceiling of the gym and giggled to himself when they burned their hands sliding down. He made other students with queasy stomachs do endless somersaults on the tumbling mats even after they turned ashen gray.

One sixth-period class, he humiliated a rather unathletic student on the basketball court. After the boy ran to the showers crying, our teacher turned on the rest of us. Suddenly I tackled him and began to wrestle him toward the sports equipment storage room. Two other students finally helped me subdue him; while the rest of the class looked on in shocked surprise. Inside the storage room, I pinned him to the floor. With the aid of my classmates, I pulled off his britches and left him pantless in a bin of basketballs.

After locking the gym teacher in his own storage area, I took his pants to the school's main bulletin board in the front lobby and pinned them up with a note reading "Mr. 's britches." Apparently he stayed in the storage area until Marshall, the custodian, noticed the sign and reunited our p.e. teacher with his pants.

Early the next morning I was called before our principal with my two primary collaborators. The principal sat looking up at me for a long moment of silence. He didn't say a thing. Apparently he was trying so hard not to laugh that he was afraid to speak. He didn't appreciate this teacher either. Still choking back his laughter, the principal began to lecture me about respect and honor. In the middle of a sentence, he lost his poise and began to laugh uncontrollably. He laughed so hard he almost fell out of his chair. Still laughing, he asked us to leave our teacher alone and ushered us quickly from his office. We could hear the principal still gasping with laughter as we walked back through the hallway to our classroom grinning in relief and shaking our heads at our good fortune.

Other times my motives weren't so virtuous, and the consequences weren't so easily escaped. Miss Cox was just twenty two years old when she was hired to teach a Brookville High School Latin class. We took Latin I, II, and III in those days.

Needless to say, some of us got really tired of Latin and were just waiting for a way to spice up those boring class sessions. Miss Cox was a nibbler. After she assigned us an in-class writing or reading assignment, she would pop open her desk drawer and reach demurely into her private stock of cookies or candies. Placing one hand discreetly before her lips, Miss Cox would chew her midmorning snacks while we all looked on hungrily.

One day I brought a live rat to school in a paper lunch bag and placed it in Miss Cox's drawer beside her stash of cookies. The rat was filling up on chocolate chips when Miss Cox reached into the drawer. Everyone was peeking around their open textbooks waiting to see what would happen. At that moment the rat jumped right out of the desk drawer and into Miss Cox's lap. She screamed, flew into the air, and fainted dead away. The classroom broke into pandemonium. The rat was running up and down the rows of desks. The boys were laughing, the girls were screaming, and Miss Cox lay on the floor unconscious at our feet.

Hearing the commotion, the principal himself charged into our classroom, took one look, and shouted above the din, "Falwell, come out here." There was no trial. He didn't even ask me any questions. He just told me to go home. Miss Cox recovered and I returned to class the next day no worse off and yet no wiser.

Just weeks later, our math teacher announced a surprise quiz at the beginning of a class. I don't know what got into me that day, but even as she began to distribute the list of questions, I whispered loudly enough for most of the class to hear, "We don't want this test. Let's lock her up in the closet so she can't give it to us." My cousin Kenneth Falwell helped me take her gently but firmly by the arms and walk her quickly to the coat closet in the back of the classroom. I shoved two empty desks in front of the door and dismissed the class.

Fortunately my teacher was a good sport and a longtime friend. I was the editor of the school newspaper that year, and she was our sponsor. She and I had a good relationship; and though the principal was furious, my math teacher didn't press charges. And after a phone call from that teacher explaining my little prank, even my mother didn't punish me.

During my four years at high school and my two years at Lynchburg College, I was a member of one of Lynchburg's neighborhood "gangs." Lynchburg is a beautiful little city built on seven hills along the James River. During my adolescent years, there were roughly seven Lynchburg gangs, each associated with a different area of our town. And though I lived just outside the city limits, I drove the few miles separating Campbell County from the Fairview Heights section of Lynchburg to maintain my membership in the Fairview Heights gang. White Rock Hill also had a gang. Cotton Hill, Rivermont, Daniels, and West End all had gangs of their own.

You can't really compare our Lynchburg gangs to the ethnic gangs of the major American cities. Our "gang wars" didn't come close to the bloody West Side Story insurrections that we read about in New York, Chicago, Miami, and San Francisco's Chinatown. In those days there was no cocaine, heroin, or even marijuana available in our town. It required a small act of rebellion to even drink a beer with the boys. And believe it or not, almost none of my peers were sexually active before marriage in the late 1940's and early 1950's. In fact, I remember hearing of only one girl getting pregnant in Brookville High School during my four years there between 1946 and 1950.

The city fathers had tried to tame even our harmless area rivalries with football, baseball, and basketball league competitions. Actually, containing our gang wars to the athletic field worked moderately well, but when the games were over we congregated in our various hangouts and plotted mild mischief of our own.

I was the ex-officio president of the Fairview Heights gang because I was the only member of the crowd that hung around the Pickeral Cafe on Campbell Avenue who had a car. There was a concrete wall across the street from the cafe that once bordered the old Marvin Bass Elementary School. When the school was torn down, the wall was left standing. The Fairview Heights gang was nicknamed the "Wall Gang" because we sat on the wall eating hot dogs, drinking Cokes, and plotting revenge on rival gangs in the city or across Campbell County.

Remember, there was no real access to television then. We had to stand in front of a downtown department store to watch Red Skelton clowning on the tiny ten-inch screen in the window. There were two movie houses playing westerns, usually with a Lone Ranger or Superman series on Saturday afternoons. Two others featured musicals or classic films from the past. We were pretty well left to design our own entertainment in those days.

The roller-skating rink at the edge of town was the scene of several serious skirmishes between the Wall Gang and a gang from Appomattox County. Our rivals came to roller skate in carloads. The gang from Appomattox showed their hostilities toward us at the rink and then, later in the evening, would drive by the "wall" and shout obscenities at us as they passed by.

Eventually the Wall Gang struck back. There were occasional fist-fights on the skating-rink floor and in the parking lot. One Saturday night a near brawl broke out among the skaters when three young men from Appomattox tripped a member of the Wall Gang who was skating backwards and didn't see it coming. A couple of fist-fights ensued. We let air out of their tires. And just below the surface, real uptown violence was brewing.

The Fairview Heights gang met every day for one whole week at the beginning of summer to plan our revenge on the kids from Appomattox. I think it was my cousin Ray Bell who got credit for suggesting our final war plan. "Buttercup" Bell was my best friend during those adolescent years. He would not measure five feet tall on his tiptoes in those days. He was small, quiet, strong, and aggressive. Bell suggested that he sit alone on the wall that next Saturday night when the gang from Appomattox came cruising by in search of trouble. The rest of us would remain hidden in the tall grass and trees nearby. When the Appomattox gang drove by the Pickeral Cafe looking for a rumble, they would see poor little Buttercup sitting alone and defenseless in the semidarkness.

That Saturday night forty of us took our hiding places around Buttercup as he sat alone on the wall. Our spy had called from the skating rink to warn us that the boys from Appomattox were on the move. We hunkered down in the grass. Buttercup moved into the light where he could be seen easily from Campbell Avenue. When the Appomattox gang drove up to the Pickeral Cafe across the street, Buttercup stood to his full height, made a gesture that is universally understood, and let off a stream of profanity that surprised all of us, including Buttercup.

Brakes squealed. Two carloads of angry kids spilled onto the street and headed in Buttercup's direction. He stood there taunting them until they were completely in our trap. With one cry, the forty of us jumped out of hiding and attacked. Buttercup stayed on the wall screaming obscenities, dancing up and down, almost beside himself with excitement. While the battle raged, four of our members broke free, ran to the cars from Appomattox and let the air out of their tires. When the tires were flat, we ended our attack and disappeared into the darkness. The police arrived at that moment and found our visitors licking their wounds.

The Wall Gang had at least one female member in those days. Rags Ragland was tough. She could play football with the best of us. One Saturday night in 1950 Rags and the guys were clowning on the wall, singing all the old radio commercials we could remember. We weren't making all that much noise, but a neighbor with a low tolerance for music called the police and they arrived with flashing lights and sirens blaring.

"You make more noise than we do," Rags yelled at the police when they turned their spotlights on her and ordered that we disperse. Rags just stared at them. Nobody moved. It was a standoff. The police searched each familiar face with a spotlight and, with one last word of warning about loud noise and latenight parties, drove away.

Rags had not moved a muscle. She just stared at the police car angrily. The neighbor had called in to complain when there was nothing to complain about. As we talked about it, we grew more angry. Finally Rags suggested we get revenge on that nosy neighbor.

There were old railroad ties piled on the lot behind the wall. The ties were soaked in tar. We dragged the sticky ties into the middle of the street directly in front of the home of the neighbor we suspected as having called the police. Somebody found a can of gas and poured it onto the ties. Someone else struck a match. Immediately the ties began to blaze. The gang cheered. Suddenly the whole street was on fire. The flaming gasoline had run down the ties igniting the asphalt. Smoke and flames erupted along the entire block. We watched with fascination as a stream of fire boiled toward the neighbor's picket fence like hot lava boils from a volcano. Suddenly a police car careened toward us, red lights flashing. Seconds later another police car appeared, followed by a fire truck. We boys ran in a dozen different directions, hiding behind the houses and in the tall weeds nearby. Rags refused to run.

Firemen began hosing down the blaze. The police ran toward Rags. She shouted at them from her lonely place upon the wall. "They went that way," she said, and police cars squealed off in the wrong direction. Finally the fire was extinguished. The smoldering ties were pulled from the roadway. And the boys came out of hiding to carry Rags on their shoulders to her place of honor in the Pickeral Cafe.

Somehow during all those adolescent years, our Fairview Heights gang escaped any serious consequences from our pranks and intergang skirmishes. There were black eyes, bruised knuckles, occasional broken bones, shattered windows, and one burned street, but for the most part we got off easy. And when the police were called, they knew us or our families and let us go with a warning. But even as an adolescent I began to understand the principle of cause and effect. Actions, responsible or irresponsible, lead to consequences. During my senior year the lesson came home with a vengeance.

Just before high school graduation, one of my "harmless" pranks resulted in rather dire consequences for me and for thirty-two members of my high school football team. The school cafeteria issued different colored tickets for each day's hot lunch. Those tickets were kept in a locked safe in the office of Brookville High School. During my senior year I learned that the safe had been donated to the school by the father of one of my classmates. After a little encouragement, that same classmate handed us the secret combination to the school safe.

Each morning after learning the cafeteria ticket color of the day, we would remove enough tickets from the safe to feed the team and would meet in the football locker room to distribute tickets to our fellow players. That way, my buddies had their lunch money to use for other, more important purposes, while we all ate in the cafeteria free of charge for my entire senior year.

It was meant to be a joke. The school made money charging a one dollar entrance fee to our football games. We were just getting our share, or so we thought. Besides, it was our senior year. No self-respecting class had ever graduated without pull ing some kind of harmless but embarrassing trick on the administration. We had found our way to get even for those four years of suffering.

Unfortunately, someone in the administration began to notice the difference between the number of meals served in the cafeteria and the amount of money collected from the student diners. Quietly an investigation was launched. The Campbell County sheriff was called. Without our knowing it, a secret search of our lockers was conducted by police and school officials together. Our basement ticket stash was discovered. The school safe was carefully monitored. We thought it all a lark, but the principal and the local law-enforcement agencies considered it a serious felony.

Finally, on one May morning just before graduation when the case against us was airtight, each of the thirty-three players was hauled from his classroom to face individual interrogation. They nabbed us all at once so we could not coordinate our stories. Our parents had been called that morning and asked to come immediately to the high school campus. "Your son is in trouble" was the only warning. In the principal's office one by one we were advised of the consequences of our "prank." The sheriff actually sat beside the principal as the penalties were handed out to us. The financial loss amounted to several thousand dollars, and the parents were asked to pay back in equal shares the total losses of the cafeteria for that school year.

I still remember sitting in the principal's office. My mother was there beside me. The principal sat on the edge of his desk, and the sheriff stood behind him. We didn't know whether we were going to prison or be expelled just weeks before graduation. I was grinning broadly, trying to bluff my way through that terrible moment when the principal finally announced his verdict.

"Jerry," he began sternly, shifting papers beside him on his desk. "You will not give the valedictorian address this year as planned!" I swallowed hard and blinked back my disappointment. Then he concluded: "We can't have a petty thief deliver Brookville's honors speech, now can we?"

My mother paid my share of the cafeteria losses. Then we walked in silence from the room. Somehow I managed to maintain my grin, but I was dying inside from the embarrassment and the disappointment I felt. It had all started out innocently enough. We just didn't think about the consequences of our "harmless prank." I was guilty as charged. We were all relieved to discover that nobody was going to jail. Nobody would be expelled or forced to miss graduation. But our joke was being treated as a major theft. An appropriate penalty was levied against each student.

When the principal told me I would not be giving the valedictorian address, I really felt the consequences of my crime. I had worked hard on my studies during those last two years of high school. I had earned my valedictorian honor by maintaining the highest grade average in my class. Now what I wanted most was being taken from me as a consequence of my foolish indiscretion. I grinned and pretended not to feel the pain, but I was feeling it terribly.

I looked awful that day. My fingers and face were bandaged. My nose was broken and swollen twice its normal size. Both eyes were black. My face was puffy and lacerated from a near fatal auto accident.

After high school graduation, I entered Lynchburg College as a pre-mechanical engineering student. At L.C. I studied math and physics, English and history, and took my first formal courses in religion. Lynchburg College had been founded in 1903 by the Disciples of Christ denomination; and though the name was later changed from Virginia Christian College to Lynchburg College, all students were still assigned six hours of Bible and theology.

My first formal study of the Bible made little or no impression on me. I still didn't know the Old Testament from the New. The notion of sin and its consequences was still totally unknown to me. But every Sunday morning my mother tuned our radio to Charles Fuller's "Old Fashioned Revival Hour." She turned the volume up so high that I could not help but listen to the happy music of Rudy Atwood and the choir and the booming voice of Charles E. Fuller warning of sin and its consequences and presenting the claims of Christ.

I had stopped attending Sunday School or church. I was totally uninterested in religion and unmoved by Mom's loving if subtle attempts "to win me to the Lord." But even in those adolescent years Mom's prayers for my undeveloped spiritual life were being heard and answered in unusual ways. For one example, during the summer of 1949, my high school principal had chosen me to represent Brookville at Boys' State, a lively experience of government in action for high school students held that year at Virginia Tech. I roomed with a Church of God boy from Wise, Virginia, whose name I've forgotten but whose life had a long-range effect on me.

The first night in our dorm room he introduced himself and in the next breath asked me if I was saved. "Saved?" I didn't even know what he was talking about, and I felt trapped and angered by his aggressive witness. But he reminded me of Virginia McKenna, and I remembered how much her aggressive style had meant in my father's life; so when my roommate witnessed I grinned back at him in silence as my dad had grinned at Virginia.

At the welcome dance that first night at Boys' State, I told my date that I was rooming with a religious nut. I ridiculed his religious preoccupation and was at first repelled by it. When my girl and I were invited to join a handful of other seniors outside for a beer, I refused, fearing that my roommate would spot me and end up preaching at me for drinking.

The boy didn't dance that night either. He told me later that Christians didn't dance. But he sat on the sidelines smiling, talking with the other seniors, and watching me like a friendly hawk. All week long he witnessed to me about Jesus and the Gospel. Before he went to sleep he read passages from the Bible and knelt at his bed to pray. Somehow he turned every conversation into an opportunity to share his Christian faith. And though I didn't give him one positive response, his words made a lasting impression on me. When we said good-bye at the end of the week, he said, "I'll be praying for you." I grinned and walked away, but his words about sin and its consequences were left echoing in my brain.

I breezed through my classes during those next two years at Lynchburg College, worked part-time as a sorter and tier at Lynchburg's Mead Corporation paper mill, and spent every spare moment at the Pickeral Cafe with my chums from the Wall Gang. We ate hamburgers, drank Cokes, and listened to Tony Bennett on the jukebox and such lowbrow pop tunes as "Good Night, Irene," "Music! Music! Music!" and "Getting to Know You," from Rodgers and Hammerstein's new musical The King and I.

With the Communist Chinese invasion of the Republic of South Korea, America had been standing on the brink of World War III. But by the time I entered college, truce talks had begun in Tokyo. In 1952 Dwight Eisenhower's election to the presidency looked certain, and lasting peace seemed just around the corner. And though our nation's economy was threatened by serious inflation, employment had reached a record high and the future seemed full of promise.

For students at Lynchburg College 1952 was the year of panty raids, flying-saucer stories, and "Ike for President" rallies. The popular song of the year would be "Too Young." Gary Cooper would win the Academy Award for his performance in High Noon, and Ernest Hemingway would publish his short, powerful novel The Old Man and the Sea.

I had no idea that at the beginning of that same year, on January 20, 1952, my life would be turned inside out. The Sunday morning began uneventfully. I awakened early to the smell of hoecakes and bacon wafting up the stairs in my direction. In those days I wondered if Mom used an electric fan to blow those wonderful smells into my bedroom on Sunday mornings. It was her way to get me downstairs to hear the weekly broadcast of the "Old Fashioned Revival Hour." From my bed I could hear the choir singing "Heavenly Sunshine" at full volume and Rudy Atwood doing arpeggios up and down the keyboard.

For a moment I lay there breathing in my mother's love but wishing she would let me sleep-in just one Sunday morning without a Charles Fuller sermon echoing up and down the stairway. Finally I succumbed to the smell of fresh molasses syrup, ran down the stairs, and entered the kitchen a playful penitent entering the skid-row mission, willing to listen to the chaplain's sermon in exchange for a hot homemade breakfast. Mom greeted me with a good-morning hug and seated me quickly at the table. Charles Fuller was just reading his text from his radio pulpit in the Long Beach Municipal Auditorium. Mom had the table set and the food in place so I wouldn't miss a word.

I humored my mother by actually listening to Fuller's sermon that morning. I don't remember his text, but I do remember feeling something that I had never felt before. As he preached, a lump began to form in my throat. And it wasn't the hoecakes or the fat-back bacon. I felt like crying, but I wasn't sad. I felt excited, but there was nothing exciting on my schedule that day. Fuller was warming up to his text, and though I was listening to his words I was remembering other words spoken at other times. Fuller said, "Are you born again?" and I remembered my roommate at Boys' State asking the very same question.

I didn't know a thing about the Holy Spirit. If anybody had told me that day that God Himself was present in our family kitchen making His move to rescue me from my own sinfulness, I would have laughed out loud. But looking back, it was His presence that I was feeling. Don't ask me to explain it. I know that God is always present in our lives. Sometimes we feel Him. Other times we don't. That morning, I felt Him there but didn't know what I was feeling. He was calling me, but I didn't recognize His voice. I just felt edgy and excited like you feel before a storm strikes or that moment in the hospital just before your first child is born.

Do you remember the story of Samuel, the young man

lying in his bed 4,000 years ago in the home of Eli, an Old Testament priest? In the middle of the night, God spoke to Samuel, and the boy ran quickly to Eli thinking the old man had called him. Three times it happened. God's gentle voice heard in the night by a suddenly awakened child. Samuel didn't recognize that it was God Himself who was calling. Then Eli explained, and when God's voice spoke again the boy answered clearly, "Here am I."

Some people have exciting conversion experiences like the Apostle Paul on the road to Damascus, complete with blinding lights and heavenly voices. For others, like myself, God came quietly into Mom's kitchen, where she had spent many years praying for me. And in that kitchen God answered her prayers and began to move me toward that moment that would change my life forever.

I didn't go to church with Mom that day. I could tell she was disappointed, but I grinned, kissed her on the cheek, and watched her leave for morning worship without me as she had for so many disappointing years. I drifted through the day in a kind of daze. Something was happening in me that I could not explain. I felt excited and anxious and happy all at the same time.

Later that Sunday afternoon I joined my friends at the Pickeral Cafe. How could I know that God had followed me there? How could I understand that it was His Spirit pursuing me across Lynchburg that day? I remember sitting alone on a stool in the restaurant. The jukebox was playing. The room was filled with noisy kids. But in and through the commotion, His voice was speaking to me. I couldn't hear words, but I knew that something strange and wonderful was about to happen. I didn't know it then, but it was God's world breaking into my world. Why it happens when it happens is still a mystery to me. But that it happens is no question anymore.

After Cokes and burgers and restless excited looks over my shoulder and around the room, I wandered across Campbell Avenue to join my Fairview Heights friends who were gathering for another Sunday night on the wall. Even I could not believe what happened next.

Right in the middle of a typical Wall Gang conversation I heard myself asking, "Does anybody know a church in Lynchburg that preaches what Dr. Fuller preaches on the radio?"

I have tried to remember what made me ask that question. I cannot. It seemed to come from nowhere. Obviously it came from Him. Nobody seemed surprised by the question, and Wilson Wright, one of the older members of our gang, answered, "Yeah, a church over on Park Avenue." He added quickly, "It's kind of a holy-roller type church, but they have good music and loads of pretty girls."

When he said "pretty girls" I cut in with "So, why don't we go?"

"When?" somebody asked.

"Tonight!" I answered.

"But we aren't dressed for church," Wilson argued against my idea, and the others finally recovered enough from their shock to join in his protest.

If nobody else would go, I decided to go alone. Believe me, the decision wasn't true to form. I had never done it before. And my friends, most of them, believed it was the beginning of a prank and that I would never do it again. But Wilson's brother Otis Wright volunteered to go with me and another close friend, Jim Moon, made it a threesome. We drove to the Park Avenue Baptist Church, parked the car, and walked up the steps into the sanctuary. The church seated just 300 people, and almost every seat was full. An usher took us to the front row and planted us there with all the congregation watching. Jack Dinsbeer, the twenty-three-year-old youth minister, was leading the congregation in an enthusiastic Gospel song.

"The windows of heaven are open," the people sang and the cement-block building literally shook with their singing. "The blessings are flowing tonight."

I looked down at the songbook the usher had handed me and was surprised to read Gospel Songs from the Old Fashioned Revival Hour. There are no coincidences when God is at work. Immediately I felt at home. The singing and the songs were familiar. My mother had piped them up the stairs and into my bedroom for almost a decade. I felt like I had been in that place before. I held the book in my hands and looked about the room.

There were twin upright pianos standing on each side of the platform. Macel Pate, who six years later would be my wife, was playing the piano on the right. Delores Clark, who five years later would marry my friend Jim Moon, was playing the piano on the left. Both girls were trying to outdo Rudy Atwood with their enthusiastic accompaniment.

"I think I'll ask her for a date," Jim Moon whispered above the singing, pointing at Macel. "Then I'll ask that one," I whispered back, pointing at Delores. It seemed an appropriately macho response. But I knew that something else was happening here. My heart was beating double time. My throat was dry and my hands trembled.

Jack Dinsbeer moved back and forth and up and down the little platform, waving his arms and shouting encouragement as he led the singing. He had the women sing a verse and then the men. He had the choir sing in harmony with the congregation. He was all over the place like a cheerleader urging every person to join in the song. Soon Jim and I quit whispering and even tried a verse ourselves. As we sang, I imagined being in Charles Fuller's auditorium in Long Beach. The voices of the people in that little church seemed to blend with voices in the Long Beach Municipal Auditorium.

I was getting more excited and more nervous. I knew something important was about to happen. A quartet sang. Jack played a trumpet solo during the offering. The Sunday evening youth choir sang just before the pastor, Paul F. Donnelson, got up to preach. Paul was twenty-nine. His sermon was full of energy, clear and down-to-earth, just like the preaching of Charles Fuller. He preached about sin and its consequences, about Christ, the cross, and an empty tomb.

Then suddenly he stopped, bowed his head, and began to pray. I stood watching him as the congregation began to sing, "Just as I am without one plea, O Lamb of God I come to Thee." A young woman walked past me to the altar and knelt to pray. A young couple knelt beside her. Before long a dozen or more young people were praying with counselors at the altar. I felt like I was being pulled by a magnet to join them there, but I also felt embarrassed and even a bit afraid. At that moment Garland Carey, an old white-haired gentle man standing in the row of pews behind me, leaned forward and whispered quietly. "Would you like me to go down there with you, son?"

"I certainly would," I answered, and without a moment's hesitation we walked together and knelt at that old-fashioned altar. Mr. Carey opened his Bible as he knelt beside me and turned to the book of Romans. He began to read and explain the plan of salvation.

"For all have sinned," he began, "and come short of the glory of God."

He explained that we are all sinners by nature and that the sins we commit, whether great or small, are simply evidence of our sinful condition.

Then he looked at me and grinned knowingly. "Are you a sinner?" he asked.

"Yes, sir," I answered.

"Of course, we're all sinners," he said. "Doesn't take much to figure that out, does it, son!" Then he turned the page and read again.

"The wages of sin is death," he said, lingering over the word and staring down at me. At first I didn't understand those six small words. "The wages of sin is death." Then I thought about my father. For fifteen years I had watched him die. He had sinned, and though the courts and the family had forgiven him, he could not forgive himself. To blot out his grief and to stop that painful guilt, my father began to drink. It wasn't drinking that killed him. It was the wages of sin.

Finally I looked back at the old man kneeling beside me. He was smiling now. "The wages of sin is death," he said again. Then he added quickly, "But the gift of God is eternal life through Jesus Christ our Lord."

I remembered those last wonderful days of my father's life. I could still see him lying on his deathbed smiling up at me. By accepting God's forgiveness for his sins, my dad had found life in this world and in the world to come. Now it was my turn to accept in my youth what my father had postponed too long.

Garland Carey was a deacon at that little Baptist church on

Park Avenue. He was old and wrinkled. It wasn't easy for him to kneel there beside me, but his face shone and his eyes sparkled as he talked. This man knew the Lord, and you could tell it in a glance. He told me the story of Jesus, God's only son, who died to pay the price of our sinfulness.

"If you confess with your mouth the Lord Jesus," he said quoting the words from memory, "and believe in your heart that God has raised him from the dead, you will be saved."

He smiled again, as if the bearer of the greatest news in history. "Isn't that easy?" he asked. "Isn't that wonderful?" And then without a pause he continued: "For with the heart man believes unto righteousness; and with the mouth confession is made unto salvation.... For whosoever shall call upon the name of the Lord shall be saved."

It seemed perfectly simple that night and perfectly clear. I was a sinner. Sin had its consequences. Jesus had paid with His own life that I might be forgiven of my sin and avoid those consequences forever.

"Would you like to ask God to forgive you, son?" he said finally. I nodded and began a simple prayer of confession. When I finished, Mr. Carey looked me in the eyes and said, "Did you call upon the Lord to forgive you?"

"Yes, I did," I answered.

"Did He promise to forgive you if you confessed your sins and believed in your heart?" he asked.

"Yes, sir, He promised," I said.

"Now do you think God could lie?" he asked, grinning.

"No, sir, I don't," I replied.

"Then what do you think God's done for you?" he asked.

And that quickly I accepted the mystery of God's salvation. In that simple act of confession and belief God forgave my sinfulness. I didn't doubt it then. I haven't doubted it to this day.

Suddenly the old man put his arm around me and began to pray his own prayer of thanksgiving for my salvation. I felt as though my mom were there beside us and Virginia McKenna and Charles Fuller and the boy from Boys' State and Mr. Logwood, my childhood Sunday School teacher. Each of them had worked and prayed for this day. Without their loving witness,

I might not have been at that service, let alone kneeling at
that altar.

For 2,000 years, men and women, boys and girls of every
race, color, and nationality have come to this moment when
they had to decide for or against God's gift. Each heard the
same claims about Jesus's life, death, and resurrection. Each
had to decide: will I believe in Him or will I walk away from Him
forever?

Fishermen standing in their boats near the shore of the Sea
of Galilee, heard His voice and were convinced and convicted by
His teachings. Their choice was not an easy one: Stay in the
security and relative comfort of their fishing business or throw
it all away and follow Him? They had just seconds to decide.
Peter and Andrew put down their nets and followed Him.

But the rich young man who came to Jesus by night and
asked quietly, "How can I inherit eternal life?" heard His invitation to follow but could not take the risk required. The Bible
says that same rich young man had too much to lose, so he
went away in sorrow. Little did he know how much he lost that
day in trying to save what he had.

And so in every generation some people decide to ask forgiveness for their sins and to acknowledge Jesus as their Savior while others shake their heads in disbelief and miss their
chance forever. That decision results in what Christians call the
new birth. The term "born again" comes directly from the story
of Nicodemus, a ruler of the Jews, another man who came to
Jesus late one night to investigate Him and His teachings.

"Rabbi," he said, "we know that thou art a teacher come
from God: for no man can do these miracles that thou doest,
except God be with him" (John 3:2).

Apparently, Nicodemus had been impressed by the teachings and the miracles of Jesus. He began his private investigation of the Master with that strange compliment question. "Verily, verily, I say unto thee," Jesus answered, "Except a man be
born again, he cannot see the kingdom of God."

Jesus knew that Nicodemus was trying to find out who
He was and what change believing in Him might make in his
own life. So before the conversation could drag down into a

theological argument, Jesus summed up everything in three short words: "be born again."

That is the beginning of the Christian's new life. Everything else follows that act. No one can really understand the kingdom of God, Jesus told Nicodemus, until he is born again.

Nicodemus answered, "How can a man be born when he is old?"

And Jesus replied, You must be born of water (natural birth) and of the Spirit (spiritual rebirth). That moment when a sinner confesses his sins and opens his heart to the Spirit of God is the moment of rebirth. The Bible only speaks of Nicodemus twice again. Once when the leaders were in an uproar about Jesus's claims, Nicodemus urged caution and came close to defending Him. Then again when Jesus was taken down from the cross and laid in Joseph's tomb, the Apostle John says that one last time Nicodemus appeared on the scene, this time to anoint Jesus's body with oil and spices.

We don't know for certain whether Nicodemus was born again or if he waited, wondered, and went away sorrowful. My father waited just a few days short of his full lifetime to say the sinner's prayer and find rebirth. I was just eighteen when I was born again. I wish I had listened to my mother earlier. I wish I had joined her in that little Baptist church on Franklin Street. I wish I had dared to take my stand with that young man at Boys' State. I wish I had started my spiritual pilgrimage as a child as have my own children. But wishing is a waste of time. At that Park Avenue Baptist Church altar I decided to postpone the decision no longer, and as Paul promised, "all things became new."

"And your name, young man?" the minister asked as I stood with thirteen other new converts at the close of the service before the happy little congregation.

"My name is Jerry Falwell," I answered.

"Well, Jerry," the pastor said, putting his arm around my shoulder, "this is the end of your old life and the beginning of your new."

And though I didn't really understand it, I look back now upon that night nearly forty-five years ago and realize it was an ending and a beginning. From that moment everything changed for me.

Faith is believing what God says in spite of the circumstances. Faith is simply taking God at His Word.

— Jerry Falwell

CHAPTER FIVE

Born Again

Episcopalians may nod and smile correctly as they hurry from the sanctuary after mass. Presbyterians and Methodists may shake hands and chat politely after Sunday services. But Baptists like to hug. On that cold winter night of my conversion, I got up off my knees, stood beside Pastor Donnelson as he introduced me to my new brothers and sisters in the Lord, and then walked slowly down the aisle among them accepting their welcome and feeling their arms around me. I thought I would never reach the front door through that gauntlet of happy huggers.

"Praise the Lord, Brother Jerry," an old man exclaimed as he almost squeezed the life out of me.

"Amen," echoed a tiny wrinkled woman whose eyes were filled with tears.

"Welcome to the family," a young couple added while they balanced their sleepy baby and both hugged me at the same time.

I could see that my friend Jim Moon was struggling up the aisle just behind me in a similar sea of hugs, best wishes, and welcomes. Remember, I was eighteen years old. During my last years at Brookville High School and my first two years at Lynchburg College I seldom went inside a church. I liked pretty girls, fast cars, latenight parties with the Wall Gang, sandlot baseball, a hard-fought football scrimmage, poker games, and beer busts. If this sudden show of affection had taken place at school or work, I would have felt suspicious or embarrassed, but these people were genuine. It was written all over their faces. Like friends and family at a maternity ward with their noses pressed up against the window, oohing and aahing a new-born child, my new friends at Park Avenue Baptist had witnessed my new birth and were welcoming me into the kingdom of God at the beginning of my new life among them.

Later I learned that even as Jim and I entered the church that night, those people began to pray silently for our salvation. A few of them recognized me as the rowdy Falwell kid from Rustburg Road whose father ran booze during the Depression and whose family had a rough and ready reputation round Lynchburg. To most of the members of that little Baptist church on Park Avenue, I was just another kid from Lynchburg College, but from the moment I walked up the aisle into their fellowship and took my seat in the front row, those who knew me and those who didn't were praying that God would speak to me through Pastor Donnelson's sermon.

When that old white-haired stranger leaned forward to invite me to kneel with him at the altar, they were all leaning forward with him. And when he knelt beside me, opened his Bible, and began to present God's plan of salvation, those dear people surrounded us with their prayers. And that night, January 20, 1952, as I accepted Christ as my Savior, almost every one of them sat patiently on the cold metal folding chairs, their heads bowed, their eyes closed, and their lips moving in silent prayer on my behalf until God's business in my life had been accomplished. Evangelism in that church was teamwork, and almost nobody left the room until the work of God was finished.

By the time Jim and I had reached the front door, walked down the stairs and through the crowded little narthex to the sidewalk, Jack Dinsbeer had left the platform by a back entrance, charged down the rickety iron steps, and raced around the church to meet us.

"Hi," he said, holding out his hand to greet us, guessing that we didn't need any more hugs that first evening in the family. "I'm Jack Dinsbeer, the youth pastor. Welcome to Park Avenue Baptist."

I had no idea of what was about to happen to me that moment at the front door of the little two-story cement-block church in Lynchburg. Upstairs in the warmth of that congregation, I had accepted Jesus as my Savior, but on the icy cold sidewalk just thirty minutes later I was meeting the man who would introduce me to Jesus as my Lord.

"Next Sunday morning at 10 A.M.," he began, "I am teaching a Bible class for young people. I want you to be there."

"Sure," I answered quickly, "we'll come. Won't we, Jim?"

Jim nodded. We were rubbing our hands together and rocking back and forth against the cold. Already our noses were red, and puffs of steam came with each breath. People were hurrying past us to their cars, but Jack Dinsbeer wasn't finished.

"There's a Sunday night youth meeting at six right here," he continued. "You'll want to bring your friends to that, and a worship service at eleven on Sunday mornings. Can we count on you to be there?"

Again we quickly nodded our consent, anxious to get out of the cold and back to the Pickeral Cafe for hot coffee and a burger.

"What happened to you tonight," Jack continued, "is just a beginning. Don't let your new faith shrivel up before it has a chance to grow."

His words sounded strange and kind of ominous. "Don't let your new faith shrivel up." There was so much about the spiritual life that I didn't understand. Everything was new to me. I had been born again. Wasn't that enough? I had seen the instant wonderful change in my father at his deathbed conversion. I supposed that the altar experience was the end of it for me. But I was wrong.

Conversion was just the beginning.

I didn't understand then the comparison between physical birth and spiritual rebirth. When I was born physically, August 11, 1933, at Lynchburg's Guggenheimer Memorial Hospital, I came kicking and screaming into the world from my mother's womb. A doctor's skilled hands supervised the process. Nurses cleaned away the afterbirth, washed and powdered me. Mother felt the pain. Dad paid the bills. I was born, and it was a messy, painful, expensive process; but it was only the beginning. I was a helpless, vulnerable infant. If Mom or the nurses had abandoned me that day of my birth, I would have died in a very short time. Instead, it had taken fifteen or sixteen years of love and care to prepare me to survive in the physical world on my own.

Spiritual life begins much like physical life in a kind of birth or, as the Baptists say, rebirth. On January 20, 1952, I was reborn at the Park Avenue Baptist Church. Deacon Carey, a wise layman and a devout student of the Bible, supervised my rebirth. Pastor Donnelson introduced me to his flock. The people hugged me and welcomed me into fellowship. I had been reborn, but in the life of faith I was still a helpless, vulnerable infant. If they had left me alone in Lynchburg with no further preparation, I might have shriveled up spiritually in a very short time. Thank God, they didn't abandon me. Many people, including Pastor Donnelson, his congregation, and friends and family around Lynchburg, contributed to those first months of spiritual growth; but it was Jack Dinsbeer, the youth pastor at Park Avenue Baptist, who made the difference.

Between that winter night, January 20, 1952, and a morning in August, seven months later, Jack Dinsbeer helped me take my first important steps toward Christian maturity. In his innocent, friendly greeting after church that night, Jack was beginning the process in me that would lead to spiritual growth and full-time Christian discipleship.

In the New Testament, Acts 9, you can read the story of the conversion of Saul, a powerful enemy of the little Christian church in Jerusalem during the first century. On a journey from Jerusalem to Damascus, Saul was blinded by a light and confronted by a heavenly voice. Apparently, he experienced his rebirth that day. Saul's conversion has been painted and sculpted, sung and preached for twenty centuries, but what might have happened to Saul if a certain Christian disciple named Ananias hadn't done the follow-up in Saul's life that his new faith required?

It was Ananias who helped Saul understand what had happened to him on the Damascus road. It was Ananias who baptized Saul, and it was Ananias who prayed with him and taught him from the Scriptures. Saul's conversion on the road to Damascus was the beginning of his spiritual life, but it was his training in the faith under the disciple Ananias that helped prepare him for his journey in faith. Even Saul's amazing conversion complete with blinding lights and heavenly voices needed follow-up. Jack Dinsbeer was the first man to really disciple me.

I dropped Jim at the Pickeral Cafe, but decided to drive home immediately to share the news of my conversion with my mother. It was late enough for Mom to be in bed. There was no light shining in her bedroom window. I walked quietly to her door and stood for a moment hoping she might still be awake.

"Jerry?" she asked.

"Yes, Mom," I answered. "Can I come in?"

Already she had put on a robe and opened the door to greet me.

"What's the matter, son?" she asked, looking first at me and then at the grandfather clock in the hall behind me.

"Nothing is the matter," I answered smiling. Then I told her. "I went forward to the altar at Park Avenue Baptist," I began. Mom's eyes lit up. She took my right hand in her hands and stood there holding me. I could feel her hands trembling. "An old man read the Bible and prayed with me."

"Oh, Jerry," she said, "that's wonderful."

Then she led me into the kitchen, where she put on a pot of hot chocolate and sat down beside me. I told her that the singing and preaching at Park Avenue was like Charles Fuller's "Old Fashioned Revival Hour." I told her about the young people and Pastor Donnelson and Jack Dinsbeer. She sat there smiling, her eyes filled with tears and her hands still gripping mine.

That next Monday morning I began another uneventful week as a second-year student at Lynchburg College. In the

afternoons I pumped gas at an Esso station. In the early evenings I played basketball with the Fairview Heights team against
our rivals from Miller Park or Cotton Hill, and after burgers at
the Pickeral Cafe I joined my friends in the Wall Gang.

I didn't feel a great deal of change in my life immediately
after my conversion during that first week of my new spiritual
journey. And though my occasional outbursts of profanity disappeared overnight, my daily routines hadn't changed. My work
and study schedule went on as normal. That Friday night the
weather grew balmy in Lynchburg. The Wall Gang met at the
Pickeral Cafe and walked together across Campbell Avenue to
our spot on the wall. We were just hanging out when Jack
Dinsbeer parked his Chevy across the street from us. He went
into the cafe and asked Mr. Pickeral a question. We could see
the old man point toward the wall and then watched Jack as he
crossed the street in our direction. After shaking hands with
Jim and me he said, "Hope you'll both be in church this Sunday
morning."

"We will," we promised in unison.

"Bring your friends," Jack said, smiling up and down the wall
at the motley Fairview Heights gang gathered there. "Do they
have names?" he added in a stage whisper, grinning.

We introduced Jack to our friends from Fairview Heights.
They warmed to him immediately. He was easy to talk to and
full of fun. Nobody guessed that he was a minister, but when he
explained the Sunday schedule at Park Avenue Baptist, the
gang, including Rags Ragland, listened with amusement yet with
growing interest. After ten or fifteen minutes of conversation,
Jack simply excused himself and walked away. My friends were
impressed.

"I like him," Buddy McCauley said. "I think I'll go with you
to his church this Sunday."

A handful of our friends laughed at that idea, but Bobby
Burks, a boy from Terrapin Hill, stopped their laughter. "Pipe
down," he uttered menacingly. "I think I'll go, too."

"Count me in," a third friend, Otis Wright, volunteered; then
he added in our direction, "What time did he say it started?"

Jim and I arrived early that next Sunday morning for Jack's

Sunday School class. We brought eight or ten of the gang along with us and sat in rows of chairs in a crowded little basement room. Jack introduced us to the other young people gathered there. Jim moved quickly to sit next to Delores Clark, one of the two pretty piano players we had noticed on our first visit to Park Avenue Baptist. I sat on the other side next to her good friend Macel Pate.

The girls were not interested in us. They had come to study the Bible and let us know it clearly from the start. Later we learned that their parents had warned them about members of the Fairview Heights gang, even newly converted members. The girls were friendly but cool and maintained their distance.

That night at youth meeting, Delores and Macel took their places at the upright pianos. Undaunted, Jim and I sat in the front row of folding chairs for the best possible view. Our motives for church attendance were mixed at best during those first few Sundays at Park Avenue, but Jack Dinsbeer didn't really care why we had come. He knew that after conversion the first step toward Christian discipleship is getting established in a local church and fellowship of Christian believers. And he wasn't particular about the motives that got us there.

"Not forsaking the assembling of ourselves together..." he read to us one Sunday from the Book of Hebrews, Chapter 10, "but exhorting one another: and so much the more as ye see the day approaching."

The language of the Bible was new to me, and though the antique English words common to the King James version were strange and sometimes difficult to understand, there was something deep and mysterious about the way they affected me. "Exhorting one another," wrote the author of Hebrews, and when I looked up "exhort" in my dictionary at home I found these synonyms: "Urge strongly, advise, caution earnestly." And when I asked Jack about the meaning of that mysterious "day approaching" he talked about death and eternity and the second coming of Jesus Christ.

Kingdom talk was totally new to me then. We were teenagers. Death seemed a million years away. We had our whole lives before us; yet we listened. Jack was not preoccupied with dying, nor did he try to scare us with an overload of hell-fire and brimstone. In fact, almost every Friday night Jack made his appearance at the wall to win and woo our friends. On Saturday afternoons he joined us for informal games of baseball or football at the park. On Sundays he organized picnics, trips to the caverns, or hikes in the foothills of the Blue Ridge Mountains. We laughed and clowned and played together as energetically as we studied and prayed and witnessed, but life took on a new, serious dimension as he talked of the shortness of our years and the length of eternity. Now, looking back, I realize how quickly life would change for all of us and how important Jack's first visit to the wall had been.

Buddy McCauley and Bobby Burks were just two of the many Wall Gang members who became Christians during those next few weeks at Park Avenue Baptist. Buddy went to Baptist Bible College, graduated, became a minister, married a beautiful young coed he met in Bible school, was ordained, and died before his thirtieth birthday of uremic poisoning. And Bobby Burks, the boy from Terrapin Hill, was converted, joined the Army, and just a few years later was killed in an auto accident on 29 South near Lynchburg.

Otis Wright was converted that very next Sunday and forty-five years later is still a close friend and co-worker at Thomas Road Baptist Church. So many of the Fairview gang found Christ that winter. And like me, they were trained in discipleship by Jack Dinsbeer and ended up in the ministry or in responsible lay positions in our church in Lynchburg and in other churches across the nation or on mission fields around the world.

Once we had taken our place as active members of the church, the process of becoming Christ's disciples began in earnest. On weeknights we often met in Jack's home for Bible study, prayer, and training in Christian witness. Jack lived in a little red-brick house on Thomas Road. His wife Madolyn fixed hamburgers and chocolate shakes for the crowd of kids that gathered. Their newborn son Wayne was held and pampered by each of us in turn as the evening progressed. Then, with burgers in one hand and Bibles in the other, we worked for the first hour reading and discussing the New Testament, especially the Gospel of John, Paul's letter to the Romans, and the short letters called First, Second and Third John.

From the first week after our conversions, Jack trained us to lead other people to Christ as we had just been led. We memorized the five or six Scriptures that outlined the simple plan of salvation. Deacon Carey had shared those same passages with me at the altar the night of my conversion. We practiced reading and quoting them to each other. Immediately Jack encouraged us to "bear witness to our faith." Hoping I would not forget the Scriptures and their order, I wrote in the margin of the Bible the passage that should follow:

After Romans 3:23, "For all have sinned and come short of the glory of God," I wrote at the bottom of the page, "Turn to Romans 6:23." After Romans 6:23, "For the wages of sin is death, but the gift of God is eternal life through Jesus Christ our Lord," I wrote, "Turn to John 1:12." I underlined "But as many as received him, to them gave he power to become the sons of God, even to them that believe on his name." The next reference followed in the margin like clues to a mystery: "See I John 1:9, 'If we confess our sins, he is faithful and just to forgive us our sins and to cleanse us from all unrighteousness.'"

The other verses followed: I John 5:11,13, Romans 10:9,10, James 2:19, Hebrews 9:27. We turned back and forth between the verses until the pages almost fell into place and the passages leapt out at us. "Remember," Jack would say "many of the people you will talk to have never heard the Gospel of salvation in their lifetime. They'll be glad and grateful that you took the time to tell them the good news."

I really related to that. I still do. I am convinced that my father would have accepted God's forgiveness gladly during those long miserable years of his unforgiven guilt, but nobody stopped him long enough to make him listen. Nobody except Virginia McKenna even tried to tell my father that he could find God's forgiveness for all his sins, including killing Garland. So he suffered needlessly. He wasted his life on the bottle and eventually died from cirrhosis of the liver because nobody had the courage to tell this powerful, sometimes frightening man the good news that God had already forgiven him.

So, it was easy for me to tell others the good news. People wear masks to hide their suffering. And if they get defensive and refuse to pull down their masks, that's all right, too. At least they will have had a chance to hear. The rest is in God's hands anyway.

In our soul-winning training sessions, Jack would remind us to explain slowly and carefully what Christ had done to save us. "Listen to the people's questions," Jack said over and over again. "Try your best to answer them from the Scriptures. And take your time. Remember, God is working inside that life even as you talk. Let God's timing be your timing."

People were friendly. They were surprised by our boldness, but they listened as we shared our faith, and often they would ask questions and even invite us to pray with them for their salvation.

We met back at the church after our Monday night visitations around Lynchburg for more fellowship and a debriefing. We told stories about what happened when people answered the door and found us standing there. Some of the stories were hilarious, some scary. There were a few slammed doors, plenty of profanity, a threat or two, even a call to the police. But most of the doors were opened in grateful welcome and relief. We found hungry, lonely people locked behind their chains and dead bolts just waiting for someone to care enough to visit. There were old people who were sick and dying and forgotten. There were children whose parents had disappeared and parents whose children had run away. We found empty stomachs and empty hearts on almost every block. And the stories of the lives that God changed along the way still inspire us.

Often Jack's living room was crowded with teenagers eating french fries and wiping away their tears. God was blessing our door-to-door ministry. Our Park Avenue Baptist Youth Fellowship was growing. Every week more young people came. Many that were led to Christ on their front porches ended up leading others to Christ the very next week. When the group began, there was just a handful. Then we grew to twenty, thirty, forty, fifty, and a hundred members. Before long most of the Fairview Heights gang were active workers in the Park Avenue

Baptist Church. We had no idea then that this same nucleus of new Christian converts would form the charter membership of Thomas Road Baptist Church just a few years later.

Nor did I dream at the beginning that Macel Pate, the eighteen-year-old piano player with short auburn hair and deep blue eyes would one day be my wife. I admit that I noticed her immediately upon entering Park Avenue Baptist that Sunday night in January. In fact, Jim and I were attracted to both girls, Delores Clark and Macel Pate, but after kneeling at the altar and giving our lives to Christ any romantic ideas we might have had were soon displaced by the spiritual rush that followed.

In the weeks that followed, Jim and I and a growing number of our friends from the Fairview Heights gang were so caught up in our discipleship program that our old interests were shelved or discarded altogether. There were no lectures against latenight poker games or beer busts. Jack didn't spend any time haranguing us against dancing or drinking or heavy dating. I know that we Baptists have a reputation for being uptight about these social practices among adolescents and young adults. It was one of the reasons I didn't get interested in the church even earlier. I was afraid it would mean the end of excitement in my life and the beginning of life in a kind of Baptist monastery.

In fact, the truth was just the opposite. My carousing days ended because something new and wonderful came into my life. I was part of an army of Christian disciples commissioned by our Commander-in-Chief to evangelize the world. No latenight poker party or beer bust could compare in excitement to those latenight sessions at Jack and Madolyn's when we shared what God was doing in our lives and in the lives of the people upon whose doors we knocked.

And though the first excitement of those early days of discipleship didn't wear off then, nor have they worn off to this day, my glands did begin to function again quite normally and my interest in pretty girls resumed its normal role in my life. That interest focused almost immediately on Macel Pate.

Macel was eighteen, a senior at E.C. Glass High School. She had a perfect smile that she used only sparingly in my direction. During those early months at Park Avenue Baptist,

Macel giggled occasionally with Delores and her other friends, but around me she remained serious, cool, professional. We studied the Bible together. We knocked on doors and witnessed together occasionally on the same Monday night team. We sat next to each other now and then on the floor of Jack and Madolyn's red-brick home on Thomas Road, but Macel remained distant, and it wasn't easy to cross the space between us.

Unfortunately, Macel already had a boyfriend. And to make matters worse, her boyfriend was the younger brother of Pastor Donnelson's wife. He was a handsome young man, popular and gregarious, a committed Christian boy who was commuting between Lynchburg and Springfield, Missouri, where he was a student at Baptist Bible College. If I thought the distance gave me a better chance, I was wrong. The pastor's wife stood in for her little brother. I couldn't steal a glance at Macel without getting a warning frown from the pastor's wife.

But during Sunday morning or Sunday evening worship, Wednesday night prayer meeting, or Sunday youth fellowship, I placed myself in a metal folding seat with a direct view of Macel at the piano and watched her with growing fascination. She was beautifully shaped, with slender arms, a tiny waist, and slim wrists and ankles. She had studied piano for more than ten years and took her music seriously. She arched her fingers and attacked the keys with determination. She played with the same excitement and joy as Rudy Atwood, Charles Fuller's pianist on the "Old Fashioned Revival Hour" radio broadcast. Her eyes only left the music to glance up at the song leader, but on rare occasions she turned shyly in my direction and once even deigned to smile at me.

Macel's smile made me weak. Her lips were perfectly bowed. She had dimples and a tiny bobbed nose. Her blue eyes sparkled when she played and her slender shoulders swayed gently with the music. I knew I was falling in love and I knew that meant trouble for both of us.

Macel's mother, Mrs. Lucile Pate, didn't care for me. She knew my family's reputation in Lynchburg and had convinced Macel that I was a "typical Falwell" and would lead her down the primrose path if she took one step in my direction. Lucile liked Macel's current boyfriend very much, but I soon learned that she would like any boyfriend who lived hundreds of miles away. Lucile Pate was very protective of her youngest daughter and didn't really like the idea of Macel seeing anyone seriously, especially me.

Macel agreed with her mother during those first few months of winter 1952. I invited Macel to go roller skating. She declined. I tried to sit next to Macel at a youth fellowship banquet. She subtly moved away. I sneaked up beside Macel on a hike through the Blue Ridge foothills. She walked quickly off to join her girlfriends. But I persisted, and gradually Macel's resistance was being worn away. My Christian commitment was sincere. She no longer suspected me. And my energy for Christian tasks was boundless. I arrived at the church before the doors opened and waited until the last song died. I never missed a Bible study or Monday night visitation. I loved to share my faith and found more and more people responsive to my personal invitation to accept Christ as their Lord and Savior.

I had no idea that my growing spiritual commitment was more effective than flowers or dinners or presents at overcoming the suspicions that Macel felt for me. And though she rebuffed my early advances, I could see that I was slowly gaining ground. Early in March 1952, twenty or thirty young people from Park Avenue were practicing for a musical presentation in the basement of our church. The piano bench was needed upstairs. The chair available for Macel was far too low for her to reach the keyboard. I took my chances and made my move.

"Here," I said, sitting down in the small chair. "Sit in my lap and you'll reach the keys, no problem."

I couldn't believe it. Without a moment's hesitation, Macel sat right down on my lap and began to play. I can still remember how wonderful it felt to have her sitting there. She was light and smelled of some wonderful fragrance. I kept my hands at my side and tried to look cool and casual. But my heart was beating fast and I wanted to hold her in my arms.

Of course, within minutes the word reached our pastor's wife of this "terrible basement indiscretion." She immediately called her brother in Springfield, and from that day their relationship began to cool. Macel's old boyfriend and I became close friends. He married a beautiful young woman and is a successful husband, father, and respected pastor today. His children attended Liberty University, and he and I are still good buddies to this day. Remember, in those days he and I were not the only suitors of the lovely and very eligible Macel Pate. And though she was always pursued by half a dozen suitors, she had not lost her heart to any man. So, by every standard that I knew, she was fair game and I was a determined suitor.

And though Lucile Pate didn't warm to my cause immediately, as the months progressed I developed other allies in the Pate family. Sam Pate, Macel's dad, was a deacon at Park Avenue Baptist. He liked Macel's boyfriend, but Sam didn't believe that any man studying for a ministry in church music could support his daughter adequately. He knew that I had well placed if questionable family connections and plans to graduate with an engineering degree. Sam Pate didn't discourage the growing interest I was showing in his little girl.

And Macel's kid brother, Sam "Sonny" Pate Jr., just sixteen at the time, was easily impressed by a ride in my 1934 Plymouth with its souped-up oversized Dodge truck engine that my brother Gene had managed to install in it. I dropped by the Pates' occasionally to pick up Sonny for a two-man game of basketball or to ride over to Meek's Delicatessen for a Coke and a hot dog. I pitched baseball with Sonny and taught him how to throw a slider and a fast curve ball. In spite of what you might be suspecting, I wasn't just using Sonny to reach his sister. I liked Sonny and enjoyed our times together. Fortunately, he liked me, too, and soon became my friend and advocate with his sister.

But my best allies in the pursuit of Macel Pate were her two older sisters, Jean and Mary Ann. The Pate family home stood at 414 Munford Street. Because Lucile Pate didn't like me, 414 Munford was off limits to Jerry Falwell, at least at the beginning of my pursuit of her daughter. The Pates, especially Lucile, had strict codes of behavior for their children and enforced them faithfully. Seeing Macel on a Sunday afternoon required the coordination of a space flight. If you walk down Munford Street from the Pates' home to Memorial Avenue and continue along Memorial for two blocks west to Stuart Street, in just three additional blocks you arrive at Miller Park. Our church stood at the corner of Park Avenue and Stuart. The building next to the Park Avenue Baptist Church housed Meek's Delicatessen. Almost every Sunday afternoon, when the dinner dishes were washed, dried, and put away, when Sam Pate Sr. settled into his recliner to read the Sunday paper and Lucile Pate prepared to take her Sunday afternoon nap, Macel and her sisters would kiss their daddy on the cheek and wave good-bye to their mom, saying, "We're going to walk over to Meek's to get some ice cream."

I would wait at Meek's with my car. As soon as Macel and her sisters arrived, I would open the front door for Macel, wave gratefully to her two sisters, and drive away. Nobody lied. Jean and Mary Ann would enter Meek's Deli for ice cream sundaes, which I gladly financed, while Macel and I would drive into the nearby countryside or just down the street to Miller Park. Most of the time we would load the car with kids from Park Avenue Baptist and take them with us on our excursions. Within an hour or two we would return to Meek's Deli, where Macel joined her sisters for the seven-block return walk to their home on Munford Street.

That left me just enough time to head over to Fairview Heights, pick up members of the Wall Gang, and drive home for a quick visit to my mother's house on Rustburg Road. Mom did not leave our house very often after Dad died. She felt comfortable there and used her time to can jams and jellies, bake fresh bread and cookies, and make banana pudding which she used to feed my troop of friends.

After a quick supper, we would rush back to church in time for a six o'clock youth fellowship meeting and the seven o'clock evening evangelistic service where the youth choir sang and Macel Pate played the piano. Lucile Pate sat in her favorite place and watched me enter the sanctuary with my gang of friends. I greeted her daughter with all the formal distance Lucile required, and not once did she suspect that I had seen Macel since the Sunday morning service.

Dad Pate suspected that more was going on between me

and his daughter than reached the eyes, but he didn't mind. In fact he encouraged it in his own way. He didn't want his daughter to starve to death married to a church musician. In fact he didn't think much of church musicians in the first place. He was an old-school Baptist from Alum Creek, a tiny, primitive isolated mountain community a few miles outside of Charleston in the rolling hills of West Virginia. Sam Sr. didn't think you needed a song leader up there "waving his arms and looking silly." In fact, you could dispense with the music altogether and just let somebody preach.

Sam Pate grew up in the mountains. Macel and I and our family have driven our four-wheel GMC Suburban into those mountains many times to visit Sam's surviving relatives. The foundations of her grandfather's home-place are still up there above Alum Creek. Macel's grandparents were dirt poor, but worked hard to care for their brood of seven children. The Pate house was papered inside with newsprint, and the tin roof barely held back the rain. But the old family home was clean and warmed by an iron stove with a blazing wood fire. There was always something to eat and plenty to wear. And somehow Grampa Pate managed to keep an old Model-T Ford running just well enough to transport goods and family down the mountain. The road to town was a nearly dry creek bed through thickets, heavy underbrush, and trees. As my friend B. R. Lakin used to say, "In bad weather in those mountains even the birds walked."

When Macel's dad was still a child, he got a job building power lines for the Appalachian Power Company. He made fifteen cents an hour and felt wealthy. As a teenager, he wasted nothing. He worked seven-day weeks and put aside money to support his mom and dad. On a nine-dollar-a-week salary he was sending money home to help pay his parents' bills. Eventually Sam bought his own Model-T and followed the construction crews building and maintaining those mountain power lines.

That's how he eventually migrated to Lynchburg in 1927, met and married Lucile Donald, and began his frugal house-building business. Sam Pate soon built his first house in Lynchburg for less than $4,000. He was tighter than bark on a tree. When Sam borrowed $1,000 as a mortgage loan at $13 or

$14 a month, the payments worried him until he paid off the house. He never carried any debt after that. He built a house, sold it, and built another. He built the family home at 414 Munford Street in 1948 and was living there when I began my pursuit of his youngest daughter in 1952.

There was never a bottle of beer drunk or a cigarette smoked at Sam and Lucile Pate's home on Munford Street. It just wasn't allowed. And the only music ever played on the old Philco radio was Christian music. Every time the doors of the church were opened, Sam and Lucile with their children Jean, Mary Ann, Macel, and Sam Jr.-were present and accounted for. There were prayers at meals and Bible readings at bedtime. At Christmas nobody opened presents until the whole Christmas story had been read again from Luke, and on New Year's Eve, after a lively and loving family dinner, the old year was ended and the new year was begun with family prayers of thanksgiving and recommitment.

The whole experience was new and exciting for me. I had never been in that kind of home. I came from a totally secular household. Except for my mother's quiet, praying presence, the Falwell home on Rustburg Road was a noisy, boisterous place where success was measured in deals hammered out and business wars won. Our house was lively, with a steady stream of Dad's business partners, rough and tumble employees, and his latenight drinking buddies. By contrast, the Pates' home was quiet, almost austere, with strict rules and carefully regulated relationships. The visitors came for prayer meetings and Bible studies. Missing church, leaving the tithe unpaid, or beginning a meal without saying grace would be like committing murder.

Dating Macel Pate was regulated like every other relationship in the Pate household. After Macel's parents, her two sisters, and younger brother Sam had gone to bed, Macel and I would sit on the sofa in the living room and talk. We would hold hands or I would have my arm around her as we talked about school or church events. Our conversations were often whispered because just behind that living room wall was the small master bedroom where Sam and Lucile lay listening. Even then I could picture Sam Sr. lying beside his wife watching the bedroom clock approach 10:15 P.M. At exactly 10:15 Sam would knock on the wall. Bump. Bump. Bump. Those three sharp raps on the wall meant I had exactly three more minutes to be gone. I never dared to see what might happen if Mr. Pate were forced to knock again.

Of course I was frustrated by the heavy handed discipline in the Pate household, but I was also fascinated by it. I had grown up in an entirely different world. I could leave home for a week and when I returned the most that would be asked was "Where have you been, son?" It just never dawned on my mom that I would be doing anything wrong or that I wasn't able to make my own decisions or to handle their consequences. But if any one of the Pate children had stayed out after 11:15 P.M., Sam and Lucile would have called out the state militia.

Between my conversion in January 1952 and the end of my first summer as a Christian in August, seven months later, Pastors Paul Donnelson and Jack Dinsbeer and the people of Park Avenue Baptist Church treated me to a course in Christian discipleship that had more Biblical content and practical hands-on training than the average seminary degree.

Both pastors compared the Christian life to a journey that began at my second birth. That journey or Christian walk took a lifetime and ended only upon my physical death, when I would stand before the Lord to be rewarded for my faithfulness. The lifelong journey was fraught with danger. I had to make my way through two different and competing worlds simultaneously: the world of God and the world of man. These worlds overlapped. The world of man was visible and run by the Enemy, Satan. The world of God was invisible and ruled by the Lord Jesus. You could see and touch, taste and feel man's world. But God's world required faith to comprehend. Man's world was physical, colorful, and alluring but ended at death. God's world was spiritual and would never end.

It was all so new and exciting to me! Suddenly all of life became a kind of battlefield. God and Satan were waging war for my soul and for the soul of every man, woman, and child upon the earth. At my conversion I was changing sides. When I knelt at the altar to ask God's forgiveness for my sins, I was deserting the

Enemy and signing up to fight on God's side. My brothers and sisters at Park Avenue Baptist were my fellow Christian soldiers marching as to war. Christ was our Commander-in-Chief. The Bible was my guide, my strategy for warfare, my code of conduct, my source of strength and wisdom. Prayer was the opportunity to communicate directly with my Commander, my Father, my Savior, and my Lord. And those front porches on which we witnessed were scenes of battle.

Because he was the youth pastor, Jack Dinsbeer became my primary trainer for the Christian journey, my master sergeant at a kind of spiritual boot camp. Those weeknight Bible study, prayer, and training sessions in Jack's home and on the streets witnessing door-to-door were the nucleus around which all my training focused. From the beginning we learned that sharing our Christian faith with those who didn't know Christ as Lord and Savior was the Christian's primary task.

I began with my friends from Fairview Heights. The wall across from the Pickeral Cafe that once echoed with gang warfare and police sirens soon became a mission field for Jim Moon and me. One by one our friends succumbed to our invitation to attend Park Avenue Baptist Church. Otis "Nubby" Wright was the first to accept Christ as Savior. We carried our wellmarked Bibles to the wall. We witnessed verse by verse to our open-mouthed friends. We carried them by the carload to Park Avenue Baptist, and we knelt beside them, one by one, as they gave their lives to Jesus as we had done.

But our training did not end with witnessing skills. There were a million things to learn. My spiritual ignorance knew no limits. The night I was converted there was a banner over the front wall of the church that read ARE YOU A TITHER? I didn't even own a Bible let alone know the Old Testament concept of giving one tenth of your income to God and to the church. I had never even heard the word "tithe." When Jack came to visit the Wall Gang that next Friday, I blurted out in front of all my friends, "Hey, Jack, what's a tither?"

There was a moment of silence, followed by friendly laughter. I had never heard of Christian stewardship or tithing. I had blurted out my question pronouncing "tither" to rhyme with "whither." Everybody had a good laugh at my expense, but then began immediately my first lesson in Christian stewardship.

In fact, Jack's Biblical answer to my naive question had immediate results. I began tithing that first Sunday. I had an income of about $25 a week pumping gas at the Esso station on Campbell Avenue. It was an Esso station then, and I had told my girlfriends at Lynchburg College that I was a salesman for Standard Oil. I was paid in cash, and I carefully counted out $2.50 into the offering plate on Sunday morning. It was like getting converted again. When the plate passed me and I dropped in that first installment in a lifetime of giving, I felt excited and committed and on the team.

Jack taught me everything, even song leading. I couldn't carry a tune in a basket, yet he made me stand up before the youth group, wave my arms, and sing with passion. Memorizing the old hymns and Gospel songs was an important and life-changing part of my early Christian education. One of the first hymns I learned God has used dozens of times to strengthen and to comfort me.

Jesus, Jesus, how I trust Him.
How I've proved him o'er and o'er.
Jesus, Jesus, precious Jesus.
O for grace to trust Him more.

I first sang this little chorus to a classic hymn during a Wednesday evening service in March 1952, the night I surrendered my life to full-time Christian service. We sang those old choruses and hymns over and over again until they were permanently written on our memories. Those same songs carried the great Biblical truths in a form that brought them immediately to mind during the times in our lives when we needed to remember them most.

Trust and obey. For there's no other way
To be happy in Jesus, but to trust and obey.

Great is Thy faithfulness, O Lord, my Father.
There is no shadow of turning with Thee.
Thou failest not. Thy compassions they change not.

As Thou hast been, Thou forever wilt be.

Onward Christian soldiers, marching as to war;
With the cross of Jesus going on before.
We are not divided. All one body we.
One in faith and conquest; One in liberty.

What a friend we have in Jesus,
All our sins and griefs to bear.
What a privilege to carry
Everything to God in prayer.

Macel played the piano and the rest of us sang until our throats hurt. And after the singing, the Bible studies and the prayer, the young people of Park Avenue would sit around Jack and Madolyn's living room until late into the evening.

Often I stayed alone with Jack after the others had gone. I look back on those long frank discussions as a turning point for my life. Jack didn't just lecture me. I asked questions, and together we looked up the answers in our Bibles. It was my first chance to see someone use a concordance. Every word in the Bible is listed there with its reference: book, chapter, and verse. If he couldn't remember an entire quote, one word would send him thumbing through that concordance in search of the text we needed. I learned to love the Bible first while studying it before the fireplace with Jack and Madolyn Dinsbeer.

As soon as I learned one simple truth from its sixty-six books, Jack would have me teach it to the others at a youth meeting or as a substitute teacher for a Sunday School class. "You learned it," he would say. "Now share it with somebody else."

I wasn't prepared to witness, yet on the first week after my conversion Jack encouraged me to head back down to the wall to share my new faith with my friends. I wasn't ready to teach, but the minute I learned the most elementary truth, Jack had me teaching it. And I certainly wasn't prepared to lead singing, but the very first hymn I knew by memory, Jack had me leading.

Pastor Donnelson and Jack Dinsbeer invited me to ride with them on pastoral calls. We visited sick people in their homes.

The pastors would introduce me and then ask me to read the Scriptures with shut-ins or pray with families unable to attend the church. I sat with the pastors in the hospital emergency ward with church members and strangers who were facing crises and even visited funeral homes to help comfort friends and families facing death.

I didn't understand it then, but these two pastors were training me in Christian discipleship and preparing me for full-time Christian ministry. Fortunately, neither man ever asked me to preach. I was terrified of public speaking. I always took courses in high school and college that did not require an oral report. I could handle a small class or sit-down study group, but on those rare occasions in high school and Lynchburg College when I was asked to speak publicly, my knees knocked, my palms grew damp, and my throat turned gravel dry. I could handle any face-to-face conversation, but groups, even small groups, left me tongue-tied and stuttering.

I suppose that's one of the reasons I planned to study journalism or engineering at Virginia Polytechnic Institute after my first two years at Lynchburg College. I wanted to serve Christ, but I knew that I could never be a preacher. I was just too afraid to stand before a crowd. As my informal course in Christian discipleship progressed under Jack Dinsbeer, I began to puzzle about the future. My family assumed that I would take my place somewhere in a family business around Lynchburg. My brother Lewis had a booming restaurant. My uncle Warren and his boys had a trucking company, gas stations, a large well-drilling firm, a busy garage, an airport charter company, and other businesses around Lynchburg. My father had established plenty of open doors in other city businesses before he died. It would have been easy to have a comfortable position and to serve Christ as a Christian layman in the community.

I had been converted in January 1952. By March of that same year under Jack Dinsbeer's intense course in Christian discipleship my determination to graduate from Virginia Tech in journalism or engineering was weakening. Then one Wednesday night in March 1952 I walked up the stairs of the Park Avenue Baptist Church expecting to attend a typical Wednesday night

Bible study and prayer service. Instead, my life was changed forever.

I don't remember the text or even who taught it that night. I don't remember where I was sitting or with whom. But I do remember the congregation beginning to sing: "Jesus, Jesus, how I trust Him."

I didn't cry. I didn't even feel particularly emotional. There was no vision. No blinding light. No miracle. No mysterious presence. I just sat there singing those words and saying over and over to myself, "Yes, I will trust Him!"

The next day I stopped by the church. Jack and Pastor Donnelson were together in the tiny church office. I stuck my head in the door. They both looked up at me and smiled. I stood in the doorway awkwardly.

"Do you guys know a good Bible school that I could attend?"

For a moment there was silence. Jack bowed his head. Pastor Donnelson looked over to his youth minister and then smiled up at me.

"Why do you ask?" he said quietly.

"Because last night I surrendered my life to serve the Lord full time," I answered. "And going to Bible school just seems the right thing to do."

When Jack finally looked up at me, he was blinking hard and smiling like a proud father who had just given birth.

The problem with too many fundamentalist evangelicals is that spiritual growth begins and ends with rebirth. In fact, I discovered early in my spiritual journey that being born again is just the beginning. From that moment, a new Christian begins a lifelong journey. Matthew, Mark, and Luke all quote variations on Christ's important words: "If any man will come after me, let him deny himself, and take up his cross, and follow me" (Matthew 16:24).

Christian discipleship following Jesus every day for the rest of your life is not an option; it is His command. It takes work, sacrifice, discipline, and determination. And what I learned of Christian discipleship at the Park Avenue Baptist Church in those short months after my conversion was wonderful; but it was only the beginning.

God never called anyone to be a quitter. The word "retreat" should not be in the Christian's vocabulary. The only way is upward and onward for the Lord.

— Jerry Falwell

CHAPTER SIX

The Good Book

Baptist Bible College! my two pastors answered in unison when I asked them to recommend a place for me to study.

"Baptist Bible College?" echoed the shocked and disappointed voices of my teachers, most of my family, and my friends when they heard the news.

The only thing I knew about that little unaccredited Bible school in Springfield, Missouri, affiliated with our Baptist Bible Fellowship, was that Macel's former boyfriend was attending there. In spite of that, I quickly agreed to enroll.

Since my conversion, the Bible had taken a central place in my life. I was reading and memorizing it daily. Each Old or New Testament passage opened windows on an exciting new world for me. How quickly I became addicted to the stories of the prophets, the priests, and the kings of Israel and the life and teachings of Jesus and His disciples. I couldn't imagine anything more wonderful than to study full-time this ancient book with its good news as modern as today's headlines. The promise of studying the Holy Scriptures at the feet of great teachers and preachers pulled me toward Springfield, Missouri, like a magnet.

My mother smiled and nodded happily when I told her, but my brother Lewis, representing the wider Falwell family, was totally against this unexpected change in plans.

"Baptist Bible College?" Lewis mumbled to himself one more time. "What is this: some kind of joke?"

Everyone including myself had assumed that I would graduate from Lynchburg College, Virginia Tech, or from Notre Dame. In spite of my occasional pranks during my high school and early college years, I had a surprisingly impressive academic record. I earned straight A's at Brookville High School and was selected valedictorian of my graduating class. At Lynchburg College I also made the dean's list. I had become a dedicated fan of Notre Dame's fighting Irish football team; and Who's Who in American High Schools included the notation "Plans to attend Notre Dame" in my short biographical blurb. And when I tried to explain to my older brother my new commitment to full-time Christian service, it only made matters worse.

"Get a legitimate, accredited degree," he urged me. "Study business; then if you're still hung up on religion, learn about the Bible in your free time."

Dad had given Lewis his Hilltop Restaurant in 1946, when my older brother had been mustered out of the Navy. In the intervening years Lewis had managed the business wisely and was buying property around Lynchburg. He and his wife Margaret had built a beautiful home in a wooded area on the outskirts of the city. His workers had dammed a creek to form Silver Spring Lake complete with a public bathhouse, picnic tables, swimming and diving areas, and small boat rentals. Lewis had plans for business expansion in and around Lynchburg, and those plans included me. My decision to attend Bible College left him frustrated and unnerved. But when he confronted me, it was one of those rare occasions when my mother intervened in a Falwell family squabble.

"Stop discouraging him, Lewis," she told my brother after enticing him into her kitchen with promises of a large dish of banana pudding loaded with fresh whipped cream. "He's doing what he believes is right," she said. "And you must let him do it."

But even my mother's soft words and banana pudding could not calm the response of my Lynchburg College math teacher, Mrs. Bahous. Somehow this sophisticated Islamic math scholar had singled me out for special attention in her classes in higher math and calculus. She spoke of integrals and differentials with a kind of poetic reverence normally reserved for literature or the fine arts. Dr. Bahous had nominated me for the B. F. Goodrich "Mathematics Student of the Year" award at Lynchburg College and was disappointed, even angered, when upon winning it I told her my plans to drop math altogether in order to attend Baptist Bible College in Missouri.

Only my twin brother Gene was not around to lobby against my decision. He had entered the Navy that same year and was on shore duty in Norfolk, Virginia, when I announced my plans to attend Baptist Bible College. Actually, Gene could care less about my academic plans. He dropped out of high school in his junior year to pursue his mechanical and farming interests. He was and is a practical man whose gifted hands and generous heart have ministered to people around Lynchburg and across Virginia. But he did not put much stake in higher education. Gene liked the idea that we had shared through childhood that I would try out for the St. Louis Cardinals and win a position on one of their farm teams in the minor leagues.

Looking back, it is fascinating to see the hand of God leading me in those seven months of discipleship training under Jack Dinsbeer and Pastor Donnelson. As I read, studied, and memorized the Bible and as I worked and played, worshipped and witnessed with my new Christian friends, my old dreams just faded away while God's new dreams took hold in me. That Wednesday night in March 1952, as a handful of friends at Park Avenue Baptist sang "Jesus, Jesus, how I trust Him," I simply surrendered my old plans and said okay to His new plans for my life. The very next day I was filling out enrollment forms for B.B.C.

Macel's family, especially her mother, cheered my decision. Lucile was glad I was getting out of town. Her resistance to my courtship of her daughter was dying down even then, but the idea that 1,100 miles of highway would slow down the natural passions growing between us brought her great relief. Macel kissed me and wished me well. We promised to call and write at every opportunity. My Wall Gang friends, most of them active members of Park Avenue Baptist by that time, waved and shouted best wishes as I drove my 1941 four-door Plymouth with its IKE FOR PRESIDENT bumper stickers down Campbell Avenue loaded down with books, clothing, and a lunch my mother packed that was large enough to get me through the first year of Bible College.

Actually, Pastor Donnelson had invited me to stop in Cincinnati, Ohio, en route to Springfield to attend the annual September Meeting of the Baptist Bible Fellowship, the fellowship to which Park Avenue Baptist Church was affiliated. The plenary sessions were being held in Lockland Baptist Church in Cincinnati, where John Rawlings was the pastor. This meeting for the denomination's clergy was held three times a year in various cities across America, and Pastor Donnelson thought I might be inspired by the great preachers who would be preaching there.

Until that time, all I knew about the Christian church was centered in Lynchburg, Virginia. I thought our church was the center of the universe. Park Avenue Baptist was growing in attendance by a hundred new people every three or four months. People were being converted at almost every meeting. The little building was jammed with new converts, and the more traditional churches across the city were watching with wonder at what was happening among us.

I had no idea that other churches like ours were springing up across America. I had no idea that there were thousands of young people just like me who were experiencing rebirth and discovering prayer, the Bible, and the excitement of Christian discipleship. And I had no idea that there were preachers like Pastor Donnelson and Jack Dinsbeer who preached the Bible faithfully with eloquence and conviction.

I sat in Pastor Rawlings's great church surrounded by two thousand clergy, lay leaders, and Bible students like myself listening to those great Baptist preachers proclaim the Word. Dr. G. B. Vick, the president of Baptist Bible College and pastor of

Temple Baptist Church in Detroit, was the first to speak. This great man of God commuted between Missouri and Michigan, pastoring a large church and administering the movement's growing Bible College. Another great pastor, Dr. Bill Dowell, was the second speaker in that long line including such other notables as Dr. Wendell Zimmerman from Kansas City Baptist Temple; Dr. R. O. Woodworth from Springfield, Missouri; Dr. Fred Donnelson, my own pastor's distinguished father; and Dr. Noel Smith, a preacher, teacher, and Christian editor.

You might not know these names or the impact of their preaching on generations of young Christians like myself. That meeting was held forty-four years ago. Many of the men are dead now or retired. But they were alive and in their prime in Cincinnati and I was spellbound by their preaching and felt the presence of God in each of their lives.

During those short days in Cincinnati I learned that there were fundamentalist Christians all across America and even around the world. That discovery was a shock and a surprise to me. Suddenly I realized that I was part of something tremendous that God was doing in the hearts and minds of people everywhere. For the first time I felt the excitement of being a part of a worldwide movement of God's spirit, and I walked from session to session with my mouth open and my heart beating in growing wonder.

I was only nineteen years old. I sat in the front row with my Bible open and my ballpoint pen in hand. I underlined their Biblical texts in my own Bible and jotted notes about their sermons in the margins. I laughed at their funny stories and cried at their examples of Christian courage or suffering. I was awed at the long Biblical passages they could quote from memory and by their skills at making the meaning of those passages crystal clear with a simple illustration. I leaned forward when they whispered and sat up with a start when their voices boomed down at me.

I remember one afternoon session of that clergy conference more vividly than all the rest. It was the host pastor's turn to preach, but the service began without him. The congregation sang mightily. Prayers were offered. The Biblical text was

read. The announcements were made. I strained to see why
Dr. Rawlings had not yet arrived. There was excitement in the
air. Suddenly the preacher appeared on the platform and walked
quickly to the pulpit. His face was flushed. Beads of perspiration trickled down his neck and wet his shirt. Even as he opened
the Bible to his text, Dr. Rawlings began to explain.

"Our church is under fire," he said. "But we will not retreat.'

A great "Amen" swept the clergy gathered there.

Pastor Rawlings spoke quietly at first, apologizing for his
late entrance and explaining its cause. At that time his congregation in Cincinnati was in a lawsuit with a woman member of
the church who had been expelled for misconduct. Pastor
Rawlings and his deacons had carefully applied Biblical principles
to her case. It had been a painful decision. They had prayed that
the woman would confess her sins privately that she might be
readmitted into the Christian community as the Apostle Paul
had instructed.

Instead the woman had appealed to an Ohio state court,
which ordered Pastor Rawlings and his deacons to place her
back in membership immediately. That day Dr. Rawlings had
defied the court and was himself being cited for contempt. He
had left the courtroom and driven directly to the church to
preach his sermon to the waiting clergy. It was my first time to
hear a preacher in confrontation with the civil authorities.

"Our religious liberties are at stake," Pastor Rawlings
warned the delegates crowded into his church for that convention. "But will we surrender?" he asked, his voice rising and his
arms outstretched.

"No," he thundered, answering his own question to the chorus of "amens" from the 2,000 people who had gathered. "Hell
will freeze over before the courts replace God's Word as the
ultimate, final, and only authority in this place. We will obey
God and no other!"

I sat in the pew shaking with excitement. If only my dad
could have heard the sermon that day. Preachers were not soft
and weak as he had told me. This man was strong and courageous, obstinate and determined. In fact, I remember thinking
as I sat listening to Pastor Rawlings that this preacher was more

like my dad than anybody I ever met. He was tough, outspoken, unpredictable, and he refused to be bullied.

I drove from Cincinnati en route to Springfield, Missouri, even more certain that my decision to attend Baptist Bible College was a good one. Still, I never dreamed that one day I would stand in a pulpit let alone face a great congregation of my own. I would study the Word, but how God would use those next four years of Bible study was still a mystery.

I moved into Berean Hall on the campus of Baptist Bible College in Springfield. Each dormitory room had matching bunk beds, desks, closets, and a community bathroom. Everybody worked part-time while a student at B.B.C. Classes were held from 8 A.M. until twelve noon. We studied the Bible mainly, with courses in systematic theology, the life of Christ, Old and New Testament, church history, world missions, English, preaching, philosophy, music, education, and a smattering of electives, including speech and journalism.

After the morning classes, students dispersed to their jobs in department stores, gas stations, and small factories across Springfield. My mother's $4,000 gift meant that I didn't need a paying part-time job. I could work in a church as a volunteer staff member rather than taking a job in the city, and that first Sunday I volunteered my services to the Reverend W. E. "Bill" Dowell, pastor of Springfield's High Street Baptist Church and chairman of the faculty at B.B.C.

At that time, High Street Baptist had more than 2,000 people enrolled in Sunday School. The junior department alone included more than 150 children ages nine, ten, and eleven. Max Hawkins, who owned the Hawkins Milling Company in Springfield, was the department superintendent. Pastor Dowell suggested that I begin my work at High Street by volunteering to teach the Bible to one of Max Hawkins's classes for eleven-year-old boys. Hawkins took one look at me and decided my interest in teaching would be short-lived. He had seen plenty of pink-cheeked Bible student volunteers take up the charge with enthusiasm and put it down again when the tedious work began. He didn't want to take the risk with me.

"I don't have much hope for you Bible student types,"

Hawkins began. "You start strong and fade fast."

I stood my ground. Finally Hawkins gave in. "Okay, Falwell," he conceded, "you can have one eleven-year-old boy. That will be your test. If you can handle one student, just maybe you can handle more."

On my first Sunday as a teacher, I met the eleven-year-old boy Max Hawkins had assigned to me. Daryl was a rather shy young man with dark brown eyes, large blotchy freckles, and curly blond hair. He had a kind of cherubic smile and the all too perfect manners of churchgrown children who can put their minds in neutral and sit through anything. If I couldn't handle Daryl, I couldn't handle anyone. One of Hawkins's aides had hung a curtain around a table and two chairs in the general assembly room. It would be our classroom. Hawkins would be watching in the wings.

Daryl was my first real congregation. I taught from the Bible and he listened. After two weeks alone with me, the poor kid got desperate or bored enough to bring a friend for company. The weeks crawled. Nothing happened. My studies were heating up. Papers were due. Daryl and his friend were faithful, but those two boys could easily be placed in one of the other classes. I was wasting my time, and after six Sundays of wheel spinning, I approached Max Hawkins with the news.

"Give me back the roll book then," Mr. Hawkins answered rather abruptly. "I'll find someone else to teach them."

Max Hawkins was a no-nonsense Sunday School superintendent. He had seen dozens of overzealous Bible School student volunteers come and go. He thought I would flop from the beginning, and he didn't even blink when I resigned. He just reached out for the roll book and stood waiting when I didn't hand it to him.

"Well," he said. "Let's get on with it."

Once again Hawkins reached for the roll book in my hand.

"I'm not going to quit," I said finally, gripping the roll book even tighter. Hawkins just shrugged his shoulders and walked away. I drove my '41 Plymouth back to Berean Hall and locked myself in an empty room to pray. The reasons for my failure were obvious even to me. Jack Dinsbeer had taught me that it takes total commitment to grow a church or a youth group or a class of two eleven-year-old boys. For seven months we had worked day and night at Park Avenue Baptist. It would take that same kind of determination to bring new life to my tiny class. I asked God to forgive me and to give me another chance.

Every day for a week I sneaked away to that unused dorm room to pray. On Saturday I called Daryl and his friend Mark and volunteered to take them out for ice cream.

All day that next Saturday Daryl, Mark, and I visited every eleven-year-old boy that we could find on park playgrounds, at the schoolyard, at the ice cream store, riding bikes on neighborhood streets, or just sitting idly on front porches. We invited the children to join our class at High Street Baptist, and I explained to their parents or grandparents or guardians who we were and why we were approaching their children. A handful promised to attend.

On Sunday I loaded my '41 Plymouth with children and drove them to High Street Baptist. The boys loved that old car. I could remove the steering wheel while driving and hand it to one of the boys. I had attached a pair of pliers permanently to the steering column and could steer with my left hand while handing out the steering wheel.

"Here," I would say quietly to an unsuspecting boy, "you take the wheel."

It was a trick I played on new boys on their first ride to church with us. The old-timers would pile into the back seat and let the new unsuspecting classmate sit by me. The excitement and the suspense would increase until finally I would remove the wheel and hand it to the eleven-year-old beside me. Invariably his eyes would widen, his mouth would fall open, and he would sit there holding the wheel looking at me with a mixture of fear and amazement.

The steering wheel trick became a kind of initiation rite to that growing class of eleven-year-old boys. I was never really certain if it was my Bible teaching or that trick with the steering wheel that drew the boys to class. Nevertheless, the class grew by leaps and bounds. Every Sunday at 9:45 A.M. I would parade a growing number of boys past a surprised Max

Hawkins. There was no room behind our little curtain for the extra children, but Max managed to widen our circle of chairs and grin one small quick grin in my direction as he hurried away.

I spent almost every school day afternoon and evening, all day Saturday, and all day Sunday working with my congregation of eleven-year-olds. We had picnics and wiener roasts, bike rides and hikes to caves in the Ozarks. I coached, umpired, and refereed endless games of baseball, football, basketball, and soccer. And we didn't just play. In just a few short weeks we mobilized and began to train a team of eleven-year-old Christian disciples who also worked and witnessed together. On Saturdays we fanned out across the city talking to other eleven-year-olds in theater matinee lines, in neighborhood libraries, in penny arcades, and in shopping centers.

The Sunday pickup route soon outgrew my vintage Plymouth, and I organized my fellow B.B.C. students who had cars to help transport the dozens of children who were swelling our curtained corner of the Sunday School assembly room. I was teaching portions of Scripture that I had just discovered myself. Sometimes I could answer the boys' questions. Other times I had to promise them that I would find the answer during the week and bring it back to them. I gave Bibles to each boy and showed them how to study, underline, and make notations in the Word. I told Bible stories. I read and discussed important Bible lessons from the Old and New Testaments. I had memorization contests where the boys would quote the verses they had learned by heart and receive prizes for their work. I found that teaching the Bible was the best way to learn it for myself. During those months, I did my best to bring to life the ancient Biblical truths and almost immediately I began to see results.

During the class sessions, children were being spiritually reborn as I had been reborn. After a Bible story about Matthew the tax collector or Peter, James, or John, the children would bow their heads and pray the sinner's prayer.

At 11 A.M. I would march the whole class into the sanctuary so that they would hear Dr. Dowell preach the Sunday morning sermon. I got friendly ushers to reserve whole rows up

◄ *Falwell family cemetery
as it appears today.*

*My grandfather, Charles William
Falwell, 1867-1939, a dairy
farmer and landowner (1895).*
▼

My father's first endeavor at age 22 (1915).
▼

*My father's oil and gas distributing company in front of our home in 1923. My father owned
dozens of filling stations all over the region and was the distributor for many more.*
▼

King David and Sallie Beasley with their 14 children in 1915.
Mother is at the far left in the back row.

My mother, Helen B. Falwell,
1895-1977 (1919).

My father, Carey Hezekiah
Falwell, 1893-1948 (1913).

My uncle Warren Falwell's restaurant and filling station, where Garland was killed in 1931. ▶

▲
Garland Falwell during his incarceration in 1930.

◀ *My father dressed in business and formal style everyday. I am accused of doing the same.*

My Grandpa Charlie standing at Garland's grave in 1931.
▼

A recent photo of the homeplace where I was born and raised. My twin brother, Gene, still lives here with his wife.

Grandpa Charlie is holding me while our nanny, Dave Brown, holds Gene.

Gene (on the right) and I are in a formal portrait at age 3.

◄ *My father as I best remember him - in his forties.*

A studio picture of Gene (on the right) and me when we were 12 years old. ◄

I posed for this picture in 1946 with my dog, Pep, and a cat whose name has slipped my mind. ►

My sister, Virginia, and older brother, Lewis, pose during a 1942 furlough after his basic training and prior to action in the South Pacific. ▼

▲ *My brother-in-law, Lawrence Jennings, standing with Dad, Gene and me in 1941, near the front steps of our homeplace.*

A TRBC dinner-on-the-grounds cele-bration in 1958.

I am kneeling (fourth from the right on the first row) in this group photo of the Brookville High School freshman class in 1946.

My college basketball team in 1955 (This fuzzy photo was lifted from an old publication of mine). I was captain and played forward on this Baptist Bible College team.

The Mountain View Elementary School, just before being razed, where I attended my first seven grades of school, 1940-46. Thomas Road Baptist Church rented this building in June 1956 for its very first meeting.

Macel and I at a TRBC staff Christmas party way back when...

The "Old Time Gospel Hour" television program began as a studio production in a local television station 40 years ago.

Tom Morrison of WSLS-Channel 10 in Roanoke, Virginia was our first producer/director for "The Old Time Gospel Hour" when it was a studio production.

◀ *This is a 1959 picture of the old "Donald Duck" building with several additions already visible.*

This was the 30'x 50' auditorium of TRBC in 1956 with many of the charter members present. ▶

◀ *We began televising our 11 A.M. Sunday service live from this sanctuary, which we erected in 1964.*

In 1964, this newly-erected 1,000-seat sanctuary was filled immediately.

▼

The steel framework of our present church sanctuary as construction progressed in 1969. This building was originally designed by Thomas Jefferson. The old drawings were modified architecturally to meet our demands.

We opened and dedicated this new sanctuary in July 1970.

This sanctuary and the educational buildings are used daily by the church and our Lynchburg Christian Academy elementary and high schools.

Our wedding, April 12, 1958. We rushed to complete the addition to our expanded church sanctuary so that our wedding could be held at TRBC. Thank God, Macel didn't know what she was getting into.

Sam and Lucile Pate, Macel's parents. Lucile died in 1973 and Sam in 1984. Both were faithful TRBC members and were always very close to and supportive of our family.

Jerry Jr. was born on Father's Day, 1962. He literally changed my life-my driving habits, sleeping pattern and values.

Macel, Jeannie, Jonathan and I at a 1971 TRBC picnic. Church member and long-time friend "Cat" Combs is seated next to me. Her husband, Calvin, was our minister of music during this era.

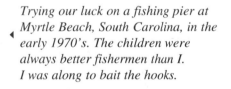

Trying our luck on a fishing pier at Myrtle Beach, South Carolina, in the early 1970's. The children were always better fishermen than I. I was along to bait the hooks.

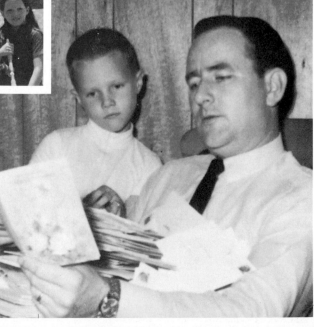

Jerry Jr. helps me open cards on my 34th birthday in 1967.

The former homeplace of the late U.S. Senator Carter Glass and other tracts of land, totalling over 5,000 acres, which comprise what is now Liberty Mountain, the campus of Liberty University.

Beginning in 1977, Liberty Mountain has been the site of a continual building program. Over 64 buildings have been constructed and over $1.25 billion invested in the acquisition, development, furnishing and operation of LU, the world's largest Christian university.

An aerial photo of a January 1977 prayer meeting in the snow, held on Liberty Mountain. This historic prayer meeting, involving students and faculty, was immediately followed by the construction of the first building on the new campus.

An aerial photo of some of Liberty's campus. The 10,000-seat Vines Center with the silver dome dominates the landscape and the social life of the university.

The courtyard with flags ▶ honors Liberty University students who hail from 50 states and 52 nations.

The "Odd Couple". ◀ This 1983 address at Liberty University by Senator Edward Kennedy was "a shot heard round the world."

The Elim Home for Alcoholic Men opened its doors in 1959. Hundreds have found new life in Christ. About 50% of all men leaving Elim have never used alcohol again.

My co-pastor, Jim Moon, and his wife, Delores, my mentor, John W. Rawlings, and his wife, Orelia, our sister-in-law, Carole Pate, with Macel and me at Smith Mountain Lake for a day of fun and relaxation.

This Moral Majority banquet in the early 1980's was one of hundreds of such gatherings of pastors, designed to mobilize the Religious Right. Syndicated columnist Cal Thomas, at the head table, was our vice-president for media relations.

The old mansion on Treasure Island was headquarters for our children's camp for underprivileged and churched youth during the 1960's, 70's, and early 80's. A James River flood in 1985 wiped out the camp. Camp Hydaway on Liberty Mountain replaced Treasure Island.

The Center, located in downtown Lynchburg, is our TRBC outreach to the inner city. Hundreds of mostly minority children and adults are ministered to daily by the pastoral and lay staff of The Center. Sunday services are also conducted and an early learning program for pre-schoolers is operated daily.

The emergence of the New Right and the formation of the Moral Majority in 1979 brought increased media coverage.

The national media in 1980 did not have a clue as to who these religious conservatives were. We slipped in under the radar in the 1980 elections, as we helped bring Ronald Reagan to the White House and to remove a dozen liberal U.S. senators.

A private meeting in 1982 with President Reagan. Among other matters, we discussed his Peace Through Strength Initiative which eventually brought down the Berlin Wall and caused the collapse of the Soviet Union. During those days, I carried his Initiative to the American public almost daily.

The Kennedy and Falwell families pose for a photo following a friendly meal together at our Lynchburg home in 1983. Later that evening, Kennedy addressed the students at Liberty University.

Bob Dole and I have been friends for many years. His wife, Elizabeth, has spoken at Liberty University. Liz's mother, Mrs. Hanford, has been a supporter of Liberty University and this Lynchburg ministry for a very long time.

A typical "I love America" rally on the steps of a state capitol in 1980. About 70 LU students travelled with me to 44 of the 50 state capitols for rallies which made a great impact on the nation. These rallies gave a great boost to the brand new Moral Majority organization.

The late Dewitt H. Braud, in the early 1980's, participating in a Liberty University walk-a-thon. Mr. Braud was Old Time Gospel Hour board chairman and a dear and personal friend.

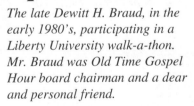

Robbie Hiner entered Liberty University as a freshman in 1971. Today, he is music minister at Thomas Road Baptist Church and, with his wife Patty, is the proud father of Christopher and Chad.

My friend, Tony Orlando, my colleague and OTGH soloist, Mack Evans, and I in Tony's Branson, Missouri theater in 1994. Mack suffered a fatal heart attack two days later.

Jack and Joanne Kemp joined Macel and me for a private luncheon following his morning message to the Thomas Road Baptist Church congregation in 1994. Jack, Joanne and their children are all committed Christians.

A November 1985 eleven-mile Walkathon by Liberty University faculty, students and administration to raise money for the university. We walked around Liberty Mountain.

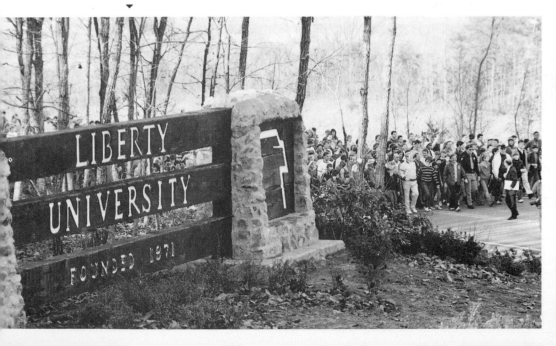

These U.S. Marines, beside Marine One, are not standing at attention for Macel and me. President and Mrs. Bush are walking just in front of us enroute to the 1990 LU Commencement platform with 20,000 persons anxiously awaiting. (President Bush asked Macel and me to ride with them on Marine One to this great event.)

My dear friend, Prime Minister Menachem Begin, awarded me the highly coveted Jabotinsky Award at the Waldorf Astoria in 1980 for my long support of the State of Israel.

Macel and I were the special guests of President and Mrs. Bush for every White House Christmas party while he was in office. Macel and Barbara have been dear friends for many years.

Macel and I met with President Ford and U.S. Senator Harry Byrd Jr. in the Oval Office in 1975. My cousins, Calvin and Doris Falwell, were with us.

In this 1983 meeting with President Nixon at his New York office, we discussed national defense. I believe President Nixon was one of the greatest men ever to lead this nation, in spite of Watergate.

A meeting with President Bush in the White House in 1991. He had just led us victoriously through Desert Storm.

Crowd surfing in the 1996 Big South Tournament with 8,000 Liberty University basketball fans and millions of ESPN television viewers looking on. Obviously, I have great faith in the love and physical strength of my LU students. By the way, we won the game!

Dining on the lawn outside the "Mansion" during a recent Commencement week celebration. My office is located inside this historic landmark.

Landing a big one, with Jerry Jr., in Alaska, 1983.

Macel, her two sisters, Jean and Mary Ann, and brother Sam.

My twin, Gene, and I in a recent photo. I am 20 minutes older than Gene, for you lovers of trivia.

This buggy on the front lawn of our home was my grandfather's and father's. Jerry Jr. found and purchased it as a Christmas '84 surprise gift to me.

My first calling and the love of my ministry-life is serving for the past 40 years as Pastor of the great Thomas Road Baptist Church.

My hope for impacting the world in the 21st Century is Liberty University, where I have served as Founder and Chancellor for the past 25 years.

My best friend and love-partner for the past 39 years is Macel. The best fun I experience in life is the time I spend with her, doing things that seldom make headlines. Here, she and I tried very hard to save three little rabbits who were inadvertently uncovered by a lawnmower at our home. We succeeded.

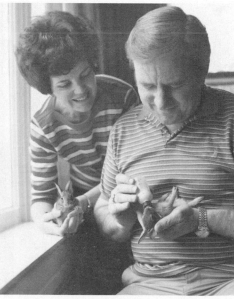

front "for Falwell and his boys." I'd have my friends from B.B.C. sitting at the ends of each row to keep order in the ranks. Remember, these were normal eleven-year-old children with the attention span of a runaway train. Daryl and Mark had been raised by Christian families, but most of that new crowd of children that we were gathering had never been inside a church before. They didn't even know enough to close their eyes during prayer or to remain silent during the sermon.

At the end of almost every Sunday worship service during the fall and winter of 1952 I stepped forward with one or more boys to submit them for baptism or church membership. On weeknight visitations to their homes, I often led parents or older brothers and sisters of my eleven-year-olds to faith in Christ. Our class moved from the curtained corner into ever larger Sunday School rooms. In just six months the class was the hottest thing in town for kids that age.

When I quit teaching at the end of my first school year at B.B.C., we had fifty-six regular members, and special class activities often swelled to more than a hundred eleven-year-olds in attendance. During those busy months at High Street, I learned that building a class required regular visitation, up-to-date record keeping, quality teaching, an exciting extracurricular schedule, bold witnessing, careful follow-up, daily nonstop prayer, and lots of dedicated helpers.

My dorm mates hated to see me coming. "Look out," the warning spread up and down Berean Hall. "Falwell's coming."

I needed drivers for the "bus ministry" we had formed to get the eleven-year-olds to Sunday School. During Thanksgiving break in 1952, my four-door '41 Plymouth sedan was replaced by a two-door '48 Plymouth coupe. It was a terrible mistake. We got as many as fourteen kids into that little car for the run to church. But the parents were beginning to fear for the lives of their children and the kids were arriving at church bent double and twisted back. So by Christmas that year I was forced to mobilize every available student car at B.B.C. on Sunday mornings to pick up kids around the city.

Now and then I noticed Max Hawkins watching me and my growing class from the shadows. "If you can teach just one," he had said, "maybe you can handle more." It was perhaps the most important lesson in discipleship that I learned during those student days at Baptist Bible College.

It certainly was my first solo experience in Christian leadership and my first opportunity to experiment with the practical side of those Biblical principles I was learning. The curriculum at B.B.C. was centered in the study of the Scriptures. Most of our professors were seasoned fundamentalist pastor-teachers such as G. B. Vick, Noel Smith, W. E. Dowell, and F. S. Donnelson. These experienced and committed preachers stood before our classes and taught the Word with practical application for our daily lives and ministries. That was more than forty years ago, but I still have the King James Bible that I carried into those classes and that I marked with various colored pens and pencils as those men of God lectured to the 300 students at Baptist Bible College.

How quickly I learned that, as a Christian, the Bible was to stand at the center of my life. Each lecture I heard and each book I read taught me more about the Word. Written over a period of 1,500 years by forty different authors spread across the Middle East, North Africa, and southern Europe, the Bible is an amazing and life-changing book. Actually it is a collection of sixty-six different books: thirty-nine in the Old Testament, twenty-seven in the New. There are a total of 1,189 chapters and 774,000 words in the King James version of that ancient text. In Bible and theology classes I learned that the Old Testament tells the story of God's love for humankind from the beginning of creation. The Bible begins in Genesis with a dramatic account of human sinfulness and of God's immediate and ongoing attempts to rescue His creation from the consequences of that sinfulness.

In the beginning, the Bible tells us, God walked in paradise with Adam and Eve. He planned for them and for each of us who would follow them a life of peace and creative collaboration with the Father. But sadly the Bible also reports in vivid detail the human disobedience that destroyed God's ideal for us and threatened to destroy all of His creation. Adam and Eve are the first to disobey. Then their son Cain follows suit and kills his brother Abel in a fit of jealous rage. By the time of Noah, "wickedness reigns upon the earth."

The Bible tells us that during those long generations after Adam and Eve sin got so out of hand on planet earth that God regrets that He has made us. The justice side of God longs to wipe out creation and begin again. But His mercy side triumphs, and God calls Noah to build an ark and save creation. After the deluge, God draws up a covenant with Noah and his family to give the world another chance.

Chapter by chapter, book by book, the Bible documents God's efforts to rescue His creation from its own sinfulness. He makes covenants with the patriarchs: Abraham, Isaac, Jacob. He promises them a great people living in a land of promise. "And from my people Israel," God promised, "will come a Messiah who will save all people from their sins."

Through Moses and Aaron, God rescues the Israelites from slavery in Egypt and leads them through the wilderness to that land of promise. He gives them judges and priests to lead them in His name: Deborah, Gideon, Samson, and the rest. He even gives them kings—Saul, David, and Solomon—when they demand to be led as other nations are led. But still the people disobey. They turn to false gods. They break the commandments. They sin boldly; while God just keeps on loving them. And when God's people are threatened by enemies from within and from without, God gives them prophets to lead them safely home. Isaiah, Jeremiah, Ezekiel, and the others call the nation to repentance. But the people disobey, imprison and murder the prophets, or ignore them altogether. And the Bible traces in vivid and horrifying detail the continued story of sin and its consequences.

The Bible is a love story. Time and time again it illustrates how much God loves the world in spite of its sinful disobedience. The Old Testament is the historic record of God's attempts to rescue humanity from its sinfulness. That story ends thirty-nine books later with the death of the prophets and the destruction and captivity of the nation Israel.

At that moment the New Testament love story begins to document God's final attempts to rescue the world from sin and its consequences. In a manger in Bethlehem a child is born. Angels, shepherds, and wise men kneel before this baby while the world sleeps. Only a handful of people recognize the child as God Himself come to rescue us. It was His last option, planned from the beginning. All else would fail.

The first four books of the New Testament (the Gospels) are the story of that child, of His life and teaching among us, and of His death and resurrection on our behalf. The fifth New Testament book records the Acts of the Apostles as they are invaded by the Holy Spirit and move out into all the world to preach the Gospel to every creature and to build the church of which we are now a part.

The historic letters of Paul and the other apostles who follow explain God's plan of salvation and lay out clear, helpful guidelines for daily living. The last book of the Bible, the Revelation of St. John the Divine, creates a beautiful and yet terrifying picture of those last days when God will reveal Himself in judgment and in grace to all creation.

The Old Testament presents Christ as the One who is to come. The New Testament presents Christ as the One who has come. In the Old Testament we have the New Testament concealed. In the New Testament we have the Old Testament revealed. You cannot fully understand the mind and the will of God without reading and understanding both Old and New Testament together. And throughout the pages of both Old and New is the central character of Jesus Christ, by prophecy in the Old Testament, by historical record in the New.

The men who wrote the Bible wrote as they were moved upon by the Holy Spirit (II Peter 1:20,21). God used their talent, their wisdom, and their words to present His truth. He used their individual personalities and perspectives to express His will for the world. And though He dictated through their lives exactly what He wanted to say, His message was also filtered through their own unique gifts, understanding, and personalities.

Read the words of Moses or Jeremiah, Mark or Paul. Each of the forty authors lived in a different time and place. Each man was shaped in a different culture and by different friends and families, by different schools, vocations, and life experiences. Each reflects his own time and place. Each brings a unique perspective to God's struggle to save the world. Each adds a very different facet to the prism through which God's Light shines, but each author unflinchingly, unswervingly, inerrantly presents the same Light.

We can trust what the Biblical authors have written to be the truth because we can trust the God who inspired each of them. They do not contradict each other. They do not make mistakes or tell lies. Although they wrote with their own words, the Bible is the Word of God. It is the only infallible revelation of God's mind and purpose for the believer. Historically, the Bible is accurate. Geographically it is correct. Theologically it is without error. Scientifically it is believable. And as literature it is unfailingly beautiful, inspiring, and captivating to anyone who comes to it with an open heart and lively mind.

The purpose of the Bible is to reveal the mind of God to every man and woman upon the earth. The central message of the Bible is the Gospel: Through the death, burial, and resurrection of Jesus, fallen man is reconciled to a holy God.

The Bible is God's love story to the human race. God does not speak today from the heavens as once He spoke. God does not walk among us as a man as once He walked. But God still desires to communicate with us, and for that purpose He has given us a Book, the Book of Books, the canon of Scriptures from Genesis to Revelation. And on each and every page of each and every book God is alive and revealing Himself to anyone who will listen.

For that purpose God's Holy Spirit has come. His Spirit lives within every believer. When we open God's book, the Holy Spirit goes to work immediately to guide our reading, to inform our minds, and to move our hearts. With each verse, His voice speaks in our hearts God's own words of comfort and direction.

By reading the Bible God informs and illuminates us with His truth. He is able to speak to us through the Bible and give us direction and guidance in our daily lives. Through the Bible God is able to direct us away from sin and into ministry and service. During those years at B.B.C. each teacher emphasized the central importance of the Bible in our lives. They told stories about the rich, productive lives of men and women through the ages who based their decisions on Biblical truth, and they warned us about the disasters and defeats ahead for those who tried to make it without daily reading, studying, memorizing, and believing God's Word.

At first the Bible seemed too large, too long, too difficult to ever read from cover to cover let alone to understand.

"Don't try to read the whole Bible at one time," Jack Dinsbeer told me early on. "You wouldn't read Pilgrim's Progress in one sitting, would you?" he asked. During my first months of Christian faith, I began reading with the Gospels and in the Psalms and Proverbs. I memorized key verses and began to sample the Old Testament story of Israel.

My teachers at Baptist Bible College helped me design a lifelong program for reading and studying the Bible, and I have maintained that program for these forty-four years. By reading just three chapters a day and five chapters on Sunday, I read the Bible completely through every year. Further, by reading two chapters in the Old Testament and one chapter in the New Testament you come close to getting through both major Testaments in about the same period of time.

To read three chapters of the Bible every day and five on Sundays is my minimal goal. Almost every day of the year I read more than that. But I never read less. I also read (almost every day) five chapters in the Psalms and one chapter from Proverbs. This way, I read through both books every month. These two Old Testament books are very special to me. The 150 Psalms lead me into worship and praise. When the Enemy is close on my trail, there is nothing like a Psalm to perk me up and renew my courage and my determination. The Proverbs of Solomon are rich in practical wisdom and full of humor. There are thirty-one short chapters in Proverbs, 915 verses. By reading just thirty verses a day, you finish the book every month, and the gold nuggets you mine in that short time are well worth the extra effort.

I like to read the Bible exactly as I read a novel, from

beginning to end. I don't like to skip around in it when I am reading for my own spiritual growth. Some people get up every day, open the Bible, and let a finger drop onto the passage they will read and study. Others begin a book and read until they lose interest and then begin again somewhere else. Yet others have a planned reading program outlined for them that they faithfully maintain.

I start in Genesis and Matthew simultaneously and read the Old and New Testaments in sequential order from the beginning to the end. I jot down the dates of each reading and many of the inspiring ideas God gives me along the way. I keep a legal pad nearby for writing longer notes, ideas for lessons, sermons, a book, or an article. Some people keep a Bible reading diary. Others use a promise box to draw a Biblical promise at the beginning or the close of every day. Early in my days at B.B.C. I learned to combine my prayer time and my Bible reading and to schedule time for both spiritual exercises at the beginning of the day. I keep a prayer list by my Bible. As God answers my prayers, I mark them off the list. I keep my relationship with God very conversational, very practical, and very simple. I begin each day reading His word and talking to Him through prayer. I read a little. Then I pray. Then I walk around the room thinking about the Biblical passage I've just read and talking to God about its meaning in my life.

In those early B.B.C. days I tried to save from thirty minutes to an hour each morning exclusively for prayer and Bible reading. For forty-four years I have continued that habit. Almost every day there is a good reason not to do it. There is an assignment due, a crisis waiting, a family matter that needs attention, a breakfast meeting, or a conference call. The demands of each new day would destroy my time alone with God and His Word if I would let them. I cannot. When I do fail to keep the appointed time, it cripples the day. When several days pass without Bible reading and prayer, the damage accumulates and my life bogs down noticeably.

Another habit that has stayed with me from those early days is tithing. I will never forget my first Sunday at High Street Baptist Church in Springfield. I was only four to five days into my Bible College experience when Pastor Dowell opened the Bible to Proverbs 3:9 and preached on tithing.

"Thou shalt bring forth the first fruits of all thine increase," he ad-libbed from the Old Testament text. "All," he said again, spelling the word carefully and looking, or so it seemed, straight in my direction.

I was just nineteen. I had $4,000 deep in my pocket to cover my education. Certainly I was not to tithe that money. My mother had already tithed it before placing it in her savings. That money represented approximately what the year's board, room, and my personal needs would be. How could I take 10 percent of my entire nest egg and give it to God?

". . . the first fruits of ALL thine increase," Pastor Dowell said again, and when the offering plate went by during the very next service, I placed an envelope containing $400 on the top of the pile. What I thought would be a crippling act resulted once again in a feeling of joy and liberation. God came first and the rest would follow. Again the Old Testament standard of 10 percent is my minimum gift. I try always to give more, but I never give less.

It was another biblical principle that proved effective in my early Bible College experience and has remained effective to this very day.

During those years in Springfield, I often commuted the 1,100 miles to Lynchburg to see my mother and to visit Macel and her family. Macel and I met and dated irregularly during 1952. In 1953 and 1954 we dated long distance. By the end of the school term in 1954, I decided to take a year off, move back to Lynchburg, and work at Park Avenue Baptist Church.

The church had faced a time of trial. Both Pastor Donnelson and Jack Dinsbeer had resigned and gone on to other ministries. The congregation was floundering. At the height of the incredible growth years, Satan got his foot in the door. Internal problems undermined what God was doing, and the people were frustrated and confused. The youth work that had grown in leaps and bounds almost died completely. It seemed an appropriate time to interrupt my studies and go to work to save our little church in Lynchburg.

Macel had corresponded regularly about the growing problems at the Park Avenue church. When a new pastor was needed, I knew the perfect man to fill the bill. Frank Wood was a friend of mine at B.B.C. He was an outstanding student and a good preacher. I told him about our church and drove him all the way to Lynchburg to meet the people. On the spot they hired Frank, and I spent the 1954-55 school year working part-time as his youth minister.

Billie Lynes and his wife Iona managed the Marilyn Shoe Store at 913 Main Street in Lynchburg. They were committed Christians and volunteered to teach classes for teenagers in the Sunday School. At five o'clock when the shoe store closed, Billie and I would grab a hamburger and go to work with the various area gangs still organized around Lynchburg.

The Fifth Street Gang was constantly in trouble with the law. We began our summer program working directly on members of that gang. The Fifth Street Gang hung out from early evening until late at night at Dabney's Cafe on Fifth Street. We introduced ourselves, explained our program at Park Avenue Baptist, and then waited to see who did not turn away.

These were tough young white kids from the poorest section of Lynchburg. There were fifty to seventy-five of them, depending upon the time of day or night, and trouble was the thing they had in common. Many of them came from broken, violent homes. Almost every one of them had been hauled by the police into juvenile and domestic relations court. Most of them had spent time in juvenile detention. Many had been sentenced to reform school or jail for robbery, arson, malicious mischief, and a variety of misdemeanor and felony charges up to and including murder. Our Fairview Heights Wall Gang were Boy Scouts by comparison. Billie Lynes and I swallowed hard on those first few visits to the Fifth Street Gang. We were only two or three years older than they were and a lot less muscled. At first only one young man showed any interest at all in attending Park Avenue Baptist. But every night for weeks in the summer of '54 we visited Dabney's Cafe offering to take the Fifth Street gang members to baseball or football games, treating them to Cokes and coffee, listening to their lists of complaints, and talking to them about Jesus and the Bible and their lost souls.

One gang member eventually accepted Christ as his Savior and began to attend Sunday School with us. But every Sunday he shied away from church and disappeared before the eleven o'clock service could begin. Then another boy accepted Christ in Sunday School and the two of them bravely stayed for morning worship. It seemed so slow. Every night after closing down the shoe store, Billie and I would head to Dabney's and go through the same frustrating routine. In months of long, hard struggle only five or six of the gang had been converted; but we prayed and witnessed and waited as the Bible instructed us.

Then one tragic Saturday night five members of the Fifth Street Gang were killed in a bloody head-on collision on the outskirts of town. All week long Billie and Iona, Otis Wright and I worked to comfort the remaining gang members in their time of grief and loss. Believe it or not, on the very next Saturday night in a totally unrelated situation another four members were killed in another drunken head-on collision.

Suddenly their resistance collapsed. On Sunday night, forty members of the Fifth Street Gang and a handful of their girlfriends volunteered to accompany us to the evening service. Billie and Iona were working late at the shoe store on an emergency inventory and could not come. Otis Wright and I loaded our cars for return trips from Dabney's Cafe to the Park Avenue Baptist Church. The auditorium seated only 300 people. The front rows were filled with Fifth Street Gang members looking tough and acting rowdy. The Pates wandered into church and thought for a moment they had come to the wrong place. Macel played the piano loudly to drown out the gang's crude comments and attempts at bawdy humor. The song leader announced the Gospel song, but nobody in the Fifth Street Gang could sing it. Finally Frank Wood began to preach.

His sermon was simple and to the point. He talked about sin and its consequences. He told the story of Jesus's death on the cross as God's act of pardon. I was amazed when the gang quieted down and began to listen. When Frank stepped to the altar to invite any sincere seeker to pray with him, all forty of the gang and their girls moved forward and knelt with him. They weren't kidding. For the first time in their lives they had received the good news that God loved them, that He forgave them their sins and offered them a chance to begin life again. We worked and prayed and taught around that altar until late Sunday night. Then we sat in a circle in the sanctuary and heard each person give his or her halting, joyful personal testimony.

"Let's go tell Billie and Iona," one of the gang suggested about eleven-thirty that night. "They'll want to know."

So we piled into cars and headed down to the Marilyn Shoe Store on Main Street. Billie and Iona had no idea of how well their prayers had been answered. They were locked in behind drawn blinds doing an inventory when half the Fifth Street Gang came pounding on the doors.

"What do you guys want down here?" Iona asked haltingly, staring into the darkness at the sea of rough and tumble faces staring back at her.

"We got saved, Iona," one of the guys shouted back. "Let us in so we can tell you all about it."

Finally Billie saw me in the crowd and unbolted the door. We crammed that little store with young people whose faces were stained with tears and whose voices trembled as they shared the excitement of their newfound faith. We spent another hour or two just rejoicing over what God had done among us.

I sat on the floor leaning up against a rack of men's socks listening to the clamor of excited voices, wondering what part God had played in the tragic deaths of those nine young people. They had died through their own drunken carelessness, yet there was no doubt that their deaths had opened the hearts of those who remained. Whatever happened, God took seriously the salvation of these boys and girls. He used those two unrelated head-on collisions as an instrument for us to harvest. As a result, all of those young people experienced changed lives. A judge on the juvenile and domestic relations court told me months later that the work load of the police and of the court had been noticeably reduced after that Sunday night service at Park Avenue Baptist Church, and the revival spread like wildfire

among the remaining Fifth Street Gang and across the city of
Lynchburg. Those young people became real evangelists. Many
of them are Christian workers three and one half decades later.
One of them, Bobby Brooks (one of the better behaved members of the gang), is a pastor now in Tidewater, Virginia.

Upon my return to Springfield in September 1955, to begin
my senior year at Baptist Bible College, Dr. R. O. Woodworth,
the school's business manager, invited me into his office and
asked me to consider working on weekends as a minister to
young adults in the Kansas City Baptist Temple. Already he
and Pastor Wendell Zimmerman had decided that I could drive
the three hour journey to Kansas City on Friday afternoons
after classes, board and room with Pastor Zimmerman's parents, and work on the weekends as a member of his professional staff.

It was my first full-time paid position as a minister. I would
receive $60 a week, board, room, and driving expenses. And
though my '55 Buick Century gulped down gas at eight miles
per gallon, gasoline was still less than twenty-five cents a gallon, and I could save enough from my salary to pay my final
year's school costs.

That Friday I packed my suit, a white shirt and tie, a toilet
kit, and my Bible and drove to Kansas City. And though a new
Kansas City Baptist Temple was being constructed on Swope
Parkway, the congregation still occupied the large store building they had converted and added to during the last years of
growth and expansion. From a handful of faithful charter members, in just a few years there were already 700 to 800 people in
Sunday worship, with Sunday School attendance often hitting
the 1,000 mark. The church office was always in a state of bed-
lam. Dr. Zimmerman and his staff of paid and volunteer personnel were crowded into little offices packed with files and
charts, boxes of Bibles and study materials. Pastor Zimmerman
introduced me to everyone and then showed me to my own
little office.

I still remember sitting alone for the first time at that barren desk with my Bible, the only book in the room, feeling as
excited and proud as a newly elected President must feel as he

takes command of the Oval Office. When Dr. Zimmerman had gone, I knelt beside the desk, put my hand on the Bible, and prayed a prayer of gratitude to God for what He had already accomplished in my life. I had felt His call to Christian ministry, but I never once dreamed that within just a few years I would be appointed to the staff of such a great and growing church.

I lived with Pastor Zimmerman's parents, Mr. and Mrs. Fred Zimmerman. Mother Zimmerman was a sweet, wonderful lady who taught Bible classes at the Baptist Temple until she was in her late eighties. She adopted me that year. Mother Zimmerman kept cookies and Cokes in the refrigerator for my late-night snacks. She kept fresh flowers in my bedroom and always left a light on for my latenight arrivals.

After the Friday afternoon drive from Springfield, I hurried to my office to prepare for the busy weekend that would invariably follow. I was appointed the new teacher of the Doers Class. These young adults were all high school graduates. Some were college students. Some had already taken positions in the professional and business world. All were single. Many of these young people would go directly into the ministry from their Kansas City Temple experience.

The members of the Doers Class were the elite new generation of educated and sure-to-prosper Baptists. Their founder/teacher was Verle Ackerman, a multi-talented musician, choirmaster, and Bible teacher who had just moved to Miami, Florida, to become an associate pastor. Eventually he would become the senior pastor of a great church in Hollywood, Florida. In the past three decades Verle has served more than once as president of our Baptist Bible Fellowship. For these past decades he has been and remains one of my best friends. But following in his footsteps then was no easy matter. The Doers Class was devoted to Verle Ackerman and determined that no one could replace him.

Because so many Doers sang in the church choir, they insisted that I follow Verle's example and lead the choir as well as teach the class. Needless to say, it was a bad idea. I could hardly sing on pitch let alone conduct a major church choir. So I dismissed the idea out of hand. "Dr. Zimmerman wants his

brother to lead the choir," I informed them, "and that's the way
it is."

The Doers responded immediately with "Okay, big boy. We'll
show you."

From that moment, Doers leadership showed me only the
back of their heads as they passed me in the corridors without
speaking. They were young, aggressive, and used to having their
own way. But I was just as young and just as determined to
succeed in my first ministry as they seemed determined to
cripple it. After praying briefly for their renewal, I left them in
the hands of God and began to build a new nucleus of leadership in the Doers Class.

In that year of service between 1955 and my graduation in
mid-May of 1956, the Doers Class had a totally new look, with
new members and new leaders as well. On Friday nights we
planned singles events, study groups, prayer and visitation sessions. I led young people to Christ, introduced them into the
class, organized and trained them into small groups, assigned
them areas of the city to visit, and celebrated with them each
new young person they introduced to Christ.

The months passed quickly. The class grew as it had never
grown. Average attendance jumped from forty to 104 during
the year. And then suddenly my term at Kansas City Baptist
Temple was over. I had announced my plans to spend just one
school year in Kansas City. No one believed me. One Sunday
morning early in May I informed the entire class that the next
Sunday would be my last. Truman Dollar, another graduate of
B.B.C., would be succeeding me. The old-timers could not hide
their looks of surprise.

Apparently there was a lot of soul-searching done that last
week. The old Doers leadership asked me to meet with them
on Friday night at a famous Kansas City restaurant whose name
I have forgotten but whose New York-style cheesecake I will
never forget. We sat at a large table in the back of the restaurant. One by one the old leadership confessed their shame for
having given me such trouble. One by one I forgave them. It
was easy to forgive. Dozens of young men and women had been
converted to Christ and integrated into the Doers Class in spite

of them. New leadership had taken their place. The year had been their loss and the church's gain.

Tears were shed. Much cheesecake was consumed. The truly penitent young people spent the evening urging me to stay with them in Kansas City, asking for a second chance. Already Pastor Zimmerman had offered me a jump in salary from $60 a week to $135, plus expenses. I was honored by their offer, but determined to move on. From that day, those same Doers who gave me so much trouble have been my friends.

Later in May I graduated with my degree in theology from Baptist Bible College. Those years in the Word were only the beginning of a lifetime of Bible study for me. I still read the Bible every morning. I have read through the Psalms and through Proverbs more than forty times since 1956. I still write in the margins of my Bible and on yellow legal pads as I read and study the Word. And even after thirty years of study since graduation I feel as though I've just begun to discover the life-changing truths in this astounding Book.

My mother never dreamed that her love for the Word would be passed on to me. And no one in the Falwell family, not even my mom, suspected that one day a Falwell would march down the aisle at a Baptist Bible College graduation to receive a diploma let alone to spend a lifetime in Christian ministry. In fact, until just a few days before the graduation exercises were scheduled to take place, no one from my family in Lynchburg had taken the event very seriously. Then suddenly Virginia McKenna, our old family friend who had spent her lifetime witnessing to the Falwells and to the people of Lynchburg, heard about my graduation.

Immediately, and without asking my mother, Virginia bought two airplane tickets from Lynchburg to Springfield. Then she drove to our home on Rustburg Road and presented one of those tickets to my mother. She and Mom were great friends, but Mother would not think of taking such a trip. The old prop airplane would skim just above the Blue Ridge Mountains on its bumpy hour-long flight to Charleston, West Virginia. After a two-hour wait and a change of planes, the flight would proceed to St. Louis, Missouri, and after another three hour wait in St. Louis, a third and even smaller plane would fly the two women to Springfield.

That airplane trip in 1956 was long and arduous for a seasoned traveler, but my mother never traveled at all after Dad died. She had grown old and tired. She had become a kind of recluse in our family home. She seldom left her warm kitchen or her comfortable living room for the short ride into Lynchburg let alone to travel across the country in three different airplanes. But Virginia prevailed. It would be Mom's surprise gift to me.

Just one hour before they landed, I learned that they were coming. I had a new 1955 Buick Century with a big engine and a small two-door body with a bright red top and a black bottom. It was a classic car that Mother had bought me the year before. She waved as I drove up to greet them at Springfield's airport. I arranged for Mom and Virginia to stay in the lovely home of Max and Lucy Hawkins. Max was the owner of Hawkins Milling and the Sunday School superintendent who had taken a risk on me with that one lonely eleven-year-old boy. Then I drove those two sweet and precious old ladies on a guided tour of Springfield, the Baptist Bible College, and down to the grand Shrine Mosque where the graduation exercises would take place.

Dr. Bob Jones Sr. preached the commencement address that year. Though he was an old man, he was still very powerful in the pulpit. The school choir sang. The graduation class was presented to the audience by the college dean. I received valedictorian honors along with my diploma. And through it all my mother and Virginia sat side by side smiling at me through their tears. Mom had given me my first Bible. In her own quiet way she had passed on her love for God's Word to me. When family and friends argued against my attending Bible College, Mom backed my decision. And she offered her own life savings to help pay my way through college.

"Study the Word," she said quietly at the beginning of those three years of Bible College training, "and God will bless you!"

And when I walked past her down the aisle at graduation, looking rather formal in my cap and gown, her sparkling eyes and proud smile added her blessing to God's blessing at the beginning of my new ministry.

I owe much of my success in life and ministry to two of the greatest women who ever lived—my mother and my wife.

— Jerry Falwell

The ultimate joy in life is
reproducing yourself in others.
— Jerry Falwell

CHAPTER SEVEN

A Call to Christian Witness

In those first months after my conversion, my prayer life was sketchy. I ended up repeating myself or going to sleep while praying at my bedside. But I kept trying. And slowly my prayer life developed muscle. My prayer list got longer and more specific. Five minutes of meaningful prayer a day stretched to ten, and ten to fifteen minutes.

Then I began to learn that all praying was not the same. There are different kinds of praying. The first real prayer that many people pray is the sinner's prayer for salvation. I had prayed that prayer at my conversion. Then my new friends taught me about prayers of thanksgiving, prayers of confession, and prayers of petition.

It was easy to pray prayers of thanks in those days. I made lists of God's blessings and thanked Him daily for everything and everyone on the list. God had changed my life and I was deeply grateful. Suddenly I began to notice all the other wonderful gifts He had given me along the way. As I drove through Lynchburg, I thanked Him for everything good that I saw. As I met with my new friends at Park Avenue Baptist, I thanked God on the spot for each of them. I took my mother in my arms and thanked God for her love to me. I felt like putting my arms around the whole world and hugging it with gratitude.

About that time I learned about prayers of confession. Almost immediately I learned that those new goals I had taken on at my conversion were easy to miss. Some of my old habits were hard to break. Some of my old responses flared automatically. Prayers of thanksgiving were almost immediately followed by my prayers for forgiveness. I was forgiven, don't misunderstand. God had saved me from the power of sin to corrupt and destroy my eternal life; but Satan was still at work trying to undermine my resolve, trying to block my path, trying to ruin my new relationships with God and with His church. Quickly I learned how important it was to see and admit my sins and to confess them to the Father.

After prayers of thanks and prayers of confession, it was easy to move on to prayers of petition. There was so much I needed from God. And there was so much that my friends and family needed. So I began to make lists of requests that I prayed for every day. People who were sick or lonely or lost. Friends and family who had needs. I prayed for my church and its work in Lynchburg. I prayed for the country and the world. And above all I prayed that God would guide and use me in the days ahead.

No longer was it difficult to pray. I began to talk to God at every available opportunity. I didn't always kneel down. I didn't have to close my eyes. I didn't have to start with "Dear God" and end with "In Jesus's name, Amen." This conversational style of praying revolutionized my prayer life. I began to understand what the Bible means by "Pray without ceasing." I talked to God like I talked to a friend, and little by little I discovered that He was hearing and answering my prayers.

From that special day in March 1952 when I surrendered my life to Christ for full-time Christian service, I knew that God would find some kind of ministry for me. But even after graduating from Baptist Bible College I wasn't sure that I could ever be a preacher. I had learned to witness face-to-face under Jack Dinsbeer at Park Avenue Baptist Church in Lynchburg. Max

Hawkins saw to it that I improved my teaching skills by practicing on that growing class of eleven-year-olds in Springfield's High Street Baptist Church. And the experience with the Doers Class in Kansas City proved that I could speak fairly effectively to a small group of fifty to one hundred members.

But until the spring of 1956 I had never preached a Sunday morning sermon to a congregation. My speech and preaching classes at B.B.C. gave me the chance to preach to professors and to my peers, but that was no proof that I could preach a real sermon to real people sitting in real pews. And I was afraid to make a decision about my future ministry until I knew for certain whether I could or could not preach.

Then without a word of warning, just two weeks before my graduation, Pastor Zimmerman told me that I would be taking his place in the pulpit that next Sunday morning. Notice that he said I would be preaching. He didn't ask me if I wanted to preach or if I could preach or if it would be convenient for me to preach that Sunday. He simply ordered me to preach, and that was that. I drove back to Springfield in shock and surprise.

At a time of crisis the first thing a Christian thinks to do is to pray. I had prayed regularly since the day of my conversion four years earlier. I prayed the sinner's prayer at the altar of Park Avenue Baptist Church. I had developed the habit of conversational prayer in the months of discipling that followed; but it was during this eventful summer in 1956 when I really began to pray in earnest.

Before my first sermon that spring of 1956, I prayed nonstop asking God to use the experience to show me whether I could preach or not. As I decided upon a text, I prayed about it. As I studied the related Scriptures, I prayed about each one of them. As I wrote my outline, I prayed about each point. And as I filled in the illustrations, I drenched each one in prayer.

This would be my first real sermon. I was frightened and unsure that I could do it. The Baptist Temple could seat at least 700 worshipers. My knees knocked and my palms grew cold and damp at the very thought of preaching before all those people. In some churches there is no way to really measure a sermon's effectiveness. Preachers preach, and after the benediction the congregation goes home. But in the Baptist Temple in Kansas City—whether right or wrong—there was a standard by which every sermon was judged. That test of a sermon's effectiveness continues in most Baptist churches to this day.

After each sermon an invitation was given for people to respond to accept Christ as Savior, to seek a deeper spiritual life, to be baptized, or to register for membership. There would be hundreds of people in attendance at the Kansas City church that Sunday morning. And though nobody would admit it, if no one came forward the sermon would be considered a flop.

I knew then it wasn't a trustworthy standard and I knew, too, that I should not have worried about such earthly results when God's business is invisible and eternal. But I was just twenty-two years old and this was my very first (and maybe last) sermon. So I prayed and I worried. I didn't just want people to come forward. I wanted someone to find Christ as Savior through my preaching. If nobody came forward to be born again, I would consider the sermon a flop myself.

There was no turning back. In just three weeks I would be leaving Springfield in search of my own ministry. What if I didn't have what it takes to preach? What kind of ministry would there be for me?

I prayed every day and every night that week. I begged God to show me through this single sermon if He was calling me to preach. "Show me clearly, Lord," I prayed, "so clearly that I cannot misunderstand what You are saying to me."

In Biblical terms I was asking God for a fleece. In this case, a fleece was not a piece of wool that once covered a sheep; although the ancient Biblical tradition originated with a piece of wool in the hands of Gideon, the judge and general of Israel, 1,100 years before Christ. The enemies of Israel had surrounded Gideon and his small army in the Valley of Jezreel. Gideon asked God for a sign that he would triumph.

"Behold," Gideon said to God, "I will put a fleece of wool in the floor; and if the dew be on the fleece only, and it be dry upon all the earth besides, then shall I know that thou wilt save Israel by mine hand, as thou hast said" (Judges 6:37).

That next morning the earth was dry, and Gideon "wringed the dew out of the fleece, a bowlful of water" (Judges 6:38). And though Gideon repeated his request for proof the next night, asking God to reverse the test and keep the fleece dry while the earth stayed damp, I asked only that God show me in that one sermon some clear sign that He wanted me to preach.

I fasted and prayed the last three days before my sermon. On Saturday night I prayed almost all night long, from sunset until sunrise. Gradually my fear lifted. On Sunday morning when I stood to speak before that large crowd of people, I felt perfectly calm. I announced my text from Hebrews and preached with a sense of total freedom. My throat wasn't dry. My palms weren't sweaty. I felt alive and at home in the pulpit; and the people, even the young ones, listened attentively. And when I led in the invitation, nineteen people responded to give their lives to Christ. It was an average response for a Sunday morning service at Baptist Temple, and as I stood at the altar shaking hands with the seekers and introducing them to the deacons who would counsel them, I continued to pray that God's fleece would be perfectly clear.

The last person in line was a wrinkled old lady I had seen a dozen or more times in the front rows of Baptist Temple. The dear old woman grasped my hand and leaned forward to whisper in my ear. "Young man," she said, her voice trembling slightly, "I am a charter member of this church. I've been sitting in these pews since Dr. Zimmerman started it. I've heard him preach and I've heard all the great preachers he's brought here, but this morning through your sermon God showed me for the first time that I've never really been born again." I felt her hands trembling in mine. She was blinking back her tears. I knew she was an authentic seeker and when she asked, "Will you pray with me that I might be saved?" I knew that God had heard and answered my prayer for an unmistakable sign.

That next week, Dr. Zimmerman asked one more time if would accept his generous offer to join his staff in Kansas City. "No," I answered, finally certain of my decision. "I'm resigning. I'll be gone in two weeks."

"Why?" he asked, sitting beside me in the front pew of his

sanctuary. "What have I done wrong?"

I told him about my fleece and the wonderful thing that happened the Sunday of my first sermon.

"Where will you go?" he asked finally, seeing that I was determined to leave Kansas City and strike out on my own.

"I don't have an idea," I answered. "I don't have any invitation at all. But I am sure there's a need somewhere."

God had given me my fleece. He had answered my prayer. That experience helped me feel confident that if I continued to seek His will in my life, I would find it even though my future was entirely uncertain.

I believed then as I believe now that God hears and answers every prayer we pray in the will of God. But some prayers require more complex answers than a fleece can provide. And there are varying periods between the time of praying and the time of inner confirmation, in those instances where the one who prays may feel uncertain and afraid.

The summer of 1956 was a summer filled with difficult prayers and times of wondering if God had really heard them. Never in my four years as a Christian had I faced so many decisions with such far-reaching consequences. Once again I turned to God for guidance, and once again He heard and answered my prayers. Only this time there was no miraculous fleece, no moving demonstration of God's presence. Even worse, this time it seemed that all the great pastors and teachers in our little Baptist fellowship disagreed with God's answer to my prayers.

I left Kansas City Baptist Temple with no place to go. As I emptied my little office into cardboard boxes and loaded them into my red and black Buick sedan, I prayed. As I said goodbye to my friends in the Doers Class and left my room at Mother Zimmerman's for the very last time, I prayed. And as I drove from Kansas City back to Springfield, I continued to pray for guidance.

Even while I prayed, I remembered an invitation to minister in Georgia that I had received six months earlier from my good friends Billie and Iona Lynes. They had moved from Lynchburg to Macon to manage a shoe store there.

"We don't have a good fundamental church in Macon that

we're happy with," Billie wrote. "Why don't you come to Georgia after graduation and we will start one together?"

I had many happy memories from that 1954-55 year we had spent together in Lynchburg working with the pastor and the people of Park Avenue Baptist. I could still see the surprised look on Billie and Iona's faces when I appeared that Sunday night at the Marilyn Shoe Store with forty new Christian converts from the Fifth Street Gang in tow. How we celebrated God's answers to our prayers that night. How I looked forward to working with the Lyneses again.

"Billie," I said over the static-laden long-distance line to Macon. "I've surrendered to be a pastor, but I have nowhere to go. You still want to start a church in Macon?"

"Sure do," he answered quickly. Then he turned away from the mouthpiece and shouted excitedly to Iona, "Jerry's coming to Macon!"

"Give me a week at home," I said. "I'm going to visit Macel. Then I'm on my way to Macon and we'll start a church."

I drove to Lynchburg praising God for hearing and answering my prayers for guidance. It all seemed so simple. I had no idea how complicated things would get and how much praying I would have to do to find my way through those next pressured weeks.

When I got to Lynchburg, I found my home church, Park Avenue Baptist, facing serious division and growing discontent. The transition between Pastor Paul Donnelson and the new pastor had not been smooth. The people were divided. The church had stopped growing. Thirty-five members, including Macel and her family, had united to ask the pastor to resign. When he refused, they left Park Avenue and were planning to begin a church of their own.

I remembered Park Avenue as the place of my spiritual rebirth. I loved and respected their founding pastor, Paul Donnelson. I was converted and discipled under his ministry. I admired and respected the second pastor of Park Avenue. He was a graduate of B.B.C. I had been instrumental in recommending him to Park Avenue Baptist. I had spent an entire year working on his staff. I loved the Park Avenue church and I loved her people. They were my spiritual family. They had given me new direction, and I hated to see them suffering and divided.

Upon my return to Virginia, I was asked to preach for two consecutive Sundays in a Baptist church in Richmond to fill in for their pastor, who had taken ill. I did that. And the second week the entire group of thirty-five Park Avenue dissenters drove down to Richmond to hear me preach. Macel and her family sat in the congregation surrounded by old friends from Lynchburg. It was the first time that anyone from my home-town had heard me preach. I had been the rough and tumble kid from the wrong side of the tracks. They sat in open-mouthed amazement at what had happened to me in those years at Bible College.

Following the sermon, Lawson "Pop" Johnson, the former chairman of the Park Avenue Baptist Church deacon board and one of the original thirty-five dissenters, invited me to dine with their group in a downtown Richmond restaurant. Percy Hall, Harold Knowles (my longtime friend), the Watts family and many others who have been my coworkers through the years were there. It was during that Sunday afternoon dinner that my friends from Lynchburg asked me to serve as the founding pastor of their new church.

I was shocked. Immediately I explained my plans to begin a church in Macon. They asked me to reconsider. So I thought the very least that I could do was to promise these old friends that I would pray about it. Sometimes Christians use that little promise "I'll pray about it" to gain time when they really want to say no but just don't have the courage to say it. But I was sincere and immediately began to pray about helping start a second church in Lynchburg.

Just a week before I had prayed for guidance, and God had answered, "Go to Macon!" Or so I thought. But when I prayed again for guidance, I felt God leading me to stay in Lynchburg. How could it be? If God wanted me in Macon, it seemed that He'd have closed the door to Lynchburg. And if He wanted me in Lynchburg, why had he let me promise that I'd go to Macon?

It was like getting two different and opposite fleeces. Both doors seemed open to me. This time as I prayed, God seemed to be leaving the decision in my hands. It was the beginning of my second important lesson about prayer. I had already learned that God heard and answered every prayer we pray, but now He was beginning to teach me about the human side of praying.

God doesn't do our thinking for us. Sometimes He provides an obvious fleece, but other times He lets us make the difficult decisions without one. Apparently God was glad for me to go to Macon if I wanted to, but He was glad for me to stay in Lynchburg. The final choice was mine. This time there would be no fleece. God wanted me to learn that making difficult decisions prayerfully is a part of being human.

At those times we need to get as many trustworthy opinions as we can gather. We need to collect every possible scrap of information. We need to examine every option and its consequences. And we need to listen both to our brain and to our heart before we decide. Then, once we've made our own decision—carefully and prayerfully—we cannot give in to the people around us who disagree, even if we love and respect those people. Once we've decided, we can't look back to worry, wonder, or regret.

The next two Sundays of that eventful summer I traveled away from Lynchburg to fill pulpits for absent pastors, the first Sunday in Roanoke and the second Sunday in a little Baptist church out in the country. Each Sunday I would see my friends from Lynchburg sitting in the congregation listening to my sermon. And each Sunday they would repeat their wish that I would help them start their new church.

During those first four weeks of summer, I prayed night and day for God's direction. But I quit looking for handwriting on the wall to direct me. This difficult decision was mine to make; so as I prayed, I began to examine the options and their consequences for me and for the people of Lynchburg.

The thirty-five dissenters were obviously Christian men and women of good will who were anxious to serve the Lord in their community. They had tried to reconcile their differences with their former pastor but had failed. They wanted to put the past behind them and to begin again. They had decided that Lynchburg was a large enough city for two churches of our

Baptist fellowship. They had promised me that they would start their new church a good distance from Park Avenue Baptist, in a largely unchurched neighborhood. They would not compete with members of Park Avenue Baptist or attempt in any way to proselytize them. They needed a pastor to help them start the church, and they believed that God had led them to me.

I loved and respected the pastor and the people of Park Avenue Baptist Church. I wanted to help heal the wounds suffered by Christian people on both sides of the battle. But I also loved the people of Lynchburg and feared that this ongoing war within my home church would cripple our Christian witness in the city. As I prayed, I grew more and more certain that if both sides would turn away from their conflict and get back to God's business, then both sides would grow and eventually be reconciled.

There were other reasons I wanted to stay in Lynchburg. These reasons of the heart were not so altruistic as the reasons of my brain, but they were reasons to be considered nevertheless. I loved the idea of living one last time with my mother in the old home-place on Rustburg Road. I craved a chance to be back in Falwell country surrounded by my sister and my brothers, by uncles and aunts, cousins, nephews, and nieces. And being close to Macel once again made me realize how much I had missed her and how much I wanted and needed her by my side.

Macel and I walked in the fields near the old family home. We talked about the future of Park Avenue Baptist and about our future together. We prayed that God would guide me in my decision. Thinking carefully about each option was the way that God was guiding me. I had promised Billie and Iona Lynes that I would help them start a church in Macon. I knew that they would be disappointed if I didn't keep my promise. And I also knew that the pastor of Park Avenue Baptist and some of his people would misunderstand and misinterpret my motive if I stayed in Lynchburg even temporarily. I knew that either decision would cause pain and problems for myself and for the people that I loved. Still, after days of struggle, I felt that my best decision would be to postpone my move to Georgia for at least a few months. And when I asked God about that decision, I felt confident that He approved and agreed.

Before making my final decision, I called the pastor and asked to see him. We sat together in his little study just off the sanctuary where I had found Christ as Lord and Savior. How many times in that same room Pastor Donnelson, Jim Dinsbeer, and I had prayed before a Sunday service or a revival meeting. The pastor and I had spent a year together working out of that office to reach the city of Lynchburg for Christ, to minister to the Fifth Street Gang, and to help meet the needs of the congregation. It was a room filled with happy memories of my first four years of Christian faith.

"They're going to start a church anyway," I began. "And they've asked me to help them get it started. Why not turn this defeat into a victory? Let the second church be considered a sister church of Park Avenue Baptist. We can pray and work together. Both churches will grow."

He listened silently while I reasoned on behalf of the new church. Baptist congregations often thrive in such conflict. We run our churches democratically. We have no pope, no college of cardinals, and no bishops. We believe in the priesthood of all believers; therefore, our pastors have to earn their authority, and our boards of deacons are set up to serve the church, not to run it.

But Baptists are human beings like everybody else. We love Christ and we are united by our loyalty to Him, to His Word, and to His promised return; but in the meantime almost everything else is up for grabs. We often act first and think and pray later. Our churches are filled with feisty, independent frontier-American types who bow to no man's (or to no woman's) authority. Of course, those independent spirits may fight and divide, but often through the division comes growth and expansion for the church and an ever enlarging witness for the Gospel. I tried to convince Park Avenue's pastor that if we worked together we could turn this little tragedy into another triumph for Christ and for His kingdom.

He listened and nodded silently. He knew that the thirty-five people were going to start their church. I reiterated their promises and assured him that we meant only good for the city, for the Kingdom, and for Park Avenue Baptist Church.

After an hour or so he seemed willing to give the plan a try. Then he excused himself, went to a nearby office, and called our fellowship's headquarters in Springfield, Missouri. I don't know whom he called that day or what exactly was said between them, but when he ended his call and came back into his office, he was no longer willing to cooperate.

An executive of our little Baptist fellowship (we don't like to call ourselves a denomination and prefer to be seen as a "movement") passed on the word to me that our plan to begin another church in Lynchburg was "unacceptable" and that the only acceptable option I had was "to leave town immediately and to let them [the dissenters] go."

The pastor stood towering over me voicing his authority and the authority of his mysterious contact at headquarters. If I stayed to help the church I would be taking a stand against men I loved and respected. If I let them scare me away, I would be moving against the voice of God, who I felt was calling me to stay in Lynchburg.

"I'm sorry," I said. "I mean you and your church no harm. I will see that the thirty-five people who have asked me to help them start a second church in Lynchburg keep their promises. But I have decided to help them and cannot back away from that decision."

How lonely I felt that day, deciding against all the advice of the authority figures in my life. But I had prayed and thought long enough. After considering all the options, I knew that I wanted to stay in Lynchburg, at least for a while; and even as I prayed, I felt that God wanted me to stay as well.

"I'll have to delay my trip to Macon," I told Billie and Iona on a latenight call. "I'm needed in Lynchburg for a while." The Lyneses understood and promised their continued prayers. But other people were not so understanding.

The pastor saw my gesture as an attack against him and the remaining congregation at Park Avenue Baptist. He began to speak against me and against the thirty-five dissenters. And the word quickly spread to Springfield and throughout our little fellowship to key pastors and powerful Baptist leaders across the country.

Before he became a student at Baptist Bible College in Springfield, he had been a member of Pastor G. B. Vick's Temple Baptist Church in Detroit, Michigan. Dr. Vick also served as president of Baptist Bible College, and the two men had developed a close personal friendship. I had a deep and lasting respect for Dr. Vick. His classes in Bible and Sunday School Administration made an important impact on my life. His sermons had informed and inspired me. I admired and appreciated his leadership of the Baptist Bible Fellowship.

Within a very short time I learned that Dr. Vick himself opposed my decision to help the thirty-five. One of the denomination's leaders called me from Springfield to warn me officially.

"You are just twenty-two years old, Jerry," he said. "You have promised to go to Macon. You must keep that promise."

I argued that I was needed in Lynchburg, at least temporarily. I explained that the people were going to start a second church whether I stayed or not and that it seemed appropriate that someone who cared about both sides would help them in those crucial early weeks.

"Those people are troublemakers," he replied. "You should not help them start a church, Jerry. A second church in Lynchburg will only cause trouble for Park Avenue Baptist and its pastor. And it won't help your future, either."

In spite of the menacing tones in that flurry of phone calls that followed, I stayed in Lynchburg.

"I will pray about it, earnestly," I promised each caller. "After all, I've just committed myself to helping them start the church. I have not decided to stay and pastor it."

"Then get out as quickly as you can," one replied. "Don't cause any more controversy than you've already caused."

Apparently the leadership of our 4,000 churches in the Baptist Fellowship had decided that if I continued with my plan to help start the second church in Lynchburg I would be "excommunicated."

"If you do not leave Lynchburg immediately," one official

caller informed me, "you will be cut off from the Baptist Bible Fellowship International. You will not be welcome to preach in our churches or to attend our fellowship meetings. We will not accept students at Baptist Bible College from your church, nor will our students be allowed to assist you in your ministry."

Those were terrible times for me. I had only been a Christian for four years. I had been converted through one of their churches and discipled by their ministers and lay leaders. I had been taught by their professors and their pastors in their Bible College. I was grateful to these men and women for giving me life. I was loyal to their school, to their missions program, and to their national leadership. My heart and soul were wrapped up in that little fellowship of Baptists; and to think that in making my decision to stay in Lynchburg I would be cut off from all of that was a real emotional blow.

But I had prayed for God's guidance. And I had thought through on the options and their consequences. I was certain that God had heard and answered my prayers. Every day I felt more convinced that He wanted me to stay in Lynchburg in spite of the threats against me. So I stayed.

It was at that time that God began dealing with me about belonging to Him alone and not to anything else on this earth. I didn't belong to the Baptist Bible Fellowship International. I didn't belong to the city of Lynchburg, the state of Virginia, or to the United States of America. I belonged only to God. It was His voice in my heart and brain that would direct me, and no other's.

I was certain I had made the right decision. I felt growing conviction that God was pleased I had chosen to stay in Lynchburg and that He wanted me there in spite of all those who were standing against me. Still, I felt alone. I went to my bedroom in the old family house. I had lost every friend I had in the ministry. I felt cut off, isolated, and abandoned. I read the Psalms of David and wept. With the Psalmist, "I cried unto God with my voice, even unto God with my voice; and he gave ear unto me. In the day of my trouble I sought the Lord" (Psalm 77:1 2).

During that time when my enemies seemed everywhere, I began to read the story of the writer of the Psalms. This man whom God loved best had been confronted by the prophet, repudiated by the people, and rejected by his family and friends. His sins had caused great hardship to those he loved and to the nation of Israel. And though God forgave David, the king still had to face untold heartache. Night after night he soaked his pillow with his tears. And though I hadn't disobeyed and displeased the Lord in the same way King David had, I needed the same kind of comfort and strength that David sang about in the Psalms.

I lay on my bed at night and prayed for God's comfort. It was another major lesson I learned about prayer that summer of 1956. There are moments in our life when we feel totally alone. At those times, talking to God is the only form of comfort available. And yet we wonder if He really hears us. Without prayer, we are isolated and alone in a very chilly universe. And though our prayers connect us directly to the Creator of the Universe, there are still times of praying when God may seem distant, a billion miles away, and we may feel alone and afraid.

Because of my decision to help found the church in Lynchburg, I was "excommunicated" from the Christian fellowship that gave me spiritual birth. I had lost everybody and everything on this earth that seemed important to a twenty-two-year-old preacher about to begin his first church. And though these were lonely, fearful times, once again Christ proved to be an ever present source of comfort. He never really left me or failed me, even though I didn't always feel His presence. After those several months of soul agony, I simply relinquished my life and my ministry to the Lord.

"God, I am yours alone," I said. "Nobody else wants me. I am no longer the property of any church or any denomination or any movement. I am totally and entirely yours. I will minister to this city. You have called me here, and here I will stay. I will reach this town for Christ and I will do it all alone if that's what it takes."

I had given my life to that little fellowship of Baptists. And when suddenly they said we do not want you, I didn't know where to turn. They said they would not accept money from my new congregation for their mission work around the world.

They said they would not accept Bible students from my new church for training in the ministry. They said they would not welcome me in a fellowship meeting, that I could not preach in my fellow pastors' pulpits and they could not preach in mine.

And though I felt terrible and alone and abandoned, it was an important and necessary time for me. During that long hot summer I turned to God as I had never turned to Him before. Let me add quickly that those men who rejected me were good men. But they allowed their zeal for a movement to get ahead of the Spirit of God in their hearts and lives. We long since have corrected all that. After fifteen years of isolation, the gap has been bridged again. We support the fellowship and are members in good standing of that body. But during that time I determined that never again will I allow my membership in a denomination or a fellowship or an organization of any kind to get in the way of my direct one-to-one relationship with the Lord.

I spent fifteen years alone and cut off. But God used those years to help me understand that my trust should be entirely in Him. The Apostle John wrote that "ye need not that any man teach you: but as the same anointing teacheth you of all things" (I John 2:27). I learned during those fifteen long years that I didn't need a fellowship to guide me. I didn't need a program to follow or a book of outlines to depend upon. I didn't need a headquarters or a hierarchy to trust in. Jesus Christ was all of that for me.

On June 21, 1956, we held our first service in the Mountain View Elementary School auditorium. I preached. Macel played the piano. And our little congregation gathered and prayed together for God's guidance for our new church and for a home that we could call our own.   On the next rain-drenched Monday afternoon I found myself with Percy Hall driving about Lynchburg looking for a place to hold the first official meeting of our little congregation. His insurance agent had told Percy that there was an empty building on Thomas Road in the undeveloped west end of Lynchburg. We parked in the rain and stared at the thirty-by-fifty-foot abandoned building standing on the corner of that muddy lot. In the early 1940's. it had been a corner grocery store. In the early 1950's. the building had housed the Donald Duck Bottling Company, a soft drink firm that went defunct.

We walked to the building, pushed open a back door, and brushed away the cobwebs and debris that stood directly in our pathway. The building was empty except for broken shelves, rusty pipes, and tattered boxes piled in one corner. A sticky coat of black syrup stained the floor and the walls and had even splashed up onto the ceiling. But we hardly noticed the mess. The possibilities of that filthy little building seemed endless, and the property surrounding it was entirely empty.

"Percy," I said excitedly, "let's find out who owns it; maybe this is the place to start."

The old building was owned by Miss Vera Thomas, the daughter of a former state senator, A. F. Thomas. The agent for her extensive properties throughout Lynchburg was John Stewart Walker, whom we approached immediately about using the vacant building to start our church.

"We don't have any money to purchase the property," I explained, "but we would like to lease it starting today with an option to buy."

Mr. Walker agreed. The rent would be $300 a month. The thirty-six of us agreed to take on that expense among us. For the next week we shoveled and pounded and polished. Old theater seats were acquired and set in place. Curtains were hung over broken or cracked windows. Hymnbooks and Bibles were collected, and an old upright piano was moved to its place near the little wooden lectern that would serve as my first pulpit.

On Wednesday evening, June 27, our congregation met in the partially restored building to hold the organizational meeting of our new church. We adopted our simple constitution and our bylaws that night. We elected our first three trustees and named ourselves the Thomas Road Baptist Church. Again we prayed that God would lead us from the very first moment of our ministry in Lynchburg. We didn't do anything without praying about it first. We believed that God was there with us from the beginning, and we asked Him to guide us each step of the way.

On July 1, 1956, our first Sunday service was held on

Thomas Road in Lynchburg. At 6:30 A.M. that first Sunday morning, I awakened in our home on Rustburg Road to the smell of biscuits, gravy, and bacon. I could hear Mom humming in the kitchen as she bustled about preparing a man-sized breakfast to get me through that first official day of my ministry on Thomas Road. I showered, dressed, and hurried to greet her. She stood looking down at me as I ate. It wasn't common for Mom to talk about her feelings, no more than it was common for me to talk much about mine. But when the radio began to play "Heavenly Sunshine," signaling the beginning of one more "Old Fashioned Revival Hour" broadcast, I could see the look of happiness in her eyes as she smiled down at me.

I could hardly believe what was happening myself. All those years I had sat at that breakfast table listening to Charles E. Fuller preach on the old Mutual Broadcasting network, wishing Mom would change the station, knowing that she wouldn't, knowing that she was hoping that God would use that broadcast to change my life. And on that Sunday morning she knew for certain that God had heard her prayers, and she stood basking in the joy of it.

There was a moment during that breakfast when our eyes met, and the glance that flew between us said it all. For so many years my mom had prayed for me. Seldom had she spoken of her hope that one day I would know Christ as Lord and Savior. And never once had she shared her secret dream that I might even be a preacher. During those high school years, I pretended not to notice the radio blaring the "Old Fashioned Revival Hour" broadcasts. I laughed or changed the subject when she spoke of God, and I refused to go to church with her.

But Mom never stopped praying for me. Years passed with no signs that her prayers were being heard let alone answered, but she continued to pray for me nevertheless. She was never melodramatic about it. I never saw her kneeling at her bedside, nor did I overhear her crying out to God on my behalf. Quietly, patiently, secretly, she prayed for me at the beginning of each day and at its end. And no matter what I did or said, she kept praying.

It was the most important lesson that she taught me about

prayer. When you want something from God, don't stop asking Him until you get it. Jesus himself told a parable about a judge who did not fear God or man but who gave in to the tearful pleas of a widow who demanded vengeance on her enemies. "I will avenge her," the judge said one day, "lest by her continual coming she weary me."

Sometimes we forget this story. We don't really believe that God hears us and is moved to compassion by our prayers. Yet Luke begins Chapter 18 of his account of Jesus's story with the meaning of the parable: Jesus told his disciples a parable to show them that they should always pray and not give up.

My mother never gave up. She wanted Christ to save me. And in spite of my resistance she even dreamed that one day God would use me in His ministry. And on that Sunday morning in June 1956 my mother knew that God had heard her prayers and that her wildest dreams were coming true for me.

We Falwells do not easily express emotion. On that morning Mom just stopped long enough to smile at me. I smiled back. We didn't speak of it then; nor did we ever speak directly to those spiritual wonders that were affecting us both so deeply. I just rose from the table, thanked her for breakfast, hugged her quickly, and walked to my car.

By 8:15 A.M. I was unlocking the old building. I pulled back the curtains so that the sun would stream into our rough little sanctuary and take off the morning chill. I arranged and rearranged the seats. I placed my Bible on the little pulpit and opened it to my morning text. I paced up and down the center aisle nervously, occasionally looking down Thomas Road for any sign that someone would actually show up that day.

I think the first couple to arrive were Lawson L. Johnson and his wife Bertha. Pop Johnson stood about six feet tall and weighed roughly two hundred pounds. His wife was just four feet eleven. But from the beginning they were tall, strong pillars that God used to help hold up our little church.

Mr. Johnson had been an employee of the city of Lynchburg, maintenance division, all the years of his life. Upon retirement at sixty-five, he began working part-time at the city jail as a deputy sheriff and a jailer. He served our church faithfully from that first day as the teacher of our adult class. He and his family were dedicated to the church. In fact, by the time Pop and Bertha Johnson arrived with all their family members, including his sister Lorna Watts and her large family, we already had a fairly good-sized congregation.

I can't name every person in attendance that morning; nor can I give credit to every man, woman, and child who invested their lives in Thomas Road Baptist Church. But Pop Johnson is a good man to represent them all. From that Sunday night in January 1952 when I was converted at Park Avenue Baptist Church, Pop Johnson had a strong influence on my life. His Bible teaching and his spiritual leadership made a strong and lasting impact on me.

I remember one incident in the spring of 1952 when I was playing left field for our baseball team in the Class A Division of the City League. It was a Sunday afternoon. Pop had gone walking after church and sat on a bench near a water fountain on the left side of the outfield.

"Boy," he hollered when he recognized me as one of the young people from the church. "What are you doing playing ball on Sunday?" I knew Lawson Johnson was a deacon at Park Avenue Baptist. I didn't have any scruples against playing ball on Sunday then, and I don't have any scruples against playing ball on Sundays now. But during the following week I read that passage from the Apostle Paul's letter to the church in Rome where he instructs the first century Christians to avoid eating meat that might offend a brother. And I realized that playing baseball on Sunday was an offense to my brother Deacon Lawson Johnson. So I quit playing baseball altogether. I had hoped to play professional ball one day. Probably Pop Johnson saved me from a lot of embarrassment.

That first Sunday on Thomas Road, I saw Pop and Bertha drive their car onto the empty field next to the church building. Pop helped Bertha from the car and then slowly reached into the back seat for the large heavily marked Bible that he would use to teach his adult class. Bertha waved at me as they started across the field toward the door of our storefront church. They were pioneers, and though they were old they were as excited about this new venture as I was. They both grinned broadly as they walked across the threshold into the combination classroom/sanctuary.

The place looked ragged and funny. There was a smell of Lysol and Clorox still in the air. Though the sun was shining through the cracked windows, the metal folding chairs we had prepared for Pop's class were icy cold. But Pop Johnson took his place at my side with the proud look of a man who was about to launch the largest Baptist church in the world. And though he didn't live to see it, that was exactly what Pop and Bertha Johnson were doing.

Just four years later, an artery ruptured in Pop Johnson's brain. Thirty-one hours later he was dead. But he left us with a priceless, prayerful legacy. Before he died, Pop's adult Bible class grew quickly to become the keystone of our Sunday School program. Everybody loved him. And everybody knew that when Pop Johnson prayed, God listened. When he died, the procession of mourners wound its way down Thomas Road for many blocks to Pop's burial place.

When we finally began our Sunday School that first Sunday morning, there were thirty-five adults and three dozen or more children in attendance. I greeted each one as he or she entered. I announced how we would divide the room into sections for our first class meetings. We took a Sunday School offering and sang happy birthday to a child. There was a short break after Sunday School.

People stood in the sunshine outside the building talking excitedly about the future of our little church and then began to reassemble as Macel played a prelude of Gospel songs on the old upright piano. Walter Mitchell was our "head usher." His wife Vergie was still cleaning up the mess from her beginners' Sunday School class when we began our opening hymn.

The trustees sat near the front of the building with their families: Macel's dad, Sam Pate Sr., Percy Hall, and Pop Johnson. Homer Wrenn was chosen our first treasurer. I remember praying the pastoral prayer, reading my text, Philippians 3:12-14, and beginning to preach my first sermon on Thomas Road. That storefront church looked very much like a cathedral to me. And the sun shone through the cracked windows making streaks of light in the dust that still shimmered in the air. The people sat in pools of light beaming up at me. It was our first Sunday, and everybody was on his or her best behavior. No baby cried that morning. No child squirmed. No adult dozed off to sleep.

And when I ended my sermon, when the invitation had finished and the people stood for a final prayer, I looked down on the fourth row and saw my mother. Her eyes were wet with tears and her face glowed.

For twenty-two years Mom had prayed for a moment like this one. Now God had answered her prayers. On July 1, 1956, I stood at the door after the service and shook hands with each member of our tiny church. "We'll be praying, Pastor," they promised on that first day. And though they were just a handful of average Christian believers, they kept their promise, and upon their prayers God has built a miracle.

The sinner's prayer is the first prayer that people pray at the beginning of their new life in Christ. It is a simple prayer. It can be prayed silently or aloud, alone or in a crowd of people, with or without emotion. Everyone says it differently in his or her own way but its theme is the same for everyone who prays it:

> Lord, I am a sinner.
> I have disobeyed You.
> I have broken Your commandments.
> I believe that Jesus died for me and rose from the dead for me.
> I believe that in His life and death and resurrection,
>   my sins can be forgiven.
> Please, Lord, forgive me all my sins.
> I confess Jesus as my Savior and Lord.
> Come into my life.
> Let Your Spirit control me forever.
> Thank you for Your forgiveness,
>   for accepting me into your family
>   and for granting me eternal life. Amen.

If you have never prayed before, this is the prayer with

which to begin. Use your own words or read the words above. Saying the exact or "proper" words is not important. God understands your heart. If you have ever told a lie when you were a child or stolen from your mother's purse or dented the fender of a neighbor's parked car, you know how terrible it is to carry that guilty feeling very long. And though it is difficult to get up enough courage to say, "I'm sorry," you know how good it feels when it's said and done. God has feelings, too. If you have ignored Him or disobeyed Him or even used His name in vain, He feels it. He goes on loving you. Nothing can stop God from loving you, but He still feels it when you sin against Him.

The sinner's prayer is saying "I am truly sorry" to your heavenly Father. In just a few sincere sentences you can be reconciled with Him again. It doesn't matter if your sin is great or small. The load of guilt you've been carrying all these years can drop away. And the great gap you've felt between yourself and God can be bridged in those few short words.

As a brand-new Christian I was amazed to learn that prayer is simply conversation with God. And often, the best and most productive kind of praying is the prayer of thanksgiving. For these thirty-five years I have begun each day with prayers of thanks to God for Who He is and for all He is doing in my life and in the lives of my family, my friends, and my church. You can't imagine how the shape of the day can be changed when you begin with prayers of thanks.

Try it! Tonight on your bed do what the Psalmist suggests. "Praise him in the night watch." Put your head on the pillow. Think back over the day and thank God for every good moment you can remember. I like to begin the day in the same exact way, saying prayers of thanks in my car on the way to my office or the airport. I turn off the radio and I spend the entire drive just remembering all the good gifts that God has given me.

"Thank you, God, for this new day . . . for my family . . . for my work . . . for my friends . . . for my health . . . for that beautiful sunrise . . . for that child's smile . . . for Your Son who gave His life that I might live free from the power of sin."

See how grateful you can be. Add to your gratitude list every possible good thing in your life at this time and in the past.

Look ahead and thank Him for the blessings yet to come. Fill your life with thanksgiving. Develop the attitude of gratitude. Even if you don't feel particularly grateful at that moment, thank Him! The very act of praying prayers of thanksgiving can transform a black and ugly day into a day of joy and wonderful surprises.

Every day I also pray prayers of confession. Just because I am a Christian does not mean that I have stopped sinning. I like the little bumper sticker that reads: CHRISTIANS ARE NOT PERFECT, JUST FORGIVEN. And though the sinfulness at my core has been forgiven, I still sin regularly in thought, word, and deed; and I need God's forgiveness daily for the sins of commission or omission of which I am guilty. At the end of the day, I confess to God everything that I can think of that I did or didn't do that dishonored Him. I take my sins to the cross. I deposit them at His feet. I ask Him to forgive me, and I leave them there knowing they are forgiven through His blood and that they have no more power over me.

Everyone sins, preachers included. Almost two thousand years ago the Apostle John made that perfectly clear when he wrote: "If we say that we have not sinned, we make him a liar, and his word is not in us" (I John 1:10).

Several times every day of my life I claim the promise of God that immediately precedes those words: "If we confess our sins, he is faithful and just to forgive us our sins, and to cleanse us from all unrighteousness" (I John 1:9).

Get away each day for a time of confession. Take time to think about what you've said and done during the past twenty-four hours. You will be amazed at how much there is to confess. And as you recall the people you may have hurt or offended, you will know why you may have so few friends or why your wife or husband or your children or parents don't smile when they see you coming. Confess to God and then ask their forgiveness. You will be surprised by the results this kind of honesty will add to your life and to the lives of those you love.

I also pray prayers of petition every day. This is also called intercession. I have a long list of requests that I bring before God daily. I pray for each member of my family by name every day. I tell God the trials that each is facing and ask Him to help them with each specific need. I pray for my ministry and for the ministries of others I know and love. I pray for people in Lynchburg and across the country that need God's special help. I pray for the city, for the state, for the nation, and for the world. I pray for mayors, governors, senators and members of congress, cabinet officials, and the President. I pray for the salvation of those who are lost and for God's guidance for those who love and serve Him.

Begin your own list of prayer requests. I have always used a legal pad. Write down on a page each individual request and the date you make it. Talk to God about your request like you would talk to a friend. Return to that request every day until you see God's answer. Then write down the answer and its date on the page. Just going back through that diary of your prayers of petition will bring joy and new faith into your spiritual journey.

You can pray any place and any time. Posture and location are irrelevant. But some places and some times are more helpful for effective, focused praying than are others. I like to pray while I am driving in my truck. Nobody bothers me there. I can drive up Liberty Mountain and look down across the Liberty University campus and even across Lynchburg as I pray. There is quiet on the mountain. I feel closer to God there above the noise and distractions of the city.

Everybody should have a place where praying is easy. Some people set aside a room (even an old closet) in their homes for prayer. They put in a light, a Bible, perhaps a notebook or diary or other Christian reading materials. They put a sign on the door: PRAYER CLOSET: DO NOT DISTURB EXCEPT IN EMERGENCY. Friends and family know that when that door is closed their loved one is at prayer.

It is good to have a regular place and a regular time to pray. Even if you have just five minutes a day for formal prayer, reserve it. Keep it sacred. Don't let anyone steal it from you. And likewise, develop the art of praying everywhere, at all times about everything. Prayer is at the center of the Christian life. When we pray, we grow. When we stop praying, we begin to die. The poet is absolutely right who wrote, "More things are wrought by prayer than this world dreams of."

What Thomas Road Baptist Church has now become is a direct result of God's answers to people's prayers. Nothing would have been accomplished on Thomas Road without the prayers of my mother and the prayers of hundreds and thousands of people just like her. For the Christian, prayer is everything. Paul wrote to the first century church in Thessalonica, "Pray without ceasing" (I Thessalonians 5:17). And Jesus himself promised us that "all things, whatsoever ye shall ask in prayer, believing, ye shall receive" (Matthew 21:22).

At the heart of every dream come true is the faithful prayer of someone like my mother. If we want to break the back of evil and to destroy the power of the Enemy working in our midst, we must pray. Nothing is accomplished without it. Whatever you need for yourself or for someone you love, for your church, for your city or your world, you can have it if you pray believing. It is His promise to us and His command.

Many theologians do battle over election and predestination. It has been my experience that the more persons with whom you share the Gospel, the more persons that get elected.

— Jerry Falwell

It always costs you something to do a work for the Lord. If it does not cost you anything, it is not worth doing.

— Jerry Falwell

CHAPTER EIGHT

Spreading the Word

At 6 A.M. on Monday morning, July 2, 1956, I unlocked the front doors of our little church in the old bottling company building on Thomas Road and entered the empty sanctuary. The cement-block building was cold and dark. I switched on a light and stood looking at the empty rows of theater chairs that we had just purchased from the old Isis Theater on Main Street. On our first Sunday many rows of those chairs had remained empty. I was determined that in the next few weeks those same chairs would be filled to capacity.

"Lord," I prayed, "there are hundreds of people near this little building who do not know You. Help me find them. Help me reach them. Help me get them inside this place!"

I remember standing in the semi-darkness of our storefront sanctuary watching the sun gradually bring heat and light to that empty place. Less than twenty-four hours before, our little congregation of dissenters had gathered in the front rows of our makeshift church. I had promised them that in just seven days we could double our attendance with new people from the neighborhood if we really worked at it.

Working to fill a church is not just an exercise in pride. At

207

the heart of my Christian faith is the strong belief that people who do not know Christ as Lord and Savior are spiritually lost and that we who know Him are responsible to share His story with those who don't. From the first day of our own conversion, we are called to Christian witness. Sharing the faith is at the very center of what it means to be a Christian, and there is no better way I know than to share it door-to-door, person-to-person in our neighborhood.

The Bible makes it clear. Jesus Himself set the example. Early in His ministry, Jesus saw Zaccheus, a tax collector, sitting in the branches of a tree near his home in Jericho. That little man—hated by his own people for collecting taxes for the Roman conquerors—had climbed into a sycamore tree hoping to see Jesus as He passed. Religious leaders ignored the man. In fact no self-respecting Jew would even speak to Zaccheus let alone enter the home of this man who collaborated with the enemy.

But Jesus looked up at Zaccheus and shouted above the noisy crowd, Come down. I want to visit your house.

Imagine how surprised Jesus's friends would be that our Lord would associate with this man let alone visit him in his home. But when the disciples criticized Jesus for inviting himself in to dine with a sinful traitor, Jesus answered simply that "the Son of man is come to seek and to save that which was lost" (Luke 19:1-10).

Jesus believed in knocking on doors and so do I. At the beginning of His ministry, Jesus told His disciples his plans for them: "Come ye after me," He said, "and I will make you to become fishers of men" (Mark 1:17). Just before He ascended into heaven at the very close of his life on this earth, Jesus commanded them again, "Go ye therefore and teach all nations, baptizing them in the name of the Father, and of the Son, and of the Holy Ghost: Teaching them to observe all things whatsoever I have commanded you: and, lo, I am with you always, even unto the end of the world, Amen" (Matthew 28: 19,20).

I had spent enough of that first summer concerned about Baptist preachers who condemned me for helping this handful of people to start their church. When Christians fight, they make the Devil happy. Our disagreements and the time we spend on them just keep us from the real work of witness. Jesus has commissioned us to be His witnesses. I determined early that Monday morning to put the old struggle behind me and to face the real work at hand.

We may have been a congregation of dissenters excommunicated from our fellowship of Baptists, and what we dreamed for our church may have been condemned by my fellow pastors and Baptist lay leaders alike; but God had called us to the task, and I stood there believing that it could be done. I was determined to fill that sanctuary if I had to fill it myself.

For that reason I began the new week before sunrise. I felt like a general about to raise an army. I pictured the building filled with people sitting in the theater chairs, standing in the aisles and along the walls. I could hear them singing the great songs of faith and reading the Old and New Testament lessons together. I could see them kneeling at the rough wooden altar to give their hearts to Christ and rising up to commit their lives to ministry. And I determined that they would join me walking the streets of our neighborhood, knocking on doors and sharing their faith with those who answered.

On Monday morning I walked up that empty aisle and knelt alone at that front row of seats near the pulpit. I was scared and excited and determined. I felt God's call to Lynchburg, my hometown, and I couldn't wait to begin.

Just days before, the volunteers and I had walled in my little office at the front of the sanctuary. Actually it was just a cubicle six feet wide by six feet long that we had built to house my desk, my almost empty file, my small collection of books and Bibles, my rolodex containing the names, addresses, and phone numbers of just thirty-five adults, and my newly installed telephone. Believe me, the office was primitive at best and dusty, hot, and crowded at worst. But it was my own, and that morning I sat at my small wooden desk feeling exactly like Eisenhower as he plotted D-Day and the invasion of Europe.

I had a large piece of poster board before me and a map of Lynchburg in my hands. I tacked the map to the poster board and put a large black dot at the place on Thomas Road that marked our church's location. Then I placed my Bible on the map, opened it to my text for that day, and read slowly the key passage from the fifth book in the New Testament. The Acts of the Apostles: ". . . and ye shall be witnesses unto me both in Jerusalem, and in all Judea, and in Samaria, and unto the uttermost part of the earth" (Acts 1:8).

These were Jesus's last words recorded on earth. Immediately after speaking them He was "taken up; and a cloud received him out of their sight" (Acts 1:9). Two thousand years ago, those words were a clear directive to His disciples. And they are just as clear a directive to those of us who follow Him today.

"And ye shall be witnesses unto me," He said. Picture it. Just minutes after giving that order, Jesus was gone. His disciples stood looking into the heavens, shielding their eyes against the sunlight, blinking back their tears of grief and surprise. He was gone and His last words echoed in their brains: "...and ye shall be witnesses unto me..."

Witnesses? The word has become so common now that we forget the impact it must have had on them. Imagine how you would feel if you had been in their place. Following Jesus for three years had been roller coaster enough, but those last six or seven weeks had been unbelievable. They had seen their teacher welcomed to the capital city of Jerusalem by huge crowds of people singing Hosanna, shouting praises, and waving palm branches. Just days later they had seen Him arrested, tried, murdered, and buried in a borrowed tomb. And just days after that they had seen Him risen from the grave, alive and well again. Then suddenly there was one more surprise. On a hill outside Jerusalem Jesus speaks His last words to them, "and ye shall be witnesses unto me," and then even as they are staring up at Him in shock and disbelief, Jesus disappears into the heavens.

They could hardly believe what they had seen and heard in those last three years let alone in those last few weeks. And yet He was expecting them to tell the world about it. They thought they would have Him around forever, that He would lead them and their people into a brand-new day, that He would always be there to show them the way. He had been their teacher, and they assumed they would be His students forever. Then suddenly it was graduation day. Their teacher was gone and they were left to tell the story, to be His witnesses.

Witnesses? It is the name that our modern judicial system gives to the person present at the scene of a crime or an accident. Have you ever been called to be a witness? If so, you know how it feels to stand up in a packed courtroom to tell judge and jury, plaintiff and defendant exactly what you saw. With one hand raised before the court and the other hand placed firmly on the Bible, you promise "to tell the truth, the whole truth, and nothing but the truth, so help you God."

It is a scary and exciting time. Everyone stares at you. The defendant saw it one way. The plaintiff saw it another way. Each witness saw it differently. But your task is to report the event exactly as you saw it, adding nothing and subtracting nothing, whatever it might cost you.

Jesus's disciples had been eyewitnesses to His ministry upon the earth. They had seen Him heal the sick and raise the dead. They had heard Him teach and preach in the synagogues, on the streets, and in the Temple. He had called them to follow Him, and in obeying His call their lives had been radically changed. Now He was calling them to testify to the world exactly what they had seen and heard. He was commanding them to be witnesses of His work in their lives and in the lives of others exactly as they had seen it, without adding or subtracting from the truth, whatever it might cost them.

And it was to be a very aggressive witness. After all, the salvation of the world depended on the story being told and told widely. "And ye shall be witnesses unto me both in Jerusalem," he began—that was their city, the capital of their nation, the place where it all began— "and in all Judea," He added. In one sense, Judea meant all of Palestine, the land of the Jews. But in a broader sense it meant anywhere and everywhere that Jews were living across the Middle East and around the world.

"And in Samaria," Jesus added. The people of northern Palestine were former Jews who had been excommunicated by the faithful of Judea for their differing beliefs. Ordering His disciples to bear witness in Samaria was more than just a sign of geographical expansion. It meant that their message must be taken outside of strictly Jewish territory into an ever widening world.

"And unto the uttermost parts of the earth," Jesus concluded. There would be no limits placed on their witness. It was His command. The circle of witness began at Jerusalem and increased in ever growing circles until it embraced the entire world.

That first Monday morning in my cramped office, I labeled the dot on the map where our church stood and the ten-block radius immediately surrounding it as our Jerusalem. I had placed the point of a compass on that dot and drawn the ten-block radius around it. I traced the penciled circle with a black felt-tip pen. The next wider circle I called Judea. That circle included a twenty-block radius from the church. The next circle included a thirty-block radius. I called that third circle our Samaria. And the rest of Lynchburg, all of Campbell County, Virginia, the states and nations beyond were "the uttermost parts of the earth."

I decided that my first task was to visit a hundred homes a day in ever widening circles. I carried my Bible and a yellow legal pad for taking notes. By nine o'clock each morning, Monday through Saturday, I left my office on Thomas Road and was heading into the neighborhood to knock on doors.

"I'm Jerry Falwell," I began when someone answered. "I'm the pastor of a new little church meeting up here at the bottling company building. We're starting a new church, and I'd just like to invite you up when you can come and attend our services!"

People stared at me through their screens. Housewives had dishes they were drying in their hands or a vacuum cleaner still running in the background. Unemployed men sat on the porch eyeing me with suspicion. Older widow ladies peeked out around their chain locks and listened to my invitation. Children cried. Dogs barked. Radios and televisions blared at me.

I was young, determined, and filled with enthusiasm for the task. I didn't preach to our neighbors on their front porches or read from the Bible at them over the kitchen sink. I was taking my own census, trying to discover who lived in each house around our neighborhood. I wrote down the names and ages of each person in every home on the block. I kept a list of their schools, their jobs, and their churches.

I wasn't out to steal souls from other congregations in the area. In fact I congratulated each person who claimed active church membership and wished them and their church God's best! But it was important to find out if each person really was an active member of another Bible-believing church or just pretending.

"I'm a member of First Methodist," one lady declared proudly.

"Wonderful," I answered, writing down the information. And then without looking up I added the question "Who is your pastor over there?"

When she didn't know the pastor's name, I assumed that there were many other things about the faith she didn't know.

"Now, I don't want to take you away from your own church on Sunday morning," I told her, "but this Sunday night I am preaching on forgiveness, and I'd be honored if you would come.

"By the way," I would add before leaving, "if you ever need any spiritual help or otherwise, let me give you my phone number. I'd be glad to have you call me."

I would leave a little card with each person. It didn't have a Scripture on it or an outline of God's plan of salvation, just the number of the church and of my home on Rustburg Road. I would tell each person that if he or she called the home number, my mom would answer and would notify me immediately. My mother acted as my answering service in those days before tape machines and electronic pagers. She saw it as her ministry and wrote down each message with care and concern.

By knocking on 100 doors every day, six days a week, I could visit 600 homes in a week's time. There were those who I really believed set their dogs on me. There were others who slammed their doors or listened impassively to my appeal. But at least two or three times a day I would hear a stranger say, "Please, Come in. God must have sent you here. I've been praying that someone would come."

Only then would I enter a home, only when I had been asked sincerely to come in. Often I would find a sick child who needed prayer, a lonely and frightened widow who needed someone to talk to, an isolated alcoholic who wanted help in drying out, a couple struggling with their marriage, a young mother recently abandoned by her unemployed husband, or various victims of physical or psychological family abuse who needed serious help in escaping their predicament. I listened to each painful story. I read from the Word. I prayed for God's healing or direction. I advised, I counseled, I referred, and I led many to salvation in Christ. Everyone received an invitation to attend services at Thomas Road Baptist Church.

Immediately upon leaving the home, I wrote down every scrap of information on my yellow pad. Soon the list of people and their problems covered dozens of pads. The rolodex was full and my follow-up list was growing longer every day.

That first week a woman in our church volunteered to come into the office on Thursdays to help me. By then I had found and borrowed an old mimeograph machine from a nearby office supply store. Together Mrs. Hughes and I launched the first Thomas Road Baptist Church weekly newspaper. I wrote out each column by hand. Mrs. Hughes shaped a headline from press-on letters and typed my column and the news of the church below.

From the beginning, we published a weekly record of the growth of Thomas Road Baptist Church in Sunday School and church attendance, homes visited, and even souls saved. I wrote articles about my dreams and the dreams of my little congregation. And though we started with just four basic services— Sunday morning Sunday School and worship, Sunday night evangelism, and a midweek prayer and Bible study session—in just a few weeks there were other events, special services, and a coming revival meeting to advertise.

Each family I visited during the week would receive our little news bulletin through the mails by Saturday morning. On Saturday afternoon each home I visited would be called by a lady volunteer from Thomas Road Baptist.

"Miss Jones?" the caller would begin. "This is Mary Smith. I am a member of the Thomas Road Baptist Church. Pastor Falwell asked me to call you. He mentioned that he had dropped by to see you on Tuesday and invited you to attend our services this Sunday. He asked me to remind you that the service begins at eleven A.M. and that he is preaching on 'How to Pray and Get Your Prayers Answered.' He also said to remind you that if ever he can help you in any way, just call the church or Pastor Falwell's home. Do you still have those numbers?"

I called those three contacts with our church my "triple whammy." a personal visit, a newspaper in the mailbox, and a follow-up call from a volunteer. And immediately these three contacts began to produce results. That first Sunday, attendance doubled. In seven days the church began to grow. Our people saw the little storefront building begin to fill with new people from the neighborhood. I explained that personal door-to-door visitation was the key to further growth, and I began to enlist men in the church to join me in that task.

I didn't ask for volunteers. I personally selected the first two men I would train to witness door-to-door. They had to have warm hearts, outgoing personalities, and a sincere burden for souls. We met on Thursday night at six in the sanctuary at Thomas Road. Already I had made eighty or ninety calls that day. The two men joined me for prayer and a time of preparation, and then they spent the next three hours with me knocking on doors in our neighborhood.

These men were being trained on the job. At first they felt kind of awkward, even embarrassed knocking on a stranger's door. Then they had to conquer their natural fear of those typical obstacles to door-to-door visitation: large dogs who chased us up the sidewalk or shotgun barrels pointed at our chests through broken screen doors. And they had to learn a whole repertoire of answers to the crazy, angry, seductive, or even dangerous questions that people sometimes ask.

These men learned on the job. They walked the streets with me. They watched me knock on doors, converse with strangers, field questions, handle problems, and counsel others before they had to do it by themselves. Actually, most home visits were uneventful. People smiled, listened, took our little schedule of events, and promised that they would consider dropping by the church.

But every sixty or seventy visits someone would ask us in. During many of those living room or kitchen encounters, a husband or wife, sometimes a whole family, would give their lives to Christ. I can still remember watching those trainees out of the corner of my eye as we led people to the Lord. They got so excited that they couldn't wait to get out the door; down the steps, and back to the church to share with the other volunteers what God had done.

After several weeks of training, each new man would train another. Before long we had ten men knocking on doors every evening of the week and all day Saturday. It was go, go, go around that place. Nobody rested. There wasn't time. What we were doing was far too important to stop even for a day. These were wonderful men whose dedication to Christ and whose skills at witnessing were influential in building the spiritual foundations upon which Thomas Road Baptist Church now stands.

Every night before our volunteers left to begin knocking on doors and every Sunday evening before our evangelistic service began, our people met to pray. Our storefront building had an air compressor room ten feet wide by fifteen feet long that made a perfect prayer room. Those first few weeks on Thomas Road we carted away the rusty old compressor, patched up the holes in the wall, added a used oil stove, swept the dirt floor, and met in the room to pray. I am convinced that behind every successful witness program is a group of Christian people who meet to pray.

I can still see those first men on our visitation teams sitting in their circle of prayer before beginning their evening visits: Percy Hall, R. C. Worley, Emmitt Godsey, Lawson Johnson, Homer Wrenn, Guy Brumfield, Jack Lawhorne, and dozens more were used by God to reach out from Jerusalem, to Judea, Samaria, and into the uttermost parts of the earth. Many of them are with the Lord now seeing firsthand the results of those early door-to-door visits in our neighborhood.

One afternoon I stopped at the edge of our church

property and introduced myself to a surveyor who was working there. I wrote down his name and address on my yellow pad. I told him about our church and gave him my phone number. That very next Sunday morning the surveyor, David Horsley, arrived at our eleven o'clock service with his wife Judy. Our little congregation welcomed them to Thomas Road Baptist Church. An usher handed them a hymn-book. The Horsleys joined in the singing and listened to me preach. At the invitation they both came forward and knelt to give their lives to Christ.

That next week David and Judy Horsley invited me to visit members of their large family who lived in homes across Lynchburg and around Campbell County. One by one the entire Horsley family became Christians. First David's father, Ray, a foreman at the Mead Corporation paper mill in Lynchburg, was converted, and then his mother, Amanda, accepted Christ as Lord and Savior. David saw God liberate his father from alcoholism. Then, just weeks later, David's sister Ann became a Christian, and her husband Ray Hudson joined her at Thomas Road Baptist Church. Also, a second sister, Faye, and her husband Bob Hubbard found the Lord. Before long the entire Horsley family had become Christians and took their place in worship and in witness with our growing congregation.

In the past three decades the Horsley family has served in many important positions throughout our ministry, and it all began when I stopped to visit a surveyor who was working on an empty lot near our old building almost thirty years ago. A s a teenager I watched my father destroyed by unforgiven guilt and alcoholism. Now when I look back on those days, I believe that if there had been someone who had visited my dad like we visit the people of Lynchburg, he would have given his life to Christ and would have found the forgiveness that would have saved his life and his soul. People were afraid to visit my father. He was tough. He was sarcastic. He could ridicule and scorn. He had built a tough facade and he hid behind that facade almost until the day he died.

I believe in ignoring the walls that people build. Behind the facades that separate us, we are all alike. We all need to know that God loves us. We all need to know that in Christ God has forgiven our sins and our failures. We all need to know that through Christ we can begin again.

If only someone had ignored Dad's scorn. If only someone had waded past his defenses and shared the faith. If only there had been men in Lynchburg in those days like the men who walked the streets with me, my father might not have suffered a lifetime of unforgiven guilt.

The Christian is a witness to the greatest story ever told, to the best news ever published on the earth. Why be embarrassed to share the good news directly? Why beat around the bush or wait until a more appropriate time or place. I believe that in witnessing we must get straight to the point and tell it like it is. People may laugh. They may ridicule. They may lash out. They may turn away in embarrassed silence. But once they know that you are sincere, they will listen, and as they listen, God Himself will break past their barriers and the truth will dawn in their hearts like sunrise at the beginning of a brand-new day. This is how the Holy Spirit works.

There will be people who do not understand, who do not open their arms immediately to accept the truth. Never mind. Let God take care of them. Make your witness clear and then move on. We walked those streets in ever widening circles from my office on Thomas Road, and on every new street God brought results we never dreamed.

There are endless obstacles placed by the Enemy in the way of our effective witness. First we have to struggle with our own fears. "I don't have an outgoing personality," some people say. "I'm not smart or good with words," others chime in. "I don't know enough about the Bible" or "I am not ready to answer the questions my friends might ask." The list of fears goes on. But these aren't reasons, they are excuses. Just share in your own words and your own way what God is doing in your life. And then let God do the rest.

You might find other kinds of obstacles set up even after you've tried to witness. People may laugh at you. They may find clever ways to make your life miserable. Or worse, they may ignore you altogether. It doesn't matter. Jesus said, "Blessed are ye, when men shall revile you, and persecute you, and shall say all manner of evil against you falsely, for my sake.... for great is your reward in heaven" (Matthew 5:11-12).

There were obstacles placed in my way that first year. I expected resistance from the Enemy and his followers, but resistance came from another unexpected quarter as well. A pastor in a church just a few miles away began to see our circle of witness moving into what he called his territory. He called me into his office and sat me down. He opened a map of Lynchburg. He showed me the area of the city that he said was mine and asked me to keep myself and my visiting volunteers a safe distance from his church.

"Are you visiting these people?" I asked him.

"No," he answered, "but that isn't your concern."

"It is my concern," I replied. "These people are lost. I don't care where they find Christ, but if no one else is telling them the good news, then I and my people will tell them."

God doesn't limit our territory. He expands it. Christ's last prayer upon this earth was for Christian unity. He wanted us who follow Him to live and work as one. But sometimes unity must take second place to witness. If one church fails in its responsibility to witness to the community, God will raise up another church to get the job done.

Every house I visited those first weeks seemed to have a radio playing in the background during the daylight hours and a television blaring at night. At first it didn't cross my mind to use radio or television in my own local ministry, even though God had used the broadcasts of Charles Fuller and the "Old Fashioned Revival Hour" as a witness in my life.

Then one afternoon in the fall of 1956, Macel and I were listening to music on WBRG 1050 on the AM dial. It was a new country and western station that went on the air just shortly after we began Thomas Road Baptist Church. Mr. Epperson, who died recently in his nineties, owned that little station and a handful of other stations in the Southeast. It was a daylight station, which meant that the sign-on and sign-off corresponded each day to the actual time of sunrise and sunset.

I decided to ask Mr. Epperson about beginning my own

broadcast on his local station. I had no radio experience. I don't think I had ever even visited a radio station. But I put on my best suit and tie, gathered a handful of Thomas Road Baptist Church weekly newspapers, and drove to the station to see the owner about buying time.

I was thinking about a weekly program on Sunday mornings just after the "Old Fashioned Revival Hour" broadcast. But Mr. Epperson, a devout Christian layman, had a better idea.

"Go on radio every day, Reverend," he advised me. "I've been looking for someone to start our broadcast day with words to the wise. You would be just perfect." His station manager, Tom Buckley, agreed heartily.

I swallowed hard, screwed up my courage, and asked him how much a daily program would cost me.

"How about seven dollars a program?" he asked. "Could your new church handle that?"

We shook hands and began a relationship that lasted many years. I would begin each broadcast day with a thirty-minute program live from the studio. WBRG had only 1,000 watts, but on a clear morning those watts carried our Thomas Road Baptist Church broadcast from the studio in Madison Heights, Virginia, to homes throughout Lynchburg, across Amherst and Campbell counties, and to communities up and down the foothills of the Blue Ridge Mountains.

The studio was in a little four-room prefab house on a large empty unpaved lot in the shadow of the transmitter and a tall, rather spindly broadcast tower. I sat at a metal desk in a studio no bigger than a large closet. My engineer sat across from me behind a glass window. In the summer when the sun rose early, our broadcast began at 6:30 A.M. As the fall and winter approached and the days grew shorter, my broadcast began at seven, and in the dead of winter we went on the air as late as eight.

The moment the broadcast began, I signaled the engineer to play my theme song. I can't even remember what it was these thirty years later. But I still remember the excitement I felt when the trumpets played and the choir began to sing. After the theme song, I reported the news of our church, the days and times of our services, and stories about people whose lives were being changed by God through our congregation's ministry.

Then I signaled the engineer to play the special song of that broadcast day. At first, I used records featuring the music of George Beverly Shea, Jack Holcomb or the Old Fashioned Revival Hour Quartet. In later broadcasts I used pre-recorded soloists or groups of singers from Thomas Road Baptist Church.

The last twenty minutes I preached and promoted the church. Because I would rush from the studio at the close of the broadcast to begin my hundred door-to-door calls for that day, I would often tell listeners which area of town I would be visiting, and when I arrived people would be waiting to greet me or ask me about our church.

Hundreds of people were reached directly or indirectly during those first years on radio. Dozens of stories could be told about the lives that were changed because they "accidentally" turned the dial that day to WBRG. One morning I walked into my tiny office to begin my prayer and Bible study for the day, and the phone was already ringing. Mrs. W. B. Cheatham was on the line, a beautiful elderly lady who lived alone in an expensive townhouse on Rivermont Avenue.

"Your program is such a blessing," she began. "Do you ever visit my neighborhood on your calls?" she asked. "I phoned to ask you to come by and visit."

Rivermont is an exclusive section of our city where wealthy business leaders of our community live. Lynchburg is a prosperous city. Captains of industry, chief executives of corporations, bankers and investors, even occasional celebrities from the world of art, literature, and music live in their beautiful homes in our city on the James River. Their Tudor and Georgian mansions, their luxury townhouses and condominiums, are safely ensconced behind high walls and guarded compounds. Electric buzzers, alarm systems, automatic gates and garage doors locked out bums, burglars, and Baptist preachers.

"You must come by," Mrs. Cheatham insisted. "I want so much to meet you and to hear about your church on Thomas Road."

Mrs. Cheatham was a longtime member and generous

supporter of the Rivermont Presbyterian Church, a very fine, solid congregation in our city; still she insisted that I visit her. This very gracious lady had a fascinating story to share. She was born and raised in Concord, a small town just fifteen miles from Lynchburg. Her husband had been a successful farmer, but he died early in their marriage and left her a young widow with five small children to raise.

Mrs. Cheatham had moved to Lynchburg. She raised her young family alone and worked hard to guarantee that each child received a good education. Her son Owen had founded the Georgia-Pacific Corporation and was at the time chairman of the board. Her son Julian was vice-president of Georgia-Pacific. Mrs. Cheatham had seen her other sons and daughters take responsible positions in business and the church.

"Will you pray with me?" Mrs. Cheatham asked at the end of our visit.

She took my hand and I spoke a short honest prayer of thanks to God for her life and the lives of her family. It was one of those visits where I was blessed by another Christian's love. Through Mrs. Cheatham I was introduced to her children and their families during the years that followed.

When we purchased and began to develop the Treasure Island Youth Camp on an island in the middle of the James River in 1963, Mrs. Cheatham called her son Owen and told him about the dormitories and craft shops, the gymnasium and the chapel we were building for the children of Lynchburg and the surrounding communities.

Just days later I received a call from the local rail yard. An entire boxcar filled with building supplies had arrived with my name on it. I told the dispatcher that I hadn't ordered the tons of plywood and other valuable building supplies.

"Well, they got your name on 'em, Reverend," the dispatcher answered. "And they come paid for. You might as well pick 'em up," he added. "Looks like they's a gift from Owen Cheatham his very self."

Mrs. Cheatham and her family were friends in need. I cried when Mrs. Cheatham died. She had loved me and my church even though she was a loyal and generous member of her own congregation. Owen Cheatham asked if I would assist in his mother's funeral. Now Mrs. Cheatham and her sons and daughters are buried in the little cemetery near their old family church in Concord, Virginia. Whenever I am in the area, I walk through that graveyard and remember how much good God did through the Cheathams in my life and in the life of Thomas Road Baptist Church. And it all began because of that little seven-dollar program on the radio.

In September of that first year at Thomas Road, I began our radio ministry. I was astounded by the results. After visiting thousands of homes door-to-door, and after inviting thousands of people to church person-to-person, I began to realize how effective the broadcast media are in getting into all those homes and presenting the message to all those people simultaneously from one convenient studio location. So it was only natural for me to begin to dream about expanding our church's electronic ministry through television.

In December 1956 I decided it was time to act. One Monday morning I drove to the small studio and office building of our ABC Television affiliate, WLVA (for Lynchburg, Virginia). In those days Channel 13 was as primitive for a television station as our storefront building was primitive for a church.

The downtown studio on Church Street was small and makeshift. Often there was only one working black-and-white camera and a one or two-man crew who set the lights and microphones and ran the camera and the control panel simultaneously. Needless to say, it wasn't a very creative medium then. It was my first experience with live television, and I was always surprised and relieved when a picture actually appeared on home screens around Lynchburg.

Still I didn't complain. The station offered to sell me one half-hour time slot a week for $90. I signed their contract immediately and agreed to report to the studio that next Sunday afternoon for a 5:30 P.M. live telecast. We had no soloists at the church at that time, so I asked a young man who sang at the Methodist church if he would be the soloist for our program. Bill Brooks agreed to sing, and Macel agreed to accompany him on the out-of-tune upright piano in the tiny studio. Together the three of us launched our television ministry called in those days simply "Thomas Road Baptist Church Presents."

Late on Sunday afternoon Macel, Bill, and I arrived at the studio with absolutely no instructions as to what we should do next. At 5:30 P.M. a red light began to flash at the studio door, and the cameraman/director motioned me to begin the program.

"Hello," I said, swallowing hard and looking to Macel and Bill for support. "My name is Jerry Falwell. I am the pastor of the Thomas Road Baptist Church."

For about two minutes I told about our congregation and its services. I told how many new visitors were crowding into our little sanctuary and how many people were getting saved. I told about the growth of our Sunday School program and of the small tent we had erected to house the expanding children's department. And I shared the good news that already we were beginning construction on a new auditorium that would double our seating capacity.

Then Macel began to play an introduction to Bill Brooks's Gospel song. I introduced Bill, and while he sang I opened my Bible and prepared myself for the short sermon that would follow. When the music and the preaching were finished, I took one last opportunity to invite those viewing to visit Thomas Road Baptist Church.

"Tonight," I said, "in just ninety minutes, I will be preaching from the prophet Jeremiah at our church on Thomas Road. You have plenty of time to eat a peanut butter sandwich, drink a glass of milk, grab your Bible, and come on over! I want to welcome you personally; so please stop me at the door and say hello!"

By the time Macel and I had our own Sunday snack in the Pate kitchen and drove back to church, the place was packed to the walls with people. No other preachers were on television then. Television made me a kind of instant celebrity. People were fascinated that they could see and hear me preach that same night in person. So our Sunday evening services were jammed. The church was growing, and God was changing lives.

One Sunday night early in our television ministry, I looked

House Speaker Newt Gingrich joins me in prayer on the platform of the 1996 Republican National Convention in San Diego.

All eleven of us on a brief vacation in 1996. Left to right, seated, Wesley, Becki, and Jerry Jr. Standing, Trey, Poppy, Macel, Jeannie, Paul, Shari, Jonathan Jr. and Jonathan.

Charles Wesley (Wesley) and Jerry Falwell III, (Trey) indulge me. (Summer, 1996)

And, so do Jonathan Jr., and Wesley indulge Trey. (Summer, 1996)

Jonathan is now my associate at Thomas Road Baptist Church. He has already proven himself an astute businessman and is planning to take my job one day-- but, I must add, not too soon. Shari is a great wife, mother and OTGH soloist. Jonathan Jr. wants to be president of the US in the next century. (Summer, 1996)

Jerry Jr. and Becki. He is the best attorney I know and his work at LU over the past nine years has been critical to the miraculous progress we have made. Becki is also a wonderful wife and mother, and has contributed greatly to Jerry Jr.'s success.

Jeannie and Paul Savas. Both are graduates of Liberty University and the Medical College of Virginia. Jeannie and Paul are surgeons in Richmond, Virginia. Macel and I are praying hard and selfishly that they will one day practice medicine in Lynchburg and bless us with beautiful grandchildren. Both are dynamic Christians.

Macel is my leading critic, finest teacher, dearest friend and the love of my life. She, more than I, is responsible for producing our great and godly children.

out on our little sanctuary packed with three or four hundred people and I noticed a tall distinguished man in his late fifties or early sixties sitting on the back row looking strangely out of place.

When the service ended, I could see him still sitting in the back of the church waiting for the room to empty. He seemed anxious and ill-at-ease. Finally just a handful of parishioners remained.

"Mr. Falwell," he said softly, motioning to me across the empty rows. "Could I see you for a moment?"

I walked up to him and shook his hand. He was trembling.

"My name is G. D. Smith. I've been watching you on television these past weeks. I don't go to church. I don't have a pastor to call, and I need one now for the first time in my life."

I could see that Mr. Smith was about to cry. Tears welled up in his eyes. He blinked them back nervously as though they were a sign of weakness. He wiped his face with a linen handkerchief as I led him to the privacy of my office. He stood at the door looking frightened and disoriented.

"How can I help you?" I asked, reaching out to end the silence.

"My son has been in a terrible auto accident. They've just taken him to the Lynchburg General Hospital. I've just left him there. His doctors say that he is near death."

Suddenly Mr. Smith stopped speaking. Great sobs racked his tall, muscular frame. Then he asked me through his tears, "Could you come to the hospital and pray with my son?"

We drove immediately to the hospital. God did spare the life of Mr. Smith's much-loved son. Later in the week I told my new friend about God's Son, Jesus, whom He did not spare. In the conversation that followed, Mr. Smith confessed his own sinfulness. He was a wealthy, influential man who had been living a wicked life. His primary goal in life was to acquire wealth. By the time I met Mr. Smith he already owned a bank in Big Island, Virginia. He owned a large sawmill and lumber company. He had become a wealthy playboy. And though he supplied his wife and family with financial support, he had given up the paternal and spiritual leadership of his family and desperately needed to be forgiven and set back on track with his wife and children once again.

Mr. Smith owned an expensive home in the Rivermont section of Lynchburg near the home of Mrs. Cheatham. He had every privilege that money and power could buy, but he wasn't happy. He felt like his life had been a failure. He needed God.

I visited the Smiths, witnessed to them, and led them all to Christ. Mr. Smith became a deacon at Thomas Road Baptist Church. His eldest son, Bobby Smith, became a close personal friend and supporter of our church and especially of the television ministry. To thank God for what that primitive little television broadcast did for his father, for his brother Lewis, and for his entire family, Bobby Smith and his wife Carol underwrote at least fifty television stations during our time of media expansion in the early and mid-1970's. Today Mr. G. D. Smith is retired, a close friend and supporter of the ministry, and his son Bobby is a member of our Liberty University board of trustees.

That first year at Thomas Road Baptist Church was perhaps the busiest year of my life. The alarm rang every morning at 5 A.M. Mom had a breakfast ready and waiting for me as she had every morning of my father's life. By 6:30 A.M. I had driven across the James River to the studios of WBRG in Madison Heights. By 7:15 I had finished my live radio broadcast and driven back to my little cubicle on Thomas Road, where I read my Bible, prayed for my growing congregation, and prepared to make a hundred house calls during that new day. Some of those calls went quickly. If no one was at home, I would only stop long enough to leave a Gospel tract and a printed invitation to attend our church. Other calls ended in long, prayerful visits. There were letters to answer and telephone calls to return. There were sermons to outline, follow-up calls to assign, perhaps a wedding or a funeral to prepare, a crisis visit to a member of our church in a home or hospital room. And every day without fail there were those hundred house calls to make.

By 4 P.M. I would drive to the First National Bank, where Macel was working, pick her up, drive her to her home at 414 Munford Street, and invite myself to dinner with the Pates. Sometimes, when I hadn't knocked on at least eighty doors that day,

I would drop off Macel at her home, grab a hot dog and a Coke at Meek's Delicatessen, and head back up the road to start knocking on doors again.

I figured 10 P.M. was the latest I could risk knocking on a stranger's door; so when my hundred doors were knocked or when the clock struck ten, I raced back across town to the Pates' house and spent the next half-hour or hour visiting with Macel in her living room. Every night, just fifteen minutes after Sam and Lucile Pate had retired to their bedroom, Sam would knock loudly on the wall signaling the end of my visit with his daughter.

By then we had talked seriously of marriage; still Macel refused to set a date. And when her father played taps on the bedroom wall, she would look apologetic, take my hand, lead me to the front door, kiss me gently on the cheek, and send me out into the darkness feeling deeply in love and anxious to get married.

By midnight I had finished my reading and was safely between the covers dreaming of Macel and planning my radio sermon for the live broadcast just six hours away.

By the spring of 1957, just about three-quarters through my first year as pastor of Thomas Road Baptist Church, the city of Lynchburg was beginning to sit up and take notice. By then our volunteers and I had visited a large number of the homes in the city at least once, and many we had visited four and five times. Most of those same homes were on our mailing list, receiving the weekly church newsletter and mailings announcing the special services and events that lay ahead. Our volunteer ladies had made at least one follow-up call to each home. The daily radio program and weekly television broadcast just put icing on the cake.

There are thousands of stories I could tell that demonstrate the power of God to change lives through Christian witness. When I think back over the years, I remember one woman in particular who wanted with all her heart to share her faith effectively with other people. But every time she witnessed, she was ignored or laughed at or scorned. Mrs. H. Wearing began to wonder if God could ever use her as an effective Christian witness.

Nevertheless, in spite of her "failures," Mrs. Wearing continued to share her faith with the people she met. One afternoon in a doctor's office in downtown Lynchburg she sat next to a man suffering with intense stomach pains. She struck up a conversation with him and discovered that he was being treated for ulcers. She could see that he was an unhappy, broken man. Realizing they were alone in the waiting room, Mrs. Wearing took out her pocket New Testament and began quietly and lovingly to tell the man about Jesus. For a moment Roy Johnson listened. His eyes grew wet with tears. His hands began to tremble. Even as she spoke, Mrs. Wearing prayed earnestly that her words would break through the man's defenses and take root in his heart.

Suddenly Johnson shouted at her, "Don't bother me with your Jesus talk, lady. I don't need God. I need a doctor." Then he cursed her loudly, banged on the nurse's window, and asked for immediate attention.

For a moment Mrs. Wearing sat alone in the waiting room feeling shocked, embarrassed, and sad. She felt terrible that she had "failed" again. Then, without even waiting for her appointment, she fled the waiting room in tears.

The man with whom Mrs. Wearing had shared her faith was a member of a mainline Protestant church. He had attended Sunday School as a child, but never once did he remember anyone opening the Bible to show him God's simple plan of salvation as Mrs. Wearing had. The man had spent his lifetime searching for answers to his questions about life and death and immortality. After trying three different Protestant churches, he began to study Nietzsche, Tom Paine, Voltaire, the Gautama, and others in his quest for inner peace. Then he gave up searching and began to drink. Johnson decided to invest his life in pleasure and to give up the search for meaning. He began to smoke and drink habitually. His health began to deteriorate. His physical and spiritual anguish increased. Finally he was rushed to the hospital with bleeding ulcers.

After being released from the hospital, the man moved into a new home near Thomas Road Baptist Church. A neighbor invited him to attend, and one Sunday morning Johnson accepted the invitation. He still remembers walking in the front door of our little sanctuary and immediately feeling that something was different in Thomas Road Baptist Church. The people sang enthusiastically. They carried Bibles and underlined or wrote in the margins as I preached. And at the invitation following the morning sermon, dozens of people went forward to give their lives to Christ. For a moment Johnson had the urge to join them. He resisted. Questions and doubts tumbled in his mind. Then the moment passed.

Roy began to attend Sunday morning and Sunday evening services regularly. One Sunday night during the invitation he even raised his hand for prayer. That night he left the church shaken. He couldn't believe that he had actually done it. He stopped by a local convenience store to buy a six-pack of beer to help him sleep.

The next Sunday night he raised his hand again seeking prayer but did not respond to the invitation to give his life to Christ. As Roy hurried from the church, a Sunday School teacher approached him and asked him quietly if he could have the privilege of praying for him during the week. Roy stopped dead in his tracks. It was the same question the woman in the doctor's office had asked him. This time he did not turn away. He scribbled his name and telephone number on a card, handed it to the teacher, and ducked out into the night. Once again he bought a six-pack to help him sleep.

The next morning at work Roy approached a friend whom he had seen at Thomas Road. "What's going on over there?" he asked. "Why am I so taken by it?" The friend was a member of Thomas Road. He, too, had felt the power of God in our worship services. He, too, had felt drawn to Christ in that place. In fact, like Roy Johnson, he had resisted the move of God's Spirit in his life until one night he could resist no longer.

Johnson's friend took Roy aside and said quietly, "Roy, it is God's Spirit you are feeling. You have been searching half your life for an answer that God Himself is holding out to you. That tent. Adults met inside the sanctuary for Sunday School. All non-adults met inside our "holey" tent.

From that first summer worship service in June 1956, we

knew a building program was necessary. Sam Pate volunteered to head the construction crew. The church offered him two dollars per hour for his professional services as a contractor and builder. The rest of the labor that went into our first new sanctuary was volunteered. We drew up plans late in our first summer for a fifty-by-thirty-foot addition to be built on Thomas Road at the back of the bottling company building.

By then we had purchased that little building and the land on which it stood. The payments on the land and building, the $49 a week for radio and the $90 a week for television, the $17 a week for mimeographing and mailing the newsletter, and my $65 a week salary left nothing to make repairs on the store-front building or to construct the additional space we needed so badly. Sam Pate and his construction crew estimated that we would need almost $5,000 to build the first thirty-by-fifty addition.

"We'll have to borrow it," I told the men after an evening of discussion with our trustees.

"But with what collateral?" Sam Pate asked, shaking his head. "Without collateral nobody will lend us that kind of money."

We had no collateral, but we couldn't grow without the extra space. Already I had written Billie and Iona Lynes in Macon, Georgia, telling them that I planned to stay in Lynchburg. I had not faced their disappointment and the censure of my Baptist friends to work in a church that could not grow.

So the next day I called S. Frank Pratt, the owner of the Lynchburg Oil Company, to ask him how I could secure a loan. When my father owned Power Oil, he and Frank Pratt became close friends. They shared trucks. They shared oil-storage facilities. They sent men and supplies to each other when they were needed. They were competitors, but even more they were friends. My dad and Frank Pratt were also drinking buddies in those days. I can still remember Mrs. Pratt coming to our house to take her husband home.

After Dad died, Mr. Pratt's oil company continued to prosper. He leveraged his funds to take controlling interest in the State Industrial Loan Corporation. That company eventually merged with the Bank of Virginia.

I went to Mr. Pratt hoping to get advice about a loan. We talked about those days a decade earlier when he and Dad were friends.

"Whatever your dad needed," Mr. Pratt told me, "he got from me without having to ask. And whatever I needed, your dad supplied. And in all those years," he added, "not a hundred dollars in money passed between us.

"'I need one of your trucks, Frank,' your dad would say over the telephone. 'Can you help me?'

"'I need to borrow some of your tools, Carey,' I'd say. 'Can you spare them for a day?'

"We were friends, your dad and I. And I miss him still."

"I'm starting a church, Mr. Pratt," I finally interrupted.

"I've heard, Jerry," Frank Pratt answered. "In the old Donald Duck building, isn't it?"

"Yes," I said, not really surprised that he had heard about us with all the noise we had been making. "But we've already run out of space. And the supplies we need to build cost $5,000."

Dear old Frank Pratt began to smile as he listened.

"We don't have the money, Mr. Pratt," I said, "and our offerings are only a few hundred dollars a week. But with the growth we're expecting, I believe we could pay it all back in just a year or two."

Before I could ask my question, Mr. Pratt picked up the phone and called his man Billy McLeod, who ran State Industrial Loan for him.

"Billy," he shouted over the phone line, "I'm sending Jerry Falwell down there. Let him have $5,000 for his church."

Apparently Billy McLeod asked Frank Pratt the name of our new church that he was about to help finance with a large and unsecured loan.

"I don't know," Mr. Pratt answered. Then he looked up at me and said, "What's the name of your church, Jerry?"

Looking back, I remember worrying how we could get the loan without collateral. I should have had more faith. God provided the money without collateral from a man who didn't even know the name of our church.

Recently Frank Pratt died of cancer in a Lynchburg hospital. He was eighty-nine years old. Just a few months ago in his hospital room, I led Mr. Pratt to Christ. I told him that I was writing a book and that I would tell the story of that first generous loan he made to us without collateral.

"Oh, don't say anything about me, Jerry," he said, grinning. "Your dad and I were friends. I did it for him just like he would have done it for me."

One day after getting that loan, Sam Pate and his crew of volunteers had purchased and unloaded on our lot almost $5,000 worth of supplies. Immediately we began to build. We walled and roofed our new thirty-by-fifty-foot addition before adding the floor. We installed little space heaters with pipes going out the holes where the windows would eventually be. We covered the rest of the window spaces with metal panes to keep out the coming cold. We needed to use the building space before rooms could be finished. We raced against winter weather and met on dirt floors in cold rooms to sing and pray and teach our children.

Our volunteers worked on Saturdays and almost every night of the week until 10 P.M. Men built. Women brought food and drink. Children swept, retrieved, and straightened nails or played with pieces of wood and pipe nearby. Just as the neighbors began to complain about the loud sound of hammers and saws that was echoing out across the neighborhood, we completed the first new addition. And the "holey" tent was removed forever.

From that day we never stopped building. First we extended the storefront building from fifty to one hundred feet. Then we added thirty-eight feet toward Thomas Road. Our church looked like a massive bowling alley, 138 feet long and just thirty feet wide. All this happened in the first year, and immediately every new inch of space was filled by new children and adults coming to Thomas Road Baptist Church because of our people's faithful and expanding witness throughout our community.

The second Sunday in June 1957, just one week before our first-year anniversary, I stood before my little congregation and announced my goal of 500 children and adults to be present and accounted for in Sunday School that next Sunday. Everybody gasped. We had begun the church just twelve months earlier with thirty-five adults and their families. But I believed that our witness had been effective and that with a week of telephoning, sending postcards, and knocking on doors we could cram our long, narrow sanctuary and every unfinished dirt-floored room with 500 people to celebrate what God had accomplished in that first year.

On Saturday night Macel and I walked from my office through the empty sanctuary.

"Don't you think you're exaggerating a little?" she said.

"No," I answered without hesitating. "I think we'll have 500 people here tomorrow and break every record in the book."

In those days a church with 500 people in Sunday School was almost unheard of in the South. Only a handful of churches across the country could count Sunday School attendance in the thousand range.

"What if you don't have 500?" Macel asked quietly. "Will you be disappointed?"

"We'll have 500," I said, looking about the empty church one last time and then switching the lights out and plunging that funny little sanctuary into darkness.

She grabbed my hand and together we walked past the piles of lumber and cement blocks toward my car.

At 7 A.M. I was back in the sanctuary waiting for the first people to arrive. By 9 A.M. the new addition and the sanctuary were filled. By 9:15 we were forcing folding chairs into every extra unfinished space. By 9:30 people were standing outside crowding around every open door and window. Ushers were counting madly. Macel went to the piano and played a short fanfare. An usher handed me the final attendance record.

"We hoped that 500 people would gather this morning," I began. "But we guessed wrong." For a moment people looked disappointed. Then they realized our faith had underestimated God's power, not overestimated it.

"In fact there are 864 people here," I shouted above the sudden surge of "Amens" and "Praise the Lords." The crowd burst into applause. Macel played the introduction to the doxology, and our people began to sing.

"Praise God from whom all blessings flow. . ."

In the crowd, I could see most of those first thirty-five adults and their families smiling at me through their tears of gratitude. What God had accomplished in those first twelve months left us open-mouthed in wonder.

"Praise Him all creatures here below. . ."

The people singing had built this place through their witness and their work, yet every knuckle they had bruised knocking on doors and every blister they had raised pounding nails or sawing plywood had reaped benefits for them and for their families that they never dreamed.

"Praise Him above ye heavenly host. . ."

They had prayed that God would use their witness to build a great and growing church, and already God was answering those prayers.

"Praise Father, Son, and Holy Ghost."

I thought the crowd would not go home that day. When the final hymn was sung and the last prayer prayed, people stood in small groups hugging, crying, laughing, and thanking God for His faithfulness.

When Jesus commanded His followers to go into all the world and preach the Gospel, He meant it. We sing about witness. We preach and teach about witness. We know that witness is at the center of our Christian faith. Nevertheless, too few Christians really take witnessing seriously. But those few believers who do witness in their own family, to their neighbors, house-to-house across their communities, and in person or through media to the whole world do see amazing results. Those who quit talking about sharing their faith and who actually do it soon discover that God will accomplish far more than they ask or dream in the process.

Try it yourself. Tell somebody today about Jesus and what He is doing in your life. Knock on your neighbor's door. Ask your boss or fellow worker out to lunch. Share your faith over coffee with someone who has never heard the good news before. Don't be afraid to witness in your own words and in your own way. And when you try, God will take your witness and multiply it.

There is a wonderful promise in the Old Testament book of Ecclesiastes. "Cast thy bread upon the waters," King Solomon writes, "for thou shalt find it after many days" (Ecclesiastes 11:1).

It is a strange little verse, but it carries an important truth. Solomon was referring to those Egyptian farmers who waited until the flood waters of the Nile subsided and then scattered rice seed upon the sodden ground. Skeptics looking on would laugh at this apparently futile act, until that day not long after when the muddy earth would spring forth in rich green harvest.

Critics laughed or scolded me when I began my visit to a hundred houses every day. They laughed at my people who took up the challenge and witnessed across Lynchburg and around Campbell County. We were meeting in an old bottling company building then, and they called us the "Donald Duck Church." Now we are one of the largest churches in the world, with dozens of other churches created through our ministry. The critics aren't laughing anymore. We blundered. We erred. We were kicked off porches, threatened by shotguns, and chased away by barking dogs. But God blessed our faithful witness, and He will bless your witness as well.

If God's people will see nothing but the goal line, will accept nothing but victory, will pay any price, will suffer any hurt and hardship, will refuse to be discouraged or disheartened, we cannot help but win; because we are charged with the power of God's Holy Spirit.

— Jerry Falwell

CHAPTER NINE

The Spiritual
Life

Before the sunrise that next Monday morning I got up, dressed, drove to Thomas Road, and tacked a sign up on my office door: GONE FISHING. The sanctuary and the surrounding grounds were knee-deep in clutter from that great crowd of 864 people who had celebrated the first anniversary of our Thomas Road Baptist Church. And though I was tempted to wade into the work immediately, I knew that I needed a day off to rest my body and my soul a bit.

I remember getting into my 1955 Century Buick and driving down Highway 501 through Rustburg, Winfall, and Gladys to Long Island, Virginia, just thirty miles away. After a drive through the farmland of Campbell County, I turned off the main road, passed through a white balanced gate, and followed a twisting gravel road to the 200-year-old red-brick farmhouse of R. B. Whittemore and his daughter Ann.

In my experience, each stage of a person's spiritual growth is associated with a special person whom God sends for that purpose. The physician Luke tells the story of a powerful Ethiopian who had journeyed to Jerusalem under orders of his queen.

Apparently he was having trouble understanding a passage of the Old Testament when God sent Philip, a Christian believer to assist him. Do you understand what you are reading? Philip asked the man.

"How can I," he answered, "except some man should guide me?" (Acts 8:30,31).

Philip rode with the Ethiopian in his chariot until the stranger understood the Gospel and was baptized. Then the Bible reports that "the Spirit of the Lord caught away Philip, that the eunuch saw him no more: and he went on his way rejoicing" (Acts 8:39).

How often God sends men or women our way just at the right time to help us when we do not understand. It was a woman and her father who helped introduce me to the deeper spiritual life. Ann was tall, twenty-five, unmarried, and a very spiritual person. Her father was a successful businessman from St. Louis, Missouri, a widower who had retired in his mid-fifties on this 750-acre ranch in southern Virginia. He, too, was preoccupied with "the deeper spiritual life." I walked to the elegant old two-story house with its white shutters and dark green trim. Smoke curled lazily from the massive brick chimney, but no one answered when I pulled on the old brass bell at the rustic front door.

Usually by the time my car had stopped in their wide circular driveway, both Whittemores would be walking in my direction waving and shouting out a greeting. This morning all was silent. I walked toward the barn where Mr. Whittemore kept his thoroughbred ponies. No one. As I turned and walked toward the nearby woods, I startled a family of pheasants that flew noisily over a nearby marsh and into a distant stand of white pine.

"Hi, Jerry," Ann called, coming up the path in my direction with her father just a step behind her.

"Praise the Lord, Jerry," her father added as he embraced me and walked me back toward the farmhouse.

I confess that whenever either one of them said, "Praise the Lord," it made me just a bit nervous. But there was something about those two Whittemores that drew me back to their home like a pair of magnets. I don't remember exactly when these strange but wonderful people entered my life the first time. But shortly after my conversion at Park Avenue Baptist Church, I met the Whittemores. It didn't take many conversations with these two warm, loving, sensitive people to realize that they had "something" that I needed and wanted very much.

"We've been praying for you, Jerry," Ann said quietly. "Are you all right?"

This spiritual pulse-taking was new to me. We Baptists are not overdosed with concern about personal holiness. We believe in Christian witness. Getting people saved is everything. And we believe that salvation is forever. Once it's done, it is done! Once you've accepted Christ as Lord and Savior, you are in. There is nothing more you need to do or not do to guarantee eternal life.

After that our Baptist code is simple, sometimes way too simple. We don't drink. We don't smoke. We don't believe in immorality whatever form it takes. We have our dress codes and a few other "spiritual" trademarks. But not much else is taboo. If you want to dislike somebody, that's fine. If you want to make war on somebody, that's fine, too. And unfortunately it seems often that if you want to ruin your health, destroy your marriage, and ignore your children because you are building a great church, there is little condemnation from your peers. We don't have very accurate ways of measuring the quality of a person's inner life, and we get nervous around people who do.

"I'm fine, Ann," I answered somewhat defensively. We continued to walk in silence. She knew I wasn't fine or I wouldn't have driven out into the country to see them. I came because I was exhausted physically and spiritually. I had just celebrated the fact that 864 people were present in our Sunday School after just twelve months' work. I had a daily radio program and a weekly television program. I was regularly visiting a hundred homes a day, preaching to ever increasing crowds and gaining a reputation about town as "the preacher to watch."

But there was something missing in my life, and whenever I recognized the recurrence of that awful hollow feeling, I got in my car and drove those thirty miles to see the Whittemores.

They had been attending our church on Thomas Road some-what regularly during the last twelve months; but they weren't impressed with the 864 attendance record or the growing mem-bership rolls. They didn't ask me about my radio or television ministry. They weren't even interested in how many homes I had visited or how many people my volunteers and I had led to Christ.

"What's happening between you and the Lord?" Mr. Whittemore asked. "That's what is important!"

It was their primary question. What I was achieving for God in my ministry wasn't nearly as significant as what He was achieving inside me. Whereas many of my fellow Baptists saw being born again as the end goal, the Whittemores saw it only as the beginning. They and their fellow "deeper spiritual lifers" believed that God's Spirit began a work in the new convert that wasn't finished until death and that the primary goal of each new convert was to participate daily in what God was doing inside his or her new life.

"More marmalade?" Ann asked as we sat together around the glass-top table in the glassed porch just off their kitchen. It was our tradition. Upon my early arrival, the Whittemores put on a pot of coffee, warmed a loaf of homemade natural grain bread, and passed me some special dish Ann had prepared for this time of fellowship.

They always began with questions about the church and about Macel and her family and about my mom. They waited as I shared all the exciting news about what God was doing through television or radio or those door-to-door visits, and they sincerely celebrated each victory and consoled me in every loss. But their real interest was not in "the visible world of man" but in "the invisible world of God's Holy Spirit." They listened to my stories of what God was doing through me, but what they wanted to hear was what God was doing inside me.

At first, I must admit, I was spooked by the Whittemores. Somebody in my church described them jokingly with this short unfair critique: "They're so heavenly minded, they're no earthly good."

In fact the Whittemores were not just spiritually minded.

Ann and her father were evangelists, missionaries, and church builders in their own right. Just a few years after this meeting in 1957, Ann married a missionary and moved to South America to begin her own ministry there. And throughout his life Ann's father used his time and his resources to help our church and others like it in practical down-to-earth ways.

But both Ann and her father had discovered another dimension of the Christian life, the dimension of the Spirit-filled life, and they were determined to introduce that new dimension to everyone who was open to it. I would have rushed right past these two people and their preoccupation with the "deeper spiritual life" if they hadn't been so patient and loving with me and if they hadn't had such strong support for their position from the Bible and from 2,000 years of Christian history.

"Turn to the Acts of the Apostles," Mr. Whittemore instructed me that morning after the dishes were put away and we sat together in their warm breakfast nook with our Bibles opened in front of us.

"That fifth New Testament book should have been called 'The Acts of the Holy Spirit,'" Ann added under her breath as we were turning to Acts, Chapter 2, Verse 1.

We Baptists like the Gospels and the missionary letters of the Apostle Paul to the people of Rome or the short letters of the Apostle John. Those books speak plainly of sin and salvation to lost Jews and Gentiles who do not know Christ as Lord and Savior. We love those great evangelistic moments in Acts, especially Peter's sermon in the second chapter that resulted in 3,000 new converts. We read and reread the story of Saul's conversion in Acts g and his famous sermon dedicated to the "Unknown God" in Acts 17 and his sermon before King Agrippa in Acts 26 where he almost persuades the king himself that Jesus Christ is Lord.

From its first words, the book of Acts is an exciting history of evangelism and evangelists that makes us Baptists stand up and shout. We love to see those early preachers confound the unbeliever with those great evangelistic sermons. And we love to picture that first century church growing and spreading across the world from the Middle East into Europe and North

Africa and even across the continents to India and the Far East.

But in Acts and even in the Gospels and throughout the letters of the Apostles there is another equally important theme that leaves many of us evangelist types confused and a bit defensive. That morning at the Whittemores' we read the story again of the disciples at the beginning of their ministry.

These were not brave men. After Jesus's death they hid in an upper room, trembling and afraid. These were not powerful men. They were fishermen and blue-collar workers. These were not talented men. There wasn't an artist, a musician, a poet, or a playwright among them. And they were not brilliant educated men. No one had a Ph.D., and though Luke was a medical doctor, there is no record that he practiced those skills during the years that followed.

Something or Someone took that handful of unextraordinary men and transformed them into a mighty, powerful force. This same crowd of men who hid trembling and afraid in an upper room after Jesus's death on the cross walked down the steps of that upper room and into the world to turn it upside down.

What happened to Peter, James, John, and the others in that upper room? What happened to Saul in his lonely sojourn in the desert? Why did Jesus Himself spend so much time alone before the sunrise walking the beaches of Galilee or hiking through the hills of Judea? Why did these men "waste" so much important time by themselves at prayer and in the Scriptures? Why throughout Christian history have the truly significant individuals all followed their example and taken time from the outward journey to work so long and hard on the inward journey?

"Read it, Jerry," Mr. Whittemore encouraged me that morning.

"And when the day of Pentecost was fully come," I began reading from the second chapter of Acts, "they were all with one accord in one place. And suddenly there came a sound from heaven as of a rushing mighty wind, and it filled all the house where they were sitting. And there appeared unto them cloven tongues like as of fire, and it sat upon each of them. And they were all filled with the Holy Ghost. . ."

That morning we read together portions of the book of Acts that showed clearly that it was God's Holy Spirit working in and through these first century believers that gave their lives peace and their ministries power. These men were not just naturally brave, talented, powerful, or brilliant. They were ordinary people who had given their lives over to the power of God's Holy Spirit, who came into their lives and used them.

History may call these early Christian leaders saints and martyrs, but they were still human, nevertheless. They had physical and emotional needs just like the rest of us. They grew hungry and tired. They felt lonely and afraid. They struggled with their sexual needs, with their ambitions, and with jealousy, anger, and grief. They knew the same temptations that we know. Just because God's Spirit lived in their lives did not mean that their humanity had ended. Every day these men struggled to overcome the "spirit of the flesh" so that the Holy Spirit of God could live within them more completely.

To the Whittemores, that struggle to overcome the natural human instincts, needs, temptations, ambitions, and desires so that God's Spirit could be set free within us and through us was the process of the "deeper spiritual life."

"He doesn't want you to achieve great things in His name, Jerry," Mr. Whittemore said that day. "He just wants you to love Him, to trust Him, to wait upon Him, and to praise Him. Then He can achieve what He desires through you!"

I drove away from the Whittemores' that day feeling spiritually fed. Don't misunderstand. Being with them wasn't easy. I felt kind of silly and ambitious and unspiritual when I was with them.

"Be sure, Jerry," Mr. Whittemore said time and time again, "that your inner spiritual life keeps up with all the tasks that you have appointed for yourself. Be sure you stay close to the Father as you rush about doing your Father's business." They taught me that God would attend to the breadth of my ministry if I would attend to its depth. As I drove back up Highway 501, the late afternoon sun made deep shadows across the roadway. Streaks of sunlight flared and flashed through the branches of the trees as I raced back to make a few important calls. I had spent a whole day away from the office. I hadn't made one of my hundred house calls. There would be a list of telephone messages, a pile of letters, and a trustees' meeting at seven. I pushed the accelerator to the floorboard.

Then Mr. Whittemore's words echoed in my mind: "Be sure you stay close to the Father as you rush about doing your Father's business." I began to pray. My car became a chapel, my dashboard an altar of worship. God was doing something special in my life, and I could feel Him doing it.

The inward journey—that personal spiritual quest to know God better and to give His Spirit complete control in one's life—begins from the moment of our conversion. But for many of us there is another time in our lives that we can look back on as the beginning of that inward spiritual journey. That evening after visiting the Whittemores was a time of beginning for me.

As I neared Lynchburg, I turned left into the road that leads down to Timberlake and parked my car in a clearing by the water. The sky was streaked with deep purple, amber, and violet. The sunset made a gold path across the lake. I walked down to the water's edge and skipped a flat stone across the surface.

"Slow me down, Lord," I prayed. "The Whittemores are right. You don't need me to break my neck building a church. You need me just to love You."

The Whittemores taught me that praise is one of the first secrets to the victorious Christian life.

"Praise Him," Ann said. "Just take time to praise Him."

She quoted the Psalmist David to prove her point. From Psalm 1 to Psalm 150 the people of God are urged to praise Him: "Praise ye the Lord. Praise God in his sanctuary:... Praise him for his mighty acts: praise him according to his excellent greatness. Praise him with the sound of the trumpet: praise him with the psaltery and harp. Praise him with the timbrel and dance: praise him with stringed instruments and organs. Praise him upon the loud cymbals: praise him upon the high sounding cymbals. Let every thing that hath breath praise the Lord. Praise ye the Lord" (Psalm 150).

Late that afternoon I walked beside the lake and thought

about Jesus walking beside the Sea of Galilee almost 2,000 years ago. He, too, needed time to praise His Father in heaven. He, too, needed to get away from the day's rush and listen to the still small voice of God speaking in His heart. And if Jesus Himself spent so much time and energy during His short ministry on this earth to build that inner spiritual life, then how much more I needed to do it.

Then I remembered a little book that the Whittemores had given me as I rushed away that day. I returned to my car, unwrapped the package, and opened the small tan-covered book with a single rose etched on its cover above the title, *Waiting On God.*

The book's author was Andrew Murray, one of those "deeper spiritual life" advocates that the Whittemores often quoted. Inside the book was a series of thirty short devotional messages, one for each day of the month. Apparently God had given Andrew Murray the friendship of Mr. and Mrs. Albert A. Head, who had blessed him with "a bright home" and "days of quiet waiting," just as God had led the Whittemores to me.

In the twilight I read the poem by Freda Hanbury that Andrew Murray quoted at the very beginning of his little book. Because that poem had such an effect upon my life and because it states so well what the Whittemores and the other advocates of this "deeper spiritual life" were saying to me, I quote it here:

Wait Thou Only Upon God
Wait thou only upon God. My soul be still,
And let thy God unfold His perfect will.
Thou fain would follow Him throughout this year,
Thou fain with listening heart His voice would hear,
Thou fain would be a passive instrument
Possessed by God, and ever Spirit sent
Upon His service sweet then be thou still;
For only thus can He in thee fulfil
His heart's desire. Oh, hinder not His hand
From fashioning the vessel He hath planned.
"Be silent unto God," and thou shalt know
The quiet, holy calm He doth bestow

On those who wait on Him; so shalt thou bear
His presence, and His life and light e'en where
The night is darkest, and thine earthly days
Shalt show His love, and sound His glorious praise.
And He will work with hand unfettered, free,
His high and holy purposes through thee.
First on thee must that hand of power be turned,
Till in His love's strong fire thy dross is burned,
And thou come forth a vessel for thy Lord.
So frail and empty, yet, since He hath poured
Into thine emptiness His life, His love,
Henceforth through thee the power of God shall move
And He will work for thee. Stand still and see
The victories thy God will gain for thee;
So silent, yet so irresistible,
Thy God shall do the thing impossible.
Oh, question not henceforth what thou cans't do;
Thou cans't do nought. But He will carry through
The work where human energy had failed
Where all thy best endeavours had availed
Thee nothing. Then, my soul, wait and be still;
If God shall work for thee His perfect will.
If thou wilt take no less, His best shall be
Thy portion now and through eternity.

Every day that next month along with my regular prayer
and Bible reading I read passages from Andrew Murray's *Wait-ing On God.* When I had finished that little classic of the deeper
spiritual life movement, the Whittemores gave me other books
by Murray: *The Full Blessing of Pentecost, With Christ in the
School of Prayer,* and *The Deeper Spiritual Life.*

After Murray, the Whittemores introduced me to Watch-man Nee. Until that year, 1957, Nee, a Chinese Christian evan-gelist, Bible teacher, and advocate of the deeper spiritual life,
had only been known in English from transcriptions of his spo-ken messages in tracts and magazine articles. Converted to
Christ as a student in Foochow, China, in 1920, Nee and the
church in China passed through a period of persecution and

suffering. During a visit to Europe in 1938, just before the terrors of World War II, Nee shared the lessons God had taught him during that decade of suffering.

Early in 1958, the Whittemores gave me the first English edition of Watchman Nee's *The Normal Christian Life*. Like Andrew Murray, Nee opened up the world of the Spirit to me.

"A forgiven sinner," Nee writes, "is quite different from an ordinary sinner, and a consecrated Christian is quite different from an ordinary Christian.... If we yield wholly to Him and claim the power of His indwelling Spirit, we need wait for no special feelings or supernatural manifestations, but can simply look up and praise Him that something has already happened. We can confidently thank Him that the glory of God has already filled His temple. 'Know ye not that your body is a temple of the Holy Ghost which is in you, which ye have of God'" (I Corinthians 6:19).

Already in those early days of my ministry the Christian churches were arguing about how and when the Holy Spirit enters the believer's life. I never found the argument interesting. God doesn't limit Himself when He works in people's hearts. Our loving Father tailors a spiritual quest to fit each believer. Read the stories of those first century disciples. Jesus dealt with each person uniquely. Lovingly and patiently He let doubting Thomas feel His nail-pierced hands. But he chased the money changers bodily from the temple. God spoke in a still small voice to Samuel, but He knocked Paul right off his horse with a blinding light and a booming voice. Throughout history, God's Spirit has worked with each person uniquely. Why should we try to limit God to one mode of behavior?

With Watchman Nee I learned to celebrate and to practice the presence of the Holy Spirit every day. I know deeply spiritual Christians who differ with one another on eschatology, church polity, or other non-essentials; I have never met a Christian who lived a powerful and productive life who didn't credit everything to the presence of the Holy Spirit living and working in and through his or her life.

I believed then, as I believe now, that there are two sides to this deeper spiritual life issue. Waiting upon the Lord, as

Andrew Murray recommends, is just one side to consider. The other truth we must not forget is that we can wait forever and never really do anything for God or the church. I believed in equal doses of work and waiting. The deeper spiritual life demands action, and productive action requires the deeper spiritual life.

During those first five years at Thomas Road I tried to find some balance between my urge to win the world single-handedly and my deep desire to grow spiritually. The struggle between those two worlds went on within me every day.

At 5 A.M., when the live radio broadcast was just ninety minutes away and I was still snug and warm in my bed, it was hard to get up in that cold bedroom to pray and to read and to "wait upon the Lord." On the other hand, during those wonderful quiet times of reading and prayer, I hated to be called away by an emergency phone call or to be interrupted by one of those chance visits a parishioner makes just to say hello.

Little by little I learned how to incorporate both worlds into my life: the practical world of action and the continuous fellowship with my Lord. And little by little I felt a calmness settle over me that can only be attributed to the presence and inward control of God's Holy Spirit in my life. All that was settled early in my ministry, thanks to the Whittemores and those great men and women of the deeper spiritual life whose writings helped to focus my life. I was beginning to learn how to be both "spiritual" and "natural" in a way that allowed me to enter into His rest and truly enjoy the Christian life.

Two or three afternoons a week, I drove out to the Whittemores' to study the Bible with them, to read and discuss the men and women—ancient and modern—who wrote about the "Christ" life. We began, of course, with Jesus Himself. He set the example for a daily balance between action and contemplation, between the outward and the inward spiritual journeys. The New Testament writings of Luke, Paul, John, and Peter all contributed in their way to the discussion. The early saints and martyrs were rich in personal illustrations from their own struggle to maintain balance in their spiritual journeys.

The Whittemores introduced me to the spiritual giants of

yesteryear and to their classic Christian writings. I began to study Martin Luther, George Muller, C. T. Studd, Rees Howells, Evan Roberts, Praying Hyde, E. M. Bounds, and dozens of others. The modern advocates of the deeper spiritual life they recommended included Andrew Murray, Watchman Nee, Norman Grubb, and Alexander Hay, the founder of the New Testament Missionary Union. Later Macel and I even drove to Ontario, Canada, to meet with Dr. Hay. He was very old, but his eyes sparkled and his spirit radiated a kind of peace that left me all the more convinced that along with my commitment to evangelism and the public and outward world of Christian action, I would also maintain a lifelong interest in the private inner world of the Spirit.

Dr. Hay suggested that we meet Jack Manley and Bill Weir, two men who had given their lives to the study of the Word, evangelism, and to the practice of intercessory prayer. We visited both men in Canada. Eventually Dr. Hay, Jack Manley, and Bill Weir all brought their ministries to Thomas Road Baptist Church, sharing with us some of their Biblical discoveries about the inner spiritual journey.

As my ministry in Lynchburg grew, greater and greater demands were being placed on me. There weren't enough hours in the day to complete what needed to be done. I needed spiritual strength to carry on and supernatural wisdom to know how to handle all the opportunities that were coming our way.

Macel and I began to drive out to the Whittemores' together on Saturdays. We sat in their kitchen and talked about the deeper things of God. We read and prayed together. And we grew closer to God and to each other in the process.

From my teachers in Bible College and from the pastors who had trained me, I had learned the very important techniques of ministry, about evangelism and church growth, about Sunday School administration, raising funds, and preaching. And the Whittemores and their friends taught me about personal holiness, about prayer and waiting, about living by faith, about trusting God and His Holy Spirit to accomplish in and through me what I could never accomplish by myself.

I was still working too hard and too compulsively. But I

enjoyed every minute of it. God had called me to this work, and I never seemed to tire of it. Still, I needed more balance in my life, and I suppose it was the Whittemores who slowed me down more than anybody else. They continued preaching the deeper spiritual life to me.

"Slow down, Jerry," R. B. Whittemore would say. "God can get His work done just as well without you. All He wants from you is your fellowship and praise."

The Whittemores thought my church growth techniques were silly and demeaning. "Are you sure you want to continue those contests for church attendance?" they would ask. "It isn't right to give away Bibles and free trips to the Holy Land for prizes," they argued. "And you really should quit publishing the number of people who were saved, baptized, or who joined the church. It isn't a game, you know. You shouldn't be keeping score."

On the other hand, my activist friends criticized me for spending so much time with the Whittemores. "Those deeper spiritual life people will lead you astray, Jerry," certain people used to warn me. "Before long they'll have you in a monastery praying and fasting instead of out here witnessing and working where you belong."

I spent those first years working for some kind of balance. I began each morning with a time of quiet prayer and meditation on the Scriptures. I tried to end each day with Macel, praying, reading, and talking together. And during the busiest of days, I practiced turning over each event to God, trusting His Spirit to minister through me to others in need. Sometimes I succeeded. Other times I failed. But throughout that first decade of ministry, through the influence of the Whittemores and their friends, I found a balance between action and contemplation that made it possible somehow to get through those trying early years and the decades of stress and tension that would follow.

Although my father was an alcoholic and had died of cirrhosis of the liver, I never thought seriously about the role of the church in helping people overcome alcohol dependency. As I entered into that inward spiritual journey and began to listen more and more carefully to God's still small voice, I began to feel a burden toward the alcoholics in Lynchburg and the counties around us. It seemed that almost every day I was meeting a person, usually a man, who was struggling against the power of alcohol or had given in to it. I was praying with these men, and they were being converted; but from the beginning I knew in my heart that something more had to be done to help them recover from the bottle and keep them on the straight and narrow.

Then one Friday afternoon in the winter of 1958, George Ragland entered my office and told me the story of his struggle against alcoholism.

"I purchased my first bottle of alcohol when I was just a kid," he told me, "for medicinal purposes. And I've been sick ever since."

George laughed, but already he had been jailed for drunkenness 141 times. George and his wife had raised six children. Actually, because of his drinking problem, she had raised them almost alone. George's wife was a nurse in a local hospital. He was a rather brilliant and totally entertaining man, when sober. As a youth he had been called into the ministry, but he was drinking so heavily, even as a young man, that he couldn't concentrate to finish school or keep a good job. Still he was a very funny man and could have competed with the best stand-up comics on radio or television.

In jail, George either preached to his cellmates or entertained them with a steady stream of raucous humor. George was the town drunk. Everybody liked him, but nobody knew what to do to save him from his drunkenness. I liked George Ragland. I wanted to help him as I wanted to help the long list of alcoholics I had begun to compile in my office. But except for Alcoholics Anonymous, which was active in those days, most treatments seemed painfully ineffective and short-lived.

I wanted to act quickly, but I had learned by then that sometimes acting without praying can be a disaster. The deeper spiritual life requires both. Macel and I began to pray specifically about George and the others. The Whittemores joined us in our praying. Then I shared my burden with the deacons at Thomas Road Baptist Church and eventually with the congregation.

God's Spirit led us as we prayed. I began to feel that we needed a farm somewhere deep in the woods and a long distance from bars, restaurants, and liquor stores, where the men could dry out and find comfort and strength within a Christian community. My brother Lewis owned a 16 acre farm at Stonewall, Virginia, just eighteen miles from Lynchburg yet isolated from the old haunts and the old drinking buddies that plagued my alcoholic friends.

Again we prayed. It wasn't long until we felt God guiding us to buy that farm and hire our first staff member to oversee it. That was in January 1959. The old farmhouse on the property was cold. Volunteers filled in the cracks in the walls and ceiling. We installed oil heaters in each room and bunks for the men to sleep on. We piled up blankets on each bed, but there was no electricity or running water.

Before we had moved a man onto the old farm, Pastor John Suttenfield, my friend from the Fairview Christian Church, called with an emergency request.

"I have an alcoholic here in my office, Jerry," he began. "He's threatening to kill himself if he doesn't get some kind of help quickly. I thought maybe you could help him."

That day I met Earl Thompson. Like George Ragland, Earl Thompson had a fatal drinking problem. If he didn't get help soon, he would die. If not from alcoholism, he would die by his own hand. As I talked to Earl, I remembered that he had been a driver for my father many years before. Actually, he had helped my dad run illegal booze into Campbell County during Prohibition. The police called Earl "Look Up" Thompson because his eyelids drooped and he had to tilt his head backward in order to look up from under them to see where he was going.

"Look Up" Thompson was a tall, muscular man. Early in marriage, he had shot and seriously wounded his wife in a drunken fit of rage. Thompson had been involved with underworld mob bosses and the numbers racket. He had served time in prison. But I liked "Look Up" Thompson. Like George Ragland, Thompson had sterling qualities just beneath that drunken self-destructive surface. As with George Ragland, I wanted to help him.

I stuffed all 250 pounds of "Look Up" Thompson into my tiny Renault and brought him home. He was drunk, delirious, and suicidal. But as he sobered up, he prayed for Christ's forgiveness and was wonderfully converted. That next day I drove George and "Look Up" to Stonewall, Virginia. These two men would be our first patients at our experimental farm for alcoholics. I called it Elim Home for Alcoholics.

You can read the story of the Old Testament Elim in the book of Exodus, Chapter 15. In crossing the wilderness, the Jews had come to the bitter waters of Marah. They were howling and murmuring with grief and bitterness. God heard their prayers and delivered them from those bitter waters. And the very next stop along their journey to the promised land was Elim, an oasis where the clean bubbling waters refreshed their souls.

Our Elim was cold and isolated, but it was an oasis. George Ragland and "Look Up" Thompson began their treatment with hope, the first hope they had felt in years. Our associate minister made them welcome. He taught them every morning from the Word. They performed household and farm chores. They fished and hunted together in the afternoons. They sat around the fireplace in the evening and talked about life before and after alcohol addiction. And at night they rolled up in piles of blankets and went to sleep.

A news reporter, James Murdock, from the *Daily Advance*, visited Elim Home in January 1959. After interviewing George and "Look Up," he wrote an honest yet compassionate account of what our church was trying to accomplish in this isolated, rather primitive farmhouse at Stonewall, Virginia. It was the first time any story about the ministries of Thomas Road Baptist Church was transmitted throughout the world over the wires of the Associated Press, and the results were staggering.

Suddenly we were flooded with applications to come to Elim Home from alcoholics and their families. Unfortunately, in just a few weeks the farmhouse was filled with alcoholics from the Lynchburg area. But Elim became a model of what could be done by any church or civic group that cared. Other homes like it began to spring up across the country. The idea behind Elim Home was so simple and so perfect. And yet it never would have happened unless we had waited upon God's Spirit to lead us. I was beginning to learn about the deeper spiritual life. I was beginning to balance action with waiting on Him. And in those coming months God showed me time and time again that He was at work and would complete what He began if we would just wait on Him to do it.

We didn't know how we could afford all the changes to the property or meet all the needs of the men. We had no money, no skills, and no experience with alcoholics. Yet just two days after the article appeared, a helicopter landed in a pasture near the farmhouse. I was talking to the men at Elim when the large noisy machine landed nearby. We walked down the steps toward the copter just as Mr. James Cooke, the executive director of an electrical cooperative for several counties of Virginia, strode toward us, followed by his key aides. Mr. Cooke, a powerful and determined man, had read the article about Elim Home and had come to help us.

"The nearest electric line is over one mile up the road," Mr. Cooke reported after a quick tour of Elim Home. "But I've called for a crew on my helicopter radio and you'll have power here right away."

"But we don't have any wiring in the house," I answered sheepishly, "and we don't have any money to hire somebody to wire it."

Again Mr. Cooke had the solution. He had already called the right person for help. George and "Look Up" Thompson had adopted Mr. Cooke and followed him back and forth between his helicopter and the farmhouse. They stood behind him smiling first at me and then at him like two overgrown guardian angels.

"I've called Dan Candler," he said. Dan Candler owned Mid-State Electric Company on Church Street in Lynchburg. (He also owned part of Candler's Mountain, which would in just twenty-five years become Liberty Mountain and the home of our Liberty University.) "Dan will get your place wired," Mr.

Cooke promised, "and will throw in a few other little things as well."

George and "Look Up" grinned even wider in coming days as those "other little things" began to arrive. A complete wiring job was followed by truckloads of stoves, refrigerators, heaters, and various wonderful appliances. Then came a plumbing supply house truck and crew to put in bathrooms, and a septic company to dig and install a septic tank.

The septic tank company contacted by Mr. Cooke was owned by Mert Floyd. After Mr. Floyd and his crew from Lovingston, Virginia, had installed our septic tank and connected our first indoor plumbing, Mert confessed his own struggle with alcohol and checked into Elim Home as a patient.

During the next few weeks, the 165-acre farm was crawling with volunteer labor. Carpenters and plumbers, painters and decorators, all had read the article and had come to donate their time and labor to the project. You couldn't see through the walls anymore, and the wind stayed outside when it was blowing. And you didn't need to pile blankets to the ceiling to keep warm. There was a kitchen and a refrigerator filled with food. There were bathrooms, bedrooms, and a living room with a reconditioned fireplace where the men could meet and talk and worship together.

The rules were (and are) simple. The men must come voluntarily. They cannot be consigned to Elim Home by wife or court. They must come sober. Elim is not a drying-out place. It is a place for total deliverance. The men must sign themselves in. They must quit drinking "cold turkey," that is without the aid of other chemicals or continued small doses of alcohol. They can't leave in less than sixty days, and they must participate freely in the activities of the Home.

The men are individually counseled by Christian professionals. They work together in small groups. They pray and study the Scriptures together. They learn vocational skills. They hunt and fish and hike the trails. Hundreds of men have been through the program. And for the past thirty-eight years the Elim Home has consistently had a list of men waiting for treatment, two or three months long.

Elim Home was one of those early exercises for me in the deeper spiritual life. During those first days of my ministry in Lynchburg I began to develop a balance between the need for action and the need to wait upon God. For some Christians, action is everything. For others, prayer is the beginning and the end. But the longer I live, the more I am convinced that in the balance of these two worlds, the inward and the outward journey, comes spiritual health.

I acted to start a home for alcoholics. But my actions were limited by my ignorance, by my lack of financial resources, and the limited resources of my people. We knew there was a need and we asked God to help us meet it. We took out a loan to buy the farm. We filled the cracks in the farmhouse walls with stucco. We put in little heaters, piled up blankets and opened the doors. We prayed and we acted. We waited and we worked.

Then God stepped in and made the difference. Suddenly from the heavens a helicopter came bearing God's gifts to Elim Home. And a small army of men and women volunteers followed while we looked on smiling in gratitude and surprise. As the years have passed, I still look on with gratitude as God achieves His purposes through our quiet prayers and our simple, sometimes primitive, acts of faith. But I've quit being so surprised by what God accomplishes when we step out trusting in His promises. What God's Spirit can accomplish in this world is far greater than our actions or our prayers. Taking time out from our busy, self-appointed agendas to wait upon the Lord, to praise Him, to honor and to love Him, sets free His power to get done what we could only dream.

Mind you, I learned early from the Whittemores that it would take a lifetime to yield every part of me to God's Spirit. Developing the deeper spiritual life means a daily process of yielding to God with successes and with failures along the way. There are times we act before we pray, and end up with a mess on our hands. There are occasions when we do it our way before we give God's way a chance, and pay the consequences for our haste. And there are times when we get caught up in our schedules and go too fast to wait upon the Lord. At those times we need Him and we need each other to help us slow down and get our priorities straight again.

In those early years of spiritual discovery, I learned that no matter how many times I forget or get too busy to wait upon the Lord, that God continues to wait patiently for me. And through the years God's Spirit has never stopped forgiving me for my forgetfulness or given up working to change me and to help me grow.

Even through those early years of spiritual discovery, God was blessing Thomas Road Baptist Church and expanding our ministry. I spent my time during the 1960's. doing what every pastor is called to do: visiting the sick, witnessing to our neighbors, praying and counseling with the men of Elim Home, training volunteers, working on the church's nonstop building program, broadcasting live from Lynchburg's radio and television stations, preparing sermons and Bible studies, guiding discussion groups and prayer meetings, holding revival meetings in nearby towns, attending pastors' seminars, reading, writing, studying, and playing an occasional game of sandlot baseball or football with the young people of Thomas Road Baptist Church, and driving my little green Renault madly up and down the streets of Lynchburg and across most of Campbell County.

After his successful stay at Elim Home, my friend Earl "Look Up" Thompson used to accompany me on those drives about the city. One day he yelled at me to stop the car, and he got out.

"I've hauled whiskey for your father. I've run liquor for the mob. I've driven through police barricades and I've outrun highway patrolmen who were chasing me. But I've never been as scared as I am with you riding around Lynchburg on your pastoral calls in this little bug."

I didn't know whether to laugh or apologize. I just sat there looking out the window at him as he held his heart and breathed heavily. Finally he shook his head, opened the door, and got back in the car beside me.

"Oh, well," he said quietly, "I suppose that being killed in a head-on collision with the preacher on his rounds is a good way to die after the life I've lived."

I laughed and started on my rounds again. George Ragland and Earl "Look Up" Thompson became my close personal friends and allies in the ministry. Through their months at Elim Home, God delivered both men from their struggle with the bottle. Actually I should say that God gave George and "Look Up" and hundreds of other men like them the power to trust Christ as Lord and Savior and to stand against that awful destructive temptation day by day and to maintain their sobriety for the rest of their lives.

Actually, more than 50 percent of the men who come to Elim Home never use alcoholic beverages again. And though we celebrate what God is doing through our ministry to alcoholics, we can't help but feel sad and somewhat frightened by what we've learned. When Elim Home opened in 1959, our average patient was sixty years of age. Today the average age of alcoholics checking into Elim Home is just twenty-seven.

That same year I took my mom to visit Elim Home. She walked the grounds and visited with the men. She shook their hands and smiled as they shared with her what God was doing for each of them. On that little farm, men's hearts and lives were being changed forever. In Christ they were finding liberation from the bondage of alcohol. They were making plans to leave Elim Home, to be reunited with their families, and to begin their lives again. It was a very exciting day.

But as we turned to walk down the stairs and back to our car, I saw that Mom's eyes were filled with tears. I didn't ask her any questions and she didn't offer any explanations, but I knew what she was thinking. If only Carey Falwell had been to Elim Home. If only her husband, my father, could have sat in that circle and prayed with those men. If only.

We drove back to Lynchburg without speaking. I could see that my mother was struggling with her questions. After about fifteen minutes of silence, Mom seemed to settle the matter in her heart. As I walked beside her toward her home on Rustburg Road, she put her hand on my arm and spoke to me.

"Do you know, Jerry," she said, "if your father hadn't died you might not have cared enough about the others to build this place."

Even as she spoke, I realized for the first time that I had not built Elim Home for George or "Look Up" but for my father,

Carey. And since that day, whenever I see the men of Elim Home entering Thomas Road Church together to worship the Lord and to praise Him for His miracle of deliverance in their lives, I picture my father walking with them, smiling and talking with them about the Lord.

That is the mystery of our Christian faith. God was at work in the life and death of my father even though I could not see or understand what He was doing. God is at work all around us in the world. Our task is not to save the world ourselves but to allow Him to accomplish His will through us. The deeper spiritual life is the path we take toward being in the center of that will. The balance between the life of prayer and action requires discipline and patience, but it is the road God calls each of us to travel.

One of the most moving stories in the New Testament speaks directly to this issue. Read it in Matthew 17 or Mark 9. A loving father brought his demon possessed son to Jesus's disciples to be healed. Apparently, before Jesus arrived, the disciples had tried to heal the boy, but they had failed. When Jesus came on the scene, the father begged Him to heal his tortured, tormented son.

Teacher, he shouted above the noisy crowd, I brought you my son, who is possessed by a spirit that has robbed him of speech. Whenever it seizes him, it throws him to the ground. He foams at the mouth, gnashes his teeth, and becomes rigid. I asked your disciples to drive out the spirit, but they could not.

For one awful moment Jesus looked with anger and disappointment at His disciples. It is one of the only times in New Testament history when we see Jesus short of patience with those who followed Him.

"O faithless generation," He said to them, "how long shall I be with you? how long shall I suffer you?"

Apparently they had missed something important along the way. He had promised them power; but when they tried to act on behalf of this poor boy they were ineffectual. He was about to teach them a lesson in the deeper spiritual life, a lesson that is as vital to us 2,000 years later as it was to those first century Christians.

What a terrible moment it must have been. For the eyewitnesses report that the moment the evil spirit saw Jesus, it immediately threw the boy into a convulsion. He fell to the ground and rolled around, foaming at the mouth.

How long has he been like this? Jesus asked the father.

From childhood, he answered. It has often thrown him into fire or water to kill him. But if you can do anything, take pity on us and help us.

"If thou cans't believe," said Jesus, "all things are possible to him that believeth."

Immediately the boy's father exclaimed, "Lord, I believe; help thou mine unbelief!"

Picture that moment. The disciples and the boy's father stand helpless before the power of evil in the life of this tormented youth. How many times I stood helpless before the suffering of my alcoholic father and in the early years of my ministry before the suffering of other alcoholics that came my way for counsel and help. Alcoholism is like a demon. It enters into a life and takes control. Like the demon in this story, alcoholism has power to damage and destroy completely. Millions of husbands and wives, children and parents, have stood looking on helplessly as alcoholism, like the demon in this story, ruins someone they love.

At that moment a great crowd began to assemble. Suddenly Jesus rebuked the evil spirit with these words: "Thou dumb and deaf spirit," He said, "I charge thee, come out of him and enter no more into him."

Suddenly the spirit shrieked, convulsed him violently, and came out. The boy looked so much like a corpse "that many said, He is dead." But Jesus took him by the hand and lifted him to his feet, and he stood up.

Imagine that moment. The power of God was demonstrated right before their eyes. They had been promised that power but had failed when they tried. Fortunately, the mystery is solved just a short while later. Jesus and His disciples go indoors, and there in private they asked the question millions are still asking: "Why could not we cast him out?"

Jesus replied simply: "This kind can come forth by

nothing, but by prayer and fasting" (Mark 9:29).

There it is. The balance again between the life of action and the life of prayer. Jesus made it perfectly clear: The larger the task we have to accomplish, the more that prayer is essential. We are called to follow His example. Early in the morning, before the crowds had assembled, before He ministered to the sick of body and spirit, Jesus sneaked away from them to pray. Read the Gospels. See how often He prayed alone or with His friends. See how regularly He attended the synagogue for worship and study of the Scriptures. See how He cultivated his own deeper spiritual life.

Some believers get carried away in the direction of action and they forget prayer almost entirely. They get bogged down in doing good. They put their bodies on the line for the poor, the hungry, and the lost; but somewhere along the way they forget to pray, to fast, to study the Word, to yield to God's will, and to wait for the power and the guidance of God's Spirit.

Others get carried away in the direction of contemplation. They become so "heavenly minded" that they are no earthly good. They spend their lives in prayer and meditation and forget that God calls them to feed the poor, clothe the naked, and preach the Word to every creature.

But when our actions are backed by prayer and our prayers lead to action, we are walking in His footsteps and we have the power that He has promised us. Elim Home for Alcoholics is a living proof of the power of prayer and action together.

I have shared the story of David Horsley, the young surveyor who was converted through Thomas Road Church early in our ministry. But I did not tell you the story of his parents, who also found Christ through our church. After their conversion, Ray and Amanda Horsley became the directors of Elim Home for Alcoholics until Ray's death several years ago. Before Ray's death, he and Amanda shared their stories with me. I want to share them with you in their words so that you will see how God works through prayer and action.

"I drank alcohol in growing amounts for over twenty-five years," Ray began. "For the last ten years of my drinking I lived for nothing other than to drink.

"Every day when I got off from work, I would get a bottle and drink until I passed out or fell asleep. I would get up and go to work so sick I could hardly hold my head up. But most of the time I would make it through my shift some way, then get off and start drinking all over again.

"This went on until my wife Amanda and my family had about all they could take. I was also at the end of my rope on my job. My boss had talked to me and told me that he had gone about as far as he could or would with me. I was staying away from work because of drinking and staying away from home three or four days at a time. My wife and family didn't know where I was. Most of the time I didn't know where I was either, or where I had been.

"On December 25, 1957, I knew something had to be done or I would lose my family and home. So I stopped drinking and struggled to stay sober until July 10, 1962. That struggle to stop drinking on my own power was terrible. I was more miserable for the last two years of struggling against the bottle than when I had been drinking. I was searching for something that would help me break this awful downward spiral. I knew I couldn't hold on much longer.

"Then my son David and his wife Judy came to Christ through Thomas Road Baptist Church. They asked me to come to church one Sunday to see them baptized. I went only because they asked me to go. I didn't dream that I would find my answers there. Then, when Reverend Falwell asked if anyone in the congregation who wasn't a Christian needed prayer, I raised my hand. I don't know why I did it. I certainly had not planned to confess my need before all those people.

"I had struggled against the power of alcoholism all my life. I had worked as hard as I could work on my own power and energy to stop drinking and to get control of my life again. But I had failed. After raising my hand for prayer, I began to feel different. Maybe God could help me. Maybe His power and mine together could make the difference.

"One week later after that baptism service, on July 10, 1962, I gave my life to Christ. From that moment, I felt His power in my life. Now, as director of Elim Home for Alcoholics, I counsel men just like myself who failed in their struggle to overcome the power of alcohol until they discovered the power of God in their lives."

"My first years of marriage to Ray passed in growing bitterness," Amanda said. "His drinking grew worse every year. There were quarrels and fights almost daily in our home. Our house was hell on earth. Eventually the children moved away. Our son David joined the Air Force and sent me a large family Bible one Mother's Day as a gift.

"I was almost completely alone in those days after the children left. Ray was out drinking most of the time. I began to look through the Bible my son had given me. I marked little verses that inspired me. One verse I could not forget. I read it over and over again: 'And ye shall seek me, and find me, when ye shall search for me with all your heart'" (Jeremiah 29:13).

"About this time I started pep pills to get up in the morning and tranquillizers to go to sleep at night. I hated alcohol for what it had done to my family. I couldn't drink it, because it destroyed every decent feeling I had. No one came to our house anymore to visit. If someone came by chance to see my husband, I didn't bother to come in where they were or speak to them. My health failed and my mind was consumed by hatred.

"I first heard the pastor of Thomas Road Baptist Church on the radio and began to think about eternity. I tried to leave the pills alone but went into such deep depression that I would take them again. I longed for an escape from life and began carrying a small gun in my pocket that had been given me for protection because we lived so far from anyone and I was alone most of the time. Many times while walking in the woods I took the gun and tried to find courage to pull the trigger, but I could not pull it.

"One day, after Reverend Falwell had preached on the radio, I knelt beside a living room chair and asked God to save me, but when I finished my prayer I felt even more despair. I had no faith and no understanding. My desperate prayer reached the roof and fell back on me. And though I continued to read the Bible and almost daily asked God to save me, I felt a growing sense of agony. Finally, though I could hardly stand to be in a crowd, I went to Thomas Road Baptist Church. If nothing happened to give me hope that day, I had decided to go home, take my gun into the woods, and end my suffering at last.

"That night in the service, trembling and wet with perspiration, I took one step toward the altar. That moment I felt God's Spirit enter my life. My fear went away. A great peace settled on me. There was no light, no voice, no special music playing. I just knew that my lonely struggle was over and that God had come into my life to help me succeed at last."

When I established Elim Home for Alcoholics, I had no idea where to turn for leadership. We had volunteers and part-time pastors who served the home, but we needed someone with real experience in this unique kind of ministry. So we prayed, and God provided exactly what we needed. For the first several years, Bill and Ethel Greene led this ministry. Bill was especially gifted for this responsibility. But, soon Ethel's health forced them to resign. At this point, God provided the Horsleys. Ray and Amanda Horsley knew how to deal with victims of alcohol and chemical dependency because they had experienced God's deliverance firsthand.

God was working in the lives of Ray and Amanda Horsley long before I thought about starting a home for men who were alcoholics, and long before the Horsleys knew that one day they would direct that home. They are just two people who illustrate the mystery of God at work in our world. Getting in touch with God's plan for the world and yielding to His will are at the center of the deeper spiritual life.

At the very beginning of my ministry, God sent the Whittemores to help me understand that our spiritual growth just begins at conversion. From that moment, we begin the lifelong task of seeking and doing God's will. He has a master plan for the salvation of the lost. By practicing the deeper spiritual life we will find our place in His plan. Through constant, never-ending prayer, disciplined Bible study, and memorization, fasting, yielding to His will, and waiting for His power and guidance we will find our way to more effective witness and more powerful Christian action.

I am convinced that if we will
attend to the depth of our ministry,
God will attend to its breadth.

— Jerry Falwell

There are some things money will do; there are some things human effort will do; there are some things human ingenuity will do; but there are some things only God can do.

— Jerry Falwell

CHAPTER TEN

A Christian Marriage

I think I loved Macel from the day I met her just after my conversion in 1952. During those years at the Baptist Bible College in Springfield, Missouri, I had written her weekly, sometimes daily, urging her to take my courtship seriously. In 1954, during a visit from Springfield to Lynchburg, I had presented her a half-carat diamond ring. It was small, but it sparkled, and when she took it I promised that one day when she married me she would get a full carat or more.

I thought that when Macel took that first diamond ring I had won the battle. In fact, years later she confessed that she had taken it thinking to herself, "Well, I can always give it back." Fortunately, she never tried.

Getting Macel Pate permanently on my team was not an easy or a simple job. It had been fairly easy to win her father, Sam Pate Sr., to my cause. And her wonderful sisters Jean and Mary Ann had been my friends and advocates from the beginning. Her little brother Sam Pate Jr. had also taken up the banner; but Macel's mother Lucile was a holdout.

When I returned to Lynchburg to help begin the church, I

picked up Macel at the bank where she worked almost every evening. She played piano at every service, and that gave me other regular chances to see her and to press my case for marriage. On Sunday afternoons and almost every evening we sat in her living room until her father banged his regular warning on the wall. I used those times to talk of marriage, a home, and family.

"Well, Jerry," she would say, "Mother doesn't really think we've spent enough time on this."

I knew we could never spend enough to please Lucile. She loved her family and she wanted them to live together forever. I could visit whenever I wanted, but I couldn't take her darling daughter away.

First Lucile bargained with Macel. "If you just wait until the new sanctuary is finished, we could have the wedding there," she said. Or, "Why not wait until summer when the weather is better?" Or, "Why not wait until fall when everybody's back from vacation?" Or, "Why not wait until spring? Spring weddings are so beautiful." Or, "Why not wait until summer when the weather is better?"

Finally in November 1957 I told Macel that I had waited long enough, and when she began to quote her mother to me one more time, I said simply, "Forget it!" and walked away.

That was the longest walk of my life. And the week that followed seemed endless. I quit visiting the Pate home. I stopped picking up Macel at the bank. I even dated one or two of the other young women from the church.

One Sunday morning Macel walked up to me after Sunday School and looked me straight in the eye. "Okay," she said. "It's any time you want."

I remember shaking my head and trying to understand exactly what she was saying. "Fine," I said, finally understanding the drift. "When do you want to do it?"

"May?" she answered.

"March," I replied.

"April twelfth," she countered.

"Okay," I said, taking her hands in mine. "April twelfth it is." When we told her mother the news, Lucile smiled and said quietly, "Why not wait until summer when the weather is-"

"April twelfth, Mom," we interrupted in unison.

"April twelfth, then," Mom answered back, and then her eyes brimmed with tears (of happiness or grief I'm still not sure); and wiping away the tears with her apron, she hugged each of us a long, lingering hug and turned back to finish the dishes she was drying.

I suppose it's hard for any mother to lose a daughter. It was just difficult for me to imagine why Lucile would mind losing her daughter to me. Actually, by then she thought I was wonderful. Every Sunday morning at Thomas Road Baptist Church, Lucile Pate sat in her favorite seat smiling up at me, supporting my ministry with her prayers, her gifts, and her well-wishes; but Lucile loved Macel and hated to give her up to anyone, even me. Finally, after she realized our decision had been made forever, she quit struggling and began to be the best friend and ally a son-in-law could have.

Needless to say, our congregation mobilized for the big event. The extension on the storefront building sanctuary was finished in March 1958, just weeks before our wedding. Volunteers rushed to paint, lay carpet, finish windows, and install the new pews we had purchased.

By our wedding night, even the river scene on our new baptistry had been partially painted. Flowers covered everything. Thirty minutes before the wedding was scheduled to begin, the 800 seats were packed. By the time the wedding march began, it was standing room only. Macel wore a modest white silk gown with white orchids and a long white veil. I wore a black tuxedo and stood with my groomsmen at the front of the church just to the right of the pulpit looking down the aisle at her.

Lucile Pate sat in the front row on my right surrounded by her family and friends. She was crying. I mean she was sobbing. And it didn't look like she was crying tears of joy. Macel held her father's arm as they walked together down the white paper carpet toward me. He looked like he was about to cry. And Macel didn't look much happier.

But she was beautiful and we were-in spite of all signs to

the contrary—very much in love, and the whole church knew it. Dr. John Suttenfield, the pastor of the Fairview Christian Church, where some of the Falwell family attended, stood in front of the congregation next to my friend from Baptist Bible College days Vann Barringer, another Baptist preacher.

The service and the vows were as traditional as you can imagine. I didn't sing to Macel and she didn't sing to me. We just stood there and said "I do" while almost a thousand of our friends sat or stood looking on with mixed emotion. They all had suspected that one day we would be married. They were glad and relieved that finally we were doing it. After all those years of waiting, the wedding itself seemed rather anticlimactic. Of course the plot that followed turned the wedding night into a nightmare for me; and though now I can look back and laugh heartily, their "dirty trick" went a long way toward helping Macel and my friends get even for all the tricks that I had played on them during the preceding years.

There was a reception following the wedding, and while I changed my clothes for our honeymoon getaway, friends of Macel from the church and from the First National Bank where she worked invited her to go on a "quick ride around town." Thinking it was all part of the evening's festivities and (as she admitted, to my shock and surprise, in an interview years later) because she "wasn't anxious to get away" and "just wanted to delay it as long as possible," she went joy riding with her friends without even telling me good-bye.

Actually, our mutual friends thought they were kidnapping Macel to get even with me. But she was more than willing to assist them in the process of getting even. And I have to admit that most of my friends, inside and outside the church, had good reasons to want revenge.

Before I tell all about our wedding night, I have a confession to make that may help you understand and forgive my friends for the dirty trick they played that evening. With all this talk about Christian faith and the deeper spiritual life, I also have a rather shallow human side. How else can I say it? I love a good practical joke. I confess it. The rumors are true. I savor a successful prank like some people savor old wine. And, as I have been reminded for these past thirty years by the woman I love, by every one of my friends, and by most of my acquaintances, sometimes my pranks border on the very thin edge of propriety.

I suppose I can blame my father's genes for these occasional undeniable urges to act in ways one might call undignified (to be kind) or just plain crude and reckless (to be more accurate). He was a prankster, too. And even my complete commitment to the Christian faith has not greatly affected the prankster side of me.

Since my earliest childhood days I could not take life too seriously, at least not for long periods of time. In my junior high and senior high school days, locking a math teacher in her closet at test time, nailing a coach's britches to a bulletin board, placing a live rat in the cookie box of a fastidious young lady professor, or getting even with the cafeteria for their menu of burned liver, creamed tuna on toast, and boiled squash seemed to be appropriate, even ennobling acts. And though the teachers, the coaches, and the administration didn't agree, from time to time I just couldn't control the urge to follow through on an appropriate if tasteless prank. Now, although I am an adult, a parent, a pastor, and an advocate of the deeper spiritual life, from time to time I still can't control that urge.

And though Macel and my other friends may have suffered from those occasional youthful pranks, they got even with me on my wedding night. "For what?" you might ask. That would be telling. But out of fairness to them for the ugly, treacherous, rotten, nasty prank they played on me that night, it is only fair to confess a few innocent, clever, winsome pranks I played on them earlier in our life together.

Without naming names (my victims know who they are and that I love them), each of my friends, family, and coworkers knows how much I enjoy an occasional cherry bomb (for the sudden, unexpected noise it makes) or an "Apple Blossom Perfume" stink bomb (for the sudden, unexpected odor that leaves people gasping, giggling, and looking desperately about the room). Over the years I have bought and used these harmless but effective devices outside the church, on pastoral calls, in businesses owned by my faithful friends and church members, and even about and around my own home and family.

On one occasion I "borrowed" a donkey from a friend's backyard, tied it alongside a busy street, posted a "Free Donkey" sign on the cute little animal's side, and listed the telephone number of a young businessman in church, whose phone didn't stop ringing for twenty-four hours, with each caller asking the same strange question: "I'll be glad to take the donkey off your hands. When can I come and get it?"

On another occasion I remember jumping into a friend's car when he wasn't looking, rising up from the rear seat, placing my finger in his back, and demanding that he drive toward the river. When he groaned appropriately that I shouldn't hurt him and begged me to let him go because he was his dear mother's only source of income, I spoke normally, gave him a friendly hug, and rode with him while he drove in circles around the parking lot muttering threats and promising to get even, until he finally calmed down and joined me in my laughter.

On a third occasion, when I was still in Lynchburg College, I saw our favorite village drunk sleeping beside the road and lifted him into my car to take him home as I had done so many times before. Only that evening I saw the open car of a friend parked nearby and moved the soundly sleeping drunk into my friend's back seat and drove away. Apparently, when my friend was halfway home, the drunk awakened and thought he was being kidnapped.

Of course Macel still remembers the three-foot alligator I put in her bathtub early one morning just before she walked into the darkened room, started the water in the tub, flipped on the lights, and screamed bloody murder at the creature smiling up at her. Our neighbors later told us they heard Macel's screams clearly in their closed houses blocks away.

I have to admit that Macel is better than most at getting even. Just before we were married and before she had her driver's license I convinced her that it would do no harm for her to drive to a drive-in restaurant a few blocks away. But even as she pulled away, I phoned a policeman who was a member of Thomas Road Baptist Church. He picked me up in his squad car and I ducked down low in the back seat while he raced after my sweetheart, his police sirens blaring. When she pulled to the curb, he approached in mock anger threatening to arrest her.

I still don't know exactly how she did it, but through her rearview mirror Macel spotted me hunched down in the back seat of the patrol car. She talked kindly to the policeman and totally reversed the prank's effects. Thinking she had been thoroughly frightened and embarrassed by the event, I got out of the police car to take her in my arms and kiss her anger away. At that very moment she and the policeman both roared away laughing at the top of their lungs leaving me by the side of the street to walk home.

I paid for all my past pranks on that long, frantic, exhausting wedding night. In fact, there isn't much to tell. I searched until 3 A.M. for my missing bride. Finally I went to my sister Virginia's home. She was a justice of the peace at that time and called the police to help me find Macel. They found her about four in the morning and returned her to me. We packed the car. About 5:30 A.M. we jumped in to begin our honeymoon at last. But when I turned the key nothing happened. Opening the hood, I found the spark plugs missing, the wires crossed, and enough other temporary damage done to my engine by our friends that leaving home was out of the question.

Now before you judge this country boy and all his crazy, wonderful friends, remember that none of these pranks bring real harm and they all make memories. So let our critics go on believing that Baptists have no fun. The truth is really quite different. In Christ our sins-and even our occasional pranks-are forgiven. We are free to enjoy God and the world He has created. And we are free to enjoy one another's love and friendship. My pranks are just another way for me to say "I love you." But don't tell that to the people on whom I play them. It could get sticky, and we "uptight" "hard-shelled" Baptists couldn't stand that.

When finally the sun rose, the damage had been repaired and we were on our way to Niagara Falls, as was the plan. Suddenly Macel put her beautiful head on my shoulder and said,

"Where are we going?"

"To Niagara Falls," I answered, "just like you planned."

"Well, you know," Macel drawled slowly, "I've never been to Miami. I think I'd like to go to Miami."

So without another word I turned the car around and drove south to Florida on the beginning of our wonderful, ever new, always exciting, spontaneous, and almost totally unpredictable life together.

Upon our return to Lynchburg, Macel and I set up housekeeping temporarily in a little cabin on Timberlake, loaned to us by my cousin Cliff Bell, while our first apartment at 2100 Carrington Road was being painted and furnished by our landlord. We paid $62.50 a month rental on that first apartment between 1958 and 1960. I was making $65 a week at the church. Macel was making about the same from her job at the First National Bank. We have never since felt quite so prosperous.

The days were filled. I drove my small Renault toward the radio station and then on to my office on Thomas Road. Macel drove the 1955 Buick toward downtown Lynchburg and the First National Bank, where she worked as a teller and loan officer. I maintained the early morning radio broadcasts, the hundred house calls a day, the weekly television program, and the various other preaching and pastoring tasks. The church continued to grow, and our volunteers continued to build, hoping to keep up with the new people finding Christ, being baptized, and becoming members of Thomas Road Baptist Church.

From the original building, we built on in all directions. Volunteer carpenters, plumbers, electricians, and general handy persons pounded, sawed, bolted, installed, swept, and painted into the night. First we extended the building fifty feet in length, and then we added another thirty-eight and one half feet toward Thomas Road. That was our "bowling alley" period. Then we started down Thomas Road with a sixty-foot-wide attached building that was two stories high. Then we attached the two buildings, removed the wall between them, and the sanctuary grew to sixty feet in width and eighty feet in length. Eight hundred people could crowd together into the rows of pews that we had finally anchored safely into place. My pulpit was upstairs down the hill, and the floor was tilted slightly. Like Topsy, the place "just growed."

It looked like Macel and I would be in Lynchburg for a long time. I began to dream about starting a family. Macel wasn't in a hurry to have children, but we both agreed that with or without them the little apartment on Carrington Road would never do. Every day I drove past a new subdivision in a pleasant suburb of Lynchburg called Vista Acres. The lots were selling for $2,000. Several good friends from the church already had homes in Vista Acres, and they encouraged us to get a lot and build a home of our own.

Finally, after the owner of Vista Acres, Mr. E. R. English, gave us a 10 percent discount on a lot on Grove Road, we took the plunge. Macel and I sat down with Macel's dad, sketched out a little ranch style house, and Mr. Pate agreed to build it for us. The 2,000-square-foot structure with the $1,800 lot would cost us $12,500. We took out a 5 percent loan, made a commitment to monthly payments, and at the end of almost every working day drove over to Grove Road to watch our first home taking shape. I can still remember walking with my new bride through the framed trenches ready to receive the concrete for the foundations, helping Sam raise the wall studs, and even climbing up the ladder to "supervise" the laying of our shingle roof.

Christmas day, December 25, 1961, the entire Falwell-Pate clan gathered in our one-year-old home on Grove Road for our fourth annual holiday dinner and gift exchange. After resisting our courtship and our marriage for almost four years, Lucile Pate, my mother-in-law, had become my primary fan and backer. During the summer and fall of 1960, Mom Pate had superintended the final stages of her husband's work on our beautiful little house, and in October of 1960 she had guided our move from the Carrington Road apartment to Grove Road. We then spent a wonderful year in our brand-new home.

That Christmas day, 1961 Mrs. Pate fluttered about our home welcoming each new guest and supervising her three daughters, Jean, Mary Ann, and Macel, as they cooked and served the turkey, ham, roast chicken, mounds of salads, cooked vegetables, and an assortment of desserts. Sam Jr. was home from college in Tennessee, and my mother had arrived from our home on Rustburg Road carrying a huge bowl of her special banana pudding, my favorite dessert.

All the Pate children except my wife were still unmarried, and because Macel was still resisting my urge to begin a family, the average age around the Christmas tree that year was far too old for Lucile Pate.

"Maybe next year," Lucile stage-whispered so that everyone in the living room, especially Macel, could hear her.

She looked at me consolingly and shrugged. They all knew what I wanted for Christmas. When Macel had asked me for my gift list, a baby boy was the only item on it.

"Maybe next year," Lucile repeated as she stood to signal the end of the family's Christmas celebration.

The traditional feast had been consumed. The dishes were washed and put away. The carols had been sung. The Christmas story had been read. The floor was kneedeep in torn gift wrapping paper and bright colored ribbons. People were edging for the door when Macel stood up and ordered quiet.

"Just a moment," she said loudly. "I have something else to give Jerry."

Everybody stopped in their tracks. Macel took me by the hand and paraded me through the crowd into our little bedroom. After she had closed the door, she sat beside me on the bed, took my hands in her hands, and said, "Merry Christmas, Jerry."

I looked at her blankly. She just sat there staring at me with a mischievous look in her eyes. There was no gift in sight. And after a quick look around the room I found no gift hidden under the bed, in the closet, or in the bathroom.

"You'll never find it there," she said softly. "He's in here," she said, placing my hands on her abdomen. "We're going to have a baby."

Believe it or not, I thought that she was kidding me. Her eyes have a kind of sparkle when she's getting even with me for a prank I've played. And that day her eyes were sparkling like diamonds. Still, I just couldn't wrap my mind around the news.

"It isn't true," I said, shaking my head and frowning at her.

"It is true," she answered. "I've been pregnant for three months, but I wanted to surprise you at Christmas."

"Prove it," I demanded, unable to believe that she had been pregnant all those weeks without telling me.

"Prove it?" she answered looking rather irate. Then she shook her head, reached into her bureau, and pulled out a stack of pamphlets the doctor had given her on staying healthy during pregnancy.

"You could get those at a bookstore," I said, glancing through them, unable to believe her still.

For a moment her eyes quit sparkling and began to flash. Then she smiled, shrugged her shoulders, and walked good naturedly into the bathroom. In three seconds she was back carrying a doctor prescribed bottle of pills "to assist in controlling nausea during pregnancy." Her name was written clearly on the bottle.

"It's true?" I said, feeling a rock-sized lump beginning to form in my throat.

"Of course it's true, you big dummy," Macel replied.

I took her in my arms and began to cry. "Can I tell them?" I asked her, pulling her toward the bedroom door.

"No," she said, shaking her head. "I think I want you to wait awhile."

"Please," I begged her, knowing that her secret wasn't safe with me for ten long seconds.

"They won't believe you," she said.

"Please, Macel."

For a moment she resisted. Then she smiled, hugged me tightly, and led me back into the living room. The whole family sat or stood exactly as we had left them. They stared silently at us.

"Well, what did she give you?" Sam Jr. asked, breaking the silence. I walked directly to the sofa where Mom and Dad Pate were sitting. "There's no maybe about next year, Mom," I said. "You are going to be grandparents. We're going to have a baby."

Lucile began to cry. Sam looked at her awkwardly, then back up at me. "Are you fooling us, boy?" he said.

"He isn't fooling, Daddy," Macel said, sitting down beside

him. "I'm going to have a baby."

Suddenly the room exploded into cheers and laughter. Then I began to cry again. I couldn't stop the tears, and my crying seemed contagious. Before long everybody was crying. Lucile jumped up and hugged me. In seconds everybody was hugging and crying and talking at the same time.

"Praise the Lord," Mom Pate said over and over again. "Jerry got his present."

Finally we settled down again into our places around the Christmas tree. Only this time we were holding hands, laughing, crying, and thanking God for our first child, who was to be born in just six short months.

The only time I succeeded in goading Macel to extravagance was in February of 1962 when we were shopping for maternity clothes. She was five months pregnant before she agreed to buy clothing that would fit her.

"But I will only use them for such a short time," she protested.

She tried on five or six different dresses that day and looked wonderful in each of them. "Which should I buy?" she asked.

"All of them," I answered. And when she tried to protest, I reminded her that this baby would not be the last.

The clerk ducked into the back room. Macel stared at me for one long moment. At first she hadn't wanted this baby. Now I was announcing that there would be more. Finally she smiled and without another word of protest bought all the dresses.

As Macel got bigger I got more anxious about the baby's birth. One evening at about eleven I announced to Macel that we were going to have a practice run to the hospital so that when the time for delivery actually came we would be prepared.

"A practice run?" Macel said.

"Call your mom and tell her we are on our way," I said.

Macel awakened her mom and told her that the baby was on its way.

"Are you sure," Mom Pate asked sleepily.

"I am sure," Macel answered.

We drove to the Pates' home. Mom charged out the door and down the sidewalk talking excitedly.

"But we were just joking, Mom," I said realizing the practice run had gone far enough.

Mom was furious. Already, just a week earlier, I had called her at her office at General Electric pretending to be a nurse from the maternity ward at Baptist Hospital. I disguised my voice and said, "Mrs. Pate, you have a little grandchild."

She gasped and then began to cry with joy. I could hear her telling all her friends at the office that she was a grandma. Finally she came back on the phone and I had to confess that I wasn't a nurse, that I was her son-in-law. That time, too, when I explained my little prank, she seemed less than happy with my "strange sense of humor" and told me so in no uncertain terms.

Then at two on Sunday morning, June 17, 1962, Macel began her labor contractions and we prepared to rush her to the hospital. I had her bag packed and ready by the door. We were well rehearsed and only paused long enough to call Mom Pate to meet us.

"Oh no you don't," she said when we awakened her. "I'm not going to fall for that trick a third time."

It took me nearly five minutes to convince Mrs. Pate that this time it was for real.

Macel continued labor throughout the early morning and most of Sunday. I stayed with her except for the time necessary to preach the 11 A.M. sermon and rush back to her bedside. Every time she had a little pain, I cried. She consoled me and held my hand through the whole experience. I thought I'd never make it. When it came time for the Sunday evening service, Macel and the doctor agreed that there was plenty of time for me to preach the sermon and return before the baby was born.

I asked a volunteer to sit by my phone in the church office throughout the service. As the service progressed I could see the volunteer staring first at the silent phone and then back up through the office window at me. The phone remained silent during the singing of the Gospel songs, during the pastoral prayer, and during the evening offering. I preached with one eye on the congregation and the other eye on that telephone.

Nothing happened until the sermon ended. Then, during the middle of my final prayer, the phone finally rang. Quickly the volunteer answered it and then began to gesture at me wildly. I ended the prayer, bolted for the door, and drove to the Virginia Baptist Hospital, breaking all of Lynchburg's automobile speed records for time and distance.

I skidded through the hospital corridors and ran directly to Macel's room. Her bed was empty. I raced back down the hall to the delivery room just as our baby was being born. I was the first nonmedical person to see my hazel-eyed, pink-cheeked baby boy. They didn't know who shed the most tears that night, the baby or his excited, grateful father.

Jerry Falwell Jr. was born on Father's Day, June 17, 1962, at 9:13 P.M. Macel had surprised me with her Christmas announcement less than six months before, but I determined that she would never do it again, and I told her so in no uncertain terms. Two years later on Father's Day 1964 Macel surprised me again.

The morning began uneventfully enough. My wife and two-year-old son had painted a little Father's Day card for me. I was sitting in the kitchen drinking coffee when Jerry Jr. toddled up to my chair and handed me their creation. It was a birth announcement:

"Dad," it began, "I am going to have a baby sister. Her name will be Jean Ann Falwell, and she's going to weigh exactly seven pounds."

I read and reread the card. Finally I looked at Macel grinning at me from across the kitchen. "What does this mean?" I said, reading the words one more time.

"I'm going to have a baby sister," two-year-old Jerry Jr. interrupted, climbing up into my lap and putting his arms around my neck.

"And," Macel explained softly, "her name combines the names of my older sister Laura Jean Pate and my second sister Mary Ann Pate. Isn't that clever?"

I stood up and walked to Macel's side. She was sipping her coffee and looking like she had just won another major victory in the prank department.

"Is this true?" I asked.

"Of course it's true," she answered. "I never joke about having babies, do I?"

I picked up Jerry Jr. in my arms and together we chased Macel around the kitchen. On Sam Pate's sixty-fourth birthday, November 7, 1964, Jean Ann was born. She weighed seven pounds, thirteen ounces. Macel had missed being exactly right by just thirteen ounces.

And believe it or not, I fell for her trick yet a third time. Our last child, Jonathan, was born September 7, 1966, exactly six months after Macel had surprised me once again.

Macel helped shape me and my ministry during those first years in the pastorate. Immediately after our marriage she went through my rather small wardrobe and tossed most of it into the garbage. I was shocked when she told me that she thought my clothes were "old, stained, misfitting, and thoroughly tacky" (a view quickly affirmed by everyone who knew me in those days). After junking my favorite shirts and ties, she herded me to a clothing store to buy a suit that fit, shirts that weren't frayed around the collars, and ties that matched the rest of my attire. People didn't recognize me for the next few days.

From the beginning Macel also took charge of our checkbook. I never figured a balance. I often overdrew. And invariably if there was money in the bank I gave it away. The bank loved Macel. After our marriage, the bank never again had overdraws on my account.

Macel likes order. When she washes the dishes, even when I'm helping, she washes all the plates first, then the cups, and then the glasses. She doesn't even mix them in the sink. She wanted a boy, then a girl, then another boy, and so she had them exactly as she ordered. She knew when and what she wanted, and each time somehow she managed to arrange it. The number seven has always been a kind of special number to Macel. And when she "ordered" birthdays, the children were born on the seventeenth, the seventh, and again on the seventh. I am spontaneous. There is nothing predictable about me except my unpredictability. But Macel is a person of order, and her sense of order and timing has been her lifelong gift to me.

In fact it was Macel whose sense of order and timing helped me learn to preach. From the beginning she was my best critic. She listened to my sermons with a tiny notebook in her hand.

She wrote down the words I mispronounced and taught me to pronounce them correctly. When I was dull and propositional, she taught me to speak in pictures. When I was long, she told me to tighten up. When I was unclear, she helped me use examples that clarified the point that I was making. And when I spoke in a monotone, she explained how I could bring variety and excitement to my speech.

In those early days I listened to sermons by Dr. B. R. Lakin, Dr. W. E. Dowell, and Charles E. Fuller, but my best improvements came when Macel listened to me. Macel is a bright and talented woman; but she didn't go to college after her high school graduation. In those days Southern families didn't see any reason for the daughter to go on to college let alone to graduate school. Out of Macel's senior class, a small percent of the girls went on to college or university classes. Macel went to work for the First National Bank and worked there until 1962, when Jerry Jr. was born.

I picked her up from work every day at 4 P.M. Macel worked with the lending officers who made small commercial loans. Often she worked with clients fifteen or twenty minutes after closing time, so I spent the extra minutes visiting with officers of the bank: Robert Morrissett, the bank president, and Gorham Walker, the vice president. One afternoon while I was waiting for Macel, I walked over to Mr. Walker's desk and greeted him.

"Mr. Walker," I began without thinking, "we are getting ready to build a new church out on Thomas Road. We have an architect working on the plans and a building committee working to raise the money."

"How much will it all cost, Jerry," Mr. Walker said, looking up from his stack of loan applications.

"The contractor guesses about $195,000" I replied, wondering how or where we could ever get such a huge mortgage loan.

"We'll loan it to you," Mr. Walker said casually.

I hadn't even dared to think about getting the loan from the First National Bank. And I certainly hadn't meant to ask about a loan that moment. Yet already, without security, the bank's vice president had promised me the money. I couldn't believe it. Macel couldn't believe it. We drove straight to Meek's Delicatessen to celebrate. I had four hot dogs with all the trimmings while Macel under mock protest consumed a giant chocolate nut sundae.

The First National Bank took a risk on our little church, and to this day, thirty-five years later, Macel and I still have our personal checking and savings accounts at First National (now named Crestar Bank), a token of our gratitude for the trust they showed in us and in the Thomas Road Baptist Church.

During the first years at Thomas Road Baptist Church, I was busy from early morning until late at night. Before I married and had children, I often worked fourteen and fifteen hour days. I enjoyed the tasks and didn't mind the early morning to late night schedule. But when the children were born, I tried to arrange to be home for evening meals and to have devotions with the children almost every night.

We read a story from the Bible. We talked about the story and its meaning for our lives. Then we knelt beside the children's beds or sat around the fireplace and prayed. We invited the children to pray their own simple prayers from the time they could utter their first words. Conversation with God became as natural for them as conversation with their family or their friends.

After evening devotions I would go to the children's bedrooms, tuck them in, and give them a good night kiss. Almost every night I spent at least a few minutes with each child alone. Sometimes those moments were special. Secrets were confessed. Fears were shared. Failures and successes were confided. Other times the moments were rather ordinary, with a quick "Good night, Dad" from a tired child lying on his pillow yawning up at me.

All our children gave their hearts to Christ at home. They heard sin and salvation explained in my sermons at church, in their Sunday School and Lynchburg Christian Academy classes, and in our evening devotions. From a very young age they comprehended the difference between the daily sins we all commit (a lie to cover a bad grade, a dollar stolen from Mom's dresser, or a hurtful word to a neighbor's child) and our basic sinful nature.

From Genesis they understood how human nature had been corrupted through the disobedience and fall of the first man, Adam. From the Gospels they learned that Christ, "the last Adam," came to reconcile fallen creation with the Father. It doesn't take long for a child to understand that his or her own disobedience of a parent or a teacher illustrates a disobedient and fallen nature. And it isn't too complicated for a child to understand why seeking God's forgiveness is even more important than saying "I'm sorry" to a parent or a friend. One by one, just as soon as they understood it for themselves, our children prayed the sinner's prayer to seek God's forgiveness and to accept Christ's death, burial, and resurrection as His atonement on their behalf.

Those intimate evening times with my children began to decrease as my commitment to evangelism and to political action required regular trips to distant locations across the country. During my busiest years as president of the Moral Majority I was traveling between 250,000 and 400,000 miles a year. It didn't take long to realize that in my desire to help save America's families I could not neglect my own. I decided early on that no spiritual or political task was important enough to destroy my own family. But I also learned that creating and maintaining a healthy family life is not an excuse to stay at home or to avoid spiritual or political responsibilities.

The ministry purchased an airplane so that I could get home by bedtime as often as possible to avoid missing those important evenings at home. But on those trips when I had to stay in a hotel or motel room overnight, our family used the telephone to keep in touch.

The moment I arrived in a distant city, I would call Macel and leave my hotel room number. Macel would post it in the kitchen, and the children would call me whenever they had the urge. And in the early evenings I spent time talking on the telephone with each child before he or she went to sleep. Often, when a meeting kept me away from my room until late, I would call Macel to say good night, and as she answered I could hear the little clicks of all three extensions being lifted. Three sleepy children had been waiting up to say, "Good night, Daddy. Call you in the morning."

During their elementary years, it was not uncommon for me to see our children during school days even more than Macel saw them. My office was just above their classrooms at Lynchburg Christian Academy. Jerry Jr. and Jeannie entered kindergarten almost without a ripple, but Jonathan made waves from the beginning.

In the morning after breakfast I loaded all three kids into our car and drove them to school. Jerry Jr. and Jeannie would run off happily to be with their friends, but Jonathan insisted on staying with his daddy. I took him firmly by the hand, led him to his classroom, and deposited him with his teacher. I was afraid to look back as I walked toward my office for fear of seeing my little son staring at me with the tears already forming in his eyes. Not long after the first bell rang, I would hear my youngest son sobbing in the hallway.

"Pastor Falwell," his teacher would say, "Jonathan seems pretty upset. He says he wants to be with you in your office and not with me in the classroom."

Then she would close my office door and leave me with my red-haired son with his big blue eyes blinking back the tears and his tear-stained freckled face. He loved being with me in my office at Thomas Road Baptist Church, but it took until the fourth grade to teach Jonathan that he had a few other grades to attend before he could join me in pastoring that great church. Meanwhile, on those days when Jonathan simply could not be persuaded to rejoin his classmates, Macel found herself actually sitting in the classroom with our determined little child.

About the fifth grade, Jonathan's sensitivity began to show itself in more acceptable ways. He was always borrowing money to help classmates buy their school pictures or get a special treat. On his eleventh birthday, Grandpa Pate gave Jonathan a fifty-dollar bill. Jonathan carried that bill folded carefully in his wallet like a treasure. One Saturday afternoon I preached at the funeral of the mother of one of Jonathan's classmates. His father had died the year before of cancer. His mother had been killed in an automobile accident. The tragedy was awesome. At the end of the funeral, Jonathan ran down the hill toward his grieving friend. We saw the two young boys standing near the hearse whispering. Jonathan reached into his wallet, pulled out his treasure, and placed it discreetly into his classmate's hand. Then he turned and ran back toward us. Funny how easy it is to forget the stubborn, belligerent tears of a freckle-faced son when he grows into a sensitive, caring young man.

Jeannie developed her own wonderful sense of independence early in her life. While she was in the fourth grade, one of her classmates asked Jeannie what it felt like to be Jerry Falwell's daughter.

"He's just my daddy," she responded, thinking the question to be quite absurd.

"But he's so special," the child continued.

"He's not as special as Keyto Cooper's dad," Jeannie answered. "He owns McDonald's." The two girls quickly agreed and ran off toward the playground together.

Since she was in the first or second grade, Jeannie showed a natural gift for reaching out to people. She invited a new girl in her third grade class to a party at our second home located on Chesterfield Road. Jeannie didn't know it, but the girl's father was an ex-felon who was trying to find a job during his probation. The little girl was very poor and had come to Lynchburg Christian Academy on a scholarship. She had developed a mean, independent spirit to survive the teasing she had faced in her former school, and she arrived at our home prepared to fight.

Jeannie wrapped her heart around that little girl and spent almost the entire party in her company. We watched our daughter ignoring old friends to help her new friend feel safe and accepted.

Jerry Jr. also showed his independent spirit from his earliest childhood years. When I began to travel regularly back and forth across the country, I often took one of the children with me on the plane. Jerry especially liked to travel and one day convinced Macel that he could make the journey alone from Lynchburg, Virginia, to Minneapolis, Minnesota, to surprise me on my forty-first birthday.

"Don't tell Daddy," he made Macel promise as she put him

on the little commuter plane to Roanoke which connected to the flight to Chicago en route to Minneapolis.

And though her twelve-year-old son had assured her that "he knew the way" and would have no trouble getting there, Macel worried that whole day and waited by the telephone until late at night with growing apprehension.

"Hi, Mom," Jerry's voice echoed across the long-distance connection. "I'm in Chicago."

Jerry's flight was to have landed in Minneapolis hours earlier, but the Minnesota flight had equipment difficulties and had been postponed until morning. It was midnight. Our son was stuck in Chicago's O'Hare terminal, the busiest airport in the world. Macel was terrified. She just knew that our son would be mugged, murdered, or molested before morning.

"Don't worry, Mom," Jerry Jr. calmly said. "I'm checking into a hotel and will call you in the morning."

Macel finally got Jerry to admit that there was a woman from the church on that same flight. She, too, was going to a hotel, but when Macel insisted that Jerry Jr. stay with their mutual acquaintance, he would have none of it.

"I don't want to stay with some lady," he argued. "I'll be fine alone."

I loved the sense of independence and self-worth the children developed early on, but even during the busiest years I tried to maintain a full, rich, loving life together with my family. Sometimes, they traveled with me. Or we spoke together in person or on the telephone every single day. We never missed a family birthday or holiday celebration. We vacationed together regularly. And we refused to let anything or anyone get between us.

One Monday morning I was going over my schedule for the week and realized that a secretary had booked me to give the keynote address at a large convention on Jerry Jr.'s birthday. It was a mistake. No one had noticed it until it was too late to get out of the speaking engagement easily. Immediately I called my son to tell him the problem.

"We have made a big mistake, son," I confessed. "But we have a family commitment never to miss sharing a birthday celebration. Here are your alternatives. I will give you the $1,000 honorarium that I would receive for the convention address and spend the next day with you, or I will cancel the booking and spend your birthday as we had planned."

One thousand dollars would be quite a birthday gift, I reasoned, especially to a young boy who was already saving for college. But without a moment's hesitation Jerry Jr. said, "I'd rather have our day together, Dad. Cancel your speech."

I cancelled it without a further word. It was embarrassing. It caused those convention officials a great deal of grief and confusion. I apologized to everyone but spent the day with my son. No matter what dream consumes us, our relationship to God and to our family must come first.

Looking back upon those busy, stressful days when our children were young and impressionable, I realize that another of the reasons they grew up healthy, half-sane, and wonderfully independent was due to the blessings of our extended family, the Pates and the Falwells. Special credit has to go to Macel's sisters Jean and Mary Ann.

Jean is four years older than Macel. She became the matriarch of our little clan upon her mother's death in 1973. She took charge of our Sunday feasts and still works hard in the kitchen to prepare and serve them. Jean is tighter than the bark on a tree; yet when there is a real need, she is generous to a fault. It was her older sister whom Macel called when our Jeannie rode her tricycle off the porch and broke her arm.

"Did you call the doctor," Jean responded quietly to Macel's tearful news.

"No," Macel answered frantically.

"Well, I'll call him," she replied, "and then I'll meet you and Jeannie at his office."

Jean has been a strong, quiet calm in the midst of our busy world these almost thirty years. And her sister Mary Ann has been there at her side every day of those years, ministering faithfully to our family. Mary Ann is more like her mother, Lucile. Unlike Jean, who likes to save, Mary Ann believes that if you can buy it on good enough terms (whatever it is), you ought to buy it. Mary Ann is generous and bighearted. She and her sister have mothered Macel and me and our children and their little brother Sam and his wife Carole, their children Kathy and Ken, and Ken's wife Debbie and their daughter Katherine, aged two, the first grandchild in our extended family.

During the crisis times in my life, my family has meant everything to me. Any helpful or courageous action I might have taken was only possible because they were there to support me, to love me, to forgive me, and to keep me on the path. Through my years of childhood and early ministry my mother was a primary guide and stay. However, because of health problems and old age, she grew more reclusive as the years passed.

Fortunately, our little family was supported by the love and almost daily presence of the members of our wider family, the Pates. In 1973, the same year that the S.E.C. mounted their charges against Thomas Road Baptist Church, Macel and I and our three young children moved from the house that Grandpa Pate built on Grove Road to a new home on Chesterfield Road. With eleven-year-old Jerry Jr., nine-year-old Jeannie, and seven-year-old Jonathan, we needed the two extra bedrooms and the large family room that our new house offered.

From the first year of our marriage Lucile Pate had established a Sunday dinner after church for our wider family. My sisters-in-law Jean and Mary Ann, who had not married, worked with their mother to put on a Sunday spread that was lavish, tasty, and prepared with love. Sam Jr. had graduated from Tennessee Temple University and joined us with his wife Carole, their son Ken, and their daughter Kathy.

No matter how busy the week had been, we knew that on Sunday we would gather around that table, thank God for His blessings, and eat heartily together. When I married Macel, I gained a family that loved and cared for me and for my children throughout those difficult years. We never needed a baby sitter. Lucile, Jean, and Mary Ann were part of the family and cooked and cleaned, counseled and consoled us and our kids at every stage of our life together.

At every holiday there would be a celebration with all the trimmings. On New Year's Eve there would be a feast for all the family, songs, best wishes, and slides or home movie shows

documenting the year in pictures. On Valentine's Day no child
or adult went without hearts, flowers, and original poetry, most
of it corny if not downright illiterate but all of it rhymed with
love. In the summers we spent vacations at Myrtle Beach or at
resorts along the river. Sometimes I would fly or drive back into
Lynchburg for special meetings or to assist in overcoming a
crisis, but always the wider family would flow together, filling
temporarily the place I had left and widen again upon my return
to include me in the play and feasting. No one's birthday was
forgotten, ever. There were parties, gifts, and surprises for everyone through all those years. And Christmas came complete
with tree, decorations, several feasts, and a pillow-stuffed Santa
bearing gifts.

My mother still lived in our old family house on Rustburg
Road. We knew that she was praying for us every step of the
way. My twin brother Gene, his wife Jo Ann, and his son Carey
Lee lived upstairs in our old home-place to care for Mom. My
brother used his mechanical gifts to improve and maintain the
house and farm that held so much of our family heritage. My
children, Jerry, Jeannie, and Jonathan, loved to visit Grandma,
Gene, and Gene's family on the Falwell farm to play beneath
the apple trees, walk across the railroad trestle, eat Grandma's
special baked apples, roll down the grassy hills, and wade and
fish in the creek where Gene and I once had our minnow trap.
At the first snowfall, we would take the children to the farm to
slide down the hillsides or go sleigh riding behind a team of
horses. During our most pressured times I liked to drive over
to the farm and walk through the fields with Gene or stand alone
on the crest of the hill and look out across the foothills to the
distant Blue Ridge Mountains.

My brother Lewis had built a beautiful brick home near
Silver Spring Lake. Our children loved to visit Uncle Lewis's
place. There were diving platforms, paddle boats, dirtbike and
minibike riding, fishing, and hiking trails. And cousins Calvin
and Lawrence Falwell and Edna Falwell Twiddy were more like
brothers and sister to me during those times. Their families
own a company which manufactures truck bodies, a well-drilling business, a large general aviation charter company called

Falwell Aviation, and other enterprises. Often they flew me on pastoral calls during times of emergency from the Falwell airport (located on the old Falwell property where the Old Fort Inn once stood) in a Falwell plane to communities around the state of Virginia. And our children loved to visit the airport that bore their name and take off on that short roller coaster runway that left their stomachs churning and their eyes bulging with surprise.

My sister Virginia Falwell Jennings, her husband Lawrence, and daughter Laura stood by me and my family during those months and years of rapid growth in our ministry in Lynchburg. Virginia served as my television secretary for those early years. She kept old television files, mailing materials, and sample premiums we gave away stored in her basement and garage, until her death in 1988.

Mom continued to pray for us every day. She attended Sunday morning services at Thomas Road. She always wore her dark hat with a veil and a long dark dress with its hemline well below her knees. She smiled and nodded at the growing number of people who recognized her and stopped to say hello, but she seldom spoke and never addressed a public gathering or a woman's group. Mom always sent her weekly tithes and offerings through the mails if she didn't feel well enough to attend the morning service. Faithfully she watched the evening television broadcast and listened to our daily program on the radio.

We drove the children for regular visits to Mom's Rustburg home. She was a lovely lady up until the end. She stood tall, slender, and erect when I was a young man, but as she aged she added extra weight and her shoulders began to stoop. She never cut her hair, but wore it in a tight bun at the back of her head as she had always worn it. And at night when she let her hair down it reached below her waist. She was sweet to the children on our visits. She couldn't really bustle around the kitchen as she once had. But she still put on her apron the moment we phoned, and by the time we had arrived the kitchen was warm and fragrant with the smell of banana pudding or hoecakes and melted cheese.

Mom was an avid reader and read every word of the daily papers, the news magazines, and the publications and periodicals we produced at Thomas Road Baptist Church. Unfortunately Mom's eyes began to wear out early in her life. By the time our children visited her, she had to use a thick magnifying glass to see the report cards or the sample artwork that they brought her. Often when we arrived on a surprise visit, the children would find their grandmother sitting at the kitchen table reading her Bible slowly and carefully with that thick magnifying glass.

Mom lived to see each of her children find the Lord. Virginia was led to Christ in 1956 by an evangelist who preached one of my first revivals at Thomas Road Baptist Church. The Reverend Carl Woodbury just dropped by Virginia's home to say hello. But while he was there, he shared the plan of salvation and prayed the sinner's prayer with my sister. Virginia accepted Christ that day and never doubted after that.

My brother Lewis was sitting on a tractor in the middle of a half-mowed field of grass when another of our visiting guest speakers walked up to him, introduced himself, and shared the Gospel with force and clarity. Lewis hadn't been interested in religion until that day in the late 1960's. when J. Harold Smith broke past my brother's defenses and introduced him to Jesus. Lewis didn't make public his decision for Christ until later in a Bob Harrington evangelistic crusade at Thomas Road Baptist Church, but his life was changed from that moment he sought forgiveness while sitting in the middle of a half-mowed field. And his devoted wife Margaret and two children, L. T. and Michelle, are all committed Christians.

My twin brother Gene has always been a loving, sensitive, quiet friend. Unlike my sudden discovery of the faith, Gene's spiritual pilgrimage has been steady but gradual. Gene and I had talked about the Lord for decades. Then in the 1970's, in a conversation with one of my associate pastors, Charlie Harbin, Gene seemed to really break through into a new dimension of faith. Later Gene shared with me that if there had been any questions about the faith before that day, during that conversation and prayer with Charlie Harbin they were settled forever.

Mom had lived to see the fulfillment of her dreams for each of her children. And she had watched with growing wonder at the work God was performing at Thomas Road Baptist Church. She had witnessed firsthand the congregation's amazing growth. She had attended the dedication of each new building and the opening Sunday worship service in each new sanctuary. She prayed daily for our special ministries, including Elim Home and Treasure Island, and for the educational work of the Lynchburg Christian Academy and of Lynchburg Baptist College. On January 21, 1977, Mom cried when she heard that 2,500 students and the faculty of our growing college met in the freezing snow on Candler's Mountain in a "miracle rally" to pray that one day a great Christian university would stand upon that place.

In 1973 Mom had encouraged my growing interest in taking political stands against the evils that threatened the nation and the world. She trusted me and accepted this rather radical change with good humor and understanding. She watched the television coverage of our bicentennial "I Love America" rallies in 1976; and as the media began to cover me and my ministry with growing regularity, Mom clipped articles from the papers and watched the evening news with gratitude to God for His loving, patient work in my life.

Television and radio reporters, newsmen, newswomen, and just plain folks from around the country began to call my mom to ask her about me. She would talk to almost anyone on the telephone and answer written questions with long personal replies. Needless to say, those who called in hopes of stirring up trouble never heard a word from my mother that they could even twist, misquote, or use out of context against me.

Almost overnight I was receiving hundreds of invitations weekly to speak or to be interviewed all across the country. Sam Pate, my father-in-law, and most of the other members of our wider family traveled with me at least occasionally within the United States, to England, and even to the Middle East, but my mom always declined. She didn't like to be in the spotlight. When I received my honorary doctorate of divinity from Tennessee Temple University in Chattanooga, Mom finally accepted our invitation to come along. She met the press in triumph. She smiled and waved at the photographers and blushed deeply when the audience applauded after I introduced her from the platform.

At Thomas Road Baptist Church I would mention Mom and have the cameras find her in the congregation. She would smile and wave politely in her little hat and long black dress. And even when she had lost her hearing almost entirely, she would nod in agreement with announcements or sermons and pretend to be hearing everything, when actually she was hearing almost nothing.

Late in October 1976 my Mom was entertaining Jo Ann Falwell, Laura Jennings Wallace (my sister Virginia's daughter), and her husband Joe Wallace in our family home on Rustburg Road. Mom was eighty-one and though she had a touch of angina and took an occasional dose of nitro when her heart beat irregularly, she seemed in extraordinarily good health. That evening as Mom stood talking to her guests she leaned back against an unlatched door. Before Jo Ann could catch her, Mom fell backwards into the kitchen, hitting her head on a table as she fell. My brother Gene was called and returned home immediately. He drove Mom to the Lynchburg General Hospital to see how seriously she had been injured by her fall.

Except for a lump on her head and a bad bruise on her wrist, she seemed no worse off after falling. Several months passed. Mom seemed to be healing nicely. Then on Sunday night, February 20, 1977, Gene found her slumped unconscious in her chair. She had just heard me preach the Sunday evening sermon on radio live from Thomas Road Church. Without any kind of warning, Mom had suffered a massive cerebral hemorrhage. Gene called the ambulance and then called me. I was just leaving the church and raced home to Rustburg Road. I arrived as the attendants were placing Mom in the back of an ambulance.

I jumped in beside my mother. She was still unconscious. The attendants hadn't noticed that her arm had slipped out of the stretcher. As the ambulance lurched forward, her right arm was pinned tightly between the stretcher and the vehicle's steel wall. With all my strength, I forced the stretcher away from the wall and freed Mom's arm. Then I cradled her arm in my hands for the rest of that long, painful ride.

For several weeks she lay in a coma in the hospital. And though she didn't seem to hear us, we often talked to her and prayed with her into the late-night hours. Her brain had suffered massive damage. We moved her to the Medical Care Center, where days later her heart failed. On April 28, 1977, my mother died at age eighty-two.

Her funeral filled the new sanctuary of Thomas Road Baptist Church with members and friends who knew and loved my mom and with students from Liberty Baptist College who knew how much I loved her. The music was triumphant. My faithful friend and mentor Dr. B. R. Lakin preached the funeral sermon. Macel and I sat in the front rows with Jerry Jr., Jeannie, and Jonathan. My brothers Gene and Lewis and their families sat with us. Our sister Virginia was too ill to attend the service. I felt sad when I noticed her empty seat in the front row, for Virginia had spent more time with Mom than any of us boys. We would all miss Mom. Not for one instant were we ashamed or embarrassed for the tears we shed that day.

Mom was not active in my life during her later years, but the moment she was gone I missed her. She had been positive and uncritical about every decision I had made. She had encouraged my move toward political action. Quietly she had supported each feeble step I took in that direction. I am sorry she died just months before the real action began. She would have loved to see what happened in those productive and amazing years immediately following her death.

We Baptists don't really believe in "sacraments" as do our Catholic, Orthodox, Anglican, Lutheran, and Reformed friends. For example, the ancient idea that communion actually bestows God's grace upon us is outside our Biblical understanding. To us, taking the bread and wine (most of us use grape juice) is a memorial of Christ's death. He is not literally present in the elements. And eating the bread and drinking the juice does not guarantee His grace in our lives. And though we may disagree with our friends about the meaning of the sacraments, we are convinced that God is present through our faith in each of them. If we sincerely seek God's presence in those acts, He is present as He promised.

Marriage is no exception. No Baptist would ever speak of the sacrament of marriage; and yet from the first moment I met Macel Pate, I experienced something new of God's love through our relationship. He was there working in and through her to bless my life from the beginning.

Baptists do believe that God has definite ideas about whom a Christian should marry. The Bible has one clear warning about marriage: "Be ye not unequally yoked together with unbelievers," commands the Apostle Paul in 2 Corinthians 6:14. From my earliest days as a Christian I was taught that we should only consider marrying someone who is also a believer. For that person's sake (as well as for our own) marrying an unbeliever often leads to great misunderstanding, friction, separation, and divorce.

But I could see that Macel and I shared the same commitment to Christ and to His church. So I opened my heart to her and to God's guidance for our relationship. We had common values and common goals for marriage and family. We talked for hours about the future. We prayed together. We studied the Bible together. And when we were married, we asked God to live at the center of our life together.

When our children were conceived, we prayed for them daily while they were still struggling for life inside Macel's womb. And we prayed for them at their birth and every day since they were born. We read the Scriptures and prayed together as a family. We attended church regularly. We worked and witnessed as a family in our church programs. We spent time with other Christian families. We went on retreats, camps, and workshops to enhance our Christian family life.

And in the process, God has also blessed us through His presence and in the lives of our children. No one, not even our Catholic friends, speaks of the sacrament of children; yet through our children we have often felt the love and comfort of God. So when people speak of marriage as a "sacrament," I may not agree that marriage is an automatic source of God's grace in our lives. But I know that God has blessed and transformed me through His presence in our marriage and in our family.

Late in the 1960's, when I was still traveling 50,000 miles a year in my Buick to hold preachers' meetings or evangelistic crusades in churches around the country, my son Jerry Jr. would often accompany me. And though he didn't mind missing school and was plenty bright enough to make up the work he had missed, that first little Cessna 310 that was given the church by a businessman named Gene Dixon made it even easier for Jerry Jr. to come along.

I can still remember my seven-year-old son standing in the front yards or lobbies of those churches selling our books and records to the people who wanted to know more about the Thomas Road Church and the work that God was doing there. One Sunday evening after the service I was surrounded by pastors who had questions to ask of me. I completely forgot my son working alone at the book table. When I finally remembered him, I hurried to the back of the rather large church where we were visiting and found him surrounded by a crowd of people buying everything we had to sell. I still had the key to our little cash box; so Jerry Jr. was stuffing the sales money into his pockets, down his shirt, and even sticking it into his socks.

"You need my daddy's book," he was shouting to the smiling crowd. "You need my daddy's records."

I had recorded a sermon on "How to Double Your Church Attendance in Just One Year." I had books describing the early stages of our ministry. At the big churches or preachers' meetings, with my help Jerry Jr. could easily sell several hundreds of dollars' worth of merchandise to pay our travel expenses. But that night on his own he had sold $2,500 worth of books and records, and he greeted me with a smile that lit up the space.

On that same speaking trip to California I played basketball with the youth group of a local church. It was a rough and tumble game. In a scramble for the ball I got shoved accidentally into the backboard post. I thought a rib cracked but finished the game and continued to other speaking assignments in Riverside and San Diego. The pain in my side did not go away. I began to find it more and more difficult to breathe without wincing. I knew I should see a doctor but had no time to stop.

Finally one night in San Diego, Jerry Jr. and I went to bed in our host's master bedroom. I confessed to my seven-year-old son that the cracked rib was really hurting me. I jabbered on about being afraid to sleep on the side where the rib felt cracked. I wondered aloud if it might break loose and puncture my lung.

"That rib is killing me," I complained to my small son just before going off to sleep.

Every thirty minutes after that, Jerry Jr. shook me gently and whispered, "Dad? Are you all right?"

Each time I assured him that I was fine, but thirty minutes later he would shake me again and ask hesitatingly, "Are you okay, Dad?"

Finally I realized that my son was staying awake all night to keep me from rolling over on that cracked rib and suffering a fatal injury. Just before dawn I found him still wide awake, leaning down over me, his eyes wide open, about to whisper one more time, "Dad, are you okay?"

He took my fears literally. He was afraid that I would die if he didn't stand guard. His all-night vigil became a parable of God's grace in my life. And when someone speaks to me of the sacrament of marriage and of family, I nod and smile and understand fully what they mean. God has used my immediate and extended family to bless and guide me from the beginning. Through their lives, I have received the gift of God's grace to me and I am grateful.

A Christian leader's spiritual
authority is established in direct
proportion to the spiritual success
of his or her immediate family.

— Jerry Falwell

No one ever achieved greatness
without experiencing opposition.
— Jerry Falwell

CHAPTER ELEVEN

The Years of Change

W e didn't dream on Christmas day that our first child would
be born into a world torn by racial conflict, riots, and
assassinations. I was born and raised in the South. My perspective on the separation of the races had been deeply ingrained in
me from my days of childhood. Lynchburg was a segregated
city, no better or no worse than any other segregated city in the
South. We had black neighborhoods with black schools, black
stores, and black churches. Restaurants, buses, parks, drinking fountains, even the city jails had special sections "for whites
only." I grew up in a strictly segregationist environment and
with a few vivid exceptions never really thought about the inhu-
manity or the injustice of the system. In Lynchburg I was isolated from the major urban population centers. I grew up where
segregation was assumed by almost everyone, black and white
alike. Nobody that I knew even suggested to me that there might
be a different, better way.

And though the races were officially separated, I had plenty
of black friends and acquaintances. Although the system was in
place to keep us apart, from my earliest years I loved and was

301

loved by black friends, neighbors, and employees of my family. A large percentage of my playmates and friends from childhood were black. David Brown, a black man, had been my nanny and in many ways had been closer to me during my growing-up years than had my own father. I had eaten and played in the homes of the black families employed by my dad. We attended different schools and churches in the morning; we rode in opposite ends of the buses, shopped in different stores, ate in different restaurants, and drank from different fountains during the daytime; but in the evenings and on Saturday and Sunday afternoons my black friends and I wrestled in the fields, stole apples and watermelon, hid in the tall grass, ate our plunder in the shade of the old oak trees, swam naked in the fishing hole, and shared our dreams and fantasies beneath the starry Virginia sky.

We knew nothing of riots, marches, or Supreme Court decisions in those early years. The issue only first began to dawn on me when I was still a student at Baptist Bible College in Springfield, Missouri. On May 17, 1954, in Brown v. Board of Education of Topeka the Supreme Court declared that the "separate but equal" tradition in our Southern states did not offer equal protection under the laws providing public education. I was twenty years old and had only been a Christian two years when the high court decided unanimously that desegregation in public schools should be accomplished with "all deliberate speed."

Six months later the civil rights era began in earnest when Mrs. Rosa Parks refused to yield her seat to a white man in the front of a Montgomery, Alabama, bus. On looking back, her act of disobedience seems courageous, appropriate, and long overdue. But in those days the incident and the controversy it stirred up across America seemed silly and overblown. We Southerners didn't think that things were so bad. But we were wrong. Few of us realized how black people had suffered. We had closed our eyes or driven around their suffering for decades. When Rosa Parks refused to budge, she launched a second American revolution; but I was too young and too excited about my newfound Christian faith to realize that one day the revolution would come to my door and change my life and ministry forever.

My own conscience slept on uneasily during the first months and years of the civil rights movement. I graduated from Baptist Bible College. I helped begin Thomas Road Baptist Church, and I courted and married Macel Pate. I still had black friends. Black people could attend our church from the beginning, although they would not think to join and we would not think to ask them.

In those early years my Southern friends, even my Southern Christian friends, did not feel the injustice of segregation or wrestle with the irony that the white Christian church had been a keystone in its destructive and dehumanizing system. And though each of us continued our commitment to the separate but equal principle basic to the notion of Southern segregation, we were beginning to feel uneasy and unsure about our stand.

Each of us at one time or the other had seen the daily indignities and the occasional terrible suffering that black people endured. And though we often defended the individual and rushed to help him during those awful moments of personal tragedy, we seldom if ever stood up against the system that created that suffering. I remember seeing it firsthand in my senior year in high school.

On a Monday afternoon in May I jumped off the school bus and walked up Rustburg Road to our family home. Lump Jones, a young black man who had worked for my family as a mechanic, drove up in my little English Austin convertible.

I dumped my books on the front porch and walked down to the driveway. The convertible had been stalling and dying in traffic. Lump had repaired it. When I asked him how it was running, he answered, "Mr. Jerry, runnin' like a charm."

I remember answering, "Well, get back in, Lump, and we'll charm it for sure."

It was one of those days when you think the rules were made for other people. I wasn't watching the speedometer. I wasn't paying close attention to the twisting road ahead. I accelerated carelessly into a narrow curve just before Candler's country store. We must have been traveling at seventy-five miles an hour around the corner when a young boy on a bicycle crossed the road ahead of me. I swerved to miss the bike, and when I swerved back the little Austin convertible left the ground and went nose over tail. It felt like we rolled over a dozen times. Glass was shattering. The car was disintegrating into large sharp fragments that spilled across the roadway. Lump and I were both thrown out as the car tumbled. The Candlers came running at the sound of the crash and found us lying beside each other bleeding profusely in the tall grass.

Mr. Duval Candler lifted us into his own car and drove us to the hospital in Lynchburg. Mrs. Lila Candler mobilized several black families who lived near her property to clean up all signs of the accident. Every broken piece of glass, every crunched-up bit of metal was carried from the highway and hidden in a junk pile at the back of the Candler property. When the police finally arrived, there was no sign of an accident. Everything had been hidden safely away.

The Candlers were friends of my family. They were acting out of country kindness, trying to protect one of their own. They had no idea how well-timed their act of kindness turned out to be on that eventful week.

I was sixteen years old. My father was dead. And when the police arrived to question me, I was still too much in shock to speak to them. My older brother Lewis was called and drove immediately to the emergency room where I was being treated. Lewis was questioned by the police. He also covered for my carelessness.

Lewis lied on my behalf. He told the police that I had been driving a jeep on the back road of our property. I could hear him covering for me as I lay on the emergency-room table where the doctors were removing glass from my arms and legs, patching up the cuts and abrasions, and bandaging the open wounds. "The jeep must have flipped over," Lewis told the police. "That's what injured him."

Once again I had been protected by a friend. And though I escaped the legal consequences of my careless act, I could not escape the physical and emotional consequences that followed for me and even more for my black friend Lump Jones. We were both torn up and bleeding when we were delivered to the emergency room. Our clothes had been shredded by the gravel. Our shoes had been torn away. Even finger and toe nails had been pulled back as we were thrown from the car and dragged and rolled along the highway.

Perhaps it was because I was white and a Falwell that the doctors and nurses went to work on me first. They were stitching the larger cuts and bandaging the other cuts to stop the bleeding. Nobody even seemed to notice Lump lying there on a table near me. He was black. It appeared that he didn't matter. And I was too much in shock to notice what was happening, let alone to come to his aid. I do remember hearing Lump ask for a mirror. As he lay untreated in the hospital emergency room, my friend wanted to see how badly he had been cut in the face.

It was then that I heard a hospital employee shout at my friend Lump, "Shut up, nigger. You're not going to Hollywood."

I will never forget that moment. I was given the best emergency treatment because I was white; while my friend Lump was left bleeding, unattended in the emergency room because he was black. Finally my brother Lewis noticed what was happening. He guaranteed that Lump's hospital bills would be paid and requested that they treat him immediately. Lump survived that terrible wreck and, thanks to Lewis, soon mended and returned to work.

Gene and I grew up surrounded by racial discrimination, but the day I wrecked my little English convertible and injured myself and my young black friend Lump Jones was a particularly painful experience. This time I had caused the suffering by my own carelessness. And four days later when the principal announced that I would not deliver the valedictorian address at my high school graduation, it was another consequence of my own intemperate acts.

Three weeks later I sat with my fellow students at the Brookville High School graduation exercises. The salutatorian gave the honors address in my place. Thirty years later, in June 1980, I would finally speak at a graduation exercise for Brookville High School. The baccalaureate service was conducted in the nearby Beulah Baptist Church sanctuary. The assistant principal, William E. Wright, explained why I had missed my first chance. The students applauded as I stood to confess how much I had learned about "acts and their consequences" in the intervening years.

Like Lump Jones, David Brown's skin color almost cost him his life. David lived in a small but comfortable room at the back of our home on Rustburg Road. He had worked beside my mother for most of his adult life. He was not married. He had no family. Every morning of our childhood David Brown was there to help my mother care for my brother Gene and me in any way he could. When we were children, he bathed and fed us. As we grew older, he helped Mother maintain the house and the grounds. He was like any other member of our family. I don't remember Mr. Brown missing a day of work in his decades with us.

Then one morning Mr. Brown did not appear at the kitchen door. Mom did not worry at first that he was not present to help cook the breakfast or do the chores. But after breakfast she checked his room to be sure he wasn't ill, then began to search for him around the property. After school that day Gene and I drove up and down the neighborhood trying to help my mother find her faithful employee and our longtime family friend.

Two days later we finally found him unconscious in the lobby of the emergency room of the old General Hospital at the end of Federal Street. He had been carried into the room three nights before badly beaten and bleeding. He had no identification. The hospital personnel on duty had placed him on an emergency bed and left him almost entirely untreated in the hallway.

My brother Lewis discovered him there and called Mother. Together we rushed to be at David Brown's bedside. One portion of his head and face had been crushed from a severe blow with a dull pipe or the barrel of a pistol. He had suffered cuts and bruises about his body and was barely alive. When we arrived at the emergency room, Lewis was talking to the nurses on duty, demanding that they treat our friend. But Dave Brown was black. It was 1949. Serious civil rights legislation was still almost a decade away.

I stood beside Dave Brown holding his hand, watching him struggle for life while the staff explained why they hadn't treated him. He had no papers. They didn't know if he could pay the bill. They had no idea how or why he had been injured. In fact, the reasons they used to explain their inhuman neglect were just excuses to cover the racial discrimination common in those years of my childhood and adolescence. However, these hospital personnel, like myself, were really unwitting servants of a sick system.

Two weeks later Dave Brown finally regained consciousness. His wounds were treated. His skull was repaired, but our friend was never quite the same again. He returned to work, but his body and brain had been permanently damaged by the thugs who robbed him, beat him, and left him for dead. He was still the same gentle person that we had known since childhood, but his speech was slurred. His responses were slow and often inappropriate. He tried hard to recover but could not. Finally he bade us a tearful good-bye and moved to live with relatives in Stamford, Connecticut.

Dave Brown died just last year. Recently my son Jerry Jr. discovered old home movies of Mr. Brown playing with my brother and me when we were just six or seven years old. I loved that man then and I love him now. I called him in his home in Connecticut just before he died. We shared our memories of those growing-up years when he acted as our second father. I wished him well and said good-bye. Just a few months later Mr. Brown died.

Lump Jones is still very much alive and living with his wife in Lynchburg. Lump has grown children of his own. He worked as a bulldozer operator for my brother Lewis until Lewis died in 1981. He still operates heavy equipment in the Lynchburg area. When I pass him at a construction site, we wave and smile and remember.

I am sorry that I did not take a stand on behalf of the civil rights of David Brown, Lump Jones, and my other black friends and acquaintances during those early years. And it

is no excuse to say that during the first years of the civil rights
movement I was busy building a church, starting a home, and
preparing for our first child. But I must admit that in all those
years it didn't cross my mind that segregation and its consequences for the human family were evil. I was blind to that reality. I didn't realize it then, but if the church had done its job
from the beginning of this nation's history, there would have
been no need for the civil rights movement.

Throughout church history, individual Christians have
risked their lives, their fortunes, and their sacred honor to
stand against social injustice of every kind. In England and in
America, Christians were at the heart of the abolitionist and
suffrage movements.

In 1823 William Wilberforce, an evangelical Christian, established the first society to abolish slavery in England. And
though that nation's emancipation act was not signed until 1833,
history credits this committed Christian as a major central force
in the overthrow of slavery in England. Wilberforce was also
an important example to the abolitionists in America, who would
eventually end the slave trade and the practices of slavery here.

To understand how preaching and prayer have helped the
people of this nation to make major moral and ethical changes
is to go back to the first great spiritual awakening in America.
In the early 1700's, before the Constitutional Convention, even
before the Declaration of Independence, Jonathan Edwards,
George Whitefield, and the Wesley family were preaching in
churches, tents, and open fields across the colonies. Their call
to repentance and to Christian love led to the founding of this
free nation.

Less than a hundred years later the president of Yale University, Timothy Dwight, began a new call to repentance in
America. The preaching of his students, Congregationalist
preacher Lyman Beecher and Yale theologian Nathaniel W.
Taylor, moved the revival further. But with the inspired preaching of Charles G. Finney, the second great awakening flourished across the newly developing land. And the American abolitionist movement was one result of Finney's preaching and of
that same great spiritual awakening in America.

In 1852, Harriet Beecher Stowe, the daughter of Lyman Beecher, published her first novel, Uncle Tom's Cabin. Abraham Lincoln said that no book influenced the antislavery movement or led more directly to his emancipation proclamation than did Harriet Beecher Stowe's novel. That book grew directly out of her Christian concern for slave and slave-holder alike.

Harriet Beecher Stowe's friend Theodore Weld was converted to Christ by Charles G. Finney. Finney hated slavery and passed on to his young Bible student an intense and Biblically based commitment to the truth that "all men are created equal, that they are endowed by their Creator with certain unalienable rights, that among these are life, liberty and the pursuit of happiness."

No man in American history did more to bring down slavery than the evangelical Christian Theodore Weld. And though Ben Franklin and a handful of Pennsylvania Quakers had formed the first antislavery society on these shores on April 14, 1775, by 1835 there were still just a few hundred antislavery societies organized across the country. Under Weld's inspired leadership, by 1840, the American Anti-Slavery Society grew to include 1,650 chapters with 170,000 members. In one year this group, staffed primarily by Congregationalists, Methodists, Presbyterians, and Baptists, worked within Christian congregations to present antislavery petitions to Congress signed by more than 400,000 Americans.

From the second great awakening in America the modern missions movement was born. And with the Gospel went hospitals, schools, clinics, moral reform, and spiritual rebirth into all the world. The American Bible and tract societies were a direct result of the revival growing in America. Even women's suffrage came directly out of the ministry of Theodore Welds Lucretia Mott, and other women born and raised in Bible-believing homes and committed to the equality of all people everywhere.

There is not an ounce of support for segregation in the Scriptures and yet isolated verses had been used with me to defend the separation of the races and to maintain the status quo. And though I read and reread those Scriptures with growing concern, I didn't see my error in time to take a stand. I regret that now.

But even then God was patiently working to change me and to help me grow. In spite of my imperfections, He was blessing Thomas Road Baptist Church and expanding our ministry. I spent my time during the 1960's doing what every pastor is called to do. The church and her ministries grew nonstop during those years. In 1962 Jim Soward joined our staff to help us expand our Sunday School ministry. Before long other capable and experienced pastors and laymen and women came on board: Jim Moon, R. C. Worley, Paul Tan, Ed Martin, Claude Carter, Robert Williams, Barbara Treadway, J. O. Grooms, Jeanette Hogan, and Jim Vineyard were just a few of the gifted and dedicated people who joined us. Without their help, the Thomas Road Baptist Church could not have continued to grow and prosper.

In 1963 we purchased Treasure Island in the middle of the James River and built a camp to serve the spiritual and recreational needs of the boys and girls of Lynchburg and the surrounding counties. On Thomas Road we built the Spurgeon and the Brainerd buildings to expand our educational capacity, and in 1964 our new 1,000-seat auditorium was opened at last.

On Easter Sunday we met to worship for the first time in our new sanctuary on Thomas Road with its great colonial pillars and graceful white arches. No sooner had we begun meeting in the quiet beauty of that place than suddenly we found ourselves embroiled in the controversy that was dividing the nation.

The civil rights issue had been boiling in the South and across the nation for almost a decade by 1964. In 1954, with Brown v. Board of Education of Topeka, segregated public schools had been outlawed. In 1956, after a long and successful bus boycott led by Dr. Martin Luther King, the Rosa Parks case was settled when the Supreme Court struck down Alabama's laws requiring segregated buses.

In 1957 in Little Rock, Arkansas, Governor Orval Faubus called out the state militia to prevent integration of that city's schools. In 1958 Faubus closed all the schools of Arkansas to avoid integration in that state. In 1959 his act was declared unconstitutional and hundreds of angry Southerners assembled near Central High School in Little Rock to protest its integration.

Marches, sit-downs, pray-ins, boycotts, freedom rides, strikes, demonstrations, beatings, lynchings, and assassinations followed quickly throughout the Southern states and around the country. In their efforts to control the violence, police and fire departments were supported by state militias and the National Guard. City, state, and national courts, mayors, governors, congressmen, senators, and our President struggled unsuccessfully to bring order to the growing chaos.

In 1960 a Civil Rights Commission appointed by President Eisenhower announced that in the past three years, 436 Americans in twenty-three states had filed complaints concerning denial of voting rights. Later President Kennedy signed a Civil Rights Act creating referees to promote and supervise voter registration.

In 1962, during the Cuban missile crisis, there was a momentary lull in the battle over civil rights when the Cold War with the Soviet Union nearly boiled over into World War III. But in 1963 the civil rights controversy reignited. Thousands of people marched on Washington, D.C., and listened to Dr. King deliver his famous "I have a dream" speech from the steps of the Lincoln Monument. On November 22, 1963, President Kennedy was assassinated, and black and white together paused to mourn this terrible, tragic act.

In June 1964, 250,000 people marched on Washington again to lobby Congress on behalf of a civil rights bill, and in July President Johnson signed the Civil Rights Act outlawing discrimination in all public facilities. That same month three young civil rights activists were murdered during a black voter registration drive.

In March of 1964, after hundreds of clergy and lay leaders marched on Selma, Alabama, I delivered my own public response to the civil rights crisis in a sermon entitled "Ministers and Marches."

Quoting Philippians 3:20, I reminded more than a thousand

of our members that the Christian's citizenship is in heaven. "Our only purpose on this earth," I claimed, "is to know Christ and to make Him known." I went on to explain that "believing the Bible as I do, I would find it impossible to stop preaching the pure saving Gospel of Jesus Christ and begin doing anything else-including the fighting of communism, or participating in civil rights reforms."

"Preachers are not called to be politicians," I declared, "but to be soul winners.... If as much effort could be put into winning people to Jesus Christ across the land as is being exerted in the present civil rights movement, America would be turned upside down for God.... I feel that we need to get off the streets and back into the pulpits and into the prayer rooms."

One week after my appeal to end the marches, President Johnson asked Baptist leaders and Baptist clergy to join the battle for civil rights. He appealed directly to Christians in the South to get behind the passage of the new civil rights legislation. In an interview with the Lynchburg News, I said the bill had been misnamed.

"It is a terrible violation of human and private property rights," I claimed. "It should be considered civil wrongs rather than civil rights." And to a local newspaper reporter I added, "I've spoken against this bill in the pulpit and I will continue to do so."

After excerpts from my sermon were published and my comments against the pending civil rights legislation were broadcast across the nation, I was branded a "racist," a "Ku Klux Klan sympathizer," a "segregationist," and "a teacher of injustice, dissension, and distrust." It wasn't true.

I was just thirty-one years of age. I was born and raised in the deep South. I had grown up in a segregated society. I had been a Christian for less than a dozen years, and though my study of the Scriptures had left me with a growing restlessness with the traditional Southern position, I felt bullied and unjustly attacked by the army of white Northerners marching into the South, demanding that we follow their dictates in the running of our community and in the ordering of our lives. I was angry that suddenly the Supreme Court, the Congress, and the President had assumed rights once granted to the states, and I protested loudly the arrogant, disruptive, and often violent wave of demonstrators arriving daily in the South. I was determined to maintain the right to decide for ourselves how we would live together, black and white.

Looking back, I realize that I was speaking to one point while civil rights leaders were speaking to another. They knew that this nation could not move effectively into our future built on inequality and injustice. We knew that the solution could not be forced by one section of the nation upon another. We were shouting across each other's heads. One day the distance between us would be bridged, but in those times of conflict and confrontation nobody was listening to the other. We wouldn't admit the injustice, and they couldn't admit our right to solve the problems on our own.

Four months later, in July 1964, the Thomas Road Baptist Church was singled out for a demonstration by young white members of the Congress on Racial Equality. CORE teenagers from northern Virginia had come to Lynchburg to "stir things up a bit." And of course they chose Thomas Road Baptist Church as an appropriate place to start.

Their "kneel-in" was planned for Sunday morning, July 19, 1964. They did not come to church to worship. They came to create a media event. I instructed our ushers to watch the demonstrators carefully but to leave them alone unless they interfered directly with our worship. I encouraged our members to ignore them altogether. Early in the morning the press began to gather. At 11:15 A.M., three white teenagers from CORE and a young black friend arrived carrying a sign that read DOES GOD DISCRIMINATE?

While we sang our hymns and prayed inside the sanctuary of Thomas Road Baptist Church, the four young demonstrators milled about the front steps talking to the press and generally creating a disturbance. I asked our head usher, Walter R. Carey Sr., to invite the teenagers in to worship with us. By the time the young men agreed to enter, the service was well under way. The main floor was packed with worshippers; so the demonstrators were shown to seats in the balcony.

First they accepted the seats. Then suddenly they refused to sit down and worship quietly. Protesting, they walked out of the sanctuary creating more disturbance. Our people tried hard not to notice. I interjected into my sermon that "Christians must harbor nothing but love for all men. However," I added, "at the same time, it is a Christian's solemn duty to stand uncompromisingly against evil in any form, without fear of the consequences." Looking back upon that day almost a third of a century ago, I realize that I was speaking to both sides that day.

After interrupting the service, the demonstrators returned to our front steps. They began another "pray-in," but when an usher asked if he could pray with them, they refused. Of course, our men and women are trained to witness. One member of the church thought this was as good an opportunity as any. He asked the four young men if they were Christians.

"No," one of them answered angrily, "and I don't want to be one either."

When the boys told local police that they planned to return again on the following Sunday to create further trouble, warrants were issued for their arrest. At their hearing in Lynchburg's municipal juvenile and domestic relations court, I assured the boys and their parents that we would be willing to forget the whole thing.

"It is not the church's business," I told them, "to go around putting people in jail."

The charges were dropped and the boys released into their parents' custody.

At their hearing, Judge Wingo asked them if they had gone to Thomas Road Baptist Church to worship.

"Yes, your honor," they answered.

"Then why didn't you stay in your seats after entering the church?" he asked.

"Because," one replied, "we didn't feel that it was morally right to worship on a segregated basis."

After the hearing, I joked about the boys, saying that there was nothing wrong with the young demonstrators that a good haircut wouldn't cure. Now I wish I had taken another approach entirely. We resented those teenage boys for their interference in the lives of our community; but looking back, they were courageous, and it is time that I for one admit it.

Earlier in the week those same three teenagers with two black friends had tried to integrate Dude's Drive-in restaurant, a popular teen hangout in nearby Altavista, Virginia. Marc Gripman, one of the CORE demonstrators, just sixteen years of age, was manhandled, punched, and knocked to the street by angry white boys blocking the doorway to the restaurant. Gripman struck his head on the pavement when he fell; and as he lay on the pavement, another angry white man drove his car toward the injured fallen boy. People screamed. Brakes squealed. The car roared away, missing Marc by inches.

Whether one agreed or disagreed with Marc's purpose or his tactics, it is time to admit and applaud his courage. In fact, it is time to admit the fact that Marc and his friends were raising important questions that I and my congregation had not answered. On the surface their angry charges were incorrect. The doors of Thomas Road Baptist Church were open to men and women of every color, race, or creed from the very first day we worshipped together. But those boys could see by just looking around our packed sanctuary that black Christians were few and far between. In Lynchburg's black Baptist churches there was an equal absence of white faces.

It wasn't the law that separated us. It was years of tradition and social conditioning on both sides. That separation was wrong, and the boys were right to point it out to us. I wish there had been another way for them to get our attention. I wish even more that we who love Christ and are committed to His church had healed our own divisions before the world noticed and condemned them.

But believe me, it wasn't the Congress or the courts that changed my heart. Those demonstrators, in spite of their courage, didn't move me to new compassion on behalf of my black brothers and sisters. The new laws and the loud protest marchers may have helped to enforce the change and to speed it up, but it was God's still small voice in my heart that was the real instrument of change and growth for me.

In my adolescent and young adult years I don't remember

hearing one person speak of the injustice of segregation. I have searched my childhood, adolescent, and young adult memories for one champion in the church or classroom who provoked my thoughts in these matters. To the contrary, all my role models, including powerful church leaders, supported segregation.

And because I had black friends from childhood, because I worked and played with my black neighbors, and because my family and I had always come to the aid of our black friends or employees who were in need, I never once considered myself a racist. Yet, looking back, I have to admit that I was one. But at my conversion, God began to work His change in me. Unfortunately I was not quick enough or Christian enough or insightful enough to realize my condition until those days of tumult in the 60's.

Now, upon looking back, I can see that from the earliest days of my new faith in Christ, God had tried to get me to understand and to acknowledge my own racial sinfulness. In Bible College, the Scriptures had been perfectly clear about the equality of all men and women, about loving all people equally, about fighting injustice, and about obeying God and standing against the immoral and dehumanizing traditions of man.

Black converts from African nations had spoken at Baptist Bible College on behalf of their needy people, and many of my fellow students were surrendering their lives to mission work on their behalf; yet there were millions of black people in America, and we heard nothing about reaching them. That confused me from the beginning.

In 1963 I was invited to preach in mission churches in Jamaica, the Dominican Republic, Haiti, and Puerto Rico. I lived in the homes of those dear Christian brothers and sisters in the Caribbean. We prayed, worked, and worshipped together. On one occasion, I was invited to speak through an interpreter skilled in sign language to a large group of deaf children in a mission orphanage in the Dominican Republic.

Before I spoke, the British-trained black pastor took me aside and advised me politely. "Reverend Falwell." he said, "in your talk with the children, please don't make any reference to black or white."

He was kind and gracious and I quickly agreed. When the talk was over and we were eating lunch in the mission dining room, I asked the pastor to explain why he had carefully instructed me not to speak of black or white. He was silent for a moment, as though he had heard the question before. Then he smiled and tried to explain.

"Almost every white American pastor," he began, "stands up before our deaf children and tells them how impressed he is with their school. Then he goes on to say something like 'I am white and you are black, yet I feel such a kinship between us.' I try to communicate his comments to the children through my hands. They are not aware of any color difference. In the Dominican Republic we are a whole range of colors from light to very dark. We work on similarities here, but you Americans come and point out the difference. I get tired of trying to explain your problem to our children."

I felt his words like a boxer feels a hard punch in the stomach. If those deaf children didn't know that there was a difference, perhaps there really was no difference at all. Little by little God was getting through to me. But years of conditioning don't just disappear overnight.

Then one Saturday morning in 1963 I sat in the end chair of Lee Bacas's shoe-shine business on Main Street in Lynchburg. It was my Saturday morning ritual to have Lewis, an elderly black man, shine my shoes exactly at 10 A.M. He could set his watch by my appearance in his chair.

"I heard your sermon on television last week, Reverend," Lewis said as he began dusting a week of dirt off my shoes. "I sure do like the way you preach."

"Why thank you, Lewis," I replied, looking closely at the thin, muscular man in his middle sixties whose curly gray hair framed his shiny, smiling face. "How are you and the Lord getting on?" I asked him, knowing already the answer.

"So good," he replied, grinning up at me. "The Lord is so good, isn't he?"

Every week Lewis shared his faith with me. And every week I left his chair feeling his ministry in my life. Then on that particular Saturday morning Lewis asked a question that he had never asked before.

"Say, Reverend," he began softly, so that no one else could hear, "when am I going to be able to join that church of yours over on Thomas Road?"

Once again I felt like a boxer who had been punched directly in the stomach. For the first time in years I was speechless. We had a growing number of black families who had heard me preach on television or radio who stopped by to visit Thomas Road on occasion, but never once had one of them asked the question that Lewis had just asked me.

"I don't want to cause you no trouble, Reverend," the old man said as he finished polishing my shoes and helped me down from the chair, "but I sure do like the way you preach and would like one day to join there with you."

I puzzled over the question that next week and in the months that followed. I had no good reason that Lewis could not join my church. He was kind enough not to ask me for an explanation, because he knew there was none. I had excuses, but I had no reasons. And every Saturday morning I had to sit there in my embarrassed silence grateful that he did not ask again.

Finally I realized that every question has an answer, even if we don't like it. I knew that it would not be easy to stand against generations of tradition. I knew, too, that whatever we did would cost us. Early in the 1960's, a musical group from Tennessee Temple University visited Thomas Road Baptist Church. The soloist with that group was a bright, attractive international student from Indonesia who was majoring in music. The moment Paul Tan began to sing, he captured the hearts of our people. When he finished his master's program at Depauw University in Greencastle, Indiana, we invited him to come to Lynchburg to serve full-time on our musical staff.

Paul served Thomas Road Baptist Church throughout those years of racial conflict and became a deep personal friend of mine. I knew the risk we were taking in inviting a dark-skinned man to serve on our church staff. And we learned a little about the cost of doing right when several of our church families quit the church in protest. Other lessons would soon follow.

Almost immediately we learned again the price of standing against segregation when in 1963 we purchased YMCA Island in the James River, one of the family recreational centers for all of Lynchburg. This picturesque natural island near the heart of the city had a footbridge from the Lynchburg side, around the turn of the century. But in 1929 an old automobile bridge had been somehow moved from downtown Lynchburg and re-erected to connect Lynchburg with the island.

On the Fourth of July, the whole city of Lynchburg poured across the bridge for a day-long picnic and patriotic celebration, with athletic events from baseball games to horseshoe competitions and three-legged races. Lynchburg's first little airstrip had been built on the island, and in the early 1900's the YMCA had built a beautiful center to administer their summer camp and city recreational programs there.

In 1963 I heard that YMCA Island was for sale. I borrowed a little boat and rowed around the Island. With every stroke I felt more and more convinced that God wanted us to buy the island and to use it in the ministry of Thomas Road Church. In the years that followed, thousands of children and young people were led to Christ in summer camps and special events on our Treasure Island. Through the island camping program literally thousands more experienced growth and development in their own Christian faith. There are ministers, missionaries, and lay leaders working across the world whose lives were changed on Treasure Island.

Because Treasure Island served the entire community, black children were welcome there. Then late one summer I got a phone call requesting that I come immediately to the home of one of our church families who had given considerable funds to the Treasure Island ministry.

"We rode down to the camp on the island yesterday, Reverend Falwell," the woman began after the necessary tea and small talk, "and we thought we saw some black campers down there, three or four of them? Did you know that there were black children on our island?"

I nodded. She and her husband looked aghast.

"Well," she said, her face beginning to redden slightly, "is that a temporary thing or was there some court order or state law that made you do it?"

"No, ma'am," I answered. "It isn't temporary and nobody made me do it."

Looking shocked and horrified, my two primary backers gave me an ultimatum. I smiled and tried to explain, but then refused to even consider ending our ministry to all the children of Lynchburg. Immediately they cut off all funding to Treasure Island and removed their membership from the church.

I am a practical man. I needed their support for that expensive free ministry to children. But almost immediately it was clear to me that their act had been a blessing. I also needed to get prepared for the days and months ahead when more people would misunderstand, take their offerings, and leave the church.

In 1967 we began the Lynchburg Christian Academy at Thomas Road Baptist Church. Bible reading and prayer had been banned in our public schools. There was real need for private schools from kindergarten to twelfth grade that included moral training and Christian values in their curriculum along with academic and athletic excellence. We wanted to pioneer such a school.

The Christian private school movement was building up momentum across the nation. Unfortunately, many of those schools were founded primarily to maintain segregation. We were tarred with that same brush. Perhaps we deserved it at first. A group of local pastors went to the media with a prepared statement deploring our use of the word "Christian" in our designated name, the Lynchburg Christian Schools.

"We [who are] sensitive to Our Lord's inclusiveness," the statement began, "and to the non-whites in our community deplore the use of the term 'Christian' in connection with the private schools which exclude Negroes and other non-whites."

I dared not contradict their statement, because we had no "whites only" policy. When Dr. Pierre Guillermin and I discussed the possibility of starting Christian Schools in Lynchburg, the idea of circumventing integration was never discussed. And though we had only white students apply during our first two years, in 1969 we took in our first black child without fanfare and have been integrated in every grade up until this day.

In 1968 the first black family applied for membership in our church shortly after Dr. Martin Luther King was assassinated in Memphis. Our board of deacons decided unanimously to accept them.

Weeks later another black man was converted in the service and asked to be baptized. I remember wondering what the reaction of my congregation or of the city would be that evening before the baptismal service began. The church filled quickly to capacity. I could hear the noisy, excited crowd as my new brother in Christ and I walked toward the baptistry.

"Well," I said, hoping to lighten the tension of that moment, "I wonder if we'll both come out of the water alive?"

The black man whirled. His eyes were opened wide. Then he saw that I was smiling. We walked together into the water. I don't know who felt better after being immersed in those waters of baptism, that new convert or his grateful pastor.

That next Saturday I sat down into Lewis's shoe-shine chair at exactly 10 A.M. Lewis greeted me and began his work. I could not wait to tell him.

"Lewis," I said quietly, "we baptized a black brother last Sunday night and admitted him and his family to membership at Thomas Road."

"I know," Lewis said quietly, his eyes quickly filling up with tears. "I know," he said again, and then he smiled up at me. "I guess it's time for me to come visit, too."

Lewis, his wife, and grown family often visited our church after that. But Lewis never joined. He was a faithful member of his own black Baptist church until the day he died. I still miss Lewis and his weekly ministry in my life. His voice was the voice of God to me. God may have used the Congress and the courts, the strident marchers and their noisy demonstrations to get my attention, but He used the quiet, loving voice of Lewis to open up my heart and to help bring lasting change to me and to my ministry.

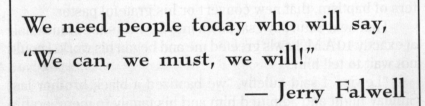

We need people today who will say,
"We can, we must, we will!"

— Jerry Falwell

CHAPTER TWELVE

Render Unto Caesar

Lynchburg's City Stadium seats approximately 20,000 people if you fill the playing field and the track with chairs. On Sunday morning, June 25, 1972, I stood with a group of my staff and family in the shade of a temporary platform we had erected at the north end of the playing field and watched the members and friends of Thomas Road Baptist Church begin to arrive. Actually, at 8:45 A.M. we gathered to pray behind a thirty-foot billboard behind the platform announcing the sixteenth anniversary of our church. Even as we prayed, we wondered if enough people would actually appear that day to fill the thousands of chairs we had placed on the grass, on the track, and in the thousands of bleacher seats that surrounded them.

Not many people thought it could be done. The church was still a teenager. In 1956 we began our ministry in the old storefront building with just thirty-five adult members and a ragtag tent full of restless children. But in the twelve years that followed, God honored us with incredible growth. In just a dozen years our door-to-door visitation campaign backed by our daily radio and weekly television broadcasts had resulted in the ninth-largest Sunday School in America with 2,640 people attending weekly.

At the end of the first ten years, the new Thomas Road Baptist Church ministries included Elim Home for Alcoholics, the Hope Aglow Halfway House for the rehabilitation and training of ex-prison inmates, the Treasure Island Youth Camp serving 3,000 boys and girls during the summer months, and in 1967 the Lynchburg Christian Academy, providing a quality academic program in a Christian setting to its first student body of 101 children in kindergarten through the fifth grades.

In just ten years, our old bottling company building had been widened, lengthened, and added to until the financials listed our properties on Thomas Road at a value of $2,199,880. And we had already outgrown our first 1,000-seat sanctuary, dedicated in 1964. At the end of ten years, our annual church budget was just over $200,000. And an additional $30,000 was raised by church members as a gift to the missionary programs of the church.

Because our buildings just couldn't handle the growth, new converts at Thomas Road were being trained and sent out across the city to form new Baptist churches. Still, between 1968 and 1972 our church experienced a growth explosion.

We were gathering in Lynchburg's City Stadium to celebrate what God had done. In the past four years, our attendance had reached and passed the 10,000-member mark. We had moved into a brand-new 3,200-seat sanctuary in July 1970. Our architects had found the historic old plans for a church designed by Thomas Jefferson but never built. We expanded those plans and erected the largest auditorium in central Virginia.

Our annual budget had gone above $1 million for the first time. The U-shaped academy building housed over 600 students in kindergarten through high school classes. The new octagon-shaped sanctuary was filled to overflowing at almost every service, and we had already outgrown the extra educational and administrative offices that housed our expanding Sunday School and mission programs. Our church campus was then valued at almost $5 million. And new people continued to arrive daily to find Christ, to be trained in the Word, and to be commissioned for Christian volunteer ministry.

On special Rally Days, we had surpassed the 10,000 mark in Sunday School attendance twice during those four years. Evangelists like Freddie Gage, a former drug addict from Houston, Texas; Bob Harrington, the "Chaplain of Bourbon Street"; and J. Harold Smith had conducted spectacular evangelistic crusades during those times. Hundreds had been converted to Jesus Christ. My brother Lewis and his wife Margaret were two of those converts during one of those crusades at Thomas Road Baptist Church.

Oliver Greene, a leading radio evangelist of that period whose ministry was based in Greenville, South Carolina, held fourteen evangelistic campaigns for Thomas Road Baptist Church during the 1950's. and 1960's. Other guest preachers, including "The Walking Bible," Jack Van Impe; Hyman Appleman, the Jewish evangelist; and Dr. Robert G. Lee, former president of the Southern Baptist Convention, held very successful meetings in our church during those early years.

I also invited leaders from very different fields to come and give their testimonies in our pulpit. Bobby Richardson, second baseman of the New York Yankees; Tom Landry, coach of the Dallas Cowboys; football heroes Terry Bradshaw, Carroll Dale, and Raymond Berry all spoke effectively to our people. I even invited one of the tallest men in the world, Max Palmer, seven feet, ten inches tall to share his testimony. When he was running for President, Governor George Wallace came by. And Senator Harry Byrd spoke to our people on more than one occasion. We were following Paul's example by using all possible ways to reach the people of our city.

By 9:45 A.M. that Sunday in 1972, the stadium was jammed to capacity. Every chair on the lawn was filled and the bleachers were standing room only. I sat on the platform next to our special guests: the country and western singer Connie Smith; Bob Harrington, the evangelist from New Orleans; and Colonel Harland Sanders, noted Christian businessman and the founder of Kentucky Fried Chicken. The Gethsemane Quartet sang a rousing song of praise. Soloist Doug Oldham had the congregation of 19,020 voices join in the "Battle Hymn of the

Republic." Trumpets played. Cymbals crashed. And I sat on the platform smiling broadly and blinking back my tears of joy.

There were literally hundreds of conversions to Christ that morning. When we gave the Gospel invitation to come forward to the platform, to pray and to receive Christ, the people came walking from the bleachers and from the chairs set up on the track and inner field.

Weeks later in headlines Newsweek magazine proclaimed Thomas Road Baptist Church "the fastest growing church in the nation." It seemed like a miracle to that handful of believers who had worked together from the beginning. And though God had blessed His people's faithfulness, in fact that astounding growth was a result of their constant faithful and sacrificial work and witness. No one dreamed that we were about to face the greatest crisis in our church's history. No, looking back, I should have known. Whenever the people of God mobilize to win the world, Satan begins to plot against them.

We had developed a concept I called "Saturation Evangelism." In sermons and training sessions I explained that "Thomas Road Baptist Church would preach the gospel to every available person at every available time by every available means." Our theme verse was found in the New Testament Gospel writings of doctor Luke: "Go out into the highways and the hedges and compel them to come in, that my house may be filled" (Luke 14:23).

We continued our door-to-door witness campaign throughout the city of Lynchburg, and across Campbell, Bedford, and Amherst counties. On our own church presses and on commercial presses throughout the city we created Gospel tracts, booklets, leaflets, educational materials, bulletins, newspapers, Bible study courses, and colorful invitations to church and Sunday School. We mailed or distributed by hand hundreds of thousands of printed pieces proclaiming the Gospel and inviting our neighbors to Thomas Road Baptist Church. We had regular ads in every weekend newspaper, on radio, and on television.

By 1971 we were distributing thousands of pieces of literature every week. As a result, that same year at least 10 percent of Lynchburg's 54,000 people were worshipping with us and another 20 percent of the population of Campbell County were attending quite regularly.

In 1968 I decided to begin a bus ministry to bring children from across the area to our Sunday School. I asked two men in the church to help me. We began knocking on doors on Leesville Road. We invited parents to come to Sunday School with their children or to send their children on the bus we would provide. Within two weeks, we had fifty riders on our first bus. I assigned that bus route to my original team. Then I took two more men to South Hill, Lynchburg, where we knocked on doors until we had filled a second bus.

Later we hired Jim Vineyard to organize and direct the volunteers who worked in the church's growing bus ministry. Every week, it seemed, another bus was filled. Before long Jim was traveling regularly to a huge site in Indiana where fleets of buses were sold at discount rates. Those buses were ten or fifteen years old. We could buy them for $600 each. Several times, ten men would travel with Jim to Indiana and each would come home driving a bus for his new Sunday School route.

On Saturdays our volunteers would work on those buses, keeping them in repair, patching seats, and painting trim. Throughout the week those same men would knock on doors and telephone their neighbors to fill the buses. As a result, on Sunday morning our fleet of forty-eight buses would make round trips up and down the streets of Lynchburg bringing as many as 2,500 children and adults to Sunday School at Thomas Road Baptist Church.

Under Jim Soward's direction, our Sunday School grew past the 10,000-member mark. We trained sixty-one brigade captains who directed our telephone volunteers. Sunday School members' names and attendance records were kept in a rather primitive but effective computer. Every Saturday the entire list was called to remind them of the next day's schedule for Sunday School and church. No one complained of harassment or intimidation. People liked being remembered and reminded. And the callers were trained to use those calls to inquire of the family's spiritual, emotional, and practical needs. When needs were discovered, callers notified other trained volunteers or the pastoral staff to help meet them.

The hundreds of Sunday School teachers and volunteers studied the Bible and were trained in educational and counseling techniques. Each of the volunteers was asked to spend two hours a week visiting and ministering in the homes of pupils and their families.

Pastors and lay leaders from across the country were watching and listening. They wrote asking questions about the amazing growth and expanding ministries of Thomas Road Baptist Church. For a while we tried to answer all the letters question by question. Finally late in the mid-1960's. we organized a special week-long pastors' and workers' conference for "Building a Super Aggressive Local Church." Hundreds came to the first session. Eventually thousands of pastors and volunteer workers from across the nation attended our annual training sessions. On that Sunday morning in 1972 when we celebrated our sixteenth anniversary in the Lynchburg City Stadium, there were thousands of pastors and workers from churches across the country who had gathered to begin their week of training at Thomas Road Baptist Church.

In 1968 Dr. Elmer Towns had written a book entitled *The Ten Largest Sunday Schools*. He listed Thomas Road Baptist Church as the ninth largest Sunday School in the nation. I had read Dr. Towns's other books and articles on church growth in America and decided to invite him to join our ministry in Lynchburg. I finally found him by telephone on a call to Canton, Ohio, early in 1971.

"Dr. Towns," I began, "you've written a great book. You've inspired me. Why don't you come to Lynchburg and help inspire the world."

He responded rather strangely and asked, "What exactly would I do in Lynchburg?"

"Help me start a Christian liberal arts college in our city," I asked him, "that will one day be a great accredited Christian university."

He was silent for a moment. I grinned, knowing the surprise he must be feeling, and continued my pitch.

"I believe there are thousands of young students," I said,

"who will catch the vision and who will carry what God is doing in Lynchburg to cities all over the continent and around the world. I want you to help me build a fully accredited liberal arts university with an emphasis on church planting and church growth. I believe our graduates could establish five thousand new churches in North America before the turn of the century and I need you to help us build that university in Lynchburg."

Dr. Elmer Towns was probably staring at the walls in momentary disbelief when I asked him to join our staff at Thomas Road Baptist Church. Many "big city folk" get that look when I ask them to come to Lynchburg. They think of my hometown as a rather primitive Blue Ridge Mountain village, a backwater on the James River. They don't believe me when I quote Thomas Jefferson's words about Lynchburg to Samuel J. Harrison in a letter dated October 8, 1817: I consider it as the most interesting spot in the State, and the most entitled to general patronage for its industry, enterprise and correct course."

John Lynch, after whom our city was named, was from a distinguished American family. His brother Colonel Charles Lynch used the law (later called "lynch law") in his effective and extralegal battle against the Tories (those early American settlers still loyal to the British) during our Revolutionary War. His sister Sarah Lynch (Terrell) helped establish the South River Meeting of Quakers and was a courageous and self-sacrificing Christian pioneer during Virginia's frontier days. And John Lynch himself was a strict Quaker whose commitment to peace with the Indians and the settlers alike helped establish the peaceful and productive city of Lynchburg among the seven hills along the James River in the foothills of the Blue Ridge Mountains.

"Enough!" Dr. Towns finally interrupted. "I'll do it."

I announced our dream from the pulpit, and that announcement was broadcast on our radio and television stations. Hundreds of young people responded during those first years. Classes were held in the educational buildings of Thomas Road Baptist Church. We bought little four-room houses near the church and turned them into dormitories for twenty and twenty-five students each. Then we bought the Virginian Hotel in downtown Lynchburg and renovated six floors of that classic old structure for 400 student residences. As we grew, classes met in every available church space, including lobbies and even on the carpeted sanctuary steps. We rented the old and vacant Brookville High School, my alma mater, and used it for classes before the building was torn down and the new Heritage High School was erected. We even used the classrooms of the defunct Ruffner Elementary School and rented a block of rooms from the Ramada Inn. Our educational dreams came true so fast that even we who dreamed them had trouble believing what God was doing in Lynchburg.

In 1971 Dr. Towns and his wife had moved to Lynchburg to help us start Lynchburg Baptist College. Today my friend Elmer Towns is vice-president of Liberty University and dean of our B. R. Lakin School of Religion. Together, just twenty-five years ago, we took our first step toward our shared dream for Liberty University and the 5,000 new churches we hoped our students would plant across America before the year 2000.

In 1972 we began Thomas Road Bible Institute. Adults across America who didn't have the time or money to enroll in a full four-year college curriculum still wanted to be trained in the Bible and in Christian theology and church history. The Bible Institute program was a two-year crash course in the English Bible. With a few announcements on "The Old Time Gospel Hour" and a direct mail invitation to our friends and supporters across the nation, hundreds enrolled during those first years.

In 1973 I had been preaching in Pensacola, Florida, when a tall, wiry man introduced himself to me at the close of an evening service.

"I am Robert Hughes," he said. "I have been wondering if you had ever considered starting a seminary in Lynchburg to help your students obtain graduate degrees in the Bible and theology?"

Dr. Hughes had earned his own doctorate in theology. He was a solid Bible student, a soul winner, a Baptist scholar of some renown, and a committed Christian and educator.

"Well, I have been thinking about that very thing," I

answered him. "Why don't you come to Lynchburg this fall and help me start one?"

Once again I got that look of amazement and disbelief. But once again the man said, "Yes, God willing, I will come!" So in 1973 in the back of an auditorium in Pensacola, Florida, I hired Dr. Robert Hughes on the spot to help us begin Lynchburg Baptist Theological Seminary.

With our rapidly growing church and plans for a major Christian university, we needed more land area and we needed it badly. Lynchburg is a small town, with an official 1980 population of about 66,000 people; 100,000 more live in the county areas around our town. And though 166,000 people may not seem like many compared to New York or Los Angeles, our total undeveloped land area did not contain many large available tracts. There was only one tract of land near the city large enough to accommodate the location of the great church and university campus we planned. Candler's Mountain with its green meadows and forested hillsides was just the place.

I loved that mountain. The Falwell home stands at the northern slope. Dad's Old Fort Inn, the Merry Garden Dining Room, and many of his other businesses were on or in the area of those 5,000 lush green acres. I grew up literally in the shadow of Candler's Mountain. I watched the sun rise and set upon it. I hiked on it and watched the seasons change the color and the shape of the woods. In the summer I hunted in its forests and in the winter I built snowmen or rode sleighs on its slippery slopes. And after my conversion I spent many hours walking on the paths or sitting beneath the trees reading the Bible and praying about the future.

The possibilities for that mountain in my ministry grew with each passing year. Then in the late 1960's I flew over the mountain en route to Lynchburg from Washington, D.C. On board the plane was my friend William H. Burruss, Jr., a timberman and large land developer who had been converted through my ministry. Looking down on the mountain and feeling all the nostalgia that it sets loose in me, I asked him who owned it and how could we obtain it for Thomas Road Baptist Church?

It wasn't just a fantasy. Too often property boundaries set

the limits on a growing ministry. We desperately needed those 5,000 acres to move effectively into the future. Bill told me that one of America's great corporations, United States Gypsum, owned 2,100 acres of that land. Apparently they had purchased Candler's Mountain but had not yet developed it. Within two weeks Bill Burruss and I flew to Chicago to see if Candler's Mountain was for sale.

"Strange that you should ask," a vice-president of U.S. Gypsum said to me that day. "We own hundreds of tracts of land across the country, but just days ago we decided to sell the exact piece of land you need."

Silently I thanked God for his reply and then swallowed hard before asking its price.

"One million, two hundred and fifty thousand dollars," he answered. I gulped again.

"We'll take it," I answered, and Bill Burruss looked at me with silent surprise. He knew we didn't even have a decent down payment on such an amount. But he said nothing.

"How would you like to pay for it?" the vice-president asked.

I knew Gypsum was selling the property to raise needed cash. I had none. "Would you consider financing it?" I said quietly.

He just laughed and shook his head.

"Could you give me a ninety-day option so we could raise the funds?" I said.

"Yes," he answered, "but you'll have to leave some earnest money."

I knew he was thinking in the hundreds of thousands of dollars.

"What about ten thousand?" I asked.

He laughed again. "Can you get ninety more in thirty days?"

"I think so," I answered quickly. "I'm certain of it."

"Then it's yours," he said.

Still dazed and excited beyond the telling, I took out our checkbook and wrote a check for $10,000 to buy the mountain we would call Liberty Mountain. And those meadows and hillsides of my childhood would one day hold a great university campus and a new plant for Thomas Road Baptist Church.

"By the way," I added as we shook hands and headed for the door, "don't cash the check for a few days. We don't have any money right now, but we'll get it."

He laughed again and, still shaking his head in disbelief, walked us to the door. In three days that first check was good. In ninety days he had the $100,000 down payment. And because of friends across the country who believed in our dream, we soon had donations, pledges, and loans to pay the rest. I shall always be grateful for what three special friends did to make this acquisition possible-Tom Phillips, Wayne Booth, and Bill Burruss.

It was our dream that one day God would use our television ministry to create and support that great Christian educational complex on Liberty Mountain with its accredited university, graduate schools, and a seminary. At the same time television would recruit our students from across the nation and around the world. Young people would come to Lynchburg, study with us, be a part of America's fastest growing church, see it expanding, see it growing, learn how it's done, catch the vision, carry the vision to their own hometowns, and translate what God was doing in Lynchburg to churches in every state of the union and every country of the world.

And God seemed to be blessing that dream. Our television ministry was growing. In 1956 we began broadcasting from one local station in Lynchburg to the people of that city and beyond to viewers in Campbell, Bedford, and Amherst counties. Then in 1959 we added a second station in nearby Roanoke, Virginia. In the 1960's. we added ten more stations throughout Virginia, West Virginia, Tennessee, North Carolina, and Washington, D.C. God was training me and my people in the wise use of this modern miracle of communication. At the same time slowly and steadily He was helping us to expand our circles of influence "from Jerusalem, into Judea and Samaria." God willing, one day we would use television to carry the good news "into the uttermost parts of the earth" as Jesus Himself had commissioned us.

Until that time, most television stations were opposed to selling time for religious broadcasting. Stations would sell everything from cars to toothpaste, but they had to give God away. Remember, television stations are profit-making businesses. To meet their public service responsibilities, stations offered some free time to the local councils of churches. So God usually ended up with the other public service presentations. And with a few exceptions religious programming found itself limited to the Sunday morning ghetto, with a panel of ministers and rabbis discussing important topics with almost nobody watching. Only those clergymen who belonged to the local councils were given time, and they ended up on the air once every fifty to one hundred weeks.

Then, just as we began to dream of using television to evangelize the nation, to create and support a great Christian university, and to recruit students for that university, America's television stations changed their minds about selling time to religious broadcasters. Or maybe we should say the prayers of the saints changed the minds of the media men. Through media and the mails, we had launched a nationwide campaign to mobilize prayer on behalf of television and its use in reviving and renewing the faith of the nation. We believe that God heard and answered those prayers. A lot of us were dreaming about the potential of television to bring Christ to this nation and to the world. Suddenly, with the move by local stations to sell time to religious broadcasters, it was our time to try.

We were standing on the threshold of an incredible opportunity to preach Christ simultaneously to every television home in the country and to create a Christian university filled with students who would return to their homes excited and trained to build great churches to evangelize our nation.

Having made the decision to use the media to reach the world with the Gospel of Christ, I called an emergency session of my staff, our television personnel, and various supporters of our media ministry. We were excited about the possibility of saturating the nation with the message of "The Old Time Gospel Hour." But the Bible was clear. The Apostle Luke quoted Jesus's own words: "For which of you, intending to build a tower, sitteth not down first and counteth the cost, whether he have sufficient to finish it?" (Luke 14:28).

National television would require a huge investment. And no one should start building a tower (even a Christian broadcast tower) without counting the cost. I commissioned a feasibility study to determine what the cost would be for us to reach out with television into all the world. Friends and advisers of our television ministry responded quickly and clearly. Our dream would require an immediate investment of somewhere between five and six million dollars.

It seemed such a small amount to begin reaching into almost every home in the nation. But the annual budget of Thomas Road Baptist Church had just reached a million dollars the year before. It would require an incredible leap of faith to raise five or six times that amount to launch our nationwide television ministry. But the people of Thomas Road Baptist Church and our friends and supporters across the country said, Take the leap of faith. We will support you.

About that time a man went to work for Thomas Road Baptist Church who had experience in raising funds for Christian ministries through selling bonds. He wrote up a prospectus outlining our dream and clearly describing the bonds we were selling to underwrite that dream. We offered 8 percent interest on the bonds (more than you could earn from banks in those days). And we promised to pay back the bond loans within a ten-year period from the day of issuance.

We mailed or hand-delivered the bond prospectus to our supporters and friends. Within a few short weeks we had our money from people who believed in "The Old Time Gospel Hour" and in our plans to build a great Christian university. Immediately, we started the school and launched our national media ministry. By 1971, the television outreach that began just fifteen years before on one local station in Lynchburg was beginning to saturate the nation from more than 300 stations reaching every state in the union.

We also followed through on our promise to begin paying interest and principal on the bonds immediately. Everything seemed to be working smoothly as we had prayed and planned. Then somebody who didn't like what we were doing notified the Securities and Exchange Commission in Washington, D.C., that we were "issuing bonds illegally."

The first I knew that anything might be wrong was in December 1972, when William Schief, then regional director of the Washington office of the Securities and Exchange Commission, contacted Thomas Road Baptist Church for information on the bonds that we had issued.

My nerve endings begin to tingle at the very first sign of government interference in the work of the church. When the S.E.C. contacted Thomas Road Baptist about the bonds, we wrote back asking why the S.E.C. was interested in our bond sale. We had developed the bond prospectus, sold the bonds, and were paying interest and principal by the book. Our attorneys were qualified to advise us each step of the way. We reviewed with our lawyers every action that we had taken during those last two years, and we felt completely confident that we had complied with every regulation governing the sale of bonds.

Mr. Schief responded that the S.E.C. inquiry was to determine if any literature had been supplied to potential buyers of the bonds that was false or misleading. We read and reread the literature that we had designed for the bonds. We found nothing wrong and answered accordingly.

Months passed. The correspondence continued. Threats were made. Rumors were spreading. We were exhausted and financially stressed, but we had acted on faith. God never promised that taking such a huge and risky challenge would be easy or stress-free. We were all working day and night. And I confess that it wasn't easy for any of us, but we were making it. God was blessing our act of faith and was providing (though usually just before the deadline) the human and financial resources that we needed to get the job done.

Then on July 3, 1973, the Securities and Exchange Commission filed charges against Thomas Road Baptist Church in the United States District Court in Roanoke, Virginia, charging the church with "fraud and deceit" in the sale of bonds to investors in at least twenty-five states. And if this horror wasn't enough, the suit claimed that Thomas Road Baptist Church was "insolvent" and could never repay those bonds.

Needless to say, we were shocked and astounded by the

charges. We met with our team of lawyers to look over the S.E.C. documents page by page. We called our own team together to examine one more time every shred of data that we had on file to begin preparing our defense. And while we were meeting, the nation's press was having a field day. Headlines in our own paper in Lynchburg quoted the S.E.C. charges: "S.E.C. Says Church Suffers from 'Gross Insolvency.'" Newspapers and news magazines, radio and television news commentators across the country echoed the charges. From the headlines just months before proclaiming us "the fastest growing church in the nation" with stories praising our accomplishment, there followed these charges of "insolvency, fraud and deceit."

One night alone in my little four-wheel-drive vehicle I sat on Candler's Mountain looking down across Lynchburg and wondering if our dreams to build a great university on that site were gone forever. And then I remembered that Jesus, too, had suffered from similar headlines. Toward the end of His life He had entered Jerusalem to the cheers of thousands who lined the road with their garments and waved palm branches in the air, singing, "Hosanna! Hosanna! Blessed is He who comes in the name of the Lord!"

But Jesus's triumphal entry was followed just a few days later by the cries of "Crucify him! Crucify him!" from that same crowd. With every triumph there is crucifixion. With every win there is defeat. But the story did not end in defeat for Jesus. After the false charges and the mock trial, after the crucifixion and the borrowed tomb, there was the resurrection. The Biblical promise is there at the very heart of our faith. "Though I walk through the valley of the shadow of death, I will fear no evil: for thou art with me. . ."

Immediately when one senses a crisis brewing it is time to pray. Facing the crisis comes later. Getting ready to face it starts now. I doubled my own prayer time. I asked others to pray with me. Eventually, the whole congregation and friends around the world joined in our prayer. And even as we prepared for the storm to strike, we prayed, studied the Word, and continued our Christian witness with all our strength.

As the national publicity against us increased, even my faith waned from time to time. There were times when I could stand in the pulpit or before the cameras and challenge our friends and supporters to help us fight the good fight. And though it didn't happen very often, there were other times when I could hardly stand before them let alone call on them to continue the fight. The claims against us may or may not have had any validity. That would be decided in court, but the rumors against us were devastating. A preacher can be found guilty of almost anything but "fraud" and "deceit." Once a man's integrity is questioned, that cloud of suspicion hangs over him and over his ministry for years, if it doesn't destroy him altogether.

I wasn't worried about my own name nearly so much as I was worried about the good name of the church that God's people and I had built together. We had worked for seventeen years to build the ministry. Now when we stood on the threshold of an open door that would expand our witness throughout the world, the S.E.C. and its charges against us threatened to close the door forever.

Have you ever opened a letter from the Internal Revenue Service to find that your taxes from some year past were being audited? Have you ever tried to find those missing cancelled checks or piles of old receipts that would prove you honest? Have you ever tried to make sense of long columns of numbers that made sense in the past but just don't make sense anymore? If you have, then you know at least a little of how we felt going back over every mailing, every letter to every investor (and there were thousands of them), every column of figures, every cancelled check, and every old receipt. Accountants and lawyers rummaged about our church offices. Great packets of data were gathered. We met often with S.E.C. lawyers and auditors in our offices and traveled to Washington, D.C., to meet with S.E.C. officials there.

We had not broken any law intentionally. We had done nothing that we knew of that could be construed in any way as illegal or even close to the limits that distinguish honorable Christian fund raising from the hucksters and charlatans that prey upon the widows of the nation. But for every piece of paper we presented, another ten pages were required. The government's questions were endless. The inquiry seemed to go on forever.

And believe it or not, we still had other things to do at Thomas Road Baptist Church besides the extra tasks brought on by the S.E.C. investigation. At the same time we were running a great and growing congregation. We had 13,000 members who needed our pastoral care. Our Christian Academy was growing every year with students filling our classes from kindergarten to high school. Our waiting list for the Elim Home for Alcoholics grew longer every day. Our Treasure Island Youth Camp for thousands of young people was in session throughout that summer on our island in the James River. And our weekly television ministry was saturating the nation. Thousands of viewers were writing to give their lives to Christ or to seek counsel or assistance. And our radio ministry, too, was growing. Handling the growing avalanche of correspondence from viewers and listeners in every state required twenty-four-hour days, endless letters, and banks of telephones.

And our Lynchburg Baptist College was well on its way to becoming a university. Already we were registering hundreds of students from across the country. They needed housing and jobs, qualified professors, and adequate classroom space. And with everything else, we continued to make those regular promised payments on the bonds to the people who had stepped out on faith to support the dream they shared with us. Running "the fastest growing church in the nation" and all these expanding, expensive ministries was taking every ounce of strength, every second of time, and every dime and dollar that everybody on our growing staff could muster.

And Thomas Road Baptist Church wasn't the only institution in my life that was growing or that needed me. My growing family needed me, too. My commitment to them was just one step above my commitment to the church and one step below my commitment to God. The Scriptures were clear on that point. My personal relationship with God came first, but my commitment to my wife and to my family followed immediately. And though I loved Thomas Road Baptist Church and though I had committed myself to the nurturing of her people and her ministries, I refused to let the pressures of being a minister damage or destroy my marriage or my family.

And my family joined with me in facing the crisis. In our family worship times we talked about the crisis and prayed for God's guidance in the weeks and months ahead. Macel fixed those special meals I like, and the children did their best to help me in those thoughtful little ways that make a difference.

It wasn't just our immediate family who rallied around during those times of crises like the S.E.C. investigation. Our friends and neighbors stood by us even when the headlines made us look like thieves and phonies. Credit for weathering every storm in my ministry must be shared with God, my family, and those special friends God provides along the way. Looking back, I want to remember a handful of those special friends (with apologies to all the others who know who they are and how much I honor and appreciate their friendship). This crisis with the S.E.C. created a great outpouring of friendship from those men and women who had supported my ministry from the beginning. How can I ever say thank you sufficiently to Sumner Wemp, Amanda Horsley, Gladys Rudder, Bill Weir, Don Norman, and so many others who prayed for me, counseled me, and held up my weary hands?

We had recently purchased Candler's Mountain for the campus of the accredited Christian University we were building. Our realtor, Byrd Mosby, a Presbyterian who only occasionally attended Thomas Road Baptist Church, had been crucial in helping us obtain the land upon which the Liberty University campus would stand as well as the various properties critical to the ministries of Thomas Road Baptist Church and Lynchburg Christian Academy. Byrd Mosby died just seven years ago; but when the scandal began to break, Mosby immediately stood up on our behalf.

I was afraid we might lose Candler's Mountain as a result of this financial investigation by the S.E.C. It had come into our possession as a kind of miracle, and I couldn't believe that God would let us lose it now. Actually, losing Candler's Mountain would have been a disaster. There was no other land in Lynchburg that could have housed Liberty University. Once again God provided friends for the rescue. Mr. Bill Burruss, who was influential in helping us obtain Liberty Mountain; his business partner, Tom Phillips, our attorney; and Mr. Wayne Booth, a local building contractor, took over the property and held it safely for us during the time of crisis.

Bill Burruss Jr. and Wayne Booth, together with their friend "Big Joe" Leonard, who owned the Leonard Tire Company in Lynchburg and once played for the Los Angeles Rams, all got saved at Thomas Road about the same time. Together they helped us financially when we were purchasing the mountain and getting ready to launch our nationwide television ministry. At church we called them the "Three Musketeers" for their ability to appear just in time to help God rescue us from another crisis.

Looking back over the crises in my ministry, there are literally hundreds of special friends I need to thank for their help in time, money, and special gifts to our ministries. Raymond Mays, the owner of a local trucking company, was one of those men who became a close personal friend and supporter from the beginning of Thomas Road Baptist Church right up through the present day. When we needed money to support the growing church or the embryonic university, Mr. Mays would stretch beyond his own means to write gifts of five, ten, and twenty thousand dollars. He would loan the ministry $100,000 at a time and trust us for its eventual repayment.

Bennie Bunnell, the owner of Bennie's Motel on Route 501 just outside Lynchburg, was another faithful friend. He loaned money to help us buy color cameras for our television ministry when we had absolutely no other way to obtain them. And the late Gene Dixon, owner of the Kyanite Mining Corporation, was another man who saw a need and reached out to help us meet it. Early in the 1960's, when I was driving 50,000 miles a year on evangelistic meetings around the country, Gene gave the ministry its first airplane, a Cessna 310. Later our own Three Musketeers, Bill Burruss Jr., Wayne Booth, and "Big Joe" Leonard presented us a new Cessna 414, a larger pressurized plane to replace the 310 and to help get us across the nation even more rapidly.

DeWitt Braud, a building contractor in Louisiana, and his

wife Lurline watched our early television programs and immediately volunteered to help us. They housed our traveling groups in their large home in Baton Rouge. They wrote generous and sacrificial checks to the ministry. They bought the ministry its third airplane, a vintage DC3. And though the plane could barely travel faster than an automobile, it would carry thirty-one people, our entire musical group, in relative comfort to our concerts in churches, auditoriums, and on capitol steps around America. Eventually DeWitt Braud sold his business, moved to Lynchburg, and continued to serve as chairman of "The Old Time Gospel Hour" board of directors. God provided DeWitt Braud as a major source of financial and moral support to the ministry, but, in the Brauds, God also provided close personal friends to Macel and me who would be co-workers with me until he went to heaven recently.

In the 1960's, when Jim Soward and I were still driving across America to preach in churches, we often stopped in Newport News, Virginia, to stay in the lovely home of Dr. Charles B. Hogan III, a dentist, and his wife Linda. Charles is another man whom God sent to be my friend. Eventually he moved his family and his practice to Lynchburg to be closer to our family and the ministry. When our children were still young, Charlie and Linda often rented a beach house in Nags Head, North Carolina, or Myrtle Beach, South Carolina, and shared that house for summer vacations with our whole family.

During the early years of my ministry, R. B. Whittemore and his daughter Ann were a major spiritual influence on my life. But during the S.E.C. crisis and the second decade of my ministry at Thomas Road Baptist, God provided another spiritual giant to help see me through the troubled times.

Actually, evangelist B. R. Lakin had been visiting Thomas Road from its earliest years to preach occasional revival meetings for our congregation. He was born Bascom Ray Lakin in the hills of West Virginia in 1901, and no one dreamed that this little country boy would one day impact the world with his dynamic preaching. He was a giant in the 1930's and 1940's, when the world had never heard of Jerry Falwell. The first evangelist to broadcast daily on national radio over WLW, a 500,000-watt station in Cincinnati, Lakin had pioneered the way for those of us in religious radio and television who would follow.

When I was a young preacher just starting my first church in Lynchburg, Lakin would drop by to preach in my pulpit and to encourage me. As we drove around Campbell County on pastoral calls in the afternoons, Dr. Lakin would tell stories about his own early years when 500,000-watt stations were legal.

"You could whisper in Cincinnati," he said, "and they could hear you in California."

He talked about announcing an evangelistic meeting on the radio and then driving down to the hills of Kentucky or West Virginia and finding thousands of people crowding the giant tents or packing the bleachers of a state fairground waiting for him to preach.

"The radio made me some kind of a star to those people," Lakin said, grinning at the memory. "I could hear them whisper as I walked from my automobile or a railroad car through the waiting crowds, 'Here comes Dr. Lakin,' or 'I touched him, Momma. I touched the radio preacher when he passed.'"

And though the world was impressed by Dr. B. R. Lakin, Lakin was not impressed with himself.

"Those were the 193'0s and the early 1940's, boy," he would tell me. "Nobody had even heard of television then. We still gathered around those big Philco radios and strained to hear the words and music through the static. Just being on that thing made you look like something special."

In fact, Dr. Lakin's ministry was something special. He was the first to use radio as a means to evangelize the nation. He employed direct mail follow-up in the 1930's and 1940's. There were no computers to assist him then. He wrote personal answers to thousands of seekers who wrote him letters filled with questions. He developed a staff of trustworthy people to help open letters and handle cash gift receipts. He remembers those days when his offices would receive three to five thousand letters a day. And though we receive more then 30,000 letters on some days in the 1980's, in the 1930's B. R. Lakin was breaking records and pioneering a whole new system of evangelism and follow-up ministries.

As our television broadcasts began to expand, Dr. Lakin stood up before the cameras and told his considerable following throughout the nation, "This is Jerry Falwell. He is God's man for this hour. Hear him!" It was a tremendous show of confidence in my ministry. His endorsement was trustworthy and far-reaching.

In 1973, Dr. Lakin was visiting Lynchburg to address another pastors' conference we were hosting. Lakin's only son had been killed in an automobile wreck; so his grandson Ronnie Lakin was driving him from Lynchburg to meetings in West Virginia. The last day of that preachers' conference, the S.E.C. announced their charges against us.

We said good-bye to Dr. Lakin that day and waved as he drove away. But on the road to West Virginia he asked Ronnie to stop the car. For a moment he sat in silence beside the road. Then he spoke quietly to his grandson.

"Turn the car around, Ronnie," he said. "We're going back to Lynchburg."

I was sitting in my office surrounded by lawyers and accountants and newspaper reporters all demanding attention when Dr. Lakin walked past my secretary, Jeanette Hogan, and into my inner office without even knocking.

"I've returned!" he announced in his booming preacher's voice. I looked up startled. The room grew quiet. The silver haired preacher stood tall and determined in the center of the room.

"I was praying over there in West Virginia," he began, "and God told me to come back here to help you."

Old Dr. Lakin spent the week. There was nothing he could do legally to end our troubles. But he ministered personally to my own tired spirit. He retold the Old Testament stories about ancient clashes between the government and the prophets. He reminded me of the New Testament stand the apostles and first century Christians had to take against kings, governors, courts, and ruling bodies. He dragged out all his best dramatic accounts of the prophets and the priests, the martyrs and the saints. And he inspired me through the telling.

"Take a fearless stand, Jerry," he would say. "Where you

are right, don't back down. Where you are wrong, apologize and make it right."

He cancelled his meetings to stay with me for one whole week. After that he called back almost every day from April until the matter was finally settled in court five awful months later. He visited regularly and prayed for us morning, noon, and night.

There is an old expression about facing crises that seems appropriate here: When it rains it pours. When the old Enemy has you down, he's going to stomp on you a couple of times for good measure. As if our crisis with the S.E.C. wasn't enough, about that time my mother-in-law, Mrs. Lucile Pate, went to her family doctor to complain of severe pains in her lower bowel. After thorough and painful testing, she was diagnosed with cancer.

Mrs. Pate had worked hard all her life. For thirty years, she shaped shoes on the assembly line at the Craddock Terry Shoe Corporation in Lynchburg. Then in her fifties she changed jobs and went to work for General Electric. At sixty-three, the doctors told Mom Pate that her intestinal cancer was fatal. But Mrs. Pate worked almost until the day she was hospitalized.

Our children stood outside that hospital room window and waved at their beloved grandma. And though we got them in to see their grandma several times before her death, at ages eleven, nine, and seven the children were too young to be admitted regularly to her bedside. They loved Grandma Pate. She had been at the center of their lives since birth, loving them, caring for them, fixing them puddings and apple pies. They couldn't believe that she was dying.

I couldn't either. Death is an easy subject to discuss until someone you love falls ill or is taken unexpectedly. We had a spare bedroom in our new house on Chesterfield Road. At night after visiting Mom in the hospital and tucking the children into bed, I would enter that empty room, close the door, and beg God to heal Mrs. Pate. I felt totally at peace about her spiritual life. She had served Christ and the church since childhood. But I needed her in my life and especially during this time of crisis, I wanted to have her present in the life of my family.

Mrs. Lucile Pate, wife, mother, grandmother, active

Christian, and mother-in-law supreme, died of intestinal cancer on November 9, 1973. Death is a time of mourning and of celebration for the Christian believer.

It is a time of celebration because we know that our friend or loved one is with the Father in heaven. We don't know exactly what heaven will be like, but we are confident that Christ will be there to wrap His loving arms around us and to welcome us home. The Bible says the streets are paved with gold. The poets describe heaven as being made up of puffy clouds. Let the poets have their fun trying to describe the heavenly regions. The Bible leaves the details to our imagination. But it is perfectly clear that at our death there is judgment, and after judgment for the Christian there is the resurrection. We receive our new heavenly bodies and immediately experience a joyful reunion with our Lord and Savior whose death and resurrection give us life forever in His presence.

But death is also a time of mourning for the Christian. The body now empty of life once held a lover, a parent, a child, or a friend. We will not see the person who inhabited that body again until we, too, join him or her in the presence of the Father. We will miss that one we loved. We will feel pain for a long time after the funeral and burial are past. Pillows will be stained with tears. Lumps will form in our throats. Memories may haunt us. Guilt over words unsaid and loving acts undone may follow us for a while. For a time our lives may feel empty and abandoned. To deny the impact of death upon those who remain is to ignore the truth of our human condition.

But for the Christian the celebration of eternity with the Father will eventually overcome the mourning that comes with death. The very next Sunday after her death, Mom Pate's two oldest daughters, Jean and Mary Ann, continued the Sunday afternoon dinner tradition for the entire family. Lucile Pate would have wanted it that way. Even as the family gathered around the festive table in the Pates' home, we felt her presence there among us, bustling in and out of the kitchen, sneaking bites to the children while chasing me from the dessert tray, and hurrying us to our places so that grace could be said and the hot meal begun.

We laughed and cried a lot that day thinking of Mrs. Pate and what she meant to each of us. After the dinner, Macel. the children, and I returned to our own home. I couldn't stop thinking of Lucile and how very much I would miss her. Finally I had to sneak away into that quiet empty room and spend some time alone thanking God for Mom Pate's life and seeking God's strength and wisdom for my own.

We have always included our children in every aspect of the crisis of death. We didn't hide reality from them. Perhaps that is why our daughter Jeannie proved to be our most helpful ally in 1984, when my father-in-law, Sam Pate Sr., died of heart failure at eighty-four years of age. Jeannie was especially close to her grandpa. He wore a pacemaker during his last six or seven years of life, and his doctor insisted that he exercise to support his ailing heart. Jeannie loved to walk with him as he made his two-mile path around the neighborhood each day. She waited patiently while he leaned against the trees or sat on a bench to get his breath and then teased or shamed him into starting the walk again.

Jeannie could charm her "papa" with a smile. Every Wednesday she took him to a nearby Wendy's for a hamburger with tomato and mayonnaise. He loved to "dine" there because they always gave his pet poodle a free burger. Grandpa was embarrassed about his failing health and insisted on putting a Wendy's napkin in his pocket at all times in case he spilled his food or needed to wipe his face.

After a bad bout of indigestion, he went to the hospital one Friday evening, and Jeannie spent the night beside his bed. In the morning, when he was feeling better, Macel convinced Jeannie that they should drive together to the University of Virginia School of Law in Charlottesville to help Jerry Jr. move into his apartment. Jeannie didn't want to go. She wanted to stay with Grandpa. But she consented to help her mom and was rushing home to Lynchburg when Grandpa died.

His death hit Jeannie hardest, yet it was Jeannie who comforted her mother when Sam Pate passed away. It was Jeannie who bustled about the family saying words of sympathy and comfort to each of us when we needed them. And it was Jeannie who went to Wendy's, got a colored paper napkin like Grandpa loved to carry, and placed it along with his favorite watch and pocketknife in his suit pocket as he lay in the open casket. It was her way of showing her love and remembering the good times she and Grandpa had shared together.

I desperately needed the support of my wife, my family, and our friends during those months of the S.E.C. investigation. It was the most difficult crisis I faced in all my years of ministry. There were times I wondered if we would survive it. Since April 1973, when the S.E.C. had begun preparing their charges against Thomas Road Baptist Church and our associates in the bond campaign, our attorneys had struggled to stop the S.E.C. and the courts from releasing to the media the papers that described their case against us.

We wanted the papers safely under lock and key for several important reasons. We didn't want the case against Thomas Road Baptist Church to be tried beforehand in the media. Releasing the papers only confused the public and prevented our side from being known. We didn't want our investors to panic, thinking their investments were lost, before we had time to explain the true situation to them. And we were negotiating at that time with a large company that might possibly provide us important financing and guarantee the value of the bonds. We didn't want the flow of negative publicity to adversely affect those negotiations.

In spite of our protests, after almost a month of struggle, the S.E.C. case was released to the waiting press. S.E.C. attorneys claimed that we had used "fraud and deceit" to sell $6.5 million in bonds to 1,632 public investors living in twenty-five different states. They had examined our financial records and claimed that Thomas Road Baptist Church "is insolvent in that its current assets are not sufficient to meet its obligations as those bonds become due and payable."

Worse, the S.E.C. attorneys claimed that we had not issued a proper prospectus on a large portion of the bond issue and that the prospectus that we had released "directly and indirectly employed devices, schemes and artifices to defraud, obtained money and property by means of untrue statements of material facts," omitted "material facts necessary," and engaged in transactions, practices, and "a course of business which operates as a fraud and deceit upon purchasers of the securities."

You can imagine what a field day the journalists and reporters had with those charges against us. And you can imagine how our investors, how our friends and supporters, how our church members, and how the general public felt the first time they read those headlines charging us with "insolvency, fraud and deceit," or what went through their minds when they saw the charges repeated on the evening news. It was terrible. It seemed that there was no way to present our side of the story and no way to reverse the negative publicity once such charges had been leveled. We were tried in the headlines and found guilty by the public before we could even state our defense.

The really scary part of it all was the possibility that the S.E.C. might force our church into bankruptcy, put us in "receivership," and padlock our sanctuary and office doors. They made veiled threats about taking this drastic action. Nationally the S.E.C. had simultaneously launched similar investigations against other evangelical media ministries. They seemed on a rampage.

I want to admit quickly that we had made mistakes. We grew too quickly. The opportunity to move into television across the nation had come without warning. The possibility of beginning a great Christian university needed immediate action. And we jumped into the bond program without enough experience, without adequate counsel, and without time to do it right.

And I also want to admit that I learned a lot from the S.E.C. charges that I might not have learned without them. First, although we were not insolvent as they claimed, we were really living on the financial edge. In our enthusiasm during that first bond campaign, we had taken foolish, irresponsible risks. Too often our financial records were kept by volunteers who meant well but didn't have adequate training or supervision. We didn't even employ an outside impartial audit firm in those days. We spent money believing that God would provide before He had provided it. That was not so dangerous when we were a little church of thirty-five adult members or even a church of eight hundred. But when we were handling millions of dollars of other people's money, taking certain kinds of risks was irresponsible behavior, and we were quick to admit it.

Second, though we did not use deceit to defraud, in our excitement to reach our goals we had included some inaccuracies in the bond prospectus. For example, we wrote that the Lynchburg Christian Academy was accredited, when in fact full accreditation was still pending. Shortly after, our schools were fully accredited as we knew they would be. But we announced the accreditation just before it happened, and that made our announcement incorrect. And we included among the church's list of assets a large gift, when in fact the donor had given us a written promise to make that large gift but had not yet actually transferred the gift to us. He did make the gift shortly after, exactly as he promised.

Perhaps you have heard the terrible expression "evangelistically speaking." It was popular in the 1950's. and 1960's. when evangelists would make claims for reaching more people than they had actually reached or when churches bragged of more children in Sunday School than had actually been present. I hate the expression. Lying, half-truths, and exaggerations should be off limits for everybody in public life, especially for those who follow the One who said, "I am the truth..." Our intentions may have been good and the figures close to accurate, but we did not meet the required criteria for a bond issue.

And third, though we had no intention to defraud or mislead, we did make a mistake in not issuing a prospectus on the sale of general obligation bonds to finance the new television ministry as was legally required of us. We didn't know that it was necessary, but not knowing was no excuse, even for Christians unskilled in the ways of law, business, and government. A Christian who whines about government intervention when in fact he has broken a law should not be excused for his ignorance. Jesus said, "Be wise as serpents." He didn't just say, "Be harmless as doves." And the S.E.C. taught me once for all time that if I don't want the government investigating me, I will be wise enough to play the game by the government's rules. And when I am ignorant or uninformed, I will find people who can instruct me before I act unwisely or even break the law. That lesson, too, was a gift from the S.E.C.

On August 2, 1973, I answered their charges in a long statement to the press that reviewed exactly what we had done and why we had done it. Such words as "devices, schemes, and artifices to defraud," I said, "are grossly misleading to the present circumstances." I explained the church's sudden growth and the need for additional funds to support and extend that growth. I admitted where we had erred and assured our supporters that their investments were secure.

"The church has yet to find one of its bondholders who feels he has been defrauded," I announced proudly. "In reality, these bondholders are friends of the church who have invested their money not primarily for financial gain but because they wish to advance the spread of the Gospel."

The S.E.C. made its charges. We replied. The battle raged on. Our people gathered to pray. Friends across the country were praying with us. It was a difficult and dangerous time. The S.E.C. was recommending that the court appoint a receiver for all the assets of the church. That prospect brought dread to my heart. I knew that turning over the control of Thomas Road Baptist Church to government appointed receivers meant giving up our freedom to control the future of the church. And that could mean the destruction of our ministry at Thomas Road altogether.

When I was down emotionally, I feared that we might lose everything. When I was up, I dared the Enemy to do his best against us. "And if we lose everything today," I once said, "we will begin all over again just up the street tomorrow." But I must admit that there were times that I felt terribly afraid and almost entirely alone.

Then on August 9, 1973, we were asked to appear in the U.S. District Court of Judge James C. Turk. An estimated 175 people jammed the courtroom and the surrounding area on the second floor of the Federal Building on Church Street in downtown Lynchburg. I parked my car about a block away and walked toward the courtroom. People rushed up to me on the sidewalk and said, "We'll be praying for you, Jerry." As I entered the building, dozens of friends and strangers crowded around to offer more encouragement. The halls and the elevator were filled with more well-wishers. By the time I neared the courtroom, I felt that all of Lynchburg and half the world were there to show that they believed in us and in our ministry, even if we had made mistakes along the way. And when I walked to the front of the crowded room, the people stood and began to applaud. I looked around at my friends and neighbors. There were tears in their eyes and smiles of encouragement on their faces.

"Don't worry, Jerry," somebody whispered loudly, "God isn't through with us yet!"

The S.E.C. lawyers sat unsmiling in their places looking straight ahead. The judge rapped for order. The charges were leveled against us. The words "insolvent, fraud, and deceit" were repeated one more time. Mr. Schief, the S.E.C. regional administrator, asked Judge Turk to appoint a receiver for the church's assets.

Our lawyers replied. All day long the discussion continued. I sat there watching Judge Turk's face, hoping for some sign of his final decision. He seemed to know from the beginning that the whole case against Thomas Road Baptist Church was a farce, a serious misunderstanding, a case of overzealous government investigators attempting to use our case to teach a lesson to charities and churches across the nation. At least, I have always felt that way.

At the end of the day, Judge Turk asked to see the attorneys from both sides and myself immediately in his chambers. In that meeting again I assured Judge Turk that we were not insolvent, nor had we intended to defraud or deceive. One more time I admitted and explained our mistakes. Then I suggested my own solution.

"Judge Turk," I said, "here is a list of outstanding Lynchburg businessmen. They are not members of Thomas Road Church. Will you appoint them as our special finance committee? Let them be my guide and counsel in all matters of finance. Let them report directly to this court as the days and weeks go by to guarantee that we are paying our debts and continuing to act responsibly. And if at any time they feel we are failing, ask them to report this to you. At that time you can do whatever you feel necessary."

The judge took the list and scanned the impressive names on it: John W. Ferguson Jr., president of the First Federal Savings and Loan; James M. Gilley, secretary/treasurer of the Burruss Land and Lumber Co.; E. R. (Ted) Harris Jr., president of Fidelity National Bank; George Stewart, president of the First Colony Life Insurance Co.; and City Councilman K. L. (Pete) White, president of Campbell-Payne Co.

On the following morning, August 10, 1973, the judge announced his verdict. On my fortieth birthday the next day, a newspaper headline declared that verdict to the world: "Thomas Rd. Church Cleared of Fraud, Deceit Charges."

In court, Judge Turk addressed the S.E.C. attorneys in these words: "As far as this court can determine, there is no evidence of any intentional wrongdoing by the Thomas Road Baptist Church."

Then he turned to address me directly. "Nothing has been said from the witness stand, Reverend Falwell," he began, "that in any way taints the good name of the Thomas Road Baptist Church."

When it was my turn to speak, I assured the court that we were grateful and that we would meet every debt obligation and continue serving God the best we knew how. I also promised that we would "refrain from engaging in any bond program or policy that would violate any federal securities law or regulations."

Then I added, "When this complaint became public, newspapers nationwide prominently reported that Thomas Road Baptist Church was being charged with fraud, deceit and insolvency.... We are hopeful that press coverage of this exoneration of fraud will be as widespread as the coverage of the original complaint."

When the hearing ended, the courtroom erupted in applause. People rose to their feet and cheered. As I tried to make my way through the crowd, I was mobbed by people whose eyes were wet and whose hands trembled with relief.

For the next three years five wonderful men met with me
and with the newly appointed and professionally trained financial officers of the church. The special finance committee was
responsible for putting our ministry on a sound financial foot-
ing. We gathered almost every week in Mr. Harris's boardroom
in the executive suite of the Fidelity National Bank. They answered our questions. They reviewed and revised our procedures. They directed our business affairs with great expertise.
They developed a system of accountability at Thomas Road Baptist Church second to none in any church, charitable organization, or even corporate business in the nation. They gave me
and my people an advanced course in finance. And they received
no pay for the hundreds of hours they gave us and for their
priceless contribution to our lives and ministry. I will always be
grateful to those five wonderful friends for their loving, patient,
professional contribution to me and to the expanding work of
Thomas Road Baptist Church.

And though I feared the national publicity would hurt if not
destroy what we were doing, in fact giving went up and stayed
up from that moment until today. In those next three years alone,
Thomas Road Baptist Church increased its budgets from $3.5
million in 1973 to $12 million in 1976. These men taught us how
to be qualified stewards of God's money. Through the S.E.C.
charges, God used these men to prepare us for the incredible
expanding ministry He had planned for us. Just ten years later,
in the 1986-87 fiscal year, we handled nearly $100 million to
finance ministries ranging from the fastest growing university in America to a brand-new television network with the
potential to bring the Gospel into homes across the nation
and around the globe.

I remember the last meeting I had with this committee of
five wonderful men. We shook hands around the table. I thanked
them one by one. And then I walked from the room and drove
up to the crest of Liberty Mountain. For a moment I sat there
looking out across our city. I remembered how terrified I had
felt when I first read the S.E.C. charges in the headlines. I recalled in the weeks that followed how I feared that Thomas
Road Baptist Church might be destroyed in a terrible scandal

just as we were launching a television ministry to evangelize the nation. And I relived those moments in the summer of 1973 when I had felt the presence of evil lurking among us as I had not felt its presence before.

Then I began to cry. God's Spirit had been with us through it all. He had forgiven us our mistakes. He had honored His people's faithfulness. And He had used the entire ugly event to teach us important lessons that we desperately needed to learn if we were to be ready for the even greater future He was planning.

Then I picked up my Bible from the seat beside me, opened to the sixth book in the New Testament, and read the words I had underlined during those terrible days of trial. Paul was writing to the Christians in Rome, who were facing their own investigation and persecution by the Roman emperor. They, too, must have wondered if they would survive their trial. Paul promised them eventual victory. And looking back, wc can see that what Paul promised came true. The Roman empire was destroyed, but the church has lived on in triumph to this day. Paul's promise of eventual victory is as trustworthy for us today as it was for that little suffering church in Rome almost 2,000 years ago: If God be for us, who can be against us?

The overcomer is one who is knocked down nine times, but gets up ten.

— Jerry Falwell

CHAPTER THIRTEEN

Church and State

On January 23, 1973, just four months before the S.E.C. began its attack on Thomas Road Baptist Church, a story in our *Lynchburg News* radically affected my life and the life of my family. Although the morning's banner headline read: "Lyndon Johnson Dies," I noticed another front-page announcement almost lost in the long presidential obituary.

Supreme Court Legalizes Abortion

"Yesterday, in the landmark Roe vs. Wade decision, the Supreme Court ruled unconstitutional all state laws that prohibit voluntary abortions before the third month. Feminists hail the decision as an important breakthrough for their cause. Right-to-life opponents of the decision promise to fight for a constitutional amendment banning abortions."

In growing horror and disbelief, I read and re-read the short article describing the historical case titled Roe v. Wade. The Supreme Court had just made a decision by a seven-to-two margin that would legalize the killing of millions of unborn children. In one terrible act they struck down all the state laws

357

against abortion and legalized infanticide across the land. I could not believe that seven justices on the nation's highest court could have so little regard for the value of human life. Apparently, there were others who shared my disbelief.

"How many millions of children prior to their birth will never live to see the light of day," asked New York's Terence Cardinal Cooke, "because of the shocking action of the majority of the United States Supreme Court today?"

The president of the National Conference of Catholic Bishops, John Joseph Cardinal Krol said, "It is hard to think of any decision in the two hundred years of our history which has had more disastrous implications for our stability as a civilized society."

I don't usually let the newspaper interfere with my breakfast with the family, but on that day my coffee grew cold and my family ate alone. I sat there staring at the Roe v. Wade story growing more and more fearful of the consequences of the Supreme Court's act and wondering why so few voices had been raised against it. Already, leaders of the Catholic Church had spoken courageously in opposition to the Court's decision; but the voices of my Protestant Christian brothers and sisters, especially the voices of evangelical and fundamentalist leaders, remained silent.

I had followed the debate on abortion with growing fascination. I had read articles by Dr. Francis Schaeffer and Dr. Jack Willke discussing the implications for a society that allows the mass killing of its unborn. I had talked to social workers, theologians, and medical personnel about the physical and psychological effects on the women who choose abortion to stop an unwanted pregnancy. I had interviewed and counseled many women (and even men) who had sought abortion to end an unwanted pregnancy because they thought it "the painless way," but soon found out the terrible emotional cost that many pay for this "quick and easy solution." I had even preached on abortion and its meaning to my people at Thomas Road Baptist Church and had used abortion as an example in several radio and television sermons during the past ten years. But that terrible decision by the Supreme Court meant that something far more drastic had to be done; but I must confess I was hoping that other Christian pastors and lay leaders would volunteer to do it.

Across the nation there were people who agreed with me that the Roe v. Wade decision was a disaster. In fact, letters, telegrams, and petitions began to stream into the Supreme Court Building in a growing flood. Court guards had to set up large bins in the basement to collect and sort the flow of mail condemning the Court's decision. The justices were being compared "to the butchers of Dachau, to child killers, to immoral beasts, and to Communists." The justices' lives were threatened. Letter bombs were received and disarmed. I was glad that people didn't like the decision, but hysteria would not undo the Court's mistake. Ugly threats and deadly bombs would only bring dishonor to the opposition and to our cause. Something had to be done to save a generation of unborn infants, but an avalanche of hatred and bile would achieve nothing.

In the spring of 1973, with the announcement of the S.E.C. charges against our use of bonds in the funding of our Lynchburg Baptist College and our "Old Time Gospel Hour" nationwide television ministry, I found myself trying to dig out of my own landslide of angry charges by the media across the nation. The problem of abortion never left my mind or heart during those troubled days of the S.E.C. investigation, but there was little or no time to take action when we ourselves were struggling to survive. Finally by the end of summer we had been exonerated by the courts. At long last the army of lawyers and accountants from Washington, D.C., had left us alone. Headlines announced our victory. By fall we were well on our way to complete recovery. By winter I could begin to think seriously again of what I should do about the Court's decision to legalize abortion.

Hoping that words would be enough, I began to preach regularly against abortion, calling it "America's national sin." I compared abortion to Hitler's "final solution" for the Jews and the Court's decision to letting loose a "biological holocaust" upon our nation. However it soon became apparent that this time preaching would not be enough. To stop the legalizing of death by abortion, opponents of the Roe v. Wade decision were protesting in the streets. For the first time in my life I felt God leading me to join them. But such a step was entirely against my nature. So I began to re-read the Biblical passages that might inform me. I prayed long and earnestly for God's Spirit to enlighten me. I talked about this life-and-death issue to my friends and even to my enemies. And I tried to stay open to the truth even when it seemed to threaten my past convictions.

It wouldn't be easy for this Baptist preacher to become politically active. I had always tried to be a responsible citizen in the privacy of the voting booth. But my teachers had taught me the concept of the separation of church and state. Somehow I thought the separation doctrine existed to keep the church out of politics. I was wrong. In fact, to our nation's forefathers, especially Thomas Jefferson and his colleagues from our state of Virginia, the separation of church and state had been designed to keep the government from interfering with the church.

Never during the founding years of this great democracy had our forefathers meant to distance the government from the truths of the Christian faith or to prohibit Christians from applying Biblical principles in their influence on the state. I had misunderstood the separation issue. In fact, it was my duty as a Christian to apply the truths of Scripture to every act of government.

Unfortunately, up until that time I had taken just the opposite position. In my 1965 sermon "Ministers and Marches" I took a strong stand against preachers taking political action. I declared that "government could be trusted to correct its own ills." I meant well, but I was wrong, and in those next few years my words would return to haunt me.

During the 1960's. millions of people seemed to be marching on the nation's capital and on courthouses, police stations, city halls, and public buildings across the country to make their stand on every kind of issue from the legalization of marijuana to ending the war in Vietnam. Some of the issues I favored. Other issues I strongly opposed. Nevertheless I refused to carry a sign and march for or against any issue, because I sincerely believed that the Christian's best contribution to social change was his or her faithfulness to our primary goals: studying the

Word, preaching the Gospel, winning souls, building churches and Christian schools, and praying for the eventual healing of the nation.

"Our role as pastors and Christian leaders," I told a national convention of clergymen, "is to attend to the spiritual needs of our people." Serving the church and letting government take care of itself had been my lifelong policy and the policy of my Christian friends and family.

Years later when my son Jerry Jr. decided to study law, my daughter had to convince her Grandpa Pate that one could be a lawyer and a Christian at the same time.

"But your mom and dad spent their whole lives teaching you children to tell the truth," Grandpa protested, "and now Jerry Jr. is going off to law school, where they teach you how to lie."

You must remember that Grandpa was born in 1900 in Alum Creek, West Virginia. There were no highways near his home. There was no electricity, no telephone. He worked very hard for the food that he ate. His parents were God-fearing, hard-working, and very poor. His philosophy of the world, of business, of politics, and law was developed in "mountain logic."

And most of the early Southern circuit-riding preachers and tent evangelists condemned lawyers, politicians, abolitionists, and suffragettes alike. "We are here to serve Jesus," they would preach. "Don't get bogged down with unbelievers and their unrighteousness."

Grandpa Pate represented generations of fundamentalist Christians for whom getting involved in law and government was out of the question. I had inherited those generations of tradition.

There were other more practical reasons that I cited against taking political action as a pastor. For one thing, I didn't have time for one more commitment in my already overloaded schedule. I was pastoring a church with more than 15,000 members. Our television and radio ministry blanketed the nation. I was writing books, teaching classes, administering our growing elementary and college programs, and traveling across the country to speak at national conventions, seminars, and workshops.

There was no extra time or energy for becoming politically involved, even in a social issue as important to the nation's future as abortion.

Besides, I didn't have a lot of background or experience in the political process. I didn't want to embarrass myself, my church, or even my Lord by wading into those political waters that were over my head. In the past, when my fellow fundamentalists had gotten involved in politics, they often betrayed their own ignorance about the problems and their naivete about the political realities that lead to a lasting solution.

This Supreme Court decision was no exception. In the immediate outpouring of public sentiment against the legalization of abortion, more than 1,000 Baptists and similar religious groups sent angry letters and telegrams to Justice Hugo Black condemning his participation in the Court's decision. There was only one problem: Justice Black had been dead for sixteen months before the Roe v. Wade decision had been made. The writers of those letters had their hearts in the right place but they were uninformed and thus ineffectual.

If I were to become involved, I knew I would have to become an expert in the complex issues and in the long, tiresome political processes that would bring solutions. There would be books, pamphlets, and legal briefs to read. There would be experts and authorities to interview. There would be strategies to outline, groups to organize, and risks to take.

Also, I became concerned that taking a political stand, even on my own time, might divide our growing congregation. I pastored a pluralistic church where people could hold various political views and still be one in Christ. Already the nation was being terribly divided over the issue of abortion. Would that also happen to my congregation?

One evening during devotions with my family, I confessed my own growing need to do more than preach against the Court's decision. I shared my fears about the death of generations of unborn children. I told stories about the people whose lives had been shattered because they consented to abort an infant and about the millions of unborn infants who would die if something wasn't done. My family sat in a little circle around the fireplace and listened. I was afraid that our children might be too young to hear the details of such a painful issue. But I knew that whatever decision I made would affect their lives as well as mine. Macel agreed that it seemed irresponsible for me to exclude them from the decision-making process.

So after Bible reading and prayers I told them everything. Jonathan was only seven, but his eyes filled with tears as I described the meaning of abortion and its effects on the unborn and their mothers. Jeannie was nine. She grew noticeably angry when she heard about the suffering. She asked questions and listened carefully as I answered them.

That night, right or wrong, I confessed my fears to my family. I doubted seriously that America would survive the judgment of God because of this "national sin." And there were so many other serious moral problems already at work eating at the heart of the nation. Finally I made this statement: "Kids, it is doubtful that you will be living in a free America when you are the same age as your parents."

Jonathan had grown more and more restless as I spoke. When I finished, he got up off the floor, walked over to the fireplace, knelt before me, and placed his hands on my knees. For one moment he looked directly into my eyes without speaking. Then seven-year-old Jonathan said one simple sentence that helped change our lives forever. "Daddy," he said, his lip quivering and his own eyes moist with tears. "Why don't you do something about it?"

For a moment I looked at my son. He stared back at me without blinking, but he said nothing more. He was waiting for my response.

Jeannie smiled at her little brother in agreement, then looked directly at me. Macel and Jerry Jr. were looking on. They, too, were silent but seemed totally in agreement with Jonathan's words. Finally Macel hugged Jerry Jr., smiled at me with knowing eyes, and stood to end our time together.

"It's time for bed," she said, and the children hugged me one by one and followed Macel toward their bedrooms. Before tucking them in, I sat for a moment by the fire and thought of the words of Jesus: A little child shall lead them. In that brief moving moment of consensus, our family began a brand-new journey together. Jonathan was absolutely right. I had to do something and I had to do it quickly.

I began to research the problem of abortion. I read every article I could find regarding the medical, ethical, and moral dimensions of the issue. I made phone calls, wrote letters, interviewed experts, listened to debates, and watched television specials and film and videotape documentaries.

During that time, I saw in Life magazine an amazing full-color picture of an unborn child approximately sixteen to eighteen weeks old. The child's eyes were closed. She was sound asleep, sucking her thumb, floating in a silken sack, waiting for that moment when she would decide that her time inside the womb had ended and her time outside would begin. She was still waiting to be born: yet already she had delicate, graceful fingers and toes. Her skin was shiny and transparent. You could see her vital organs shadowed in shades of pink and red. Her heart, already beating 120 to 160 times a minute, was pumping blood that she herself had made to her perfectly shaped arms, legs, and torso and then back through her heart again through a web-like maze of microscopic veins.

In that picture I saw a tiny trusting child whom God had created. Regardless of the human reasons behind the child's conception, God loved her. It didn't matter if her human parents wanted her to live or die. God wanted her to live. The Supreme Court of the United States of America had made a terrible mistake. Because of their decision, that tiny unborn miracle of God's creation could be killed with the consent of her mother, the medical profession, and the highest court in the land. I was growing more and more certain that my position against abortion was valid when the results of the Court's decision convinced me without a doubt that I had to act.

From a fairly accurate estimate of 100,000 abortions (legal and illegal) every year before the Roe v. Wade decision in 1973, the number of abortions in this country jumped almost immediately to a million a year. The Supreme Court had loosed a slaughter on the land. And the more information I gathered about the problem of abortion, the more I realized that there were other crises facing the nation that required immediate political action from men and women of Christian faith.

The traditional American family was being threatened by economic pressures, physical and emotional abuse, sexual immorality, and divorce. Illegal drugs and alcohol misuse were reaching epidemic proportions across the generations from elementary school through the adult years. Pornography had become a major American industry, and pornographic materials were flooding the mails and being sold to children in neighborhood grocery stores or shopping centers. And abortions in America would soon reach 1.5 million victims a year. The general moral standards of an entire generation seemed to be lowering steadily, and the courts and the politicians seemed silent if not supportive of the dangerous and deadly trend.

I continued to preach and teach against abortion. As the Biblical truths and medical data became clearer in my mind, my sermons and lectures became more informed and more determined. As the horrifying information about the related crisis threatening the American family came pouring into my life, my focus widened and my commitment to Biblically based, thoroughly Christian social action deepened. I was calling my people at Thomas Road Baptist Church to action, and through our "Old Time Gospel Hour" national broadcast I was reaching out to other clergy and laity across the nation.

People were shocked and surprised by the changed emphasis they heard in my preaching. Until the 1970's. I had been a typical Baptist pastor who was opposed to Christians, especially the clergy, getting involved in political action. Suddenly I was calling for all-out political involvement by the Christian community. I had read and reread the stories and the sermons of the Old Testament prophets and their call to justice. I had restudied the life and teachings of Jesus, with His love for the little children and His command to see that no harm should come to them. I read the letters of Paul, Peter, and John, the books of Acts and Revelation. I felt a growing commitment to take my stand prophetically against the influence of Satan in our nation and through our nation to the world.

In my book *If I Should Die Before I Wake* I retrace the

history of God's dealings with me about the abortion issue. I don't want to repeat that whole story here. I will only share one brief Biblical account that God used to help set me in my new direction. At the heart of my decision was a story repeated by Matthew, Mark, and Luke in their New Testament accounts of the life and teachings of Jesus. In Matthew 22, Mark 12, and Luke 20, the eyewitnesses document what happened that day when Jesus's enemies, the Pharisees, gathered to trick and trap Him in a public debate.

Is it lawful to pay taxes to Caesar, or not? the Pharisees asked, looking around at the crowd, knowing that either way Jesus answered He would be in trouble. If He answered, No, don't pay taxes to the government, the soldiers would arrest Him and throw Him in jail. If He answered, Yes, pay your taxes, He would offend the people who hated the government and wanted to see it overthrown. Jesus didn't answer immediately. Instead, He called for a Pharisee to hold up a coin used in paying the tax.

Whose image and inscription is this? Jesus asked.

Caesar's, answered the Pharisees.

"Render to Caesar the things that are Caesar's," Jesus replied, "and to God the things that are God's."

On the surface, it was a clever answer. Both sides were satisfied. But it wasn't only clever. It was wise and true and filled with meaning. Jesus's answer cut to the heart of our human predicament. We live in two different worlds simultaneously. The world that God is building in the heart of men and women is an invisible world based on eternal values. The world that man is building is a world of cement, steel, and glass based on human values that rust, corrupt, and die.

The trouble is that we live in both worlds at the same time. We who are committed to the invisible world of God and to His values cannot simply stand aside while the other world destroys itself and the world we share. In that confrontation with the Pharisees, Jesus also reminded us subtly that though our first allegiance is to God and to His goals for this planet, we must still be responsible citizens, willing to play our part in maintaining the world of humankind.

There was a second important reminder for me in that story. When Jesus said, "Render to Caesar the things that are Caesar's, and to God the things that are God's," He was not just telling us to be responsible in both worlds. He was also reminding us that we live in two worlds simultaneously and that we need to keep the worlds apart. Each world works differently. What we do in God's world and with His people has different rules from what we do in the world of government, with elected officials and volunteers. America is not a theocracy, a government with God as its Commander-in-Chief. America is a democratic republic with a man (perhaps one day a woman) as its chief executive officer. In God's world, we decide by God's rules. In a democratic republic, we work together, governed by the will of the majority. In God's world, we submit to Him. In man's world we submit to God and to the law of man.

But there is a third important truth implied in Jesus's simple story. Jesus made this third truth clear by the example He set in His life and by His death. God used this third truth to challenge me to political action. Although we live in two worlds simultaneously and although both worlds are to be kept separate, when there is a conflict between the worlds, the world of God takes precedence over the world of man. When we feel the law of man is unjust or contrary to the law of God, we work to change man's law. And if the law of man actually comes into conflict with the law of God, we disobey man's law and pay the penalty.

We cannot forget God's law as we live in man's world. We must try to live by God's law in both worlds, whatever it may cost us. We must work to convince others that God's law is right and will bring health and long life to the nation. We do not insist on others believing as we believe or worshipping as we worship. We protect the freedom of every person in the land. But if we feel a law is wrong or harmful for the nation, we must work tirelessly to change it. And we must use every legal tool available to us to accomplish that end.

During my first years of ministry, I had given to God what was God's and had almost eliminated my responsibility to Caesar (government) altogether. I had paid my taxes, of course. I had voted. I had occasionally made a call or written a letter or carried on a conversation to influence public policy. From time to time my sermons commented on issues of significance to the nation. But to work hard to change public policy or to dedicate time and energy to influence government regarding abortion, the destruction of the family, alcohol and drug abuse, national defense, pornography, and general moral decay would be a new and mind-boggling experience for me.

I was already preaching national repentance and individual spiritual revival and renewal from my pulpit at Thomas Road Baptist Church. And I was speaking against abortion through our radio and television programs to homes across the nation. It wasn't enough.

I began to urge my fellow Christians to get involved in the political process. I encouraged them to study the issues, to support qualified candidates who stood for the renewal of morality and good sense in the land, or to run for office themselves. I pushed for Christians to use their churches to register voters. I dared Christians to go door-to-door getting out the vote, making the issues known, campaigning precinct-by-precinct for the candidates of their choice and using their cars and buses to get voters to the polls.

In 1975 the nation's bicentennial celebration was only a year away when we began to dream about influencing the moral and ethical course of the nation in an even larger way. Don Wyrtzen had written a stirring musical entitled I Love America. We chose seventy students from a rapidly growing pool of talented students from our college and trained them for a musical ministry. In 1976 those students, a support team, and I visited 141 cities in America, performing, preaching, and praying in huge churches, public auditoriums, and great coliseums to standing room only crowds of enthusiastic grateful pastors and their people.

This musical presentation was the first offensive we launched to mobilize Christians across America for political action against abortion and the other social trends that menaced the nation's future. We were calling America back to God. We reminded the tens of thousands who watched our program that we were living in a nation threatened by godlessness. We warned them that our leaders were making decisions that could destroy the moral foundations upon which the country was built. And we challenged them to do something about it in their towns, in their states, and in their nation.

The student performers were given college credits for this long but fascinating tour of the nation's towns and cities. They traveled on ministry-owned buses followed by two tractor-trailer trucks carrying the stage equipment and costumes, sound systems, and lights. I would fly to meet them in the next city on our itinerary, arriving from my own pastoral and broadcasting tasks in Lynchburg just in time to have dinner with the pastors and lay leaders of the city. During dinner and in an after-dinner address, I confessed how long it had taken me to take a political stand and the mistakes I had already made along the way. I challenged them to study their Bibles, to pray, to study every issue before us, and to join us in taking a stand against the forces of evil at work in their towns and around the country.

The pastors were then escorted to reserved seats in the front rows of the city auditorium, where I honored them and their families. Then the lights dimmed. The snare drums and tympanies rolled. The trumpets played a fanfare and seventy wonderful young people sang their hearts out to an inspired crowd who usually responded with an enthusiastic standing ovation. Then I concluded the evening with a Biblical challenge to the Christians gathered in those large auditoriums or coliseums to unite with their brothers and sisters in Christ to save the nation.

Pastors who attended the *I Love America* rallies and heard my call to political action invited me to address their denominations' state and national conventions. I began to receive invitations to appear on various television talk shows to discuss the matter of Christians in politics. And because I had seen the power of the media to change lives and affect the course of history, I accepted. Presidents and deans of other Christian colleges, Bible schools, universities, and seminaries invited me to address their student bodies.

My board of directors purchased or leased private planes

to get me back and forth across the country in time to maintain my preaching and teaching schedule and my responsibilities with our various growing ministries from the pulpit of Thomas Road Church, Elim Home, the Lynchburg Christian schools, and our college to our radio and television broadcasts.

And all the work and travel seemed to be having results. Our letters indicated a ground swell of enthusiasm for political action by evangelical, charismatic, and fundamentalist Christians together. Churches were getting organized. Voters were being registered. Campaigns for qualified Christian candidates were being mounted. For the first time, significant political issues were being raised and discussed by church groups and interchurch fellowships. Local races were being won. State and national polls were showing signs of positive change. We seemed to be making headway in our campaign to mobilize the church to help save America.

About that time, a Gallup poll discovered that 34 percent of the American public professed to be born-again Christians. We were mobilizing a potential army numbering in the tens of millions. The fight was on!

Generally, the people who stopped long enough to listen and to ask questions, to dialogue, and to debate have been informed and informing in our times together. I learned plenty during these last years, and often it was those who began by criticizing me who helped teach me the important lessons.

In 1981 a young woman reporter heard me speak against abortion in a press conference room in a large international airport. Then it was time to catch our plane, and Macel and I started down the concourse surrounded by reporters asking one last question and security guards trying to control the crowd. Cameras and tape recorders were rolling. Flashbulbs still blazed. Startled passengers who happened to watch our media "circus" pass must have wondered how anybody could tolerate this kind of attention very long. For a moment we paused before boarding.

The young woman shouted above the din. "Mr. Falwell, one more question please."

I smiled in her direction.

"You say you are against abortion?" she said.

"Yes." I smiled again and nodded. Everybody knew exactly how I felt about abortion, because I had taken a clear stand against the killing of 1.5 million unborn babies in our country every year. However this reporter had something else in mind. "But what practical alternative to abortion do pregnant girls have when they are facing an unwanted pregnancy?" she asked.

"They can have the baby," I answered quickly, too quickly to suit the bright young woman who was questioning me. "Do you really think it's all that simple?" she asked quietly.

The rest of the press corps had grown strangely silent. They knew that something special was happening between us. This reporter hadn't just asked another question to fill her evening news slot. The look in her eyes made each of us know that her question came from deep and private places down inside her.

"Most of the girls in this country facing an unwanted pregnancy are young and poor and helpless," she said, taking advantage of the silence. "They are sometimes victims of incest or are made pregnant by men who misuse and even abuse them. Some are as young as eleven and twelve years old. Many of them would be kicked out of their homes, their jobs, and their schools the moment their pregnancy even showed. Some would be beaten, their lives threatened by the uncaring and often violent men who made them pregnant or worse yet by their own families."

The young reporter paused. The crowd of journalists looked in my direction.

"What are you doing for women who want to keep their babies but can't find any way to do it?" she asked. "They have no money for medical treatment let alone to pay for the delivery of their child. They have no way to support themselves, no place to live while they are pregnant. They are young and poor and powerless," she said, her voice rising and her face beginning to flush.

"Reverend Falwell," she concluded, "is it really enough for you to take a stand against abortion when you aren't doing anything to help the pregnant girls who have no other way?"

I escaped into the sanctuary of that airplane with the

woman's question still echoing in my mind. "What are you doing for women who want to keep their babies but can't find any
way to do it?"

From that little confrontation, our Liberty Godparent Home
program was born. Any young girl or woman in America who
finds herself in an unwanted pregnancy and doesn't want to
abort the child can check into a Liberty Godparent Home for
the duration of her pregnancy without cost. When the baby is
born she can keep the child or have it adopted into a Christian
home through our Liberty Godparent Adoption Agency. Already
there are hundreds of homes springing up across the nation.
Thousands of pregnant girls have gone through the program.
Our goal is to have 10,000 homes by the year 2000 to save the
1.5 million unborn babies being aborted every year.

Of course there is the possibility that someday we may have
a pro-life Supreme Court with the power to make a difference. A Court reversal on the Roe v. Wade decision could
save millions of unborn babies and reverse this great American tragedy.

In the long run, Jesus Himself showed us through His words
and actions why there are times when we must take a political
stand. Picture one special moment in His life almost 2,000 years
ago. Jesus was about to die. He knew the end was coming. But
there was so much to say and do in those last days. So He hurried back to Jerusalem to try one last time to help the people to
understand His mission among them.

On the day history calls Palm Sunday, Jesus entered the
capital city in triumph. Eyewitnesses reported that He received
a hero's welcome. Cheering crowds greeted Him with waving
palm fronds along the way. Immediately, in the shadow of the
temple, He began to teach them about the end of the world. He
even promised that in a short time the massive building blocks
of their esteemed temple would be thrown down to the ground.
The more He taught, the angrier the crowds became at Him.
Already threatened by His teaching and jealous of the attention
the people were showing Him, the leaders began to plot his
assassination.

Apparently the disciples hurried Jesus to the relative quiet of a nearby hillside covered with olive trees. Tell us, they said excitedly, when shall these things be?

They wanted to know when the world was going to end, but Jesus wouldn't say. He told them to keep alert. He warned them that it could come any day. But He wouldn't tell them when. Nevertheless, on one end-of-time issue He was perfectly clear.

"When the Son of man shall come in his glory," He began, "and all the holy angels with him, then shall he sit upon the throne of his glory: and before him shall be gathered all nations: and he shall separate them one from another, as a shepherd divideth his sheep from the goats: and he shall set the sheep on his right hand, but the goats on the left."

Jesus was describing the final judgment. The disciples must have crowded in with growing interest. What subject could be more important to them? What subject could be more important to us 2,000 years later?

"Then," Jesus continued, "the King shall say unto them on his right hand, Come, ye blessed of my Father, inherit the kingdom prepared for you from the foundation of the world....Then shall he say also unto them on the left hand, Depart from me, ye cursed, into everlasting fire, prepared for the devil and his angels."

This is terrifying stuff. Jesus Himself promised His disciples that at the end of life there will be a judgment. I still remember how I felt when a math teacher began a lecture with those awful words: "Tomorrow you will be tested on this material!" When we were warned that there would be a final accounting, we listened with both ears. We kept notes. We paid attention. I still hear students asking, "But what will we be tested on?" It must have been their question that day as they sat together beneath the trees on the Mount of Olives. It certainly should be our question today. At that final judgment, what will we be tested on?

You can read Jesus's own answer in the first book of the New Testament, Matthew 25:31-46. In those fifteen verses Jesus separates the people of the world into two categories at the final judgment: the sheep (the righteous) and the goats (the unrighteous).

He also described in exact detail the standard by which every man or woman will be judged.

To the righteous, He said, "For I was ahungered, and ye gave me meat: I was thirsty, and ye gave me drink: I was a stranger, and ye took me in: naked, ye clothed me: I was sick, and ye visited me: I was in prison, and ye came unto me."

And when the righteous muttered in astonishment, When did we see you hungry and feed you? or thirsty, and give you drink? When did we see you a stranger and take you in? or naked and clothed you? Or when did we see you sick or in prison and came unto you?

Then Jesus spoke the words that have challenged men and women to take action on behalf of the needy for the past twenty centuries: "When you have done it unto one of the least of these, my brethren, you have done it unto me."

And when the unrighteous asked that same question, wondering why they had been condemned for all eternity, Jesus answered again: ". . . as ye did it not to one of the least of these, ye did it not to me."

Jesus ended the story with these moving and unforgettable words: "And these [the unrighteous] shall go away into everlasting punishment: but the righteous into life eternal."

I don't know how you feel about the meaning of this great Biblical passage. We Baptists believe that in spite of a person's unrighteousness, when you ask God to forgive you and truly receive Christ as your Lord, you are forgiven. It is finished. There is no more danger of the judgment. But we still take this passage and Jesus's warning in it very seriously. While we believe in the premillennial, pre-tribulational coming of Christ for all of His church, we believe every person will give an account to God.

Jesus didn't paint this vivid picture of our final test to begin an ethical system based upon our good works. He isn't keeping track of the number of babies we save from abortion or the young women we house and help. He isn't adding up the tons of blankets we provide the street people or the number of ex-prisoners enrolled in our halfway house programs. We don't pile up points to be saved. The Bible says, "For by grace are ye saved through faith; and that not of yourselves: it is the gift of God: not of works, lest any man should boast" (Ephesians 2:89).

However, we don't believe that Jesus was just setting a kind of impossible standard either. This story wasn't told just to show us how unrighteous we are. He didn't talk of sheep and goats to illustrate how much more grateful we should be for His act of salvation. Jesus didn't play jokes on people. He was serious when He spoke those words on the Mount of Olives, and we should take them seriously.

The needs that Jesus spoke about were practical, human everyday needs: hunger, thirst, being a stranger, nakedness, sickness, and imprisonment. The list is a call to seek justice and mercy on behalf of all who suffer. When I was a young Christian, I heard sermons preached by my fundamentalist brothers against the "social Gospel." Looking back, I can understand why they were fighting the theology of those mainline Protestant and Catholic churches that had surrendered the Gospel to become a public charity. And they were right to warn those churches and churchmen and women who did not seem interested in the human soul but only in the welfare of the human body.

However, preaching against the "social Gospel" became for some fundamentalists and evangelicals an excuse to ignore Christ's call to feed the hungry and to heal the sick. No longer can we divide the church by those standards. Today's Christian community must preach the Gospel clearly and at the same time put its faith into practical action on behalf of all those who suffer.

When we began the first Liberty Godparent Home, it was to obey Christ's command. It took all kinds of political expertise to get the subsequent homes approved by local, state, and national government agencies. It required working hand-in-hand with the departments of welfare, probation boards, and representatives from the offices of mayors, governors, attorneys general, and even the Congress. It is a political process to save the unborn babies and to help and house the women facing unwanted pregnancies. But it is worth it!

If only I could take you through our first Liberty Godparent

Home at 520 Eldon Street in Lynchburg. That gracious old Victorian residence, replete with gables, turrets, and gingerbread trim, sits in a quiet middle-class neighborhood not far from Thomas Road Baptist Church. We loved that house the moment we saw it. We scrimped and saved and begged to get enough money to buy and to prepare it. Volunteers worked for weeks painting and patching, pounding and sawing, putting up curtains and laying down carpet. Telephone lines were laid for the hot line that would take thousands of emergency calls from young girls and women across America who found themselves pregnant and didn't know what to do (1-800-54-CHILD). We later moved to a larger facility and now, thank God, are moving to a brand new facility, recently contributed by friends who care.

For some, like JoAnn, making that call for help meant risking her life. Late one night one of our volunteer operators picked up the phone and heard the frantic voice of a frightened fourteen-year-old girl. She was whispering. Her words were unclear and garbled. She was near hysteria.

"Could you speak slower and a bit louder?" our operator asked. "I'm having trouble hearing you."

"My name is JoAnn," the young woman whispered as slowly as she could manage. "I can only talk a few minutes. My father is drunk downstairs. I can hear him snoring, but if he wakes up while I am calling you, he will kill me."

I used to laugh when a teenager talked of death that way. Then I learned the hard way that parents do kill their teenagers and that teenagers do kill themselves. Now when a young person speaks of death, I listen carefully.

"Could you give me your phone number and address?" our operator asked, taking the girl's tearful warning seriously.

"I can't tell you," the girl answered sadly. "If you show up here, I'm dead."

Then, without warning, there was nothing but a dial tone. Only the loud dial tone could be heard. The girl was gone. And there was no way to trace her. Our operators are helpless at a time like this. They can only wait and hope that the troubled teenager will find the courage and the means to call again. Several hours later, some time in the middle of the night, JoAnn dialed again.

"I am fourteen," the girl whispered. "My mother was hurt in a bad car wreck and just stays in bed. She can't move. We have to change her diapers and the bottle that drips food into her arm. She is like a vegetable. After my mom's accident, my daddy started having sex with me. I was eleven. I tried to pretend I was asleep. Sometimes when my daddy came after me, I got into bed with my mom, but she couldn't help me. Now I think I'm pregnant. I don't know for sure, but I think I am. How can I find out?"

The operator stayed on the line, trying to get JoAnn's address, offering her words of comfort and advice, knowing that the appropriate city officials in Detroit had to be notified. The girl was sharing more of her heartbreaking story, but she was still too afraid to give her address or phone number.

"If you come here," she said, "my dad will know I called. He says he'll hurt me if he catches me telling anyone."

Our trained volunteer kept trying to get more solid information. The girl would not budge.

"I have three young sisters," the girl confessed toward the end of the conversation. "Now my daddy's having sex with two of them."

Finally the operator convinced the girl that she would only be safe if someone from the Liberty Godparent ministries could get there to help her. At 2 A.M. the girl's line went dead again. By 8:30 A.M. that next morning the operator had notified our director, who called a social service agency in Detroit. Before noon the director of that agency called our offices with the full account.

"The girl's story is a nightmare," the social worker began. "Her mother is completely paralyzed and totally helpless. The little girls, ranging in age from eight to fourteen, have been trying to nurse their mother without any outside help for more than three years. When we entered the house, the father was still drunk and asleep on the sofa. He was holding the twelve-year-old girl in his arms even as he slept. The mother's bedclothes had not been changed in days. There were more than twenty cats on the premises. The smell of human and animal excrement was overwhelming. The fourteen-year-old is in our clinic being tested for venereal disease. She is pregnant. The two other girls show definite signs of sexual molestation. All four girls, even the eight-year-old, show signs of physical abuse."

JoAnn had seen our toll-free number on a television ad for the Liberty Godparent Home program. She asked the social worker in Detroit if she could come to Lynchburg and talk about her unborn baby with "the nice lady on the telephone." Within twenty-four hours JoAnn had been signed over to our custody by her father, and a Liberty University student who was returning to school drove her to the Liberty Godparent Home, where she stayed for five months.

During her time with us, JoAnn was given a room, fresh clothing, three solid meals a day. She was counseled about her baby. Our young women are free to keep their children or to have them adopted by a qualified Christian family through the Liberty Godparent Adoption Agency. Our medical and dietary counselors prepared JoAnn's body for a safe, healthy pregnancy. Our teachers began her high school program and taught JoAnn some of the basic skills she would need to care for herself and for her child in the days ahead. And our pastors and counselors led JoAnn to Christ and helped her begin the long-term adjustment to the psychological trauma she had suffered since her childhood. JoAnn worshipped with us at Thomas Road Baptist Church every Sunday. It was at our altar that she confessed her faith in Christ.

Talking about people like JoAnn is not enough. Jesus would have us spend every resource at our command to rescue such a child. Where there is suffering, we must act. And if our action requires political involvement, so be it.

It is my conviction that whatever is required to make a good Christian also makes a good citizen.

— Jerry Falwell

We must never forget that liberty
was born in the heart of God and
that freedom is the most basic
moral value of all.

— Jerry Falwell

CHAPTER FOURTEEN

The Moral Majority

In 1978 my ministry in Lynchburg was featured in a front-page feature article in the Wall Street Journal. That article coined the name "the Electric Church" to describe preachers who had launched national radio and television ministries. An executive editor of the Wall Street Journal, Fred Zimmerman, had been a friend from Baptist Bible College days in Springfield, Missouri. Fred's dad had been the pastor of the Kansas City Baptist Temple and my employer for a time. It was Fred Zimmerman who recommended that reporters from the Wall Street Journal feature the story of Thomas Road Baptist Church and "The Old Time Gospel Hour" in their article. From that moment, the crowd of reporters and journalists from across America and around the world who covered my ministry seemed to increase in size and energy every day.

In 1978 and 1979 we took another musical team from Liberty University to almost 150 American cities. *America, You're Too Young to Die!* was a special multi-media presentation with music, pictures, and drama. This rather sobering indictment of the sins of the nation and the dramatic call to spiritual renewal filled auditoriums and coliseums all across America.

Pastors and lay leaders were responding with growing enthusiasm to the challenge. They were organizing their churches, speaking and leading discussions on the issues, and participating in voter education and registration drives. Many of those clergymen, for the first time in their ministry, were taking prophetic stands on issues of critical importance to the church and to the world.

And though our supporters far outnumbered our critics, there were clergy and laity alike who stood against us. In cities across the country, from my own pulpit, and on radio and television I made my defense: "If the leaders of Christendom in the nation don't stand up against immorality, we can't expect anyone else to lead. I believe it is the duty of Gospel preachers to set the pace. When sin moves to the front, preachers and Christians everywhere must speak out. I will as long as I have breath."

In April, 1979 our musical team began a series of state capitol performances of the *I Love America* presentation. We began on the steps of the nation's Capitol in Washington, D.C. Our programs began at 11 A.M. and climaxed during the lunch hour. Elected officials, governors, legislators, attorneys general, and state treasurers stood beside us on the steps and made their own individual pleas for a return to morality. Thousands of our supporters, plus state employees and private citizens who chanced by and journalists on the lookout for a good story, crowded around to hear our young people sing and stayed to hear me speak.

"We have to pay the price for freedom," I said over and over again to those who stopped to listen. "If we're not willing to pay the price, God will give us what we want. Remember! He repeatedly sold His people into bondage. The book of Judges is the story of one bondage after another. When the people cried out for mercy, God sent them a deliverer. For a short time they walked with God and really honored the Lord; then they forgot Him, and once again their nation fell. I think our country is now at the point where we could fall. I don't think that is alarmism; I think that's fact, unless we repent now. The question is, if we repent and get right with God, will God bring us out? I really don't know."

I dealt specifically with the moral problems of abortion, pornography, the 50 percent divorce rate, moral permissiveness, a soft attitude toward Marxism-Leninism, our nation's military unpreparedness, and the general breakdown of traditional family values. I called for massive voter registration campaigns. I urged the religious right to stand up and be counted.

And though my words sounded ominous, I always concluded each patriotic rally on the steps of each state capitol building with God's promise: "If my people, which are called by my name, shall humble themselves, and pray, and seek my face, and turn from their wicked ways; then will I hear from heaven, and will forgive their sin, and will heal their land." (2 Chronicles 7: 14)

We visited forty-four state capitols during that year, and in every new city we visited the crowds got larger and more enthusiastic in their response. At every capitol I met with pastors and Christian lay leaders from across that state. I presented the problem. Our nation was facing perilous times. And I pointed to the role that they and their churches could play in the solution. And they responded in growing numbers all across America. We were collecting a massive list of clergy and laity who were committed to widen their ministries to include political action. The evangelical, fundamentalist, charismatic Christian communities were coming to life. The country was being changed. But all the time I was working to mobilize the Christian church to take action, God had an even larger work in mind.

In May 1979 I called a group of conservative leaders to meet in my office in Lynchburg, to talk about the future and to organize for the long, hard struggle ahead. In spite of everything we were doing to turn the nation back to God, to morality, and to constructive patriotism, the national crisis was growing quickly out of hand!

Since Roe v. Wade, more than a million and a half unborn babies were being aborted every year. The divorce rate had skyrocketed. The sexual, physical, and emotional abuse of children, wives, and the elderly was becoming common practice. The traditional American family was being threatened as never before in the history of the nation. Pornography was flooding

the mails and being sold to children through their neighborhood stores. Drug and alcohol abuse and addiction had reached
down to the elementary grades. Courts seemed to favor the
offender; and law-enforcement agencies, social action organizations, and welfare groups seemed helpless to stem the growing tide of injustice, immorality, and crime let alone to assist
the growing number of victims. Something more had to be done
than preaching on television or singing on the steps of the state
capitol buildings of America.

Between 1973, when the Supreme Court's decision legalizing abortion was announced, and 1979, when conservative leaders from across America came to Lynchburg to "draw up a plan
to save America" I had been in training. Now it was time to act
seriously.

In 1976 the Gallup poll organization had announced that
sixty to seventy million Americans had experienced a newbirth
relationship with Christ. I knew that if even a small percentage
of my Christian brothers and sisters could be mobilized to action, we could reverse the nation's downward spiral and set
America back on the straight and narrow path once again. But
in 1979, in the meeting in Lynchburg with my fellow conservatives from across the country, a new idea dawned.

At a lunch break, Paul Weyrich, one of my very dear friends
and a great American, looked across the table at me and said,
"Jerry, there is in America a moral majority that agrees about
the basic issues. But they aren't organized. They don't have a
platform. The media ignore them. Somebody's got to get that
moral majority together."

There are millions of men and women in America who
shared common moral views and human values who were not
evangelical or fundamentalist Christians. There were Protestants from the mainline denominations. There were loyal members of Roman Catholic and Orthodox congregations. There
were practicing and non-practicing Jews. There were atheists
and agnostics who had no religious affiliations at all, but who
were just as afraid of the darkening cloud upon the nation's
horizon and just as willing to take their own personal risks
against the storm as we were.

Since becoming a Christian I had lived a rather separatist life. I believed that "being yoked with unbelievers" for any cause was off limits. I didn't even get along very well with other kinds of Baptists, let alone with Methodists, Presbyterians, or Catholics.

To help you understand my dilemma, I need to explain the separatist position that evangelicals and fundamentalists have traditionally maintained. By the way, at press conferences or on television talk shows, when I am asked what the difference is between an evangelical and a fundamentalist, I usually give this tongue in cheek reply: "A fundamentalist is an evangelical who is mad about something."

Actually, evangelicals and fundamentalists agree on most important doctrinal issues: the infallibility of the Bible, the deity of Jesus Christ, the fact of a trinitarian (Father, Son, and Holy Spirit) faith, and the necessity of every human being having a personal experience of rebirth through Jesus Christ in order to gain admission into the family of God.

We believe that God loves everyone equally. We believe that all human beings are sons and daughters of Adam and therefore members of the human family in equal standing. We further believe that the death of Jesus Christ on the cross is adequate to provide salvation for all who believe in Him. However, we likewise believe that the death, burial, and resurrection of Jesus Christ are efficient to save only those who believe. We reject the philosophy of universalism-that everyone will eventually go to heaven regardless of what they believe. We reject the concept that there are many roads to heaven and that we are all working for the same place. We believe that God's simple plan of salvation is embodied in the person of Jesus Christ, God's Son, and that when Jesus said "I am the way, the truth, and the life," (John 14:6) God made it clear once and forever that faith in Christ alone saves the sinner.

On that premise of the exclusivity of salvation in and through Jesus Christ, we further accept the teachings of Paul that all marriages should be within the spiritual family. To do otherwise is to be unequally yoked together. We also teach very carefully that business partnerships, and other deep-rooted involvements and relationships, should meet this same criterion. Even in our pastoral associations and conventions, we are very careful to include only those who are of like mind and faith. In other words, we are committed to theological purity and to maintaining the sanctity of our Articles of Faith.

This position parallels the position of Orthodox Jews, conservative Roman Catholics, and other similar religious bodies. It is not elitism. It is not a feeling of spiritual superiority, although we are often accused of this. We feel very strongly that it is a commitment to the teachings of the Bible. And we are quick to point out that Bible-believing Christianity of the New Testament variety continues strongly after 2,000 years of opposition and persecution because of a firm commitment to Bible separatism.

Therefore, when I began considering how to put together a political organization that included all Americans I was faced with a terrific problem: my own personal psychological barrier. All of my background from Baptist Bible College and other places and persons providing my religious training made it difficult for me to consider such a prospect. And yet I was convinced that there was a "moral majority" out there among these more than 200 million Americans sufficient in number to turn back the flood tide of moral permissiveness, family breakdown, and general capitulation to evil and to foreign philosophies such as Marxism-Leninism.

For that reason, I determined to find the way it could be done. During those days the late Dr. Francis Schaeffer was a great help to me. Time magazine referred to him as "the Guru of the Evangelicals." In his speeches and writings, he spoke of "co-belligerents." He declared that there is no Biblical mandate against evangelical Christians joining hands for political and social causes as long as there was no compromise of theological integrity.

Dr. Schaeffer pointed out that the Bible is filled with stories of the yoking together of persons from various philosophical backgrounds for the purpose of carrying out a cause that was good for humanity and pleasing to God.

I was also aware that Roman Catholics, Jews, Protestants

from various denominations, Mormons, and other religious groups would be very wary of working with an evangelical and fundamentalist minister in any enterprise. As a matter of fact, I was not sure that we could marshal together sufficient numbers in the cross-section of the religious community and the nonreligious community to make an impact on the nation.

However, after I had settled in my own heart that it was possible to be involved in political and social issues as a Bible-believing Christian without violating the Bible that I believe and love, the job was now clearly to begin the task of creating such a "moral majority."

And if ever there was a time when God needed a job done, it was during the 1960's. and 1970's. The future of our nation was at stake. I believed (and I still believe) that God has special plans for this great, free country of ours. I believe America has a responsibility to share our spiritual and material wealth with the rest of the world. I sincerely believe that Satan had mobilized his own forces to destroy America by negating the Judeo-Christian ethic, secularizing our society, and devaluating human life through the legalization of abortion and infanticide. God needed voices raised to save the nation from inward moral decay. He needed people from across the country, regardless of their religious affinity, to renew their commitment to the basic human values upon which the nation was founded. And we could help organize that constituency.

All across the land people were just as afraid of the dangers that threatened the American family as we evangelical and fundamentalist Christians were. It wasn't necessary to be born again to hate abortion, the drug traffic, pornography, child abuse, and immorality in all its ugly, life-destroying forms. Whatever plan God had for this free nation was being threatened, and we needed to draw together millions of people who agreed on these basic issues to take a stand with us and to turn the nation around.

In that spirit and to accomplish that end, in June 1979 we organized the Moral Majority Incorporated, a political lobbying organization, and the Moral Majority Foundation, an educational foundation to publish newspapers, do radio and television programs, and conduct lectures and seminars across the country.

Our first board of directors included D. James Kennedy, pastor of the Coral Ridge Presbyterian Church in Fort Lauderdale, Florida; Charles Stanley, pastor of the First Baptist Church in Atlanta, Georgia; Tim LaHaye, pastor of the Scott Memorial Baptist Church in El Cajon, California; Greg Dixon, pastor of the Indianapolis Baptist Temple; and myself. We hadn't reached out very far in those first days, but we had begun. For some of us, just reaching out to other Baptists and other Presbyterians was a rather large step of faith. And God used that little step of faith to begin a journey that would reach out to change the nation.

Immediately we announced our fourfold platform: We were pro-life, pro-traditional family, pro-moral, and pro-American (that included favoring a strong national defense and support for the state of Israel). Suddenly we found ourselves flooded with calls, letters, and telegrams from around the country from Protestant pastors and lay people who wanted to join the team. Then Catholic priests and Jewish rabbis began to ask for information. There followed a flood of inquiries from individual Americans, believers, unbelievers, and those still struggling with belief, from every class, color, and creed, from tiny towns and the great cities. Everybody wanting to know: What is the Moral Majority and how can we join in?

In order to get a Moral Majority mailing list started to all these people, I borrowed $25,000 from Bob Perry, a businessman in Houston, Texas. We explained the Moral Majority dream and we asked people who shared that dream to join with us in volunteering their time, their talents, and their gifts. In just a few weeks, from contributions received by return mail, we had repaid the $25,000 loan, organized a small staff of full-time, part-time, and volunteer workers to handle the letters and telegrams, the speaking requests, the organization of Moral Majority chapters across the country, the development of promotional materials, film and video presentations, and political action information and here's-how kits.

Within three years, we had a $10 million budget, 100,000

trained pastors, priests, and rabbis, and several million volunteers. In Washington, D.C., for example, in just one day 569 preachers who belonged to the Ministerial Alliance there joined hands with the Moral Majority and began to work with other volunteers across the nation on behalf of defeating an anti-moral ordinance in the nation's capital. Approximately 500 of those ministers working in our nation's capital were black. Our Moral Majority quickly developed our own rainbow coalition of men and women from every race and color, every political and religious belief. I found myself sharing the platform with Roman Catholic priests and nuns, Orthodox rabbis, Mormon elders, and pastors from Southern Baptist, Methodist, Presbyterian, Assembly of God, and Nazarene churches.

This was not nor was it ever intended to be an evangelistic enterprise. The Moral Majority was not a religious movement. People of like moral and political values were uniting to save the country. We came together around shared moral issues in our country's time of crisis. This was war, and temporarily it was necessary to put aside the issues that divided us to work together for the goals we had in common. To win the war against crime and immorality, to save the American family, to stop the killing of 1.5 million unborn infants every year would take everyone willing to take a stand regardless of his or her race or religion, social class or political party.

To save the children, Baptist preachers found themselves marching arm in arm with courageous little Catholic nuns who had already taken their lonely stand against abortion and those who ran the abortion mills. In their struggle to save abused children and old people who had been forgotten, rabbis in their dark suits and little caps and Orthodox priests in their ornate vestments walked in solidarity with Quakers and Mennonites who had already led the way. Episcopalian laymen filled their Mercedeses with kids from Assembly of God churches to drive into the inner city to work with boys and girls who were trapped by drugs or sexual bondage.

Baptists and Catholics, Mormons and Jews, believers and unbelievers took to the streets to organize for political change. We registered voters. We informed them of the issues. We put maps on the walls, circled precincts, and urged volunteers to go door-to-door on behalf of candidates who supported their simple goals and to work against the candidates who did not support them. We published lists of candidates and their voting records on all the important issues, without officially endorsing any candidates. We trusted each person to make his or her decisions on whom to support.

We held rallies and parades. We filled tiny churches and great coliseums. We produced television and radio promotions and were interviewed by almost every talk show host on almost every local television and radio station in America. We mailed out millions of brochures and letters. We answered hundreds of thousands of requests for information and for aid. We manned banks of telephones and assembled huge computerized mailing lists, all to raise the moral conscience of the nation and to mobilize people of like mind to take political action.

And in the process, we helped elect a President. In 1980, Ronald Reagan filled a vacuum on the political scene. This former governor of California seemed to represent all the political positions we held dear, and his own moral and spiritual commitments seemed genuine and relevant to his campaign agenda. So we threw our growing political weight in his direction. We registered millions of new voters. We mobilized thousands of precinct workers. We used media and personal appearances to bring new life back into the political system. We did our best to excite and inform millions of people who had stopped voting and who had quit caring about government or about who governs.

And when the votes were counted, those candidates across America who supported our cause had gained a significant victory. "Reagan would have lost the election by one percentage point without the help of the Moral Majority," pollster Lou Harris exclaimed. I replied, "It was the American people, not the Moral Majority who elected Ronald Reagan . . . but we helped."

As the final results were tabulated in the important state races for national office, we discovered how important our help had been. Out of forty-three races in which a Moral Majority chapter was involved, the morally conservative candidate won in forty. And of the thirty-eight political incumbents our people opposed, twenty-three were defeated. In less than two years we had mobilized a powerful and effective political army, and on his first inauguration day, Mr. Reagan gave us a sign that our trust had been well placed and that the nation's course was on its way to being corrected. Our new President quoted the text I had been quoting in my speeches across the country on his behalf:

"If my people, which are called by my name, shall humble themselves, and pray, and seek my face, and turn from their wicked ways; then I will hear from heaven, and will forgive their sin and will heal their land." (2 Chronicles 7:14)

Immediately the nation's media published articles creating suspicion that Jerry Falwell and the Moral Majority would attempt to dictate national morality and give religious tests to candidates (Washington Post) or criticize the private lives of our elected officials (Associated Press). I denied the charges. In fact, of all the candidates our people had supported in the election of 1981, not one was a fundamentalist. "I would feel comfortable voting for a Jew or a Catholic or an atheist," I told the press, "as long as he or she agrees with us on the vital issues." And the private religious lives of the elected officials "are their business," I added, "just as long as they keep their public responsibility to the voters who elected them."

And when suspicions were raised that we were trying to stack the new administration with Moral Majority members or supporters, I replied, "I haven't asked for any of my friends to be put in the administration. We simply want to be friendly supporters from the outside."

Winning these political victories had not been easy or risk free. For example, in 1980 we took our I Love America musical program to the steps of the state capitol in Madison, Wisconsin. We never knew for certain how large or friendly these open-air crowds might be. We were accustomed to the occasional heckler and to fanatics from the lunatic fringe. I was receiving scores of death threats every month by mail or telephone, and though we ignored most of them entirely, no one could know the difference between a crank call and the warning of a crazed but serious would-be assassin.

At that time the University of Wisconsin had one of the largest cells of avowed leftists in the nation. Needless to say, this organized group of radicals had little tolerance for the political message of the Moral Majority and no sympathy at all for my spiritual message of repentance and renewal. As our crew set up the portable sound systems and microphones, we noticed people in the growing crowd wearing hammer and sickle armbands. A local police officer pointed out the professional demonstrators who were gathering among the pastors, priests, and laity who made up our typical state capitol crowd.

Promptly at 11:30 A.M. our musicians from Liberty Baptist College began to play and the singers joined in the song. People flocked out of nearby government buildings and offices to sing along. Our Wisconsin supporters swelled the crowd to several thousand strong. Most of them were friendly and enthusiastic. Then without warning the professional agitators went into action. From the back of the crowd, a group of demonstrators began to chant: "Damn Jesus Christ! Damn Jesus Christ! "

At first I tried to ignore them. Our crew just turned up the sound levels and for a moment the voices of our singers almost drowned out that ugly chant. Then more demonstrators arrived carrying signs and shouting their own profanities. I stepped to the microphone to pray. There were three or four hundred chairs in the front of the crowd for the pastors, city and state officials, and our special guests. People were turning in their chairs and straining to see what the commotion was about. The chanting grew louder and the obscenities more profane.

Suddenly it seemed that the crowd of protesters had grown to three or four hundred strong. They had locked arms and were surging forward through the audience. Men shouted. Women screamed. People who had come with their lunches in hand to enjoy the musical presentation scrambled for safety. The ministers from across Wisconsin stood for a moment looking at the demonstrators moving toward them. At that moment, one of the pastors shouted at me. "Preacher," he said, "don't pay any attention to these people. We can take care of them!"

At that moment he locked arms with pastors and members

from other churches around Wisconsin who stood on either side of him. They turned to face the noisy mob. Other pastors and priests joined arms and turned to face the demonstrators. The crowd of angry chanting students drew closer. Our choir continued to sing nervously as the arm-band wearers approached waving their fists and yelling obscenities. Suddenly the two lines met, ministers and marchers facing each other directly. Nobody backed away. Nobody flinched. I cleared my throat and continued to speak. While I spoke of the moral and spiritual dilemma facing the nation, the other preachers stood facing the demonstrators eyeball-to-eyeball in a kind of nervous truce. When I finished my full address, the security officers motioned me into a door that led directly into the capitol.

"Those ministers saved the day," one policeman said as we walked through the marble corridors to another exit a hundred yards away. "They stood right up to those punks," another added. "Who would have expected it from a bunch of preachers?"

There were a lot of people surprised to see what a small bunch of preachers could do when they had united with men and women of like moral values to take an organized political stand. Television and radio broadcasters had never given the conservatives of this country a chance to be heard. With the size and effectiveness of the Moral Majority, they could no longer ignore the conservative viewpoint or the millions of silent Americans who believed it. Newspapers and news magazines had ignored or satirized us in the past. Now, we were front-page news. And universities from Berkeley to Harvard, where radical students once ruled the day, finally opened their doors to people with another view.

At Princeton University a bomb threat forced the evacuation of Alexander Hall just before I was scheduled to address the student body. We ignored the bomb threat and went ahead with the convocation. At Yale University, a group of students held a "secular humanist vigil" to protest my appearance, condemning bigotry, chauvinism, oppression, nuclear war, and Jerry Falwell (as though I advocated those positions). At Harvard University, as I began my address, a well-organized group of students rose and began to chant in unison: "Hitler

rose, Hitler fell; racist Falwell, go to hell." From Berkeley to
Harvard protesters met my arrival waving signs and carrying
banners. At almost every stop noisy radical students greeted
my introduction with boos, hisses, catcalls, and loud angry cries
of protest.

But those students weren't to blame for their bad manners
or their lack of truthful information about me and the cause I
represented. I was a victim of students who had themselves
been made victims by the liberal press and by the liberal educational system. The press consistently compared me to the
Ayatollah Khomeini, Adolf Hitler, and Jim Jones. They portrayed
me as an absolutist who wanted to impose my fundamentalist
views on everybody else. They said I was sexist, racist, and
anti-Semitic. They labeled me a demagogue and my "followers" dupes and crazies.

Like the press, university executives and faculty alike had a
field day personifying me as the epitome of evil. For just one
example, Yale University President Bartlett Giamatti warned
his entering freshman class that I "have licensed a new mean-
ness of spirit in the land, a resurgent bigotry that manifests
itself in racist and discriminatory postures, in threats of political retaliation, in injunctions to censorship, in acts of violence."

No wonder some university students protested my appearances. If I had believed what they had heard about me, I would
have protested them myself. These young people could not help
it if they had been brainwashed against me and against my conservative positions on politics and morality. Apparently, they
weren't aware that conservatives have valid positions that can
be supported with facts and historical data, not just by rhetoric
and hysteria.

So in those early 1980's, in almost every university, a noisy
minority of the students booed and hissed when I was introduced. Then after the rowdies were calmed and the hysterical
led away, the students listened. Sometimes they interrupted
my speeches with questions or with accusations, which I was
glad to answer. Other times they waited until the end of the speech
to dialogue openly and honestly with me. And invariably when
the evening ended, the students' attitudes had changed.

When the Harvard kids began to chant: "Hitler rose, Hitler fell; racist Falwell, go to hell," the noisiest and less coherent of them had to be removed. The rest stayed to banter.

"Are you a racist?" one finally asked.

"I was at one time," I answered truthfully. "But the rumors you hear about me today are largely untrue."

"Then why don't you have any black members in your church in Lynchburg?" a student shouted.

"That's the kind of rumor I mean," I said, smiling back at him. "We have four hundred members of Thomas Road Baptist Church who are from ethnic minority groups. And eleven percent of the Liberty University student body would be minorities. Now let me ask you and your administration a question!"

The students and their teachers grew silent, knowing what might be coming next.

"How many black students, professors, or administrators do you have at Harvard?"

There was a brief, embarrassed silence. Then the students and the faculty began to laugh nervously, looking up and down the rows of white students, white faculty, and white administrators. Apparently, Liberty University had a higher percentage of blacks than had Harvard University, the "bastion of liberalism."

The university students consistently ask the same questions and invariably they are surprised to hear my answers:

1. I did not found the Moral Majority to enshrine into law any set of fundamentalist Christian doctrines. Roman Catholics make up at least 30 percent of our membership. Other members come from almost every Protestant denomination, and there are Mormons, Jews, agnostics, and atheists as well.

2. I oppose abortion but I would accept legislation that would permit abortion for women who are victims of incest or rape or in pregnancies where the life of the mother is at stake.

3. I believe that sexual intercourse belongs in a loving, caring monogamous family relationship. I do not oppose birth control in this free, pluralistic society. And though many of

my Catholic brothers and sisters in the Moral Majority disagree with me here, I personally favor the use of appropriate birth control methods in the prevention of unwanted pregnancies.

4. Although I see homosexual practice as a moral wrong and do not favor their being singled out as a specially protected minority, I do not want to deny homosexual men or lesbian women their civil rights or take away their right to accommodations or employment or even their right to teach in public schools as long as they don't use the classroom to promote homosexuality as an alternative life-style.

5. I support absolute equal rights for women. But I opposed the Equal Rights Amendment as flawed and not the appropriate or necessary tool to achieve that full equality.

6. I oppose the world's growing stockpile of nuclear arms and I fear its eventual use in the destruction of much of God's creation, but I believe in the development and maintenance of the strongest possible national defense as a deterrent to war. I am also opposed to any steps we might take toward unilateral disarmament or non-verifiable bilateral disarmament.

7. I want our children to be able to pray in their schools but I believe that the prayers should be voluntary, nonsectarian, and that no public official should write or mandate a prayer. Further, no child should be intimidated or embarrassed for not participating.

8. I believe in a pluralistic, democratic society where all the people are free to speak, where the majority rules but where no minority is exploited or discriminated against, where every race, color, or creed has equal access to justice and opportunity, where no one needs to be poor or hungry or afraid.

9. I do not believe in book burning or censorship of any

kind. The press has often accused me of book burning. It isn't true. It has never been true. Our library at Liberty University has or will have every book by every author that any great university might have to support its academic offerings. We have a matchbook we distribute to make our point. "Moral Majority Book Burning Matches," the cover reads, with our logo emblazoned in red, white, and blue. "See official book list inside." When you open the matchbook to see the books we recommend burning, you will find a blank list and the words "That's right, there aren't any!"

10. I believe in America's unswerving support of the state of Israel and of the support of Jewish people everywhere. But I believe equally in working for peace in the Middle East, in respecting and supporting our Arab friends and allies, and in assisting the poor, the hungry, the dispossessed, and the homeless of that troubled region in every way we can.

11. I believe that we should go all out to control the illegal flood of harmful drugs into this country and to do everything possible to stop their use among our people. Drug dealers should face stiff sentences and heavy fines for their crime. Drug addicts should be given every possible assistance in overcoming their addiction.

12. I believe in the free enterprise system. I have seen the options and found them wanting. I look on socialism as mutually shared poverty. But I also believe that we must continue to struggle to bring justice, equality and a fuller measure of mercy and generosity through our free enterprise system. The exploitation of workers, the misuse and abuse of power and wealth, the unequal and discriminatory distribution of profits should have no place in America's practice of capitalism.

My university student hosts dialogue and debate with me often until late at night about these and dozens of other important issues. They come prepared to interrupt and heckle. They leave better informed and somewhat surprised. All the students don't end up agreeing with me; but many if not most of them are amazed to learn that they have a large number of beliefs and values in common with the man they had been taught to hate. And more important, they discover that there is a danger of being misinformed and misled by television, radio, the press and by their own professors even in this great free nation of ours. At the close of most evenings, as I walk back through the once hostile crowds, the students are smiling, reaching out to shake my hand or even standing to their feet applauding. The overwhelming majority have now become my friends.

Other meetings have turned violent. In San Francisco, just before the Democratic Convention in 1984, in partnership with Paul Weyrich, I convened a special conference on the family for 400 invited delegates from around the country. We wanted to influence the Democratic agenda by our presence in their convention city; but once the news of our meeting appeared on the front pages of the city's papers, our hotel was besieged by hundreds of hostile and boisterous demonstrators representing radicals of every persuasion. They chanted. They yelled obscenities. They wore outlandish costumes. They carried signs and painted graffiti. They threw objects. They threatened me and the other delegates, and they massed at every entrance to attempt to block my departure from the hotel.

One hundred and fifty of San Francisco's riot police on foot and horseback were called in by Mayor Dianne Feinstein to help control the growing crowd of demonstrators. The "president of the National Prostitutes Association" joined a group of transvestites dressed in nuns' habits who called themselves "Sister Boom Boom and her Sisters of Perpetual Indulgence," and other radicals in the streets to protest my "racist, sexist, warmongering, anti-human-rights" positions. An effigy of President Reagan was hanged and set on fire next to mine. The crowds grew larger and more boisterous. The police moved in and began to make arrests.

At the conclusion of our two-day conference, the Cable News Network had requested a long in-depth interview with me in a nearby television studio. The police had insisted that I move in and out of the hotel in total secrecy surrounded by guards. But my seventeen-year-old son Jonathan had been out in the crowd throughout those two violent, disturbing days. Nobody had recognized him. He wore ragged clothing. He had a large press pass pinned to his jean jacket, and he carried a camera and a recorder. For hours he had mingled in the angry crowd, interviewing their leaders, trying to understand exactly who they were and what they were after. During that time, he spent a great deal of time getting to know Sister Boom Boom.

When the police moved into arrest the primary troublemakers, Jonathan jumped into the back of the paddy wagon carrying some of the radicals. He began taking photos and asking questions for his tape recorder. During the few minutes before the paddy wagon pulled away, Jonathan heard the radicals saying strong things about me.

"Falwell hates homosexuals," one gay man claimed. "He wants to deprive us of our civil rights. He wants to stop our teaching in the public schools. He wants us registered and monitored. He wants us deported or placed in camps."

Jonathan, still in disguise, tried to deny the charges, all of them. "As I understand Falwell," my son began, "he doesn't hate homosexuals. He doesn't want to deprive them of their civil rights. He doesn't want them registered or monitored, deported or placed in camps. He just wants them to know that God loves them and will help them find a better way to live."

In that noisy wagon, Jonathan tried to explain my position. These young men, all as serious about their causes as was Jonathan, talked and argued with my son.

Later, after my interview at the Cable News Network studio, I walked into the room where Sister Boom Boom sat waiting to be interviewed. My son sat nearby. I walked up to shake the "sister's" hand. Jonathan said, "Hi, Dad." Boom Boom's eyes opened wide with surprise. He looked at me and then back to Jonathan. "By the way, Boom Boom," I said, "I want you to meet my son."

It was one of those strange, unreal moments. In that crowd of television personnel and radical demonstrators, I looked at my son and at Sister Boom Boom and felt like reaching out to

hug them both. The radical homosexual activist in his mock
nun's habit and outlandish makeup. Jonathan in his jeans and
ragged shirt. Both young men strongly committed to totally
different philosophies. Both of them willing to risk their lives
to make their views known.

The tragedy in Sister Boom Boom's life was that no one
had ever shared with him the redeeming Gospel of Jesus Christ
or offered him the love and spiritual help and support that he
needed. But by the grace of God, my son Jonathan could have
been walking in the same direction as Sister Boom Boom. It is
so important that we clearly and sensitively show persons everywhere that while we oppose sin, we love the sinner.

I suppose one of the most painful times of misunderstanding during the early Moral Majority years, was the flurry of
headlines in early winter 1980 misquoting me about "God not
hearing the prayers of the Jews." An avalanche of invective followed that false charge from Jew and Gentile alike.

Of course anyone who knew me realized immediately that I
would never intentionally say anything to offend my Jewish
friends. My friendship with the Jewish people and my personal
support for Israel go back to the beginning days of my ministry. But one quickly learns that when you walk into the political
arena, truth is often drowned out by half-truth, hyperbole, and
outright lies. Terrible misunderstanding is bound to follow.

In 1957 when our congregation at Thomas Road Baptist
Church was still restructuring the bottling company building
into a sanctuary, vandals attacked our new front windows with
a series of well-placed rocks. In its next edition, our Lynchburg
newspaper printed a photo of me standing by the broken windows with one of the large stones in my hand.

The very next day we received in the church mailbox a
check to cover the cost of replacing the windows and a letter
promising to repair the damages, signed by Mr. Abe Schewel,
president of the Schewel Furniture Company in Lynchburg.
The Schewel brothers, Abe and Ben, were the principal officers in a chain of furniture stores located across Virginia. They
knew well from their own Jewish heritage the problem of van-
dalism and wanted to express their immediate and practical

sympathy with our little Baptist church.

The support of the Schewel family for my own family and our ministries at Thomas Road Baptist Church has grown over the past decades of friendship. In more recent times, the Schewels have provided furniture for our Liberty Godparent Home, Liberty University, and for various other of our ministries with emergency or specialized furniture needs. And another member of the Schewel family, Senator Elliot Schewel, worked on our behalf to get Virginia's General Assembly to give tax-exempt status to Liberty University.

For the past decades, critics of my ministry tried to drive a wedge between me and the Jewish community around the country. They forgot that the Jews and I share a common Judeo-Christian heritage. They forgot that my Master was a Jewish rabbi and that the writings of the Law, the Prophets, and Wisdom Literature of the Old Testament are as much a part of my faith as are the Gospels and the epistles of the New Testament.

And when they criticized me for visiting with Egypt's President Sadat and Jordan's King Hussein, they forgot that I have also visited Israel more than twenty-five times in the past twenty-five years to discuss with several prime ministers and other Israeli officials how peace might be reached in that troubled region.

Almost monthly I was invited to address Jewish groups across the country speaking in synagogues from Los Angeles to Washington, D.C. My close friend Jerry Strober is an American leader of the Herut Party, and Merrill Simon, a Jewish author, introduced to me by Prime Minister Begin, wrote a book titled *Jerry Falwell and the Jews* illustrating my longtime friendship with the Jewish people and with Israel. In 1981 in New York's Waldorf-Astoria Hotel, Prime Minister Menachem Begin awarded me the Jabotinsky Award, the highest honor an Israeli prime minister can bestow on friends of Israel for their friendship and service to that land.

Still the critics railed against me for my "anti-Semitism." The Carter-Mondale campaign committee even released a television commercial just before the 1980 election stating that "Dr. Jerry Falwell has said that God doesn't hear the prayers of

Jews." Then it went on to warn that "if Reagan goes on to the White House, Falwell will come with him, and they'll purify the land as someone else did some years ago."

The Moral Majority filed an $11 million lawsuit to stop the media slander. When the Carter-Mondale campaign committee realized they could not support their claims, they withdrew the commercial and we withdrew our lawsuit.

Being misunderstood by your critics goes with the territory of political involvement. Unfortunately, being misunderstood and roundly condemned by your friends happens regularly as well. My brother in Christ Dr. Bob Jones called me "the most dangerous man in America" and in his magazine Faith for the Family Jones asked my fellow fundamentalists to "turn their back on the Moral Majority and seek the soul-satisfying contentment of being a scriptural minority."

In June 1980 the Fundamental Baptist Fellowship passed a resolution condemning both me and the Moral Majority with these words: ". . . Moral reformation is not the mission of the Church but instead the preaching of the saving grace of Christ."

Before his death my good friend B. R. Lakin heard the wild charges against me. He knew that I was a practicing fundamentalist by doctrine, by conviction, and by practice. But he also took time enough to see why I was joining with other Americans who were not fundamentalists on behalf of the future of our nation. He answered my critics in his own wonderful way.

"They can't tree the 'coon," he said with a grin, "so they shoot the dog who can."

Early in the summer of 1983 in a press conference Senator Ted Kennedy held up a colorful plastic Moral Majority membership card with his name printed on it. To the smiling press corps Kennedy quipped, "I know Jerry Falwell needs help with the Moral Majority, but this is ridiculous."

I still don't know how the senator got that card. It might have been someone's idea of a good joke or a Kennedy staffer's trick to get on our mailing list and find out what the enemy was doing; but when the media swarmed to get my response, I said simply, "I hope he'll keep it. No one is above redemption."

Out of that brief encounter Cal Thomas, my longtime friend

and then a vice-president of the Moral Majority for media relations, called Kennedy's office and invited him to speak at Liberty University. Kennedy was courageous enough to take the challenge, and on October 3, 1983, before 7,000 Liberty University students, staff members, and friends he delivered a powerful and moving address.

He began his remarks by saying to the students, "Most of you probably think that it is easier for a camel to pass through the eye of a needle than for Ted Kennedy to speak at Liberty Baptist." The students roared with laughter. Kennedy completed his address with a challenge to me. "If you'll give your great student body an extra hour out after curfew tonight, I promise I'll turn on 'The Old Time Gospel Hour' and watch it through."

We were billed by the media as "the odd couple." Most of my critics and friends alike condemned our joint appearance. But in this great pluralistic nation closing our eyes and ears to each other's positions only leads to a breakdown of communications and the end of the search for truth. Senator Kennedy, his sister Jean Smith, and his daughter Kara ate at our home that evening with Macel, Jerry Jr., Jeannie, Jonathan, and me. We talked openly about our disagreements. We listened carefully to each other's positions. Kennedy fielded questions from the Liberty University students. He was impressed by their knowledge, their brightness, and their commitment to Christ. They, too, were impressed by his openness and his courage.

Later on a trip to Palm Beach, Florida, I was invited to visit again with the senator in his home. I met his gracious mother and though she was quite ill, we talked and had prayer together. On the beach behind their Florida home, Ted Kennedy and I walked together and talked frankly about the crises confronting America and the solutions we each held for those crises.

In 1984 I arranged for Senator Kennedy to join me in addressing the National Religious Broadcasters' convention in Washington, D.C. Since our debate there, I have spoken twice at Harvard, Kennedy's home front. In the process of all those quips, debates, and dialogues between us, we both have found new appreciation and new understanding of what we are trying to accomplish for the nation. And though a minority of our supporters on both sides criticized us for our times together, each of us decided that our search for understanding is worth the risk of being misunderstood.

During those years since 1979 when the Moral Majority was organized, I committed myself to representing the conservative cause and to getting our political and moral values heard and better understood across this nation. I worked hard to help organize and train an army of conservative activists who would take to the streets, door-to-door, on behalf of those conservative causes and the candidates who represent them. I traveled 250,000 to 400,000 miles a year, speaking millions of words on thousands of platforms in every state. I appeared on hundreds of television and radio programs. I was interviewed endlessly by television and radio networks and by journalists from what seemed to be every newspaper or news-magazine in the world.

It has been a long, hard fight. But we won plenty of victories along the way. In 1976 the evangelical-fundamentalist vote went two to one to Democrat Jimmy Carter. In 1980 we turned the vote around and delivered two to one to Republican Ronald Reagan. And in 1984 we helped deliver 85 percent of the conservative religious vote to the Reagan-Bush team.

For seven years we worked to register new voters, millions of them. For seven years we traveled across the country mobilizing and training millions of volunteers to walk the precincts. We raised and spent tens of millions of dollars educating the electorate and advocating our conservative agenda. We raised the conservative consciousness of the nation and we saw our political goals and our moral values finding wider and wider acceptance.

On January 21, 1985, Macel and I were invited to the President's second inauguration. Arctic air froze the capitol grounds. The windchill factor had dropped to thirty-five degrees below zero. The festive, colorful traditional outdoor inauguration events were cancelled because of the biting, dangerous cold. A small number of guests were invited inside the rotunda of the capitol building to see the President sworn into office. Macel and I stood near Vice-president Bush's family during that moving occasion.

"Four years ago I spoke to you of a new beginning," the President said, his voice echoing in that marble rotunda and from it throughout the world. "And we have accomplished that. But in another sense, our new beginning is a continuation of that beginning created two centuries ago when, for the first time in history, government, the people said, was not our master. It is our servant; its only power that which we, the people allow it to have."

The speech that followed proved that in fact, the nation was experiencing "a new beginning." President Reagan had been faithful to the conservative agenda. He had inherited a nation facing imminent disaster. Everyone listening to his voice remembered well the domestic catastrophe approaching in the early 1980's, 13 percent inflation, 21 percent interest, a dying stock market, and massive unemployment. The Supreme Court had legalized abortion and in those few years since Roe v. Wade, almost 15 million unborn babies had died legally in their mother's womb. Pornography was available to children on drugstore and grocery store counters. Patriotism, religious faith, and the traditional American family had fallen on hard times.

And internationally we had compounded our dilemma. Our military establishment had been virtually dismantled. We could hardly defend ourselves. We had been politically bludgeoned into giving away the Panama Canal. Ninety people, including sixty American citizens, were being held hostage in our Iranian embassy. We had capitulated to the adherence of a flawed Salt II Treaty and were close to becoming victims of nuclear blackmail at the hands of the Soviet Union.

As the President spoke I reviewed one more time why I had interrupted my own primary task of evangelism and church growth to take up my responsibility as a citizen. The nation was in peril and something had to be done to save it. Six years had passed since we founded the Moral Majority. Millions of religious conservatives had been registered to vote. Important issues had been raised. New conservative leaders had been elected. Tens of thousands of pastors, priests, and rabbis had become more involved in the political, social, and moral issues. twenty-five thousand retail stores had removed pornography from their shelves.

All the polls were in agreement: America had moved to the right politically and theologically. Conservatives had become the largest voting bloc coalition in the nation. There was a new feeling of pride and hopefulness in the land.

In his speech, the President made it clear that the American people had realized the danger and were taking giant steps toward political and economic, social and spiritual health. I felt relief, joy and gratitude as the President spoke. I had been one small part of that mass of Americans who were taking control of their government once again to steer it back to the course set by our forefathers more than 200 years ago.

"We are creating a nation once again," the President concluded, "...vibrant, robust and alive.... Our nation is poised for greatness.... Let us stand as one today: one people under God determined that our future shall be worthy of our past.... The American sound is hopeful, bighearted, idealistic ...daring, decent, fair. That is our heritage....We raise our voices to the God who is the author of this most tender music. And may He continue to hold us close as we fill the world with our song in unity, affection, and love. One people under God, dedicated to the dream of freedom that He has placed in the human heart, called upon now to pass that dream on to a waiting and a hopeful world. God bless you and may God bless America."

Two years later, in 1987, I stepped aside from the presidency of the Moral Majority and returned to my first calling at Thomas Road Baptist Church and Liberty University. I had promised five years of my life to political leaders in 1979, as they urged me to step forward and mobilize religious conservatives in America. I actually gave eight years of my life to this cause. While I shall always be a voice for the moral and social issues, I have never been confused about God's call on my life.

Sometimes, Christians must be willing to work together with persons with whom we have major theological differences in order to cure serious societal problems, and even to save the culture. But, in the doing we must not violate our theological integrity.

— Jerry Falwell

Do not try to implement God's vision. God is always right on time. there are no panic buttons near the throne. The Holy Trinity has never gone into emergency session. Everything is under control and going according to plan.

— Jerry Falwell

CHAPTER FIFTEEN

The Journey Ahead

L ife is a journey. Even if we don't know our final destination, we are traveling from the moment we are born until the day we die. We who call ourselves Christians believe that the journey begins and ends with God. He created us at the beginning of life and He will welcome us home when this life is over.

In the meantime, we are citizens of two worlds, this world that we can see with our eyes and the next eternal world that we see only through the eyes of faith. Like the children of Israel who moved through the desert toward their promised land, we Christians move slowly through this life toward the better heavenly world that God has prepared for those who love Him.

In the words of the old American spiritual:

> This world is not my home.
> I'm just a-passing through.
> My treasures are laid up
> Somewhere beyond the blue.
> The angels beckon me
> From heaven's open door.

> And I can't feel at home
> In this world anymore.

It is easy to forget that we are on a journey. Like the children of Israel we want to get out of the desert sun and lie down in the shade. But God calls to us as He called to them: Don't stop! Keep moving. You're almost home. And He promises us as He promised them that one day when the journey is over we will hear Him say, Well done, good and faithful servant. Welcome home!

There were those Jews who refused to obey God's command. They lay down in the desert, and the Bible says that you can still find their bones out there along the way, bleached white as the desert sand. But there were other Jews who fought their urge to give up the journey. They followed God all the way. They refused to lie down even long enough to rest, and one day with great rejoicing they reached the promised land.

Read the history of Israel or read the history of the New Testament church. Review the past 2,000 years of Christian history. Since the beginning of recorded time, God has called people to follow Him. They begin the journey enthusiastically, and then little by little they give up or they lose their way. But there is good news. Throughout all those centuries of history, whenever God's people get tired of traveling, God revives them. And when they get off the track, somehow He reaches out to guide them back on His pathway once again.

Looking back on my own life, I see how easy it is to wander off the pathway, to get bogged down in tasks along the way and to forget the spiritual journey altogether. But each time I have needed warning and new direction, God has provided it. He has plans for us that we never dream, and day by day He is preparing us, guiding us, getting us ready for what lies ahead.

God uses the Scriptures to re-direct us. He guides us through our times of prayer and meditation. God may use a sermon, a hymn or Gospel song, another person's Christian testimony, or spiritual books and pamphlets to keep us on track or to get us back on track again. Sometimes God even uses strangers to change our direction. We must always be sensitive to the possibility that God is using those people who suddenly invade our privacy with words of advice or even confrontation. In recent days God used two strangers to change my course and set a new direction in my life.

I shall never forget a young man named Philip, a black student from an Ivy League university, who had the courage to deliver God's message to me. For several weeks in the fall and winter of 1985, Philip had been calling Duane Ward, my administrative assistant at that time, to request a "brief meeting" with me. Duane was not trying to be difficult by turning down his request. My schedule was simply overloaded. There was no time for a meeting with a stranger. But somehow Philip convinced Duane that his desire had deeply spiritual consequences for me and should be honored.

The meeting occurred in December 1985 in the Butler Aviation boardroom at Washington's National Airport. I shook hands with this bright, handsome young man and told him we had about fifteen minutes before I must fly on to my next appointment. We sat down alone in the boardroom. His eyes were piercing, yet I felt love shining through them. And though I began the meeting anxious to get on to my next responsibility, the moment Philip began to speak I sensed that I was in the presence of a twenty-one-year-old servant of the Lord and that I should listen carefully to what he had to say.

Philip's sincerity came through quickly. His warmth and the importance of his mission were written all over his face. He made no wild statements. He had heard no voices. He had seen no visions. He spoke quietly and simply. Apparently God had been impressing on the heart of this young believer to deliver a message to me. I had never heard of Philip before, I have not seen him since, but in those fifteen minutes he spoke God's words to me.

Philip said that God was changing the direction of my life. He asked me to be open and sensitive to the leading of the Holy Spirit. He told me that my "greater ministry was about to begin." He told me that "a new touch from God was going to be on my life in the future." He said that "some new directions would soon be revealed to me." He further indicated that I would need to spend more time in the presence of God than ever I had before to be fully equipped for the awesome tasks and responsibilities ahead.

Our meeting may have gone longer than fifteen minutes. I really don't remember. I was too taken by what this young man was saying to pay attention to the time. I wrote words and phrases that he said to me on a yellow note-pad I carry and I listened carefully to every word he said.

Mind you, I have had hundreds of people offer me a "message from God." Most of those past encounters were a waste of time. I believe that God speaks to his children firsthand through the Bible and other inspirational means. I believe that God speaks to us through His people as we meet and talk with them every day. Still I am very slow to take seriously these "special messages from God" or the people who claim to have received them. But that short meeting with Philip was different. I never doubted for one second that Philip was sent by God to Jerry Falwell.

In the months that followed, I remembered Philip and his words almost every day. To this moment I carry in my pocket that very worn and folded yellow legal page on which I wrote down the notes of his conversation. I thank God for those words every day.

Just four months after Philip's visit, God used another stranger to help change the direction my life was taking. A prominent American clergyman who asked to remain anonymous called me for an appointment. And though I knew the man's name and reputation, we had never met. "Dr. Falwell," he began, "you have no reason to trust what I am about to say to you or to even take it seriously."

As I sat in my office staring across the room at my visitor, I thought of Philip and of our short time together in that Washington, D.C., airport. Once again I had that feeling that I could trust the stranger who was speaking to me. It wasn't a common occurrence for me to get "messages from God" from perfect strangers, but I had read about the process in the Old and in the New Testament. And at various important times in my life I had experienced these special words from friends and family and even an occasional stranger. Once again I felt in my heart that I could trust this man as I had trusted Philip just four months before.

"For the past months," my visitor continued looking rather sheepish, "I haven't been able to get you out of my mind. In my private times of prayer and study your name keeps popping into my head."

I looked carefully at the man. I knew he had nothing to gain by telling me this. He is a well-known, well-established clergyman in his own right. But for some reason God had placed me and my future in his heart.

"When I prayed," he told me, "I found myself praying for you. And when I studied the Bible, I kept thinking about the meaning of the verses for your life."

It was a strange but wonderful feeling to hear the man describe how his burden for me continued to grow until he could ignore it no longer. Finally he called to make this appointment, and with tears welling up in his eyes he sat across the room from me quoting the Scripture that God had laid on his heart on my behalf.

"It seemed that every time I turned to the Old Testament," he said, "God led me back to these two same verses. And," he continued as he opened his Bible and turned to the prophet Isaiah, "I grew more and more certain that it was these two verses that God wanted me to pass on to you:

"Remember ye not the former things, neither consider the things of old.

"Behold, I will do a new thing; now it shall spring forth; shall ye not know it? I will even make a way in the wilderness, and rivers in the desert" (Isaiah 43:18,19).

When he finished reading, I didn't say a word. We both sat in silence for a moment. Then my new friend spoke softly.

"God is about to redirect your paths," he said. "He has something new and wonderful for you to do, and though it will be very difficult, He has promised to give you strength and comfort along the way."

I felt awkward and a little embarrassed. But his words confirmed what God had been telling me in my own times of

personal prayer and Bible study. This man had no way of knowing what was going on in my own heart. He didn't know about
Philip or about Philip's message. And yet there he was in my
office telling me practically the same things. Immediately I
thought about the Apostle Paul quoting an ancient Old Testament rule, who made it perfectly clear how we can test the
trustworthiness of such "messages from God."

"In the mouth of two or three witnesses," Paul wrote, "shall
every word be established" (II Corinthians 13:1). God was using this second man to confirm the young Ivy Leaguer's word
to me.

Neither Philip nor the clergyman was superpious. They
didn't even say that they carried God's word to me. They just
felt that God had laid me on their hearts and that to be true to
Him and to themselves they had to tell all about it.

"God is about to elevate you," my visitor concluded. "You
are a pastor and a teacher, but God needs you to also be a Christian statesman."

After the man left, I knew that he was right about God
changing the direction of my life. But I wasn't convinced at all
about the "statesman" part. I was exhausted from seven years
of doing battle as the founding president of the Moral Majority.
I needed time for prayer and renewal. I needed time to pastor
my church and to direct the church's enterprises. And I needed
more time for my wife and family. These messages from my
two visitors helped me know for certain that it was time to make
the changes necessary.

Just five months later, God directed me to announce to the
world that I was headed back to basics. I didn't know what the
future would bring. And what I thought it would bring was entirely wrong. I was standing at a crossroads in my own spiritual
journey. And God used two strangers to help point the way.

In the fall of 1986 I wrote a letter to 1.3 million families who
are the backbone of support to our ministries around the world.
The letter began simply: "God has told me what I must do."

Immediately I explained that I had not heard any voices.
Nor had I seen any visions in the night. But I was confident that
God had made His will known to me about my immediate future,

and I wanted to share the news immediately with my faithful friends and partners in ministry. I knew the first steps I had to take to obey Him, but I had no idea of the crisis that God was preparing me to face.

"As of this date," I said, "Wednesday, October 29, 1986, my priorities are changing drastically. Involvement in political issues and campaigns will no longer claim the majority of my time and energy."

For the past seven years I had given most of my time to political causes associated with the renewal of our nation's spirit and the change of her political and moral direction. Those years as chairman of the Moral Majority had taken a tremendous toll on my ministries at Thomas Road Baptist Church. Looking back, I felt that my decision to enter into the political arena had been right and necessary. But looking to the future, I knew that God wanted me to return to the basics of my own spiritual journey.

For several years I had been wanting more time to study the Bible seriously. I needed more free hours to pray and to think about the problems of our day and about God's unique Biblical solutions. When you are flying 400,000 miles a year; when you are preaching and teaching almost every day; when you have articles and books to write or edit, press conferences and television programs to prepare for, endless meetings to attend, piles of letters to answer, and long lists of phone calls to return, it is difficult to find adequate time to develop that side of one that the Whittemores called "the deeper spiritual life."

Whatever you do, your life is just as busy as mine. You feel the same pressure I feel. You suffer the same stress in your territory that comes with mine. And sometimes in all that business it is easy to lose track of the spiritual journey, to wander off the trail, to get lost, bogged down, and disoriented. The Old Testament stories of God's people in the desert who got off the trail, who forgot or refused or got too busy to follow God, should instruct us. God could only wait so long for those who fell behind. Finally, when the unfaithful, distracted, lustful people refused to hear His warnings, the faithful people of God had to leave them and continue their journey toward God's promise. Those who got off the trail to follow pagan religions and practices, or to just rest along the way, soon realized their mistake. But then it was too late for those who quit the journey and "left their bones in the desert sun."

Taking time to study the Word seriously once again, to pray regularly again, to recall the hymns of the faithful again, to talk about one's own spiritual journey again, is the beginning of getting back to basics. No task is as important as spending time on the deeper spiritual life. No responsibility should get in the way of one's spiritual journey.

Even during those past seven years of political and social involvement I had not neglected my family. But too often our times together had been on the run. A central part of the spiritual journey is to provide leadership for the family. Quality leadership demands quality time spent together. Getting back to basics meant getting back to more quality time with my growing family.

During those seven years, so much had changed in their lives, too. Jerry Jr. had graduated in June 1987 from the University of Virginia Law School. Jeannie was a student at the Medical College of Virginia in Richmond. Jonathan was studying for the pastoral ministry at Liberty University and planned to go on to seminary and a full-time role at Thomas Road Baptist Church.

Even Macel had decided to join the students in our family. She had enrolled at Liberty University in 1983 and graduated in 1987 at age fifty-three with a 4.0 grade point average. Since the children were grown and taking their own adult roles in society, Macel was even thinking about getting a graduate degree and finding a meaningful professional vocation.

I missed leisurely time with my family and I missed just being in our lovely old home on Piedmont Place. God can charge spiritual batteries when you're puttering about the house. I know people who have their best prayer times while they are baking bread or planting flowers. And there is no better place to read and study the Word than in the quiet comfort of your home. Unfortunately, sometimes even our homes quit being a safe retreat.

Through the late 1970's. we were living in the subdivision

in Windsor Hills on Chesterfield Road. Our home was easily spotted, and as my media exposure increased, the threatening phone calls multiplied. Before long people were driving by our yard in a growing parade of noisy cars and flashing cameras. When the media were particularly critical of something I said or did, irate visitors would throw eggs against the house or set off firecrackers in the mailbox.

Eventually the bomb and kidnap threats got out of hand. Claude Brown, one of our close friends and a member of the Old Time Gospel Hour board of trustees, decided to take the matter in his own hands. In 1979 he took Macel house-hunting. No property seemed appropriate until one day they discovered a historic old plantation house just four minutes' drive from the church and ten minutes' drive from the university.

The house was built in 1834 by the Hutters, a prominent Lynchburg family, near the site where the Battle of Lynchburg was fought during the nation's Civil War. The hardwood walls and floor are held together with wooden pegs and wooden butterflies. I love the high ceilings, the tall windows, and the handshaped wooden beams. The Hutter house now sits on seven acres of lawn in one of the oldest stands of white oak trees in the nation. Some of the majestic trees are eight feet in diameter and over 600 years old.

When Claude Brown and Macel found the house, it was in a sad state of disarray, but immediately Macel saw the possibilities. Unfortunately, the house at $160,000 was outside our price range. So Claude Brown bought it, paid for it, and gave it to the Thomas Road Baptist Church. To insure our family's security, the board financed an eight-foot-high security wall around the entire property with an automatic gate and security shack for a twenty-four-hour guard.

Once again we found a place where our family could grow closer to God and to each other. I suppose that stand of white oaks and the birds and squirrels in their branches are echoes of the lost garden where God walked and talked with His creation. Somehow I find strength for my spiritual journey in that place. Getting back to basics meant spending more time there in the garden listening for His voice.

There are approximately 200 gray-tailed squirrels living in
the white oak trees. In 1986 a baby squirrel was found suffering from exposure and hunger by a security guard who nursed
it back to health. Now "Max" the squirrel lives near our back
door. Whenever he sees me coming, he runs across the driveway, climbs up my pant leg, and sits on my shoulder begging
for a peanut. You should see our guests who spot the attack
squirrel just as he climbs up my leg and begins to scold me
noisily.

I wanted more time at home to spend with Macel, Jerry Jr.,
Jeannie, Jonathan, and even Max the squirrel. So much had
happened to my family during these last seven years when I
served as founder and president of the Moral Majority and had
to travel constantly. I wanted to stay home for a while. I wanted
to be available to my wife, my children, and (eventually, I hoped)
my grandchildren. I wanted to walk through the fields and visit
the cemetery once again where my family lie buried. I wanted
to read the names on those tombstones and remember the
important place that each person filled in my life. And while
standing there remembering their lives, I wanted to think and
pray about what really is important for me to be and do during
those remaining years of my life and ministry.

God called me to be a preacher and a pastor, nothing more
and nothing less. Even during the busy political years, I maintained my responsibilities at Thomas Road Baptist Church; but
getting back to basics meant for me getting back to that original call to ministry that I had experienced as a youth. No matter where I traveled, no matter what country I was in, no matter what exciting task I found myself caught up in, I knew that
God's call to ministry was forever and that I would never be
happy to stay away from my flock very long.

That little congregation begun on Thomas Road just thirty
years earlier with thirty-five members had become one of the
largest Baptist churches in the world with more than 20,000
members. My church needed me back in the pulpit where I
belonged. I wanted to pastor my flock again and to administer
more responsibly my great and growing staff of full-time, part-
time, and volunteer personnel.

I missed having time to pray with my people who were sick or dying. I missed sharing in the celebrations of marriage, the dedication of the children, the midweek Bible studies and prayer meetings. I tried to be responsible and to assign qualified, experienced pastors to take my place, but I wanted more time to share in person with my people. That meant getting back to basics.

The local church is the front line in the war that God is waging with the Enemy. The real action does not take place in Supreme Court chambers or the marbled halls of Congress or even in the Oval Office. The real battle takes place with people who are afraid, sick, angry, or alone. The world will be won one by one. And the local community of faithful believers is the place where lives are really changed forever. I was called to work on the front lines of ministry, and I believe that the local church is where it happens.

Of course, Thomas Road Baptist Church has grown larger than most local churches. That doesn't make us better or more successful. It just makes us different. To help other churches better understand how we grew and to train young men and women to duplicate our ministry across the nation and around the world, we began in 1971 our little Lynchburg Baptist College. By 1985 our college became Liberty University, a fully accredited Christian liberal arts college with 7,500 students. By 1996 there are already seventy-five undergraduate majors and/or concentrations and many graduate programs offered or being initiated. We are training journalists, scientists, educators, preachers of the Gospel, and professionals in dozens of significant fields. But at the heart of every program is our desire to train young men and women who can build up local churches around the world where lives can be transformed by the Gospel of Christ.

I get excited about every new open door for Liberty University, its students, and its staff. Every day something new happens that gets us closer to our dream of a world-class university in Lynchburg. What God is doing at Liberty University is a constant source of surprise and joy to all of us. But I have even larger dreams for our university. I am convinced that our

student body can grow to 50,000 students early in the twenty-
first century. I am certain that we will become a world-class
university training champions for Christ in every important field
of study. What Notre Dame is to Roman Catholic youths and
what Brigham Young is to Mormon young people, Liberty University will become to the Bible-believing fundamentalist and
evangelical students of America. And I am asking God to give
me more time to guide and to fund that dream.

The growth of Liberty University has been miraculous indeed. If I had known in the fall of 1971 how difficult the creation of an accredited Christian university would be, I might
not have started the school. I share this story to help you understand how God can re-direct one's spiritual journey and give
one strength for each great task along the way.

In the early days, we had to gain academic approval from
the Virginia Council of Higher Education. At the same time we
had to apply for candidate's status for accreditation with the
Southern Association of Colleges and Schools (SACS) in Atlanta. We passed those two hurdles. They were not easy. Great
men like our president, Dr. A. Pierre Guillermin; our former
dean, Dr. J. Gordon Henry; and other committed co-laborers
like our former provost, Dr. Earl Mills, played vital roles in
achieving accreditation from the SACS organization in 1980.
Our wonderful faculty at Liberty University also worked day
and night to bring about the academic excellence that the university now enjoys.

Membership in the National Collegiate Athletic Association (NCAA) was also a great step forward for Liberty University. The development of a full-blown Division I, NCAA athletic
program is now a reality in sixteen sports for men and women,
including football. No other dictinctively evangelical Christian
university in America enjoys regional academic accreditation
and competes athletically, including football, at the NCAA Division I level. The LU Debate Team won the national champion-
ship during the 1994/95 and 1995/96 scholastic years. For perspective in just how outstanding the LU Debate Team really is,
Harvard did not make the top ten in the 1995/96 year. The LU
Men's Track and Field Team ranked fifth in the nation in dual

meet competition for the 1995/96 year. Our basketball team received a bid to the NCAA Tournament and went to the "big dance" as one of the "Final 64" in 1994. We played the defending National Champion North Carolina Tarheels on March 18, 1994 at Landover, Maryland in the U.S. Air Arena. The CBS Television Network carried the game to the world for three hours as we almost made sports history, leading North Carolina 46-45 with 9 minutes and 47 seconds remaining in the game. Our lack of depth cost us the game in the final minutes, but the world suddenly realized that Liberty University is for real. Our baseball team also received a bid to the NCAA playoffs in 1993, joining the "Final 48." Liberty University is getting larger and better, in every field, with every passing year.

One of the big challenges facing the young Board of Trustees for Liberty University during our first year of existence in 1971 was how to keep our university Biblically and theologically sound in generations to come. History told us that most of America's major universities, including Harvard, Yale, Dartmouth, the University of Pennsylvania, and the others had been established by conservative Bible-believing Christians for the purpose of training servants of God. In our own lifetimes we had watched too many denominational schools move from their original doctrinal positions to become something the founders did not have in mind.

It was this concern that caused Thomas Road Baptist Church to become the spiritual parent of Liberty University. In 1967, Thomas Road Baptist Church was forced to form a corporation called Old Time Gospel Hour Incorporated. In the Commonwealth of Virginia, state law at that time had never allowed a church to own more than twenty acres of property. This is an archaic law, but it was considered very important by the founders of the nation, who never wanted another Church of England or any state church to dominate government.

Churches like Thomas Road Baptist with extensive youth camp programs, large parking lots, and other properties related directly to their ministry have been forced to form subsidiary corporations to hold those properties in excess of twenty acres. Therefore the Liberty University board of directors

decided to place all university properties permanently in the
name of the Old Time Gospel Hour corporation so that Thomas Road Baptist Church would have influence over the doctrinal position of Liberty University in the generations to come.

What we were trying to achieve was much the same as the
Roman Catholic, the Episcopal, Presbyterian, and Methodist
church structures. The Vatican in Rome virtually owns all Roman Catholic properties throughout the world. In the state of
Virginia the Roman Catholic archdiocese headquartered in
Richmond actually holds the properties of all its churches and
some schools in all its dioceses including Lynchburg. The Episcopal Church structure is very similar to the Roman Catholics'. The Presbyterian Church achieves the same goal through
its presbyteries, and the Methodist church through its conference organization. The philosophies behind the major denominations are sound ones. It was their desire that the theological
integrity and the spiritual purposes of their churches should
never be challenged by new adherents in centuries to come.

However, a conservative evangelical or fundamentalist organization had never obtained tax exemption in the state of
Virginia under that same structure. While I will not go into the
details that made tax exemption unavailable to Liberty University while it was owned by the Old Time Gospel Hour corporation, this in fact was the case. We therefore found ourselves in
seven years of litigation, ending with our appeal through our
own Lynchburg City Council to the General Assembly in Richmond for a tax exemption.

This was a major hurdle. If a tax exemption could not be
granted us, it would have been impossible to carry out the
dream of a 50,000-student Christian university in Lynchburg.
We had learned that other states would allow us the privilege
of tax exemption under the structure we were desiring if we
moved the university to one of those states. But my heart is
tied to Lynchburg. And though our Old Time Gospel Hour
board of directors were not emotionally tied to this city, I would
have been deeply grieved to move the ministry from my home-
town. It was quite an emotional dilemma for all of us.

What a happy day it was that Friday, March 27, 1987, when

our governor, Gerald Baliles, signed into law the tax-exemption bill covering Liberty University, our Liberty Godparent Home for unwed mothers, and the offices of our entire ministry. The Virginia State Senate voted 37-3 in our favor, and the House of Delegates voted 82-14 on our behalf.

The struggle to get the university accredited and the years of litigation to get tax exemption for the church's growing ministries all required incredible energy, but God provided strength for that amazing journey. The prayers and gifts of our friends and our partners made it possible. But more, the realization of our tax-exempt status could not have been accomplished without the assistance of the Lynchburg City Council, the Lynchburg Chamber of Commerce, certain wonderful business leaders here in Lynchburg, including Kenneth "Pete" White, the longtime owner of our Holiday Inn; Preston Wade, chairman of the Wiley and Wilson Engineering Company, my cousin Calvin Falwell; and other key people too numerous to mention. We also had two excellent lobbyists in Judge Junie Bradshaw and former attorney general Tony Troy. Our local attorney, David Petty, coordinated and led this very successful effort. And, of course, without Senator Elliot Schewel and our four State delegates—Lacy Putney, Joe Crouch, Royston Jester, and Vance Wilkins—the goal could not have been achieved.

Overcoming this last obstacle—the granting of tax exemption without surrendering the theological future of Liberty University—called all of us to realize that our God in heaven is faithful. He will provide strength for the journey even when we have no idea where it might be coming from.

Our television ministry had expanded from one tiny local station broadcasting a thirty-minute sermon to people in Lynchburg and its immediate environs to "The Old Time Gospel Hour," available to millions of regular viewers weekly from coast to coast. And in 1986 we purchased the Liberty Broadcasting Cable Network to expand our television ministry even further. I wanted to see that network become a twenty-four-hour source of 100 percent Christian programming that would reach through satellite into every home in the nation.

Our other ministries also needed my time and energy. Our

Liberty Godparent Homes were spreading across the country. Hundreds of professional staff and thousands of volunteers were determined to save those 1.5 million babies who were being aborted every year. We wanted to rescue millions of mothers from the psychological burden that abortion often brings and introduce those new mothers to Christ as Savior and Lord. Our Elim Home for Alcoholics is filled to capacity, and programs like this were being duplicated on an ever-increasing scale. All these ministries needed my attention once again.

Because I had been focusing on the political scene and spending too little time raising the needed funds for these outreach programs, we had to borrow money to maintain these local and national ministries. I was determined to take time to pay back those loans and to raise hundreds of millions of dollars to adequately endow Liberty University, the Liberty Broadcasting Network, and the other ministries specializing in services to alcoholics, ex-prisoners, women and girls facing unwanted pregnancies, the hungry and destitute, drug addicts, and our mission and Christian service programs around the globe.

"God has changed my course," I announced in my letter in October 1986. "It is time to get back to basics!"

When the letter went out announcing my change in course, some headlines across the country read "Jerry Falwell Leaving Politics."

Reporters by the dozens called asking for interviews, trying to confirm the rumor. Thousands of my friends wrote, telephoned, and wired trying to be certain that the news was true. "Is the Moral Majority finished?" one reporter asked.

I laughed. In fact the work of the Moral Majority had just begun. Early in 1986, when the Moral Majority was taking a terrible beating from the press, we created the Liberty Federation to handle the broader political issues. But once again we weathered the storm of angry and often unfounded media attacks. And in 1987 the Moral Majority and its reputation across the nation was healthier than ever before. The Moral Majority was not "finished," as our critics exclaimed. Rather, I felt, we had accomplished our original mission on which we started in

1979. The "Religious Right" was now formed and in place forever. The Moral Majority organization was no longer needed and when it was dismantled it was strong and healthy.

To support that fact, Vice-president George Bush called me in 1986 to quote from a national survey that the presidential pollsters had just completed. "I have some interesting news for you, Jerry," the Vice-president announced. "We asked people across the country to rate the people and the organizations they respected most. 'Jerry Falwell and the Moral Majority' are second only to the President," he concluded.

The Moral Majority was alive and well and working. I could have continued to act as the president of the Moral Majority and the Liberty Federation. But there were thousands of exciting, knowledgeable, articulate men and women who had taken their places of conservative leadership across the country. In the beginning they needed me out there running from place to place, sticking my neck out, taking the risks, firing the opening rounds, and gathering like minds together. By 1987 there were thousands of other qualified, creative, committed conservatives on the firing line, taking leadership, and getting the job done. And I was free to get back to the original tasks to which I had been called.

I do not regret spending the eight years, 1979-1987, as I had spent them. Religious conservatives had become a part of the political fabric in America, and ever shall be. It seemed we had succeeded in the first stages of our task. America was turning around. Thank God we were, as a nation, headed in the right direction once again, at least for the moment.

So by the end of October 1986, I was certain that God was releasing me from the busy world of political-social action to focus more of my time and energy on the ministry. Obviously I will always be committed to this nation and to its political, moral, and spiritual direction. If new dilemmas arise that need my attention, I will return to the front lines without a moment's hesitation. In my letter to our faithful friends and supporters I said, "If someone tells you that Jerry Falwell is getting out of politics, don't you believe him."

I didn't know how prophetic that one line would be. Just six months after God called me to pull back from politics and to focus on my own spiritual life and ministry, a new dilemma arose that only God could anticipate. Looking back, I am still amazed at how He worked to prepare me for the new journey that lay ahead.

Let's face it. Just when you feel that you are certain about the direction of your life's journey, God may step in with more surprises. I decreased my political time and emphasis to get back to basics. I wanted time to deepen my personal relationship with God. I wanted time for home and family. And I wanted to return to those tasks that came up from my original call to ministry: pastoring and preaching, guiding the university, and evangelizing the world through the media.

And God honored my decision. The Thomas Road Baptist Church, Liberty University, "The Old Time Gospel Hour," and all our ministries have taken on new life since my decision to get back to the basics. I have felt a new power in my preaching. I have felt my prayer life deepened and my Bible study enriched. I have sensed the hand of God upon me in a very special way in the ten years since that letter went out announcing my new direction.

But then, in March of 1987, God surprised me once again. Apparently God had His own ideas about my future. He was using my decision to get back to the basics to prepare me for one of the most difficult tasks of my spiritual journey to that date. This was all part of my spiritual preparation for the sudden, unexpected task that lay just months ahead.

Meanwhile, as I left the political spotlight, organizations like Focus on the Family, Concerned Women For America, American Family Association, The Christian Coalition, The Rutherford Institute, and others began filling the gap caused by the dismantling of the Moral Majority.

It is not the boulders ahead of us
which wear us down. It is often the
grain of sand in our shoe. God
never puts more on us than He puts
in us to bear up every burden.

— Jerry Falwell

In the life of a believer, nothing happens by chance, fate or fortune.

— Jerry Falwell

CHAPTER SIXTEEN

The PTL Scandal

On February 28, 1987, I was in Florida attending a convention when once again God stunned me with information that ultimately led to a brand-new task. I had thought my next months and even my next few years would be relatively tranquil. I would pastor the people of Thomas Road Baptist Church. I would serve as chancellor of Liberty University and as president of the Old Time Gospel Hour. After seven years in the political spotlight, I would have time for myself and my family once again. The press would not hound me day and night. The requests for television appearances would end. I was looking forward to that time of peace and quiet with all my heart.

But my idea of the journey ahead was very different from God's idea. At that February 28 meeting, in the corridors of the Breakers Hotel in Palm Beach, Florida, God led me down a new pathway that would change my life radically. It all began with a short conversation with my old friend Dr. D. James Kennedy, a Presbyterian pastor from Fort Lauderdale, Florida, with a nationwide television ministry. We greeted each other near the coffee shop and talked briefly about our mutual concerns in religious broadcasting.

"I am really concerned about the stories circulating about a major broadcaster," he told me. But before he could fill in the details our conversation was interrupted.

"Pray for this broadcaster," he whispered as we went our separate ways. "If the rumors are true, they will have far-reaching consequences for the entire body of Christ."

I had heard no rumors, but I know Jim Kennedy and trust him. His brief word to me was not delivered in the spirit of judgment, nor was it thoughtless gossip. The Apostle Paul wrote that if someone is caught in a sin, those who are spiritual should restore him gently, but to be careful "lest thou also be tempted" (Galatians 6:1).

Because there were people all around us, my friend went into no detail about the PTL "rumors." Just a few days later I called him at his home to find out the details and to determine how I might help. I had seen what damage false rumor can do. If rumors of scandal about a fellow television minister were spreading, I needed to verify or disprove them. Traditionally, television ministers don't have many friends who will confront or correct them. I was doing for Jim and Tammy Bakker and for PTL exactly what I hoped my fellow television preachers would do for me.

Jim Kennedy told me enough that day for me to realize that the problem might be serious. I had no idea of just how serious it was. When I asked Jim Kennedy about the source of his information, he gave me the name of the preacher who had told him about Jim Bakker's alleged "moral and financial dilemma." I called that preacher, the Reverend John Ankerberg, and asked him directly about the charges.

Like my friend Jim Kennedy, John Ankerberg also seemed to have a genuine concern for Jim and Tammy, for their family, and for their PTL ministry. He was also concerned about the future of television evangelism. Apparently newspaper reporters were already chasing down the rumors. Soon the public would be hearing about sexual and financial scandal at PTL. Something needed to be done and to be done quickly to help limit the fallout that would affect all television ministries and bring shame and reproach to the larger Christian family.

We Christians have very specific guidelines from Christ himself for handling such crises with our brothers. Jesus said it this way:

"Moreover, if thy brother shall trespass against thee, go and tell him his fault between thee and him alone: if he shall hear thee, thou hast gained thy brother.

"But if he will not hear thee, then take with thee one or two more, that in the mouth of two or three witnesses every word may be established" (Matthew 18:15,16).

Apparently, Jim Bakker had not had the opportunity to meet with his brothers concerning the charges against him. On Thursday, March 12, John Ankerberg sent me the draft of a proposed letter to Jim Bakker asking him in the spirit of Matthew 18 for a meeting to discuss certain matters which concerned Bakker and alleged improprieties. Ankerberg suggested that he, TV evangelist Jimmy Swaggart, and I all sign the letter, in hopes that in a meeting with Mr. Bakker we might face the issue squarely, prove or disprove the charges once for all time, and seek God's direction for the future. (At this time, no one had even imagined that Swaggart himself would be embroiled in his own moral scandal scarcely a year later.)

With the rumors growing and the prospects of a damaging and revealing *Charlotte Observer* story just days away, we had to act quickly.

We needed an immediate meeting with Jim Bakker to confront him with the rumors. If he denied them, we would help him make the truth known. If he affirmed them, we would help him deal with the matter personally on a Scriptural basis and we would do our best to help the PTL ministry survive the firestorm of negative publicity that would follow.

At this point, people who don't understand how our independent broadcast ministries are organized might wonder why leaders from other religious broadcasts would get involved in the trials and tribulations of another man's ministry. Each national television ministry began independently of the other. We all come from very different theological and philosophical backgrounds. Our broadcast organizations don't usually have any formal ties with a denomination. I didn't even know that Jim Bakker had recently promised the Assemblies of God denomination that in case he died, the PTL ministry would be come their charge. In reality, in spite of his tenuous relationship with the Assemblies of God, he just reported to his own board like the rest of us. He was directly accountable to no one but his own conscience and the consciences of the board of directors that he himself had appointed.

Unfortunately, too many of these boards are made up of staff members of the broadcast and by clergy or laity who are loyal and supportive to the television evangelist who employed or appointed them. All too often, the boards are "yes" boards. They simply do what the chief executive asks. His accountability to them is only as effective as the board itself. Unfortunately, such board members often end up telling the evangelist what he wants to hear and not what he needs to hear.

Apparently, members of Jim Bakker's board were not confronting their chairman with the growing rumors, if, in fact, they had heard them. Consequently, they were not prepared to deal with the devastating charges about to be leveled at the man and his ministry by the *Charlotte Observer*. And the consequences to PTL and to all of the other television ministries would be disastrous if something wasn't done immediately.

If the media were about to announce that a Catholic cardinal or the archbishop of a major Catholic archdiocese was having a sexual affair and had built a $5 million house on a lake with church monies, the Pope himself might intervene. Most of the major Christian Protestant denominations have some kind of national structure to deal with scandals and crises in their religious communities. But the independent, nondenominational media ministries have been accountable only to their own internal boards. And Jim Bakker's board, for whatever reasons, had allowed all these personal and fiscal rumors to grow without confronting him. As a result, there was no one to intervene but a handful of us who had independent ministries of our own.

As far as I knew at the time, it was just an unfortunate and misleading rumor that any one of us, or that the group of us, was interested in some kind of takeover of Jim Bakker's PTL ministry. In the days ahead, first Jimmy Swaggart and then I would be accused of hatching a takeover plot. When Jimmy Swaggart thought it best not to sign the Ankerberg letter, he wrote a reply stating his reasons clearly. The contents of that letter were made public and were then used against Jimmy Swaggart by his critics. I print the following excerpts of that letter:

"Frances [Swaggart] and I have discussed this letter [the proposed Ankerberg letter] . . . at great length," Jimmy Swaggart wrote to John Ankerberg on March 12, "and [we] are not comfortable with it and I will explain...."

Swaggart then warned Ankerberg that Jim Bakker "will take that letter and show it over television, deleting the parts they do not want read. They will say, 'We had to take these two men—Swaggart and Ankerberg—off television, and they went on a witch hunt to hurt us....' "

Then, after explaining that he had already tried several times to confront Jim Bakker and his associates privately with the growing list of charges against them, he came to this conclusion:

"As far as I am concerned," Swaggart wrote, "Matthew 18 has been satisfied with these people...."

Then Jimmy Swaggart told Ankerberg what he thought would happen next to Jim Bakker and the PTL ministry:

"The *Charlotte Observer*," he wrote, "will do its part...."

Swaggart knew the charges against Jim Bakker were about to be released by that major American daily newspaper. Once the nation had read those charges, it would be too late to do anything in private to help save Jim Bakker's ministry or to help lessen the suffering those charges would bring to the whole Body of Christ and the various other television ministries.

"The Assemblies of God has finally started to move on this," Swaggart confided next to Ankerberg, "and they will do their part."

Swaggart himself was a member of the Assemblies of God denomination at that time but was later defrocked. He knew the rules that Jim Bakker had broken and the standard procedures of that denomination for investigating the charges being leveled against him. He knew that the thirteen Assemblies of God presbyters would defrock Bakker and once again the disgrace would have implications for us all.

Then, in that same letter of March 12, after warning Ankerberg that there was no chance that Bakker would step down for any type of rehabilitation, Swaggart painted a picture of the actions that he feared Jim Bakker and his associates would take to defend themselves against the charges.

"First," he wrote, "they will try to lie their way out of it, but the documentation should be irrefutable. Then they will pull out of the Assemblies of God."

"Their last step," he warned, "will be to institute a barrage, which has already begun, to elicit sympathy from the general public...."

Frankly, Jimmy Swaggart predicted exactly what Jim Bakker would do. He also predicted the consequences that he himself would suffer when Bakker began his self defense:

"If there are severe difficulties and problems," Swaggart wrote, "I will bear the brunt of it—no one else."

In fact, Jimmy Swaggart became the brunt of an incredible Bakker campaign to discredit him and his ministry. He was accused of mounting a campaign to take over the PTL ministry for himself.

But those awful days were still ahead of us. I knew almost nothing of the Bakkers or their style. And I had only talked to Jimmy Swaggart a few times in my life. I was just concerned that someone should do something quickly to find out the truth and to do whatever was necessary to help limit whatever damage might follow. And it was obvious that speaking directly to Jim Bakker about the charges against him was the first step that had to be taken by someone to help avoid the consequences of a major religious scandal. Unfortunately, Jim Bakker and his family were in Palm Springs, California, where Tammy Bakker had been treated for chemical dependency for the past eight or nine weeks. I didn't want to add to the burden of the Bakker family in the middle of Mrs. Bakker's treatment at the Betty Ford Clinic.

Yet, in just days, we were advised that the whole world

would hear the news. Once again the cause of television evangelism would be embroiled in scandal. So to avoid any unnecessary hurt to Jim and Tammy and their family, and yet to learn if the rumors were true or false, I had my associates Jerry Nims, Mark DeMoss and Warren Marcus deliver Ankerberg's unsigned letter to Bakker's second in command at PTL, the Reverend Richard Dortch, who was in Tampa, Florida, at that time.

"Jerry Falwell has no interest in participating in public gossip," they told the Reverend Dortch, "but he is willing to discuss these allegations face-to-face with Jim Bakker in the spirit of Matthew 18 to find out if they are true and to offer his concern and counsel as a pastor and a Christian brother."

One day later, on Friday, March 13, 1987, Richard Dortch informed Nims that Jim Bakker would like to see me in Palm Springs the following Tuesday, March 17. But Mr. Bakker refused to meet with John Ankerberg or with Jimmy Swaggart. He asked to meet only with me.

I had only met Jim Bakker two or three times in my life at meetings of the National Religious Broadcasters in Washington, D.C. In 1984, on a family vacation, Macel, the children, and I had spent fifteen minutes driving through Heritage Village without even stopping. I seldom watched even brief moments of the Jim and Tammy show. As a result I knew almost nothing about Jim or the inner workings of his PTL ministry.

Because the Bakker family was staying together in Palm Springs for Tammy's treatment, Bakker asked if I would fly there to meet him. On March 17 I met with Mr. Bakker in a private room in a Palm Springs hotel. I opened my heart to him. I told him the rumors that were spreading. I asked him for the truth. He responded openly. He confirmed the rumors about a fifteen-minute Florida hotel-room encounter with Jessica Hahn seven years earlier. He was obviously ashamed and embarrassed by the entire matter. His heart seemed to be broken. His spirit was humble and contrite. He knew his reputation and his life-long ministry were being threatened. That conversation was an unforgettable and moving experience.

"You are the first person in seven years," he told me, "who has cared enough about me to confront me with this sin. I am guilty," he said. "But I raped no one. There was no physical assault. It was a lonely time in my life. I had worked myself into a state of exhaustion. In the process, I thought I had lost Tammy. I tried to make her jealous. It was a terrible and foolish mistake."

He told me that no intercourse occurred. He said he had been momentarily impotent. He said no PTL funds were used to pay the "hush money" to Miss Hahn.

Now many versions of that fifteen-minute hotel tryst with Jessica Hahn have been printed and telecast in lurid detail. Soon after his Florida encounter, Jim said he had asked Tammy to forgive him. She forgave Jim and asked him for his forgiveness as well. Together, he said, they had received wise and expert Christian counseling. Jim convinced me that they had been reconciled to God and to each other, and he seemed truly grateful that God was putting their lives and their marriage back together again.

He didn't tell me anything about the other alleged sexual or financial improprieties that would soon be announced in headlines around the world. He only told me his version of the Jessica Hahn story; and with that limited evidence to guide me, assuming his story was true, I felt that if he made a clear and clean public confession to his church and submitted himself to the restoration program of the Assemblies of God, he could possibly recover from the shame and eventually return to his ministry. I was familiar with the two-year period of restoration and renewal that the Assemblies of God denomination offers to its erring clergymen. I knew Jim would have to leave his ministry at least temporarily, but I felt that if his story proved true he might eventually be forgiven and reinstated by the presiding presbyters within the Assemblies of God and by his PTL partners and friends as well.

Less than an hour after Jim shared his version of the Jessica Hahn incident with me, he suddenly turned to me and to others in the room with a request that shocked and surprised us all. "Jerry," he said, "I want you to take over PTL."

We had left the private room at the back of the hotel suite and were standing in a conference area with Pastor Dortch;

the PTL attorney, Roy Grutman; and my associates Mark DeMoss and Jerry Nims. The room grew silent.

I stared in disbelief as Jim revealed his plan. He proposed that on the following day, Wednesday, March 18, I would assume leadership of the PTL Television Network, Heritage USA, and the various ministries of the Heritage Village Church and Religious Ministry in Fort Mill, South Carolina. His old PTL board would meet that same day to ratify the decision, to dissolve their own board, and to transfer control of the entire PTL ministry to me and to a board I would appoint.

"You are the man," he said with growing certainty. "I will place my ministry entirely in your hands tomorrow."

Jim spoke spontaneously, as though the idea was being born at that very moment. Every man in the room seemed stunned by Jim's suggestion. He wanted to appoint Rex Humbard and Richard Dortch to the new board. The rest of the appointments he would leave to me. I listened in silent surprise.

You need to understand that I hardly knew Jim Bakker. We had never spoken more than simple words of greeting to each other at our two or three chance meetings at the National Religious Broadcaster's convention. On the surface, the whole idea didn't make sense. We seemed so different in our approach to ministry. I was a fundamentalist. He was a charismatic. I was an independent Baptist. He was a member of the Assemblies of God denomination. I was called to one kind of ministry. He had very different dreams. Was it God leading Jim Bakker to ask me to take on this awful responsibility, or was it Jim's own desperate and unwise decision?

During the several hours in that Palm Springs hotel, decisions were made that would shake the world. My decision to accept the chairmanship of PTL was based on several considerations. I had a genuine spiritual concern for the Bakkers and the survival of the PTL ministry. I also realized a grave responsibility to the family of God at large to attempt to rebuild the credibility of the Gospel ministry that certainly would suffer great injury. I also knew that this calamity, coupled with the possible collapse of a major television ministry, would do great harm to every other media ministry in America, and perhaps

even to every Gospel-preaching church in America. I could not
say no and walk away. I accepted.

We had prayer together at the conclusion of this six-hour
meeting. My associates and I drove immediately to the Palm
Springs airport and flew back across the nation to Lynchburg.
On the flight my stomach churned. I had just promised the
members of my church and the people across America who
support our ministries that I was "getting back to basics." I had
promised that I would cut back on all those responsibilities that
would take me away from Lynchburg or interfere with our ministries there. I wanted out of the public spotlight. I wanted to
escape the endless rounds of press conferences, television and
radio interviews. I wanted time to pray, to read the Bible, and
to be with my family and friends. I wanted privacy for a change
and a little time to enjoy it.

"You are the man for this job," Jim Bakker told me. "You
are the only one I know who could do it."

I arrived in Lynchburg wondering if this was the change in
direction that God had announced to me through the visits of
the young man Philip and of the distinguished American minister who promised that "God was about to use me as a Christian
statesman." As I drove my truck through the darkened streets
of Lynchburg, I wondered how I would explain this dramatic
turn of events to Macel and my family. To volunteer the time
and energy that it would take to help save the ministry of PTL
seemed totally out of touch with my new goals; and yet I couldn't
help but wonder if this new responsibility was exactly what God
was preparing me to face. I knew a terrible storm was brewing,
and I hated to think that once again I would have to be God's
lightning rod at the center of that storm.

My decision had to be made immediately. The storm was
about to break in full fury. Jim Bakker had shared only bits and
pieces of the impending scandal. Already the details of his brief
affair seven years earlier and the alleged exchange of cover-up
funds that followed were known to the *Charlotte Observer*, the
outstanding newspaper that serves the Heritage USA area and
both the Carolinas. Eventually there would be a whole list of
fiscal and moral charges dumped on Jim's doorstep. The

Jessica Hahn scandal would be just the first of many damning stories, and it was scheduled to run in the *Charlotte Observer* on that very next weekend.

After learning about the *Charlotte Observer* article that was being carefully prepared to confirm and substantiate the rumors about Jim Bakker, the newly appointed PTL attorney, Mr. Roy Grutman, contacted the editors of the paper and asked if they would postpone publication of their PTL story from Saturday, March 14, until the following Friday, March 20, 1987. In exchange he promised them an interview with Bakker and Dortch, who had until that time refused to talk to them.

To their credit, the editors of the *Charlotte Observer* agreed to delay the article as an act of fairness. They had the facts. They could have rushed to publish. But they waited, and they are to be commended for that gift of time.

Still I had less than one full day to select and recruit a board of directors. I arrived home in Lynchburg on Tuesday night, March 17. On Wednesday night, March 18, the old PTL board would assemble in Charlotte to ratify a new board and then resign. On Thursday, March 19, the *Charlotte Observer* had been promised its interview with Jim Bakker. On Friday, March 20, the whole world would know about the scandal. With almost no information about the extent of that scandal and with no real inkling of the incredible financial dilemma facing PTL, I had to make my decision.

Immediately upon my return to Lynchburg from Palm Springs on Tuesday night, March 17, I shared the news with Macel. Late into the night we talked and prayed.

On Wednesday morning Jack Wyrtzen, founder of Word of Life Ministries in Schroon Lake, New York, was our guest preacher in the Liberty University chapel. As we waited for the chapel service to begin, I told Jack about the impending PTL scandal and about Jim Bakker's request that I step in to help save his ministry. Without a moment's hesitation he said, "Looks like God has opened the door, Jerry. And like it or not, you are the only man I know who would dare to walk through it."

That night I was connected by speakerphone to the conference room in Charlotte where the old PTL board was meeting.

I agreed to their request that I step in as chairman of PTL. They ratified the membership of the new PTL board, which included Jim Bakker's two nominees: Richard Dortch, currently the president of PTL and the interim host of the PTL show, and the pioneer televangelist Rex Humbard. At the same time they ratified my nominees: Ben Armstrong, executive director of the National Religious Broadcasters; James Watt, former Secretary of the Interior; Charles Stanley, another television preacher and a former president of the Southern Baptist Convention; Thomas Zimmerman, Assembly of God leader; Jerry Lipps, owner of Jerry Lipps Truck Lines; Sam Moore, the president of the Thomas Nelson Publishing Company; Richard Lee, pastor of Rehoboth Baptist Church in Atlanta; Dewitt H. Braud, a developer and Board Chairman of the Old-Time Gospel Hour; and my associate, former business executive Jerry Nims.

Following their unanimous ratification of PTL's new board membership, the old board resigned and the meeting was adjourned. I told Macel that the transaction was history. Thursday morning, I told my children, other family members and my associates. Somehow they knew that I had just made the most difficult and controversial decision of my lifetime in ministry. Neither my friends nor my enemies would understand. Once again I would find myself at the center of a media fire storm. By involving myself in the PTL scandal, I was risking our own ministry in Lynchburg. We had no idea what price we would pay for my decision to begin this new journey.

Still I felt I had no choice. As Jack Wyrtzen said, "God has opened the door." I had no choice really but to walk through it. Besides, there were more than 500,000 PTL partners to think about. They were my Christian brothers and sisters. They had invested millions of dollars in building the PTL network and Heritage USA. Tens of thousands had bought expensive lifetime memberships as well as various timesharing programs in the hotels, condominiums, chalets, bunkhouses, and campgrounds at that 9,500-acre Christian conference center. Millions more watched the various PTL television programs and were inspired and informed by their ministry. And the whole world was looking on to see if we who call ourselves Christians could recover our integrity and put back together the pieces of Jim and Tammy's shattered dream.

That next afternoon, Thursday, March 19, the editors and reporters from the *Charlotte Observer* were waiting to see if the PTL attorney, Roy Grutman, would produce Jim Bakker and Richard Dortch for an interview as promised. In fact, he did. The newspaper people gathered in their conference room in Charlotte, North Carolina, waiting for Bakker and Dortch to confirm or deny the rumors against them. At exactly 2 P.M. Jim Bakker dialed into that meeting on a speakerphone from Palm Springs, California. At the same time, Grutman and Dortch called in from PTL headquarters at Heritage USA. My associates and I were also present from Lynchburg on that historic conference call.

Jim Bakker read a rather long statement over the telephone that was printed verbatim the next day in the *Charlotte Observer*. Very few if any reporters quoted Jim Bakker's text. I think it is important to look carefully at the words he spoke that day. I was shocked and surprised as I listened. It was my understanding that he was going to confess his own errors, to seek forgiveness and to resign from Christian leadership until an appropriate time of healing could take place in himself and in his ministry.

But Jim Bakker is a master communicator. His "confession" turned out to be a rousing self-defense complete with the passing on of blame for almost everything to his unnamed enemies. I sensed no repentance. He was angry and belligerent. His words should have been a warning to me of the troubles that lay ahead.

Bakker began with the accusation that for many years "Tammy Faye and I and our ministries have been subjected to constant harassment and pressures by various groups and forces whose objective has been to undermine and to destroy us."

After explaining that their "physical and emotional resources have been so overwhelmed that we are presently under full-time therapy at a treatment center in California," Jim Bakker resigned.

"I have decided," he said, "that for the good of my family, the church and of all of our related ministries that I should resign and step down immediately from PTL."

In the very next sentence he added, "I have also today resigned from the Assemblies of God [denomination]."

Of course Jim Bakker did not explain why he was resigning from his own denomination that day. Now we know that they, too, were investigating the charges about to be levelled against him by the *Charlotte Observer*. And they, too, after examining the evidence against him, would find those charges to be valid.

Instead of listing the charges and confessing his guilt, Jim Bakker blamed his enemies for forcing him to resign and accused the *Charlotte Observer* of leading an unfair crusade against him.

"I am not able to muster the resources needed," he said, "to combat a new wave of attack that I have learned is about to be launched against us by the *Charlotte Observer*, which has attacked us incessantly for the past 12 years."

After that broadside at his state's biggest newspaper, Jim Bakker said that he was ". . . appalled at the baseness of this present campaign to defame and vilify me."

Over the years I had heard from various PTL insiders that the *Charlotte Observer* had been unfair to Jim and Tammy Bakker. Without checking out their stories, I just assumed that it was another case of liberal journalism versus my conservative, Christian brothers and sisters.

I was wrong to make that assumption. In fact, the editors of the *Charlotte Observer* may have erred occasionally in their reporting about PTL, but for the most part, they were professional, fair, and restrained in comparison to what they might have reported given the growing scandal at PTL.

After blaming the newspaper for his problems, Jim Bakker went on immediately to deny the sexual charges that it was about to make against him.

"I categorically deny that I've ever sexually assaulted or harassed anyone."

The only confession he made for his encounter with

Jessica Hahn in that Florida hotel room was strangely worded once again to defend himself and to effectively pass on the blame to others.

"I sorrowfully acknowledge that seven years ago, in an isolated incident, I was wickedly manipulated by treacherous former friends and then colleagues who victimized me with the aid of a female confederate.

"They conspired to betray me into a sexual encounter," he claimed, "at a time of great stress in my marital life. Vulnerable as I was at the time, I was set up as part of a scheme to co-opt me and obtain some advantage for themselves over me in connection with their hope for position in the ministry...."

After shifting the blame to his enemies, Jim Bakker immediately added these words:

"I have sought and gratefully received the loving forgiveness of our Savior who forgives us of our sins," he said. "I have told Tammy everything and Tammy, of course, has forgiven me, and our love for each other is greater and stronger than it has ever been."

For a moment, I thought Jim Bakker was really confessing at last, but immediately he added, "Now, seven years later, this one time mistake is seized upon by my enemies to humiliate and degrade me to gratify their envious and selfish motives.

"They have falsified, distorted and exaggerated the facts so as to make the occurrence appear many times worse than it ever was."

Jim Bakker did not really confess to any sexual indiscretion and he ignored altogether the various charges of fiscal irresponsibility that the *Charlotte Observer*'s investigative team had gathered against him.

"In retrospect," he did confess, "it was poor judgment to have succumbed to blackmail."

He went on to explain that he paid the money "to protect and spare the ministry and my family," and "to avoid further suffering or hurt to anyone to appease these persons who were determined to destroy this ministry."

Then he added, "I now, in hindsight, realize payment should have been resisted and we ought to have exposed the blackmailers to the penalties of the law. I'm truly sorry for all that has happened in the past or any harm that may have occurred.

"I bear no malice to anyone," he hastened to add. "I forgive those who have borne false witness against me."

Then after promising to pray for the future of PTL and Heritage USA, in the last long paragraph of his telephone statement he added:

"I've asked my friend, Jerry Falwell, to help me in my crisis. The PTL Board of Directors has accepted my resignation, appointed Jerry Falwell as chairman of our board of directors requesting him to designate a new board of directors. He has done this and the old board has accordingly resigned."

In conclusion he added, "I ask the prayerful support of our friends and foes for the preservation and advancement of God's work and the future of PTL. God bless you and good-bye."

The statement was a masterpiece of confusion. It raised far more questions than it answered. Without proof, he was blaming unnamed enemies for his own problems. And though he admitted that he was "truly sorry for all that has happened in the past or any harm that may have occurred," he took no real blame for any of it. In fact, he concluded by forgiving "those who have borne false witness against me" without stating, let alone disproving, any of their claims.

And though few members of the press looked closely at Bakker's resignation speech, the resignation itself and my appointment to his place of leadership was reported widely.

That Thursday night, while Macel and I sat in the Liberty University auditorium attending a concert by the Bill Gaither Trio, our switchboard in Lynchburg lit up like a Fourth of July fireworks display. Reporters from newspapers, radio stations, and television networks from around the world were calling to confirm the PTL story. And with their frantic calls, my new journey officially began.

By Friday, March 20, reporters from around the world were crowding into Lynchburg. That night from my Thomas Road Baptist Church office I was interviewed by all the major television networks and cable news services by live satellite feed.

Vice-president George Bush was one of the first to call to wish me well. Billy Graham called shortly after to encourage me and to assure me he and Ruth would pray for me. Senator Jesse Helms and many other friends and well-wishers called to encourage me that day and to promise their prayers for the troubled days ahead.

The first meeting of the new PTL board was scheduled for Thursday, March 26, at the PTL headquarters at Heritage USA. I had less than a week to prepare for that meeting. The press was having a field day. The Jim Bakker, Jessica Hahn story was making headlines.

I met close friends and associates of PTL and of the Bakkers who were suffering with them. I prayed for them. I cried with them and I shared their growing concern. It was clear from that start that God had led me to share this very difficult moment in the life of PTL and its partners across the nation and around the world. I knew that whatever tragedy they were facing was already my tragedy. Because we were brothers and sisters in Christ, their suffering had already become my suffering. And if I could do something to help, I must do it.

Of course I had no idea where God was leading. Fortunately the journey began one step at a time. When I started down that PTL road, I had no idea how difficult the trip would be. I don't think I would have begun the journey if I had known what I would face along the way.

Jim had told me about his 1980 Florida encounter involving John Wesley Fletcher and Jessica Hahn. And after hearing his painful story, I felt certain that Jim had been forgiven for his adulterous act. I was hopeful that with a public confession and a time of discipline and healing he would return to his position with the PTL ministry.

But with the *Charlotte Observer* story and its shocking aftermath, I began to realize that the scandal was far greater than my worst dreams. Already more stories were appearing about sexual and financial misconduct at PTL. All the facts needed to be gathered and analyzed. Difficult and life-changing decisions had to be made about Jim and Tammy's future and about the future of the Heritage Village Church and its PTL ministries around the world.

Before the PTL board meeting on March 26 at Heritage USA. Dr. Charles Stanley had asked to be excused from membership and was replaced by the Reverend Bailey Smith, another Southern Baptist preacher and also former president of the Southern Baptist Convention. The Reverend Dortch, acting president of PTL and host of the PTL show with other PTL executives, had prepared an overview of the financial conditions of the ministry for our consideration. I advised the board of my March 17 meeting with Jim Bakker. I suggested we become a "one-year board." This was negated by the board. Jim Watt said, "We are here for the duration." For two and a half hours the new board asked questions about PTL and its future. The answers were unsatisfying at best. I finished that meeting feeling restless and uncertain.

More than 300 accredited journalists gathered at a press conference following our first board meeting to seek answers to the growing list of embarrassing questions about PTL's apparent mismanagement. I was determined to find those answers before the next board meeting, just four weeks away. I promised the press "a full accounting" within the next thirty days.

During the next month I felt we were stonewalled at every effort to get our auditors into PTL headquarters to get a close look at the financial accounts. I had been officially ratified chairman of the board, and yet when I asked for financial records they were slow in coming or didn't appear at all. I heard rumors that the paper shredders were running overtime in that pyramid-shaped wood and glass PTL headquarters building at Heritage USA.

To add to my growing suspicions, disgruntled PTL employees were calling me in the night to report various rumors about fiscal mismanagement. One anonymous PTL staffer called to warn that large bonuses were being lifted by "top level staff members" even while the ministry faced financial ruin. Others called to report on the repressive working conditions at PTL. Apparently, subtle orders had been given employees to say nothing to me or to those who represented me. It was a very cultic atmosphere, and I began to feel even more afraid about what I would find when the books were finally opened.

At that point I began to question my decision about helping PTL during its time of crisis. I had nothing to gain by continuing in this difficult position and I had a lot to lose. Already donations to my own television ministry had dropped by more than $2 million. National credibility for media ministries had suffered a broadside. Other ministries were beginning to suffer financially. Friends and foes alike were also taking me to task for associating with PTL at any time let alone during their time of scandal.

I had accepted the responsibility of chairman of PTL in good faith without knowing many of the pitfalls ahead of me. I was being hindered in my attempts to get to the bottom of the rumors of executive misconduct and financial mismanagement. And as the evidence of the widening sexual scandal became known to me, I felt like throwing up my hands and walking away from the entire catastrophe.

Apparently word got out that I was thinking seriously about resigning as chairman of the PTL board. On April 22, 1987, Jim Watt, a long-time intimate friend of Reverend Dortch, flew to Lynchburg and discussed the matter with me. Jim Watt had been Secretary of the Interior under President Reagan. I had suggested his name for the PTL board because I considered him a Christian gentleman of impeccable integrity.

"Jerry," he said to me that day, "if you remain as chairman of PTL you have my unswerving loyalty. But if you are thinking about resigning, I would like to know in advance so that I could select a new charismatic board to succeed the current members."

At this same time, I learned that Jim Bakker himself was about to demand my resignation as chairman of the board and was apparently about to attempt to reinstate himself as chairman and to return to his role as host of the PTL program.

I confessed to Jim Watt my own uncertainty about continuing as chairman, and I advised him of the ever widening scandal that threatened PTL's very existence. In fact, I told Jim that the next day, Thursday, April 23, I was scheduled to meet with John Ankerberg in Nashville to hear the new evidence he had compiled against Jim Bakker and his close associates.

It was easy to understand why Jim Watt didn't want to hear any new charges about his friend Jim Bakker's sexual or financial misconduct. By then we were all tired of the headlines and just wanted the whole nightmare to go away. But as chairman of the PTL board I had no choice. If more scandal was about to surface, I had to know about it. If there was more hard evidence against PTL management, I needed to know. Only the whole truth would set us free to begin the task of healing that would save PTL. To ignore the truth or to cover it up or to deny it out of hand would simply cause us more suffering in the long run.

The next day, Mark DeMoss, Jerry Nims, and I met with John Ankerberg in Nashville. He had assembled a group of people who were willing to testify in court as to the alleged inappropriate, immoral, and even illegal practices of the PTL leadership. I was shocked into silence as they presented their evidence against Jim and his associates.

It was at this meeting on April 23, just five days before our third PTL board meeting, that I heard charges about Richard Dortch's participation in the Jessica Hahn trust fund payments. I still felt confident that Mr. Dortch's motives were above reproach. But he had made a serious blunder in judgment to attempt this cover-up, and the consequences would affect us all. I also heard more evidence regarding financial mismanagement by PTL executives who were paid huge salaries and bonuses from ministry funds and a special account. And I heard that day specific charges of Jim Bakker's alleged sexual misconduct and of alleged sexual promiscuity associated with him and other former leaders in the ministry.

We also met separately on that day with four presbyters of the Assemblies of God denomination. Already rumors were circulating that I was trying to "rob the PTL ministries from their rightful inheritors, the Assemblies of God denomination." So meeting with four of the thirteen clergymen assigned the general supervision of that denomination's clergy was an important step. I wanted to know for myself their denomination's attitude about my role in this complex and tragic scandal.

In that second and totally separate April 23 meeting in Nashville, Tennessee, the Reverends Carlson, Flower, Hudson and Stenhouse, four of the thirteen Assemblies of God presbyters, assured me of their confidence and of their prayerful support. They acknowledged their own investigation of the charges against Jim Bakker and they expressed their gratitude to me for taking on this "impossible task."

On the trip home to Lynchburg, I felt a knot growing in the pit of my stomach. What I had learned made me physically ill. The PTL tragedy had the possibilities of becoming the worst public scandal in Christian history. If an ancient pope went bad, only a handful of historians might ever know it. Even the Elmer Gantrys among us had a limited impact on the public at large. But with modern television saturation reaching almost every home in the world instantaneously and simultaneously through beams bouncing pictures off distant satellites, the PTL scandal could shape the world's opinion of the Christian church for an entire generation. But for the grace of God, the next few weeks would be a disaster of epic proportions for the cause of Christ, and I had walked right into the middle of it.

The very next night, Friday, April 24, I was sitting with Macel at Liberty University's junior-senior banquet when Mark DeMoss called me out of the room. I excused myself from Macel and those who were dining with us, walked to a nearby telephone, and listened as Mark told me of the Larry King show. John Ankerberg was interviewed on the show that night. The Reverend Ankerberg repeated to Larry King and to King's viewers across the nation most of the charges against Jim Bakker and his associates that had been shared with me and my co-workers in Nashville slightly more than twenty-four hours earlier.

I did not know that Ankerberg was going to appear on "Larry King Live." Nor did I know in advance that he was going to recapitulate that long list of accusations against Jim Bakker and his associates on that program. Weeks later, when Ken Woodward, the religion reporter from Newsweek magazine asked Ankerberg if I had known about his appearance on the show in advance, he said, "How could Falwell know? I didn't know myself until just hours before the program when Larry King invited me to appear."

Some journalists ignored this fact and suggested that Ankerberg and I had conspired in our Nashville meeting to hurt Jim Bakker further. Television, radio and newspaper reporters across the nation picked up this totally erroneous story and spread the lie. Throughout this sad and sordid scandal, I did my best to protect all parties from unnecessary personal suffering and embarrassment. And to question John Ankerberg's motives for raising these issues is really quite unfair. In fact, Ankerberg's own ministry was damaged, at least temporarily, by his courageous attempt to get the truth known.

Newsweek's Ken Woodward is one of a small handful of journalists who seem to love to pick on Jerry Falwell and his conservative evangelical Christian brothers and sisters across America. Don't misunderstand me. I respect and appreciate the press. I am not afraid to appear before reporters on any occasion to discuss any questions they might have. I don't even mind it when reporters gang up against me or try to pin me to the wall with their questions.

In fact, I like a fair fight, but there are a few journalists who, in my opinion, are often unfair, bigoted and unprofessional. ABC's Ted Koppel and CNN's Larry King are just two of the outstanding journalists who deserve credit for their coverage of this PTL affair. They were professionals on the scene examining the facts and allowing those facts to speak for themselves. And in the process, the truth was advanced and the public was informed. Seldom, if ever, do these professional reporters reveal their own personal opinions, let alone launch unfair and unsupported personal attacks.

In spite of what some journalists reported to the contrary, John Ankerberg and I did not conspire to hurt Jim Bakker through John Ankerberg's appearance on "Larry King Live" that night after our April 23 Nashville meeting. It was a difficult and very private decision for Ankerberg to reveal before a national television audience the growing list of charges against Jim Bakker. He said he decided to take the risk because of rumors he had heard that Jim Bakker was about to make his move to return to PTL. John Ankerberg refused to sit by and watch in silence while that happened. He was convinced that Jim Bakker had lost his right to lead the PTL ministry, and that unless the public knew the full extent of Bakker's financial and sexual misconduct he might win the day and regain control of PTL.

In fact, the rumors that Bakker was already attempting a comeback were true. Upon my return to Lynchburg from Nashville on April 23, I had received a long telex from Mr. Bakker asking me to "turn the PTL ministry over to charismatics, appointing James Watt as chairman of the board, with Rex Humbard and Richard Dortch remaining." In his telex, Jim Bakker warned me that he had given "all the documentation on what is being done on both sides of this issue" to two major journalists, and though they were "sworn to secrecy unless something happens," that "no matter what happens to me they will write the true documented story of this unprecedented event in the history of Christianity."

The threat in Jim Bakker's telex was not veiled. "I will not fight you if you ignore my wishes," he wrote, "but I must let you know that what you are embarking on will truly start what the press has labeled a 'holy war.' "

I don't know yet what Jim Bakker thought I was "embarking on." He seemed to be implying that I was conspiring against him in some way to steal his television ministry. In fact, I was only doing what he and his total board had appointed me to do. I had volunteered to help salvage all that he and his partners had built together. The PTL program and the Inspirational Network, Heritage USA, the Heritage Village Church and Missionary Fellowship, and their evangelism and "People that Love" programs around the world were certainly worth saving. But it was becoming more and more obvious to me that Jim Bakker had become the ministry's own worst enemy. I knew that the only way possible to restore integrity and public confidence in PTL was to institute a new day of leadership there and to put in place a new group of executives who would be careful and prayerful stewards of God's money, with direct accountability to the PTL board, to the PTL Partners, and to friends and faithful supporters of the PTL ministry.

During those next few days before the April 28 board meeting, I hardly slept. It was becoming terribly obvious that the task I had undertaken was far more serious and far more difficult than I ever dreamed. My friends and co-workers at Thomas Road Baptist Church and at Liberty University were giving me expert counsel on both sides. My wife wasn't sure if I should resign or continue as chairman of PTL. My son Jonathan said, "Don't you dare quit!" My spirit offered a rebuttal. The board meeting was just a few days away; still I felt uncertain about my decision.

Several of my very intimate friends in the Baptist ministry advised me to "get out!" They were echoing what I thought to be the general sentiment for those first tumultuous weeks. But then the first round of criticism and misunderstanding seemed to end. I began to feel a change in mood. Here and there Christians began to sense the implications of this disaster for the future of the whole body of Christ. More and more charismatics and non-charismatics alike began to call and promise me their prayerful support. Ministers representing every denomination, even Catholic priests and Jewish rabbis, began to write or telegraph their cautious encouragement. A few brave strangers on the street even approached me to shake my hand or pat me on the back and say, "Hang in there, Jerry! I'm with you!" And though I felt like resigning at the upcoming board meeting, there was a voice inside me joining with their voices saying, "Hang in there, Jerry! I am with you, too!"

On Saturday, April 25, Jim Bakker issued a statement from his home in Palm Springs denying Ankerberg's charges. "I have never been to a prostitute," Bakker said, "and I am not or have ever been a homosexual."

Our newest board member, the Reverend Bailey Smith, a pastor and former president of the Southern Baptist Convention, was interviewed in Atlanta that same day and said, "It comes to the point where it really doesn't matter whether some things are true. If the perception is true, it hurts his integrity. Bakker, I think, has lost the right to lead. He needs to be forgiven, but the place of leadership is another matter."

On Sunday, April 26, on the CBS news program "Face the Nation," I refused to answer questions about the reports that Jim Bakker wished to be reinstated; but when the reporters asked me to give my own opinion about the possibilities, I had to say forthrightly that Bakker's return to PTL "would guarantee, in my opinion, the doom of the ministry."

The night before, I got just two hours' sleep. I was exhausted. I stumbled into my bedroom after midnight and found Macel still waiting up for me. I sat on the edge of the bed with my head in my hands, trying to get my thoughts into focus. We both knew how much easier it would be to simply walk away from the entire mess. We knew, too, that if I didn't resign at the coming board meeting, I would have to stay for the duration and that could mean years of struggle ahead.

So many different groups of people were being affected by my decision. First, my own family was involved. I could not allow this new pressure to consume what little time I had left to be a husband and a father.

Second, I had a 22,000-member church to pastor, 7,500 university students and a staff of 2,300 people to supervise. These faithful people needed and deserved more quality attention from me.

Third, there were millions of active supporters of our own ministries that depended on me to complete effectively what we had begun together. How would they feel about this sudden apparent change in the direction of my life?

Fourth, there were approximately 10,000 fundamentalist and evangelical religious leaders, primarily pastors, who were also vitally concerned with what happened at Liberty University. After all, I had the academic and spiritual development of their own children or students to think about. I had promised to guard the spiritual integrity of our university. How would they feel about this sudden involvement with PTL?

Fifth, there were the PTL Partners and friends who were asking "Who is Jerry Falwell and what are his plans for our ministry?" The Partners, the friends and the staff of PTL were all waiting to see what next step I would take.

Sixth, I had two different Pentecostal publics, the mainline

Pentecostal denominations and the other independent charismatics to serve faithfully. I had to see that no war developed between the charismatics and the fundamentalists.

Seventh, I had the greater family of God at large to think about. Christians, both Protestant and Catholic, were watching this media scandal with growing concern about its negative impact on the future of the body of Christ.

Eighth, I had the general American public watching me on television, listening to me on radio and reading about me in every newspaper and news magazine in the country. They weren't just making judgments about me as the scandal unfolded but about the Christian gospel as well. I had spent my adult life hoping to be a positive influence for Christ and for His kingdom. The PTL scandal seemed loaded with negative possibilities.

I felt like a juggler keeping eight balls in the air simultaneously and wondering when one or all of them would fall on my own head.

Macel lay beside me in the darkness aware of the debate that raged in my head. I fell asleep for a while. Finally she took my hand and held it tightly. Already the sun was beginning to rise. The sky was turning from black to dull gray. It had been the longest night of my life, and I still didn't know whether to resign from the PTL or stick with it until God made it clear that I should resign.

"Who else could do it?" Macel asked. "And anybody who could do it wouldn't want the job," she added.

I lay back against the pillow before beginning that next eventful day. Apparently God wasn't going to direct me clearly before the board meeting began. So I just decided to quit thinking about it and to trust Him to guide me when He was ready.

I slipped into the next room for prayer and Bible study. After showering, I dressed and headed for the airport. In spite of my confidence that God would direct my path through the day ahead, I dreaded the board meeting and the press conference that would follow. Over three hundred accredited journalists were admitted to that media event. I flew to Charlotte tired, concerned and unsure about my decision whether I should quit or continue as chairman of the PTL board.

When we arrived in Charlotte, I asked that the board meeting location be changed. Our hosts looked surprised but cooperated fully. On my first visit to the PTL headquarters just four weeks before, I had an eerie feeling that we were being spied upon electronically. At the time I laughed it off, thinking I had read too many newspaper accounts of the bugging of the American Embassy in Moscow. In fact, just days after that second board meeting, during an electronic sweep of the World Outreach Center at Heritage USA, an electronic device was discovered which, we were told, could be used to monitor conversations.

The board met in the presidential suite of the Heritage Grand Hotel. Our PTL attorney, Roy Grutman, had just returned from Atlanta, where he had taped sworn depositions from the growing list of eyewitnesses who came forward to testify against Jim Bakker and his associates for their sexual and financial misconduct. For a few minutes before we sat down for business, we talked informally about the financial dilemma the ministry was facing and about the implications of the growing scandal.

Even as we began that informal time together, I didn't know what I was going to tell the board members about my decision to stay on or to quit as their chairman. But as the moments passed and as I thought about the implications of this unbelievable scandal for Christian broadcasting and for the Christian church around the world, I knew that I could not quit.

Just days before this second board meeting, a young businessman read a verse to me from the New Testament that "God had placed in his heart for me:" "And Jesus said unto him, No man, having put his hand to the plow, and looking back, is fit for the kingdom of God" (Luke 9:62).

During that informal time, I couldn't get that verse out of my head. God was answering my prayer for His direction in my life. I realized that there was no turning back. Even as we shared briefly before convening the meeting, I knew that God wanted me to continue as chairman of PTL. I had begun the task because Jim Bakker asked me into that position. I would end the task because God wanted me to stay.

"I am here for the duration," I said after we began the board meeting officially with an opening prayer. "Let's get on with it!" When I had first arrived on the grounds nearly one half hour earlier, I was still unsure. Now my heart was fixed.

We began our official business in the presidential suite not knowing what might happen next. We were told that a television cameraman videotaped two white Cadillacs speeding away from the Bakkers' home in Palm Springs on Sunday, April 26. No one seemed to know for certain who the cars were carrying. Bakker had written in his telex that he was meeting with charismatic leaders who would form a new PTL board. Gossip from Tulsa said that Jim Bakker and other charismatic leaders would be flying into Charlotte on Oral Roberts's airplane to attempt a takeover at the board meeting or in the huge press conference that followed. Of course, this all was eventually discounted as myth.

But at that tense moment, none of the rumors could be discounted. We didn't know where Jim Bakker was or what kind of surprise he might be planning. It was bad enough to deal with the massive financial and sexual scandal with the whole world watching without wondering if the scandal might be enlarged by a face-to-face confrontation with Jim Bakker and other religious leaders.

I had done my best to prepare for every possible emergency. David Heerspink, our chief of security at Lynchburg, and three of his plainclothes officers were in the lobby with my written authorization to prevent any kind of disturbance at the board meeting or the press conference. We desperately wanted to have an orderly and successful board meeting. We wanted to get down to the business of correcting the problems and healing the inequities. It seemed to me that certain PTL officials had prevented a close look at the books until that time. We were determined to end the stonewalling and discover the truth for ourselves.

The next few hours were perhaps the longest and most difficult of my life. The board discussed many of the sexual, financial, and administrative questions that had been raised. As the evidence piled up, I knew for certain that there was no

easy way to escape the consequences of the financial mismanagement and sexual misconduct that plagued this ministry. No
aspirin could end the pain. No simple bandage could bind the
wounds. Radical surgery was required to save PTL, and as the
meeting progressed it became more evident that the radical
surgery would have to begin with the Bakkers themselves.

That was a very difficult decision. The board cared for the
Bakkers and for their family. We knew how much of their own
time and energy they had poured into the PTL ministry. We
knew, too, of the years of personal sacrifice they had invested
traveling across the country, holding meetings in little churches,
or pioneering in primitive Christian television or building PTL
and Heritage USA from the ground up. There probably had
been no large salaries, no generous expense accounts in those
early days.

We understood that Jim and Tammy both grew up in poverty and had spent much of their ministry living on relatively
small salaries. Nevertheless, the $1.9 million the Bakkers re-
ceived from PTL in 1986 alone and the approximately $4.6 mil-
lion in salaries and bonuses that they had received in the last
thirty-nine months went far beyond the limits of a tax-exempt
charitable Christian ministry. No rationalization could soften
the impact of the financial excesses we were discovering. The
board voted immediately to cut all further salary payments to
the Bakkers.

Dealing forthrightly with the Jessica Hahn cover-up attempt
was perhaps the most difficult item on our agenda that day. We
learned that $265,000 had been used to buy silence from, and
settle with, Miss Hahn and her representatives. For agreeing
to keep secret her brief Florida affair with Jim Bakker, Miss
Hahn was to receive money from the PTL coffers.

Unfortunately, the Reverend Richard Dortch, Jim Bakker's
successor as PTL president and television host, had approved
and administered the payment of the money. He had designated
$265,000 of PTL monies to buy the silence of Miss Hahn. He
had persuaded a building contractor, Roe Messner, who was
owed millions by PTL for unpaid construction bills, to hide the
cover-up expenditure on a building invoice. Mr. Messner is one

458   Falwell

of the largest church builders in America. (Following Jim
Bakker's subsequent imprisonment, Tammy Faye divorced him
and married Mr. Messner.)

I personally believed Richard Dortch's chief fault in this
affair was intense loyalty to his boss. He had served the Assemblies of God church as a pastor and denominational executive with an enviable record.

We needed Richard Dortch to continue as host of the PTL
program. We needed him to bridge the gap between the Bakker
era and the future ministry of PTL. But as the painful discussion continued, it became obvious that to save PTL and to restore trust in its leadership, Richard Dortch, too, would have
to be included in the radical surgery performed that day.

Mr. Dortch was a member of our board. He sat with us in
the meeting room that day. The strain of that two-hour discussion showed clearly in his face. Finally there was nothing more
to say. A motion was made that Mr. Dortch submit his resignation from the board and from his ministry at PTL. The motion
carried. Board member Sam Moore abstained. Board member
James Watt voted no. All other members voted in favor of the
motion.

Every man around the room shared in the agony of that
moment. Mr. Dortch and Roe Messner, in our opinion, had made
bad judgment calls in their attempts to protect the reputation
of a man they loved and of a ministry they respected. As a result, each man paid a tremendous price in personal and public
suffering for his misguided loyalty. Mr. Dortch was later convicted and imprisoned for this misguided judgment.

PTL was facing a financial catastrophe. PTL owed its building contractor millions of dollars, and yet construction on the
hotel towers and various other expensive projects at Heritage
USA was continuing. PTL owed $8 million to various TV sta-
tions in its network. A $2 million mortgage payment was due.
The next payroll for more than 1,500 PTL employees was just
days away, and there was approximately $200,000 in the minis-
try bank accounts.

Dealing with the growing charges of sexual misconduct
was bad enough; but we were also confronted with the very

real possibility of investigations pending by the United States Attorney's office and officials of the Federal Bureau of Investigation and the Internal Revenue Service. That day we also learned of a class action suit against PTL and against us, the new board, for $601 million, blaming us for the financial mismanagement we had inherited.

About an hour into our board meeting that day, the Reverend Rex Humbard resigned from the board.

"Have we done anything wrong?" I asked this elder statesman of the evangelical movement and a longtime television preacher. "Do you know something we don't know? Is there any advice you would give us?"

Mr. Humbard just smiled and shook his head sadly. "No," he explained. "I've just been around a little longer than the rest of you. I've spent fifty-four years in ministry and I'm tired. I've been through one investigation by the S.E.C. and the IRS. I just don't have the energy to go through another."

We were all experiencing a very painful event. But there was a growing feeling among the remaining board members that PTL could and should be saved. Whatever bad one could say about Jim Bakker and his personal and professional mismanagement, there was good to be said about Jim Bakker's accomplishments in television and at Heritage USA.

The Bakkers began the current PTL broadcast just thirteen years earlier in Charlotte, North Carolina. We board members were amazed to learn what the Bakkers had accomplished in that short time. Through their PTL program—also called "The Jim and Tammy Show"—they had ministered daily to thousands of grateful people across the country and around the world. In recent years the Bakkers had also pioneered in missionary evangelism, starting PTL programs with national hosts in native languages from Japan to South America.

The new PTL board was also impressed by what Jim and Tammy Bakker had accomplished at Heritage USA, the third-best-attended theme park in the nation in 1986. Jim had a dream to build a conference center where Christian clergy and laity alike could gather in style and comfort to hold great conventions or to spend a relaxed and spiritual family time together.

Apparently more than 500,000 PTL partners shared the Bakkers' dream enough to invest their time and money in it. They, too, were tired of second-rate Christian camps and ugly rundown conference centers. They wanted a place to vacation with their families where they could enjoy all the benefits of a quality resort without the disadvantages and dangers often associated with places like Las Vegas, New York, or Miami Beach.

Jim Bakker's dream was contagious. Even the most adamant critic was won over to Heritage USA on the first visit. I still remember how impressed my family members were on our fifteen-minute drive through Heritage USA in 1984, and that was before all of the current facilities had been constructed or the exciting, entertaining, and inspirational daily activity schedule had been fully developed.

Hundreds of thousands of enthusiastic PTL partners traveled to Heritage USA for conventions, conferences, marriage seminars, Bible training programs, and for family reunions or weekend vacations. They loved the place and donated millions of dollars for its construction because they believed in Jim Bakker's dream and in all the new and exciting construction projects that he was planning for the future. Tens of thousands invested in lifetime memberships and timesharing programs. As a result, Heritage USA grew from that humble rustic campground begun in 1978 to a vast and imaginative Christian conference center visited in 1986 by more than six million people.

Besides the 504-room Heritage Grand Hotel and the almost completed twenty-one-story Heritage Towers addition, there is the wood and glass World Outreach Center, the Upper Room where people can pray or find Christian counsel twenty-four hours a day, the 3,500-seat outdoor amphitheater where the life of Christ is portrayed in a moving passion play, the Barn auditorium where camp meeting services are held and lively Gospel and folk music concerts are presented, and the vast and modern PTL television studios where large audiences can watch Christian television programs in production almost every day.

The Heritage Island Water Park provides wonderful fun for families who visit Heritage USA. And scattered around Heritage Lake there is a colorful carousel, a roller-skating rink and youth center, a picturesque shopping mall built in the late nine-teenth-century style of Main Street USA. There are also lodges, lakeside chalets, camping and recreation vehicle areas, mobile home parks, and inexpensive eating and entertainment zones stretched across the 2,500-acre wooded area with its lakes and streams, gentle rolling hills, and green meadows.

Millions of visitors come to Heritage USA to join in the festive New Year's Eve celebration or the annual July Fourth picnic and fireworks display or to see the million lights that decorate Heritage USA at Christmas-time. Many return every year for seminars, conferences, or family vacations; and more and more people are moving permanently to Heritage USA to live in the single residences or condominiums in such beautiful residential neighborhoods as Mulberry Village, Wood Ridge, and Dogwood Hills.

Jim Bakker's dream for Heritage USA included ministries to people with even more practical needs than a time of family rest and inspiration. Fort Hope, for example, is designed to help America's street people find new life in Christ through counsel-ing, educational and vocational training, and sound Biblical teaching. The "People that Love" ministries distribute food, clothing, and practical Christian services to the poor and needy across the Carolinas and through "People that Love" centers around the nation. Heritage House was opened in July 1984 to care for women facing unwanted pregnancies. A twenty-four-hour hotline also offers immediate help to other women who need Christian counseling to get them through an unwanted pregnancy. Kevin's House is another creative ministry aimed at helping the physically handicapped.

At our April 28 board meeting we discovered that the scan-dal we were facing threatened the survival of the entire PTL ministry. It was immediately apparent that only God could save PTL, but before the end of that difficult meeting the new board had determined to do its best to help Him save it.

Minutes after our meeting adjourned, I stood before the largest press conference I'd ever seen. Accredited journalists from around the nation filled the Heritage Grand press room. Television cameras representing all the major networks in

America and from news services, foreign networks, and stations around the globe were aimed in my direction. Dozens of microphones would carry my voice simultaneously to millions of viewers in America and around the world who were following the scandal at PTL. Reporters with their pads and pencils or their little hand-held recorders had gathered to witness the tragedy of the PTL ministry.

"I wish to make an appeal to the churches in America," I began that day, "in parallel with President Reagan's declaration of May seventh as a National Day of Prayer, to join all of us in a day of repentance and of prayer."

That press conference seemed a perfect time to remind the nation that prayer was our only solution for the world's problems, as well as for the problems that we were facing at PTL. "I am convinced," I said to that waiting press corps, "that these dark and difficult days can be turned around. If God's people will pray for repentance, for revival, for spiritual awakening, and for a quick resolution of the issues facing us here in Charlotte, the overall body of Christ can enjoy a much needed divine healing."

For seventy-five minutes I answered questions raised by the press. I announced the changes we had made that day in PTL personnel. I listed the $60 million-plus in debts that we were facing. I promised a full accounting of PTL's financial situation in the days ahead. I refused to comment on the alleged sexual improprieties, telling the press, "It is not our role to get into these personal issues." But I promised there would be no more attempt to cover up. "For spiritual reasons," I said, "I am offering any person who is accused the privilege of sitting down to face their accusers one by one." I announced "a voluntary moratorium" on lifetime partnerships in Heritage USA until we could determine their legal status. I promised that the board "is committed that none of the creditors will lose a dime." I noted, too, that the board was optimistic about the future, "but cautiously so."

That same day I decided to address almost 1,500 members of the PTL and Heritage Village staff. I didn't know if they would welcome me in silence or throw song books in my direction.

Instead, the moment I entered the auditorium, they stood to their feet cheering and applauding what the board had done.

"I love every one of you," I said to them. "I don't have a hit list; I'm not mad at anyone. I believe God led us to assume this responsibility at this hour."

Again they applauded enthusiastically. It was one of the greatest affirmations of confidence and respect that I have ever received. And when I said, "We must all enter a new era of accountability to repent, confess, and seek revival," that great crowd of faithful PTL employees cheered again.

That night I flew back to Lynchburg. All the networks interviewed me live on the evening news. At 9 P.M. I was interviewed on "Larry King Live." It enjoyed the largest audience in the history of that popular nighttime talk show. At 11:30 P.M. I appeared live on Ted Koppel's "Nightline."

The whole world was watching the growing scandal at PTL. For the days, weeks, and months that followed, headlines would announce each new development in the religious story of the century. I was convinced that God would rescue PTL from collapse, and I was praying that He would help shield the entire Christian church from further heartache and humiliation. I felt confident that PTL partners and millions of other concerned Christians would rally to save that ministry with their prayers and with their generous gifts. And I trusted that my own ministry would not suffer too greatly in the process.

On that Tuesday night I lay down beside Macel in our home in Lynchburg. The camera crews had gone for the night. My hard-working associate Mark DeMoss had herded reporters, staff members, and associates out of my life for that day. We were alone at last. Macel grabbed my hand and looked into my eyes.

"How was your day?" she said with a twinkle.

"Oh, it was fine," I answered; and for that rare, wonderful moment we rejoiced together. God had been with us that long and terrible day as He had been with us each step of our journey together, and we lay back with tears of gratitude and relief in our eyes.

Then, on Tuesday night, May 26, Jim and Tammy Bakker

made the first of two consecutive appearances on Ted Koppel's
"Nightline." From their $650,000 home in Palm Springs, the
Bakkers charged that I had stolen their ministry. And they promised to "set the record straight" on the Wednesday night, May
27, "Nightline" program. On that program, once again Jim
Bakker would minimize his seven-year-old Florida hotel encounter with Jessica Hahn. He was still denying the seriousness of
his sexual offense, whereas we had learned from trustworthy
sources what really happened in that Florida hotel room. Not
only had Jim Bakker had sexual intercourse with Jessica Hahn,
but another close associate of Bakker's had used the young
woman a second time and a third associate had gone to the
room seeking sexual intimacy but found the young woman pros-
trate, frightened and exhausted on the floor.

On the same May 27 "Nightline" program, Jim Bakker would
deny that he had ever had any homosexual affairs, challenging
his accusers to present actual proof when in fact, we had sworn
and taped depositions taken by the PTL attorney from eyewitnesses to Jim's alleged homosexual acts or advances and what
we believed were well-supported accounts of other sexual misconduct in the ministry.

On "Nightline," when Ted Koppel asked them to explain
the excessive salaries and bonuses of $1.9 million in 1986 and
$640,000 in the first three months of 1987 alone, the Bakkers
smiled and played coy.

"Jim and Tammy are a tad flamboyant," Bakker would
admit.

"I probably am well known for my shopping," Tammy Faye
said sweetly. "[It's] better than a psychiatrist," she added.

During that television interview before the nation, the
Bakkers claimed that the old PTL board of directors had, literally, urged the huge salaries and bonuses on them. But following the program, the *Charlotte Observer* polled the old board
and found that they didn't even know about many of the large
bonuses.

Our new PTL auditors had discovered an executive payroll
account. Accountants would release large sums of money to
the Bakkers and their aides on orders from Bakker, leaving a

trail of confusing paperwork so that nobody working in PTL could know who was actually on that payroll or how much those persons were paid.

On the program the Bakkers smiled and talked about feeling sorry for any wrongs that they might have done, whereas I had in my hand their request for severance pay and benefits from the PTL ministry at $300,000 a year lifetime salary for Jim, $100,000 a year for Tammy, hospitalization insurance, bodyguards, rights to books and records, a church-owned house and its furniture in Tega Cay, a year's free telephone use, secretarial help and maid service.

"I don't see any repentance there," I told the assembled press on the same day as Jim and Tammy's second appearance on "Nightline." "I see the self-centeredness, I see the avarice that brought them down."

I hated having to stand before the media that day and tell them the truth about the Bakkers' obvious and unrepented excesses, but I didn't have a choice. An estimated 20 million viewers watched the Bakker's performance May 27 on "Nightline," giving Ted Koppel's program its biggest audience ever. Even Johnny Carson forgot to watch his own prerecorded "Tonight Show" because he was too fascinated by the Bakkers.

I knew without a doubt that, in order to protect PTL and to prevent the Bakkers from regaining power over the finances of this ministry, their half-truths, folksy stories and outright lies had to be confronted with the truth. The PTL Partners had been victimized long enough. Jim and Tammy Bakker had been accountable to virtually no one. It was my unfortunate task to hold them accountable at last.

When the press asked if I could forgive the Bakkers, I answered, "I don't know of anyone, certainly not Jerry Falwell, who hasn't forgiven Jim and Tammy, but," I added, "it is one thing to forgive someone who errs; it is something else to allow those errors to go on and on forever."

Over the years Partners and friends of the ministry had given hundreds of millions of dollars to support the PTL dream. In spite of their generous and sacrificial giving, we discovered that PTL was actually over $70 million in debt, not $60 million as we first thought, with $23 million in delinquent payments. Television stations had to be paid or the ministry would be cut off the air. Staff salaries were due. Buildings were half completed and maintenance demands were escalating. Creditors were contemplating expensive lawsuits that threatened the very existence of PTL and Heritage USA. Even a small handful of one or two hundred PTL Partners who still wanted Jim and Tammy returned to PTL were organizing to launch lawsuits against us.

The Internal Revenue Service and the U.S. Postal Service were investigating the possibility of criminal charges against the Bakkers and their former aides. The United States Justice Department announced that it was coordinating a multi-agency inquiry into the Bakkers' misuse of funds. Rumors were circulating that Jim and Tammy Bakker would end up in jail. Sadly, as the world now knows, Bakker, Dortch and others did go to prison for their crimes.

Then, on June 12, 1987, our PTL attorneys filed for protection under Chapter 11 of the federal bankruptcy laws.

"This is not a sign of failure or shame," declared our attorney Roy Grutman. "PTL has assets far above its known liabilities."

Grutman went on to explain that under the chaotic mismanagement of the Bakkers, PTL could no longer survive without protection under Chapter 11. I had opposed this step until I realized we had no other choice. Under Chapter 11 protection a bankruptcy court judge permits a debtor organization to suspend payments temporarily to creditors and prevents civil court actions from being taken against it.

That action would give PTL's new team of skillful and trustworthy financial managers a chance to file a plan with the court outlining how it intended to reorganize its finances and to satisfy all the legitimate creditors' claims. When we were granted Chapter 11 protection for PTL, we were given a chance to work things out for the future of that ministry without creditors threatening to impose lawsuits against us that would require selling off the PTL/Heritage USA assets and as a result destroying the ministry altogether.

In spite of all the tragic charges piling up against them, Jim and Tammy Bakker made one last attempt to regain control of PTL. They made a quick visit to Heritage USA and announced their plans "to be back on television in thirty days." They returned to the PTL parsonage at Tega Cay and for a short time threatened to maintain possession in spite of the planned sale of that expensive home to help pay off the growing PTL indebtedness. Finally they asked the famous San Francisco criminal lawyer, Melvin Belli, to represent them in an attempt to regain control of PTL through the civil courts. Their photogenic counsel spent a few days in a flurry of television appearances claiming that the Bakkers had a case.

Jim and Tammy brought Belli into the picture probably in hopes of putting fear into the old PTL team that was standing with us. It didn't work. Mr. Belli had had a distinguished legal career. But when he agreed to represent the Bakkers, Belli was about to celebrate his eightieth birthday. He was, to say the least, past his legal prime. Like the great baseball pitcher Tom Seaver, who had just resigned from the game, told the nation, "There comes a time to hang it up." When Belli accepted the Bakkers' case, he had, in my opinion, already passed the time in his own distinguished legal career.

In a rather embarrassing confrontation on Fox Broadcasting with our PTL attorney, Roy Grutman, Melvin Belli heard the real case against the Bakkers and got angry and frustrated when he tried to reply. While still on camera Belli took off his microphone and marched out of the studio. He was to appear with Grutman on the "Nightline" program that same evening. After his earlier confrontation with our attorney, he requested of Ted Koppel that I appear with him instead of Grutman. I accepted gladly. Then Belli changed his mind again. When Ted Koppel wouldn't allow him to appear alone on the program, Belli refused to appear at all.

About the same time, the Bakkers left the PTL parsonage in South Carolina and went into seclusion. They issued a short statement of support for the new PTL team and promised their prayers for the future of the great ministry they founded.

The rest of the story is known to the world. The criminal

investigations intensified. Indictments and criminal trials followed. Christian leaders went to prison. The national and international media had a field day. The cause of Christ sustained great injury.

Our Board worked diligently during those traumatic summer and fall months of 1987, in conjunction with the bankruptcy court and trustee. With the help of a supportive public and our ever-faithful God, we raised many millions of dollars to bring about a measure of stability and to continue operations. The world will never forget my televised journey down the PTL water-slide, business suit and all, as I kept my word at the conclusion of a successful $22 million fund-raising. But, in October, the Board felt that we had done all we could in our efforts to rescue this ministry, and we resigned to the bankruptcy court.

Since our tenure, the Inspirational Network has been purchased by a large evangelical ministry and continues to operate as a strong Christian cable television outreach. The campground continues to operate as a for-profit Christian family ministry.

Obviously, the original PTL ministry does not exist in its former greatness and style. The glitter and glamour are gone. The Jim and Tammy Show is no more. Many PTL partners and investors suffered financial loss. And due to the massive negative broad-brushing assault of the national media against Christian broadcasting in general, financial giving to many media ministries nationwide, including ours in Lynchburg, diminished substantially for several years.

In retrospect, considering the end result of the whole sordid affair, I was again forced to look back on my more than six months at PTL. What positive good, if any, was accomplished by my involvement in this ministry? Did I make a mistake accepting the interim chairmanship of Heritage? Would it have been better for all concerned if I had stayed away from the entire situation?

Over the past nine years since the PTL affair, I have spent a great amount of time thinking about this. Long ago, I came to certain conclusions which have reinforced by convictions about God's sovereignty in His dealings with His children.

First, I am convinced that God led me to Heritage in 1987. My heart was right and I earnestly sought His will in the matter. I can therefore claim the promise of Romans 8:28 that "eventual and ultimate good" did and will evolve from my participation in Charlotte.

Second, while I originally felt that my primary mission at Heritage, U.S.A. was to save the ministry and thus hopefully prevent massive damage to the cause of Christ, I have long since realized that this was not God's purpose for sending me there.

It is now my strong belief that God sent me there to bring an abrupt end to the immorality and financial fraud of this "religious soap opera" that had become an international embarrassment to the Christian gospel. If I had not accepted the leadership responsibility at Heritage, it is likely that the corruption would have continued unabated for a very long time.

In hindsight, we all now realize that PTL had been a moral cancer on the face of Christianity. Heritage had become the Mecca of the "prosperity theology" movement. God wanted it terminated. I now clearly see that Jehovah God gave me the very unpleasant and painful, but necessary, task of exposing and calling a halt to this modern Sodom and Gomorrah.

I have perfect peace that I did the Lord's will at PTL. I also sincerely pray the Lord will choose someone else for the next such mission.

Jim Bakker has recently written a book entitled *I Was Wrong* in which he openly admits how wrong he was. I met with him personally while he was in prison. I have read his ministry letters through the past three years. I believe he is sincerely repentant. I am sure God has much for him to do in the future. But, I doubt that he would have come to such contrition and arrived at such a spiritual height without the personal tragedy he has experienced during the past nine years. This is the way God deals with all of His children as He conforms us to the image of His Son.

There is one more very positive thing that happened in my life through my experiences at Heritage, U.S.A. As a pastor who has spent most of his 44 years of ministry among Baptists, my appreciation of and respect for my Pentecostal brothers and sisters reached another dimension at PTL. I came to know personally some of the sweetest Christians I have ever met while at Charlotte. My relationship with charismatic Christians across America and the world has been radically improved. While we continue to have some theological differences which are not essential to salvation, these issues should not hinder our fellowship. Since my time at Heritage, they have not hindered mine.

I must make one final statement about Heritage, U.S.A. While the media left the impression that everyone at PTL was wicked, this is simply untrue. The vast majority of the people I met there were godly. The residents are dedicated and loving followers of Christ. Most of the staff and workers I found to be exemplary saints. The supporters and partners are among the finest Christians I have known. The musicians, administrators and preachers were, in the main, above reproach. Unfortunately, a small minority of leaders brought shame upon the entire family.

There are far more valleys than mountain tops in the Christian life. God sends us two bad days for every good day in order to keep us looking towards Him.

— Jerry Falwell

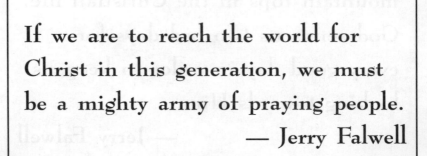

If we are to reach the world for Christ in this generation, we must be a mighty army of praying people.

— Jerry Falwell

CHAPTER SEVENTEEN

On to the Third Millennium

I had entered 1987 with a fresh commitment to my ministry in Lynchburg. With Moral Majority behind me, I was very excited about becoming a small town pastor again. The challenge of returning to Liberty University and training young champions for the service of Christ had captured my attention. Needless to say, I had not planned on the March through October excursion in Charlotte. This changed everything. I was literally caught up in a whirlwind. Those nearly seven months were the busiest and most emotionally draining days of my life. I am not exaggerating when I say that what I described in the last chapter is only a surface treatment of the most demanding challenge Jerry Falwell had ever faced. I returned to Lynchburg from Charlotte in late October virtually exhausted.

Actually, I had been preaching at Thomas Road Church every Sunday morning and evening during my PTL days. I was flying back and forth from Lynchburg to Charlotte almost daily. Mark DeMoss, my most capable assistant and dear friend, was at my side almost every moment. My son, Jonathan, helped me

473

day and night to carry the heavy load of leading the Lynchburg and Charlotte ministries. Warren Marcus, executive producer for our Old Time Gospel Hour television ministry, picked up the added responsibility of managing the PTL television programming. We four almost lived together during those stressful times.

Meanwhile, my absence from Lynchburg during the Moral Majority years had created some major administrative and financial problems for the University and the Old-Time Gospel Hour. In addition, Liberty University depended heavily on the subsidies that came regularly from our television ministry. Because of the national credibility problem caused for media ministries by the PTL scandal, our anticipated TV contributions for the year following this debacle were diminished by $25 million. This "bleeding" continued for the next four years. Looking back now, I can only worship God for His timely leadership in returning me to Lynchburg at the precise moment I was desperately needed.

After cancelling most of my scheduled outside commitments, I began devoting my time and energies exclusively to analyzing our financial problems and, with the help of our very capable and dedicated leadership team, devising a plan to work our way out of a very serious dilemma.

I actually did not know at that time just how serious our situation really was. Since 1971, we had acquired a 5,000 acre campus for Liberty University called Liberty Mountain. We had erected and furnished more than 60 buildings. Our enrollment on campus had grown to more than 5,000 students and was now the largest evangelical university of its kind in the world. We had already invested more than $200 million in the buildings, campus, improvements and capital furnishings of this beautiful school. We had never had conventional long-term mortgage financing. We had obtained short-term funding for each dormitory or classroom as we erected them and then quickly raised the capital funds through our television ministry to pay off these loans. Suddenly, however, PTL had made it impossible to raise these funds as we had in the past.

We concluded that we must find long-term financing and,

simultaneously, down-size our staff and operations. It was very painful to me to see our staff reduced from 2,300 persons to 1,800 almost overnight. These families losing their jobs were my friends. I was pastor to most of them. But, there was no alternative. To compound our troubles, we then encountered unexpected difficulties in obtaining mortgage financing. Over the next four years, we went down one dead end road after another. Adding insult to injury, the media smelled blood and beat us up mercilessly.

Finally, in early 1992, I called a meeting of our creditors to whom we owed about $100 million. I explained our situation to them and then asked them to work with us in an out-of-court debt restructuring plan. Over 95% of them agreed to work with us. We were forced to make special arrangements with a few. A small number were unwilling to cooperate in any way and God wonderfully provided the funds to pay them. Someday, I must write another book to tell how miraculously God provided and enabled us to meet every seemingly impossible challenge.

As I write these words, our debt has been dramatically reduced. During our first 25 years at Liberty University, God has enabled us to raise approximately $1.25 billion for this miracle school's creation, development and operation. Our student body has grown to a record enrollment. The 1996/97 enrollment, resident and external, surpasses 14,000 students from 50 states and 52 nations.

In the midst of these several recent years of financial crises, struggling to survive, Liberty University, amazingly, continued to grow in every way. Art and Angela Williams gave us the 12,000-seat Williams Football Stadium in 1989. Only eternity will reveal the major role Art Williams, one of America's leading entrepreneurs, played in rescuing and building this Christian university. The Williams family and Boe and Myrna Adams gave us the 10,000-seat Vines Center arena in 1990. The Dan Reber and Jimmy Thomas families completed construction on the huge Reber-Thomas Dining Hall in 1993. These three multi-million dollar edifices were given us in the midst of our life and death financial struggles.

God has, day by day, met our every need. Besides these

families and others who have been led by God to provide major financial gifts during our recent "walk through the valley," thousands of additional faithful saints have given sacrificially at the grassroots level. Some have forgiven debt. Many of our faculty and staff have gone beyond the call of duty, working long hours for less pay than they could have earned elsewhere, all because they felt the call of God upon them.

I dare not mention names of co-laborers for fear of inadvertently overlooking someone. But, I would be remiss if I did not salute a few of God's "angels" who helped me through the difficult decade now concluding. I must thank George Rogers, our 77-year old vice-president of finance and administration for his unswerving integrity, devotion and skilled and diligent labors. Dr. A. Pierre Guillermin, our president who joined me in 1967, has provided direction and wisdom during the storm, which has profoundly affected every part of this ministry.

Jim Moon, my loyal co-pastor, who has given me 40 years of his life and has stood by me every step of the way, has provided stable leadership in these challenging days. Mark DeMoss became my close friend in the 1970's, because of my relationship with his great father, the late Arthur S. DeMoss. Mark was a student then. He later became my personal assistant. Mark has wisdom far beyond his years and has meant more to me than feeble words can express, especially in recent years. Other special friends "have stepped up to the plate" in significant ways during my dark night. I think of Sam Pate, Randy Scott, the late Dr. Charles Thompson, Dan Reber, Jimmy Thomas, Harvey Gainey, Marion Compton, Kenneth Seaton, Wayne Booth, Wally Hilliard, Wilbur Peters, Jerry Lipps, Jack Bolling, Don Hershey and many others. Thank you, dear friends.

I have had three primary mentors during my 44 years in the ministry. Dr. B.R. Lakin taught me to lead a large ministry. Dr. Francis Schaeffer taught me what is really important in life. They are both in Heaven. Dr. John W. Rawlings, at age 82, is still holding forth. "Dr. John" continues to teach me the importance of vision and local church ministry. I am deeply indebted to these men and I could not have found my way without them.

Macel has been my most important and effective teacher

since I first met her in 1952. That is another book and I also plan to write it. Her wisdom, patience and steadfastness have been my anchor throughout. God knew what I needed. I am so impatient and aggressive. My motor is running endlessly, even when I am sleeping. My philosophy is always "let's do it now." Macel is my rudder and brakes. She is my caution sign on the road of life. She is tender and loving. I am a rocket ship always just off the launching pad. She is the only person in the world who can perpetually keep me under control. I repeat, God knew what I needed. She is the reason I have not self-destructed many times during the past four decades.

Jerry, Jr. finished the University of Virginia Law School in 1987. Again, God's timing was perfect. PTL exploded in 1987. Our ministry problems began erupting in 1987. Jerry began practicing law and business in Lynchburg, immediately after passing the Bar exam and marrying Becki Tilley in late 1987. And Jerry, Jr. became our ministry in-house counsel in 1987.

He never had time to relax or to gradually build his practice. Jerry, Jr. was instantly caught up in our legal and financial problems. He was a quick learner. God sent him to me just in time. While we employ many attorneys for the legal needs of this large and complex ministry, Jerry is the best attorney I know. This is not an exaggeration. At age 34, he is more responsible, humanly speaking, for the miraculous financial survival of this ministry than any other single person. This young man has guided me, this ministry and our many law firms through the "financial and legal white-water rapids" of the past nine years. Meanwhile, Jerry and Becki have been blessed with Trey (Jerry III, born 7/26/89) and Wesley (Charles Wesley, born 8/25/93). I never dreamed, when Jerry, Jr. was growing up in our home, that God was preparing him to help me lead this ministry into the 21st Century.

Jonathan is four years younger than Jerry. Unlike his soft-spoken older brother, he is a highly-energized extrovert. Like his father, he has a pastor's heart. Having completed his undergraduate and seminary work at Liberty University, this tall red-headed spiritual leader is now my associate and church administrator at Thomas Road Baptist Church.

Following his graduation from Liberty and during his Seminary years, Jonathan built a very successful film and video production and duplication company. This entrepreneurial experience has helped equip him to assist me in my pastoral ministry. I must confess that he has already taken the church to another dimension with his administrative and creative skills. My heart rejoices as I witness the obvious anointing of God on Jonathan's life and leadership. He and Shari, his musically talented wife, have a very handsome son, Jonathan, Jr. (born 3/14/96). It is a special privilege indeed when God allows a pastor to labor alongside his son. I am twice-honored as I work daily at the church and university with both of my sons.

Jeannie was five years old when she told her grandfather, Macel's dad, that she would one day become a doctor and take care of him. She is 31 now and is a surgeon in Richmond, Virginia. Besides practicing general surgery, Jeannie is an assistant professor of surgery at the Medical College of Virginia. Her husband, Paul Savas, is an orthopedic surgeon now completing his residency. Jeannie and Paul graduated from Liberty. They are now praying about and planning for children. They are very committed Christians who share their faith with others. I often say, with tongue in cheek, that Jeannie is the only perfect member of our family. For all of her life, she has been a "daddy's girl." I have no need of social security, a retirement fund or any such thing. I have Jeannie.

Macel and I consider our children to be our primary ministry under Christ. Nothing thrills us more than to watch our children, their spouses and our grandchildren following the Lord. We are grateful to God that He has used us to establish and lead a worldwide ministry, but it is our highest desire that we will be best known for having built a strong and successful family.

In three years, we enter the 21st Century. I am hopeful Macel and I can be allowed continued good health for another 25 or 30 years. I have so many dreams and visions for Third Millennium ministry. Of course, that is all in His hands. But, in my heart of hearts, I truly believe the best is yet to come.

God has a vision for you. Don't settle for second best. Don't ever retire. Don't ever quit. Let your vision become an obsessive reality.

— Jerry Falwell

You are never really fulfilled in life until you recognize your vision and fulfill it.

— Jerry Falwell

A Pastor's Dream

As I face the Third Millennium at age 63, I find myself dreaming as never before. If God has anointed me with any exceptional calling, it is as a visionary. God may call me home today, and I would have no regrets or complaints, but, in my heart of hearts, I actually believe that He is going to give me another 20 or 30 years. If you read some day soon that "Jerry Falwell has died," be assured that I was greatly surprised. I am "dreaming dreams and seeing visions" in the same way I have over the past 44 years of my ministry. I am claiming Joel 2:28 as my verse for the 21st Century— "And it shall come to pass afterward, that I will pour out my spirit upon all flesh; and your sons and your daughters shall prophesy, your old men shall dream dreams, your young men shall see visions."

My burning obsession is to cooperate with God in building the greatest Christian university in the world, in history. I truly believe the only way I can evangelize the world in my generation is to train "Young Champions for Christ" at Liberty University. For all these years, I have been living and serving under the burden of what I call **The Original Vision**. For more than a quarter century, since God first wrote this Vision upon my heart, I have been writing and re-writing it, revising and updating it and communicating it to all who will listen. I will end this book by sharing the Vision with you. This is what makes Jerry Falwell "tick."

The Original Vision

Habakkuk 2:2-4 (KJV) "And the LORD answered me, and said, Write the vision, and make it plain upon tables, that he may run that readeth it. For the vision is yet for an appointed time, but at the end it shall speak, and not lie: though it tarry, wait for it; because it will surely come, it will not tarry. Behold, his soul which is lifted up is not upright in him: but the just shall live by His faith."

God gave me **the vision** for Liberty University more than a quarter of a century ago. I have heeded Habakkuk 2:2 through the years by writing and re-writing **The Vision** hundreds of times.

The Original Vision for Liberty University, when its doors opened in 1971 to 154 students, was to build a distinctively evangelical Christian liberal arts university which would be, for evangelical students, a world-class institution comparing favorably, in every way, with Notre Dame and Brigham Young in what they provide for Catholic and Mormon young people.

The Vision calls for: (1) academic excellence, (2) strong spiritual values, (3) a commitment to the Christian worldview, (4) a behavioral code based on traditional and moral principles and (5) an intercollegiate athletic program competing at the highest level. In 1971, there was no such university in America.

The Vision further calls for dedicated men and women on the staff and faculty who are in agreement with the stated purpose of the founders. This liberal arts institution, according to **The Vision**, was created to train principled world leaders for future generations, in every imaginable vocation. Its Seminary and Schools of Religion would train the pastors, missionaries and Christian workers who would take the Christian worldview and gospel into the marketplace and the ministry; into the classrooms and into government; into all of America and into the world. **The Vision** committed us forever to the Judeo-Christian ethic, political conservatism and the American economic system of free enterprise. We would always oppose political liberalism and economic socialism.

The Status of the Vision Today

More than 25 years and $1.25 billion later, Liberty is poised to change the world by producing the **"Young Champions For Christ"** who can make a difference. We have a beautiful $200 million campus with 64 buildings on 5000 acres called Liberty Mountain. More than 14,000 students are presently enrolled with over 6,000 resident students in our dorms, classrooms and dining hall daily.

Liberty is regionally accredited by the Southern Association of Colleges and Schools (SACS) and nationally accredited by Transnational Association of Christian Colleges and Schools (TRACS). We have 26,000 alumni of our resident programs who are serving Christ and humanity as physicians, attorneys, businesspersons, educators, pastors, missionaries, evangelists, professional athletes and in numerous other vocations. We hold membership in the National Collegiate Athletic Association (NCAA) and compete athletically in 16 sports, including football, at the Division I level. **The Vision** is rapidly becoming a reality. We are not there yet, but the goal line is much closer than it ever was before.

The Original Vision was for an enrollment of 50,000 students early in the 21st century. At this re-writing of **The Vision**, our dream, which was first publicly stated in 1971, seems more and more attainable. The LU School of LifeLong Learning (LUSLLL), which provides adult education through External Degree Programs, is our fastest growing school at Liberty. It is now believed that a resident enrollment expectation of 10,000 students on campus in the early 21st Century is very realistic, and we should surpass an enrollment of 40,000 in our distance learning programs at LUSLLL in that same time period... totalling 50,000 in the entire student body.

The Vision also calls for a world-class Christian university which will, through its various ministry-training programs, produce the **Young Champions For Christ** who can be God's instruments to save America and evangelize the world in our generation. We now have thousands of pastors, missionaries, Christian teachers, youth and children's workers who are making a difference worldwide. We have thousands more in law, medicine, government, education, the sciences and arts, business and many other professions worldwide who are impacting society for good.

This **Vision** is a lofty one indeed. But, in my heart, I believe more now than ever before that God will finish what He started. Philippians 1:6 promises: "Being confident of this very thing, that He which hath begun a good work in you will perform it until the day of Jesus Christ." Liberty is now widely acclaimed as **The World's Most Exciting University**. It is also the largest distinctively evangelical Christian university in existence. I continue to write and re-write **The Vision**.

The Original Vision called for ten unique features at Liberty University which cause this institution to stand alone today. Those ten unique features are:

1. Academic excellence in a Christ-centered environment. While Liberty is accredited by the Commission on Colleges of the Southern Association of Colleges and Schools to award associate, bachelor, master and doctoral level degrees, it does so without compromising its commitment to the principles of God's Word.

2. An action-oriented curriculum.

3. A vision to change the world.

4. An uncompromising doctrinal statement, a Christian worldview, an absolute repudiation of "political correctness," a strong commitment to political conservatism,

total rejection of socialism and strong support for America's economic system of free enterprise.

5. Behavioral standards which include the prohibition of drug, alcohol and tobacco use, coed dorms and sexual promiscuity.

6. A dress code, curfews and respect for authority.

7. A superb non-tenured teaching faculty. Graduate assistants do not stand-in for faculty. All our faculty members actually teach their classes.

8. Competitive NCAA Division I athletic programs for men and women, including football.

9. Tuition costs which are in the bottom 10% of all private colleges and universities in America.

10. Required attendance at Convocations for all students and faculty three times weekly. (Over 95% of all students also attend church at least once weekly.)

As far as we know, no other accredited liberal arts university in America can make these same ten claims. I ask your prayers that we will have the Divine wisdom necessary to lead on as **The Original Vision** becomes a 21st Century reality.